# LONDON IN LOCKDOWN

*Jilke Golbach* is Curator of Photographs at the Museum of London. Prior to joining the museum in 2019, she worked as Assistant Curator at the Barbican Art Gallery on 'Dorothea Lange: Politics of Seeing' (2018) and 'Strange and Familiar: Britain as Revealed by International Photographers' (2016). She holds MAs in Art History, from the University of Amsterdam, and in Cultural Heritage, from University College London. Her ongoing doctoral research at UCL explores urban heritage, cultural regeneration and the right to the city.

*The Museum of London* tells the ever-changing story of this great world city and its people, from 450,000 BC to the present day. Our galleries, exhibitions, displays and activities seek to inspire a passion for London and provide a sense of the vibrancy that makes the city such a unique place. The museum's collection of photographs encompasses an estimated 180,000 items, comprising a visual encyclopaedia of London's physical and social fabric.

*Hoxton Mini Press* is a small indie publisher based in east London. We make photography books about London – we love and breathe this city – with a dedication to lovely production and local, urban stories. When we started the company people told us 'print was dead'. That inspired us. Books are no longer about information but objects in their own right: things to collect and own and inspire.

# LONDON IN LOCKDOWN

*Written by* Jilke Golbach

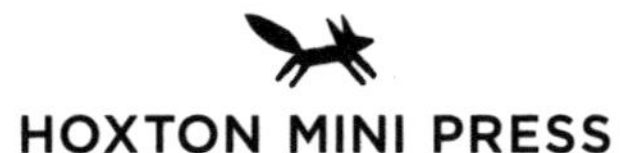

HOXTON MINI PRESS

# Contents

# Introduction

Photography has long thrived – even been brought to maturity – in disaster zones. Natural catastrophes, humanitarian crises, extreme poverty and violent conflict have all made powerful subjects for generations of photographers. In many ways, the coronavirus pandemic represented just such a moment of disruption and crisis. In April 2020, author Arundhati Roy described the pandemic as 'a portal, a gateway between one world and the next,' pointing out that historically, 'pandemics have forced humans to break with the past and imagine their world anew.'

Confronted with this rupture, it is perhaps no wonder that 2020–2021 gave rise to a new creative impulse. Recognising that nothing would be quite the same way again, many artists felt an urgent desire to document their lived experiences during this moment of transition. 'Photographers thrive on any change from the normal, and when an event like the pandemic lands on your doorstep it is almost what you have been waiting for,' says Chris Dorley-Brown, whose work is included in this book (*Deserted London,* p.34).

Here in London, the pandemic put the brakes on fast-paced metropolitan life, forcing us to slow down and take stock. The photograph – that most instantaneous, democratic and reproducible of mediums, especially in the internet age – served as a tool to record the evolving drama of it all: the facemasks and other PPE, the empty streets, the collective claps for the NHS, the socially distanced interactions through front-room windows. Such images do not however fit comfortably within the framework of 'crisis photography'. Unlike natural catastrophes or human conflict, the virus has been a nebulous threat. It has upended lives and pushed time out of joint, but it has also prompted moments of peaceful respite.

Photography was always going to play an important role in documenting such a multi-dimensional event, but we might wonder what ultimately registers on the camera from prolonged periods of confinement, rising and

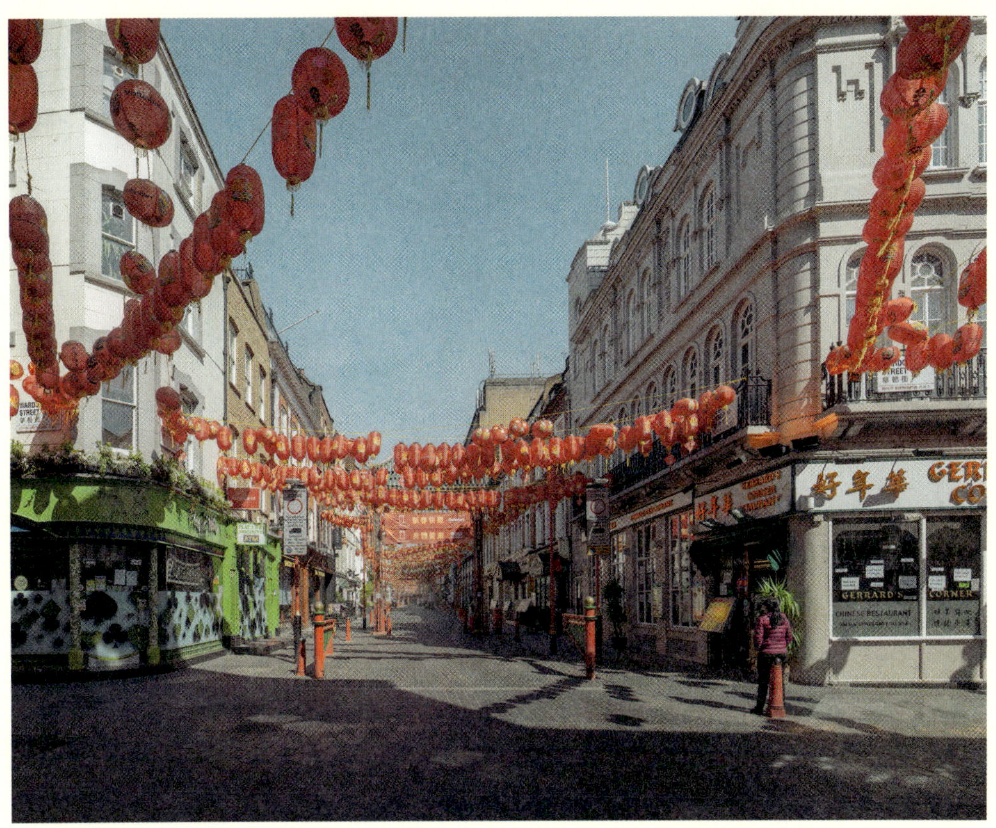

Chris Dorley-Brown, *Gerrard Street, 2020,* from the chapter *Deserted London* (p.34)

falling case numbers, boredom, loneliness and the monotony of the 'new normal'. What could photographers focus on when they themselves were rendered immobile and the actual sites of the tragedy (hospitals, morgues, care homes) were for the most part strictly off limits? And what will it mean to look at these images months, years – even decades, perhaps – on from the start of the pandemic, which, at the time of writing, is still running its course across the globe?

* * *

*London in Lockdown* is the result of a collaboration between the Museum of London and east-London-based independent publisher Hoxton Mini Press. The book originated in our shared passion for documenting life in this diverse, ever-compelling, electric city and our fascination with photography's role during the pandemic. Through the images of 24 photographers, this book

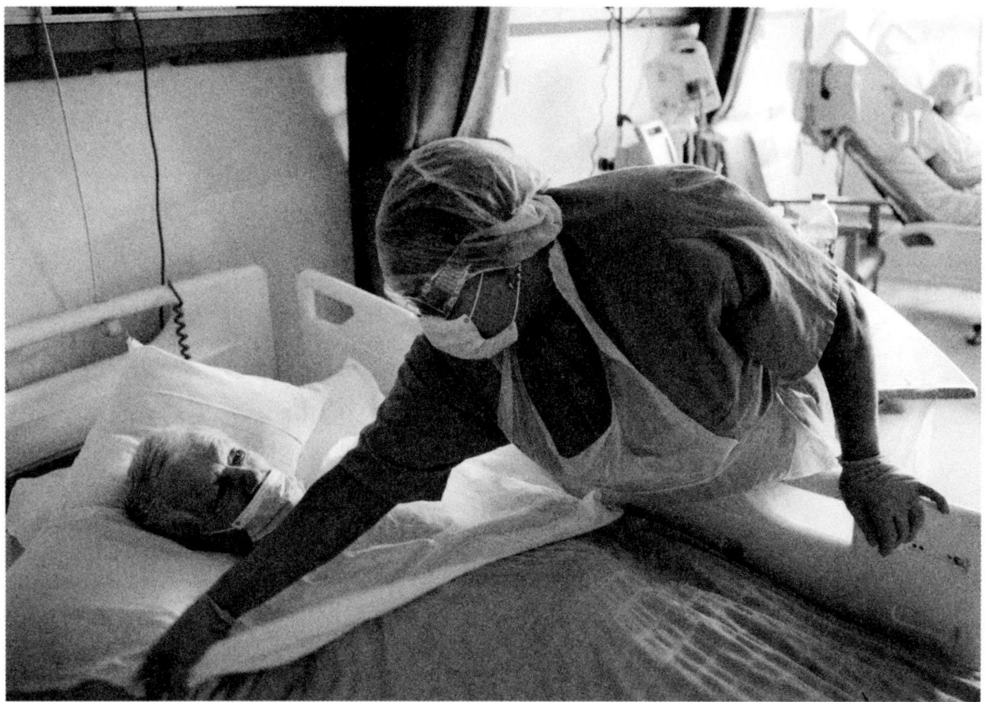

Giles Duley, *Charles Pannett Ward, St Mary's Hospital, 2020,* from the chapter
*Inside the Red Zone* (p.60)

showcases some of the most exceptional bodies of work made in London
over that time. It brings into focus the fragmentary experiences of lockdown
life in the capital, from deserted city streets and hospital wards to community
support networks and domestic confinement. Each of these two dozen
image-makers grapples with the dislocated nature of existence during coronavirus in a unique and personal way, exploring what it has meant to live in
London under the shadow of this existential, yet invisible threat.

When the UK government announced the first nationwide lockdown on
23 March 2020, the significance of the pandemic as an era-defining moment
was immediately apparent: nothing of this scale had happened in Europe since
World War II. Attempts to historicise and make sense of this simultaneously
disorienting and transfixing event emerged almost immediately. In July 2020,
historian James West Davidson wrote in *The Atlantic* that if a future history
textbook were to describe the year so far it would concentrate on 'matters of
life and breath'. He was writing about the pandemic, of course, but also the
death of George Floyd in Minneapolis – an event that shook America and

much of the world. As I write, the ripple effects of this convergence of a public health crisis and renewed calls for social justice and equality are still unfolding, but it is likely that 2020 will be seen as a year that defined the decade to come.

In response, a broad range of cultural organisations and archives sought to record the pandemic as collective memory in the making. At the Museum of London, we embarked on *Collecting COVID*: an expansive curatorial project to gather objects and first-hand experiences of the pandemic that would allow us to tell the story of this extraordinary period of time to future generations of Londoners. Hundreds of items soon came flooding in: diaries, sound recordings, homemade masks, NHS support signs, viral tweets, pandemic dreams and, of course, a huge pile of photographs.

Documenting history while still living through it is an exciting but daunting task. How do you decide what is worth saving? What might be considered meaningful in the future, and where do you begin when you cannot see an end? Without the benefit of hindsight, and with experiences shifting as the pandemic progressed – from initial outpourings of charity and community spirit to increasing frustration, protest and lockdown fatigue – the burden of living through and writing history weighed heavy on the Museum's curatorial team.

The challenge of capturing, collecting and representing the pandemic through photography also draws attention to the camera's long and complex relationship to questions of truth and the archive. The central question on my mind throughout this period of time revolved around the notion of what a photographic record of the pandemic might eventually amount to, and in what ways it would come to matter.

What would photography be able to communicate to future generations about our lived experiences of the pandemic? How could it possibly represent the fragmented nature of this crisis, which sharpened social divides of class, race, age, gender and ability, the wounds of which are likely to take decades to heal? How would certain images be reinterpreted, reshaped, sanitised or even distorted over time? And what tricks would memory come to play as current events receded into a more distant past?

* * *

In order to look forward, it proved useful to look back. Diving into the Museum's diverse collections to unearth objects of previous times of emergency – from past plagues and wartime stories to the polluted air of Victorian London and the 1950s' Great Smog – offered fertile ground from which to consider our contemporary predicament. The Blitz in particular became a significant point of reference. With common allusions to the 'battle' against Covid, the virus as 'enemy', hospitals as 'frontlines', and key workers as 'heroes', the language of war has consistently been invoked in how we talk about the pandemic.

Looking at the visual record of World War II in Britain, two things came to the surface that helped to interpret and frame the imagery of the pandemic. The first is that both photography and the conditions of crisis engender new ways of seeing; the idea that a state of emergency casts everything in a different light. It is this heightened sensibility, the psychological product of exceptional circumstances, that finds its way into the frame. Each of the photographers in this book has had to figure out different ways of working during lockdown. Their collective record demonstrates the power of photography to reflect the human condition, to communicate moods and states of being, to challenge and provoke, to connect us to others, and to detect beauty and joy alongside pain and suffering.

The second thing our archive brought to light had to do with how photography contributes to the construction of historical narratives and our tendency to use images to produce singular ways of seeing the past – things in need of critical attention. In the case of the Blitz, the best known imagery of the attacks tends to be shrouded in narratives of unity and victory – ideas that were actively propagated at the time and subsequently consolidated in the archive. We get a picture of 'Blitz spirit', which foregrounds resilience and bravery over the grim realities of living in a city under attack. This collective memory of ultimate triumph – of Londoners simply 'keeping calm and carrying on' – is coloured by a retrospective nostalgia.

In depicting the coronavirus pandemic, we might be wary of such unifying tropes and clichéd views; we must recognise that photography can only ever show part of the picture. There is work to be done, for example, in challenging the idea that the coronavirus was a 'great equaliser': an indiscriminate threat that affected everyone in equal measure. If anything, the pandemic proved the opposite – we know for a fact that the virus has disproportionately affected the lives of people of colour, that in some sections of society children have gone hungry, that women's wellbeing was hit significantly harder than men's, and

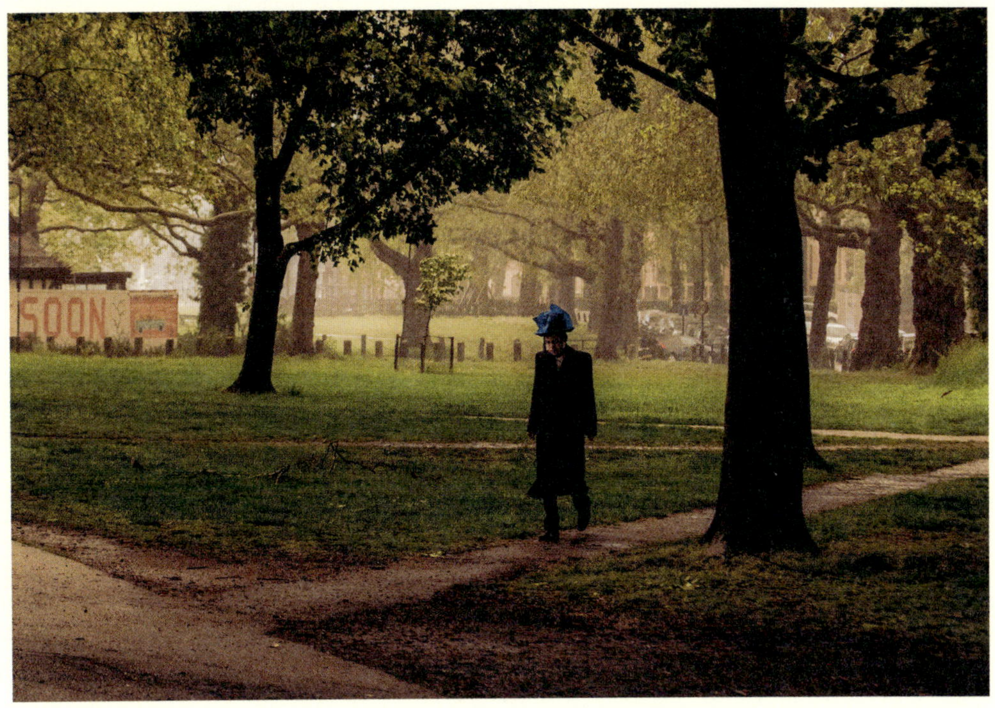

Grey Hutton, *Clapton Common, 2020,* from the chapter *The Ties That Bind* (p.88)

that the lockdowns only amplified socio-economic inequity. Ensuring these facts are recorded demands our continued attention, alongside an ongoing examination of what other truths remain obscured from vision.

* * *

*'London has become merely a congeries of houses lived in by people who work. There is no society, no luxury no splendour no gadding & flitting. All is serious & concentrated. It is as if the song had stopped – the melody, the necessary the voluntary. Odd if this should be the end of town life.' [sic]*

Virginia Woolf wrote these words in the early days of the Blitz, when the eerie silence of London's blacked-out streets made her feel as if the city had lost its song. Their meaning resounds today, finding an echo in Simon Norfolk's impressions of the empty, pandemic-struck city, *Lost Capital* (p.124), some 80 years later. 'London looks magnificent whilst looking as if it has been hit by a neutron bomb,' Norfolk wrote. 'I never imagined the apocalypse would be so quiet one would hear in Piccadilly the song of a blackbird.'

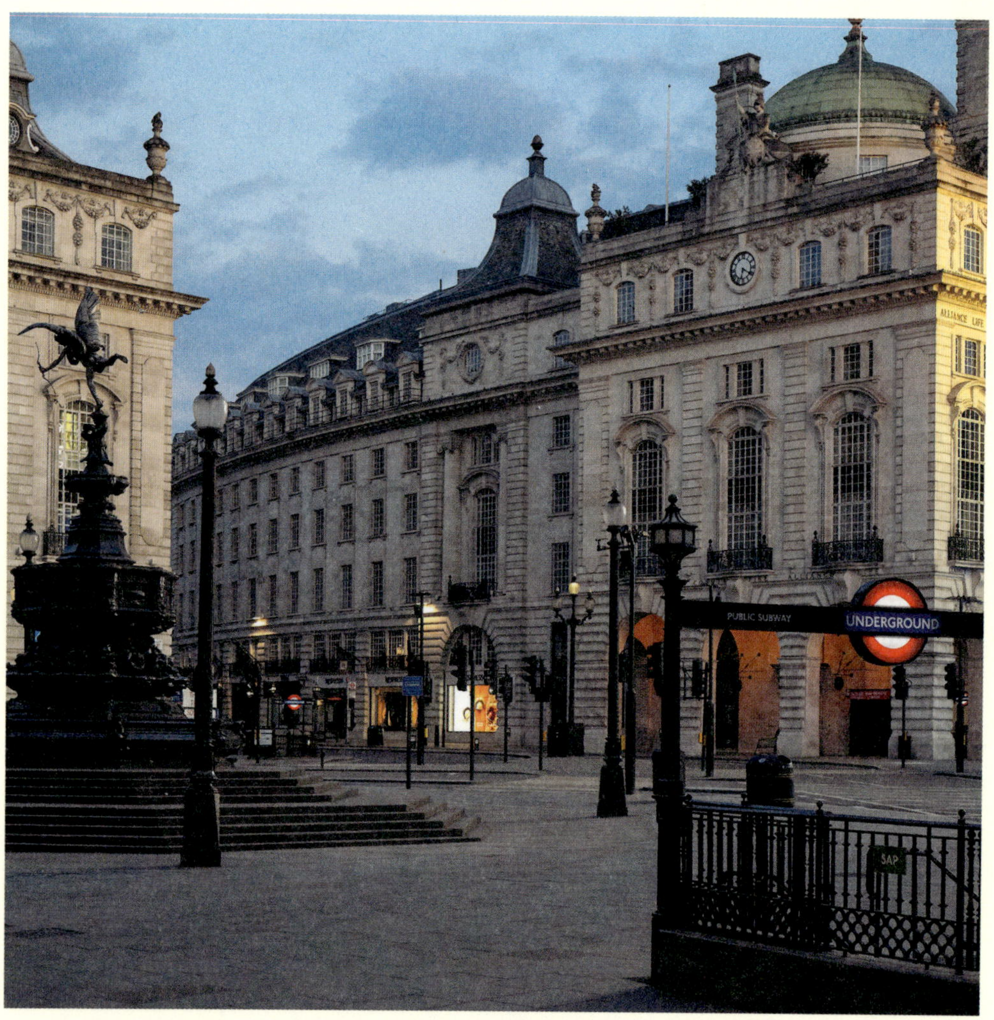

Simon Norfolk, *2020,* from the chapter *Lost Capital* (p.124)

In both these reflections, there is a sense of being present in the eye of
the storm – of a familiar world rendered unfamiliar, a tension in the air offset
by a strange quietude. Perhaps this is what it feels like to pass through
Arundhati Roy's 'portal' or 'gateway' into a different world: a moment of
suspension experienced as distinctly bittersweet.

During the first few months of lockdown, when we did not know what
was to come, there certainly was a feeling of hopefulness – despite the worry and
fear – about the possibility of emerging from the pandemic different, or even
better. It fostered a moment of self-reflection in which we could imagine

living more balanced, less toxic lives – both for ourselves and the environment. 'It was a bit like when you go to a new country and you see things for the first time,' said photographer Roy Mehta of his project *Lockdown* (p.198). 'Almost like you see that new country from a naïve point of view. After you've been there for a while you see it in a different, deeper way. This in a sense was a way of examining what we were going through.'

The idea of stepping over a threshold into a different world has been most perceptible in London's cityscape, which transformed into a ghost town overnight. Like Virginia Woolf in the 1940s, we wondered if the pandemic would come to mean the end of city life. This empty London evoked post-apocalyptic visions of a ruined city: deserted, abandoned and uninhabited. A number of photographers – among them Norfolk, Dorley-Brown and Hannah Starkey (*Empty City*, p.158) – ventured out to capture these once-in-a-lifetime views, conjuring images of the capital as a slumbering giant.

Freed from the hubbub and detritus of 21st-century life, the city seemed to open itself up to individual projections and imagined scenes, chance encounters and humorous coincidences. More than one photographer in this collection noted how they began to see London as a stage set, rich with layers of meaning; a carefully designed architectural backdrop populated by a cast of ever-changing characters.

For some, this meant capturing individual subjects and telling their stories through portraits that speak of fleeting connections and briefly shared moments. Alys Tomlinson's encounters with 2020's school leavers (*Lost Summer*, p.206), for example, stand as semi-formal portrayals of milestones left uncelebrated. For others, it meant watching the light bounce off the glass-and-steel buildings of the City, or dappling through foliage onto the waters of the River Lea. 'This new City is a sad and lonely place,' wrote Starkey at the time of creating her project. 'An ecosystem that has lost its pulse. I've become a light-catcher. A handy skill in an empty City.'

In the bright, beautiful spring of 2020, the sunniest on record, the light – that all-important thing for photography – transformed our everyday surroundings, drove us outdoors to whatever green space we could find and awoke the natural world around us. Atmospheric light, twilight, dawn and dusk are all employed as metaphors for transition in these bodies of work. In Mehta's ethereal landscapes and Celine Marchbank's wilting flowers

(*Shot in Isolation*, p.228), for instance, the first and last light of the day calls attention to natural cycles of growth and decay. In tracing nature's subtle transformation – an antidote to the anxiety produced by endless cycles of distressing Covid news – their images remind us that we are part of something bigger; that we might both learn to live in the moment and transcend it.

The scale of the pandemic, and the question of how you might capture something so uncontained, is reflected here in the images that convey a sense of alienation and distance. The estranging views of Jemima Yong (*Field*, p.150) and Mimi Mollica (*Moon City*, p.110) make the world appear as if it was viewed from another dimension. They stand in contrast to the projects that explore new-found attachments to place and feelings of belonging to local areas, previously unknown neighbours and the microcosms on our doorstep. In *Evering Road* (p.176), Christian Sinibaldi spent two months portraying the people on his street in Hackney: 'I started understanding the history of the road, and people started opening up to me. It gave me a sense of perspective and a real understanding of where I live.'

For many, the act of photographing is an urge, a necessity. This indelible need is brought to the fore throughout this book. With lives prised open in close confines, diaristic experimentation with the camera became a gift, an anchor, a means of escape. Photographers like Olivia Arthur (*Small Changes*, p.116), Philipp Ebeling (*Closer*, p.216), Lydia Goldblatt (*Fugue*, p.46) and Will Hartley (*While You Were Sleeping*, p.100) turned their gaze inwards, examining what it is that matters to us most intimately. Their introspective ways of seeing explore simultaneously shrinking and expanding worlds. In tender close-ups and pictures of the minutiae that surround us, we find a loving portrayal of what it means to be alive.

This is not to say however that the stark realities of the pandemic are absent from this collection. The struggle of life and death in British healthcare institutions was documented by war photographer Giles Duley, whose chapter *Inside the Red Zone* (p.60) stands out for its singular imagery of intensive care units at a time when photojournalists were banned from accessing such places. Andy Sewell's chapter *Food Banks* (p.132) and Grey Hutton's *The Ties That Bind* (p.88) are a testament to community groups and volunteer organisations that stepped up to meet the pandemic's many social challenges, while difficult-to-capture experiences of ill health, fear, frustration and grief

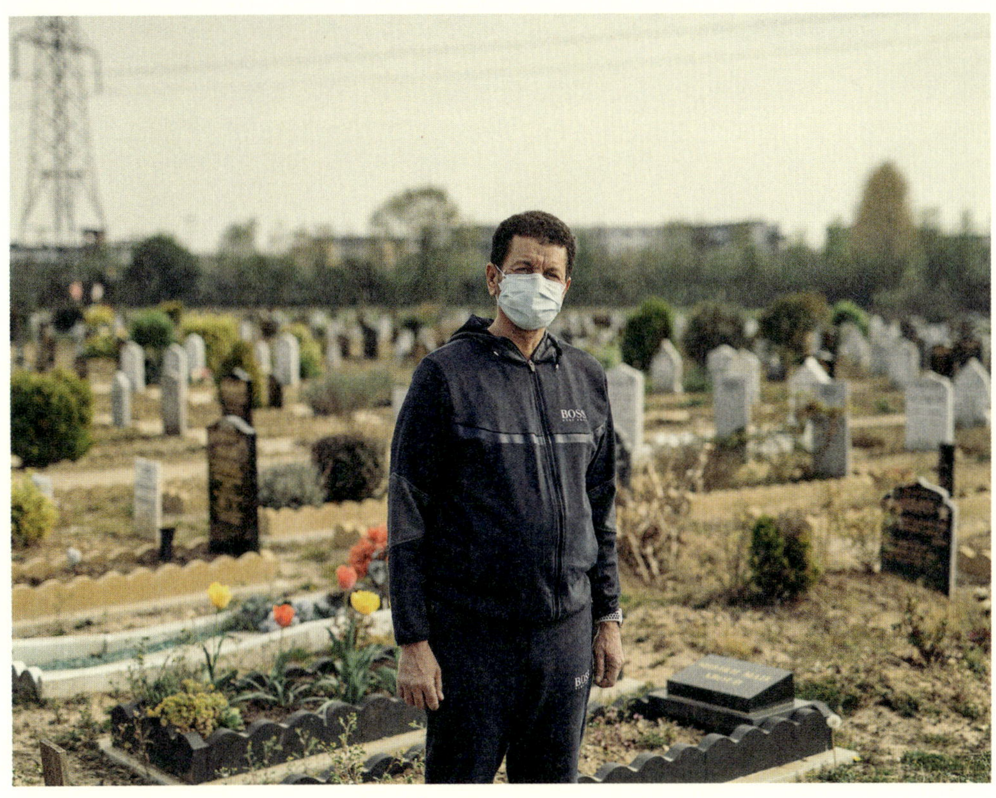

Spencer Murphy, *Funeral attendee, Waltham Forest Muslim Cemetery, 2020*,
from the chapter *Our Bullet Lives Blossom as They Race Towards the Wall* (p.18)

are complicated in photo essays like Spencer Murphy's. In *Our Bullet Lives Blossom as They Race Towards the Wall* (p.18), Murphy shows how closely these states of being are intertwined with broader issues of social inequality, racial injustice, and the government's handling of the crisis.

* * *

Such common themes and shared subject matters weave together experiences and impressions that surface throughout this book, but there are still connections, juxtapositions, associations and disjunctions that await interpretation and discovery. The question remains as to when we will have enough distance to reflect on it all. At what point will we know whether we have indeed been 'forced to break with the past' as Roy predicted? For now, as I write, we are learning to live with the virus – the rollout of the vaccination programme is bringing some optimism and hope for greater liberties, although fighting

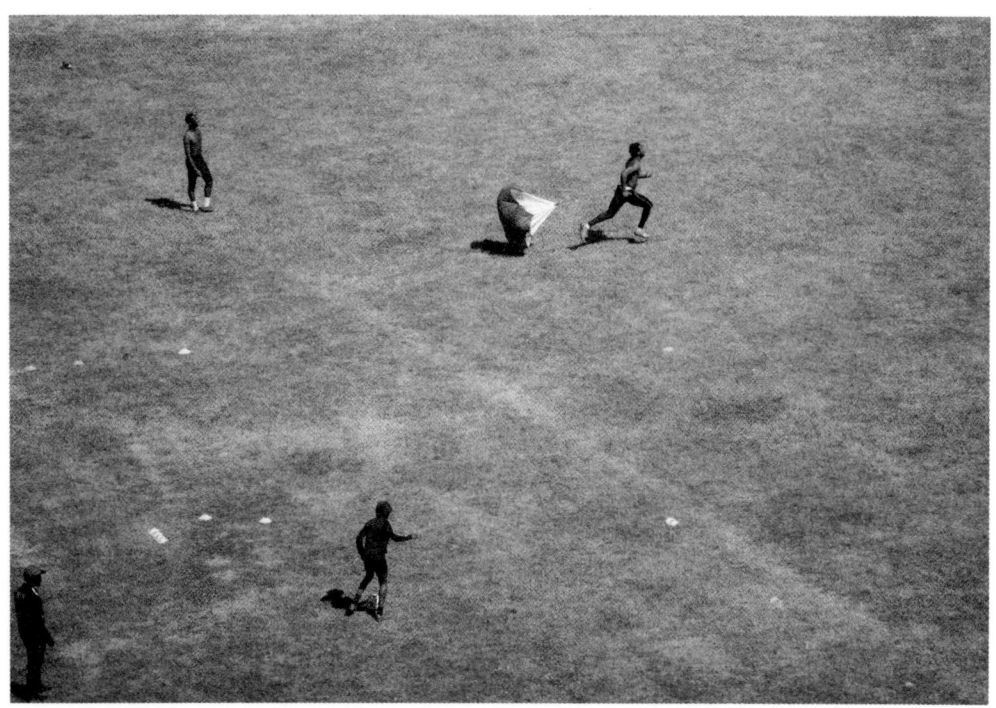

Jemima Yong, *South east London, 2020,* from the chapter *Field* (p.150)

pandemics in the plural might well turn out to be the grand challenge of our age.

    This set of images does not aim to make a chaotic world more coherent, but rather render it more complex. This book reveals how photography, in its many different applications, is a site of encounter: with the city, with urban nature, with ourselves and others, with painful truths, with closeness and distance, mundanity and transcendence. The pandemic offered us a different window from which to look out onto the world; one in which time temporarily congealed and an awareness of our fragility and mortality generated a new consciousness of being. Let's continue to look.

Jilke Golbach, June 2021
Curator of Photographs at the Museum of London

# Spencer Murphy
## *Our Bullet Lives Blossom as They Race Towards the Wall*

'In my lifetime I'd never seen anything like it,' says Spencer Murphy. 'I just felt compelled to go out and record what was going on, because I didn't know how long it was going to last for. It all seemed so strange. What I was seeing as I was moving through the streets just felt so cinematic. There was a nervousness in the air, and I wanted to try and capture something of the mood in that moment.'

From Tottenham and Hackney to the borders of Essex, Murphy covered some 40 miles on his bike in the early stages of the pandemic, his camera always in tow. In his poetic and provocative series, Covid rears its head in masked faces and padlocked swings, in Boris Johnson's pixelated image and wildlife reclaiming the streets of suburbia. Imbued with a sense of estrangement, Murphy's account of life under lockdown is as much a personal quest for the existential as it is an indelible record of the socio-political realities of the pandemic. Income disparities, racial injustices, the Tory government's handling of the crisis, the work of the NHS and the rise of 5G conspiracy theories are all brought into focus through graffitied slogans and powerful juxtapositions. 'It became a bit of a mental health thing for me, making sense of what was going on. Meaning was heaped onto everything. I'd sit on my balcony, a robin would come within close distance of me and it just felt way more poignant because of what was going on. I think everyone's emotions were heightened, and a lot of what I do tries to speak to that sensibility.'

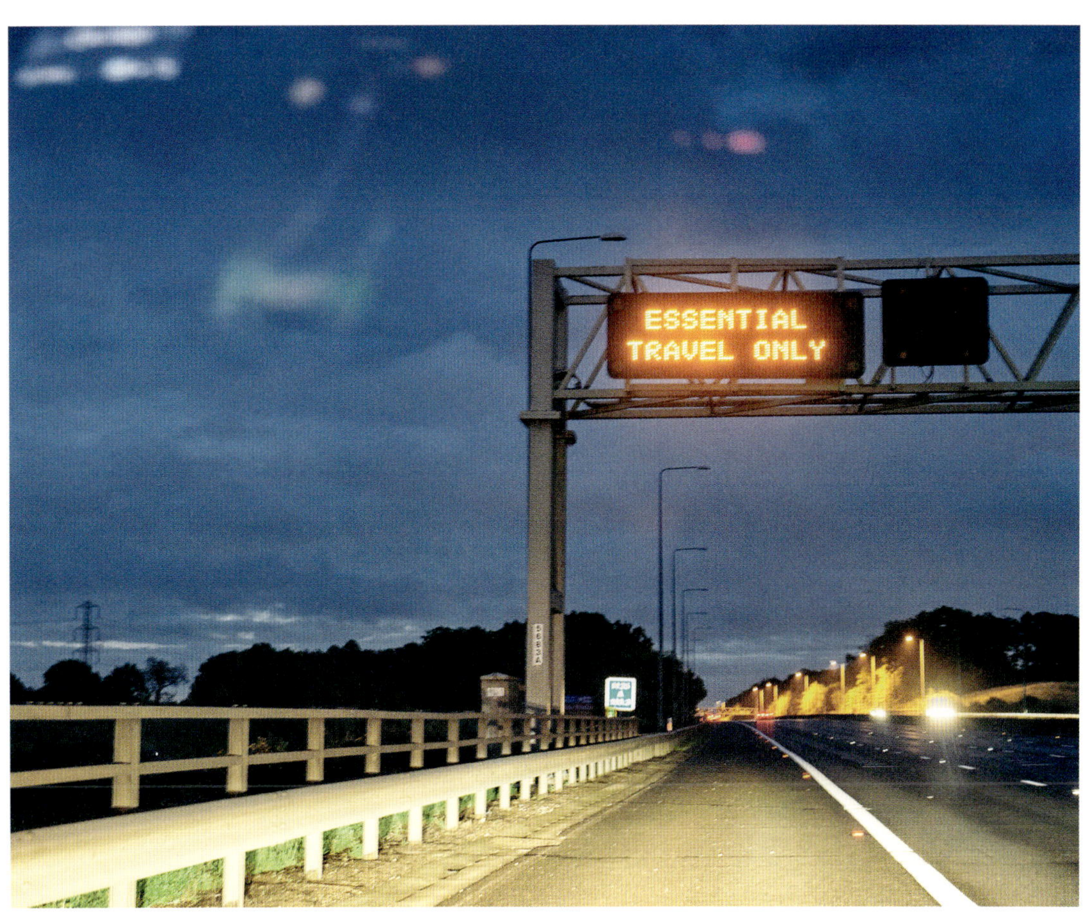


*'Essential travel only', M11 motorway, 2020*

Spencer Murphy

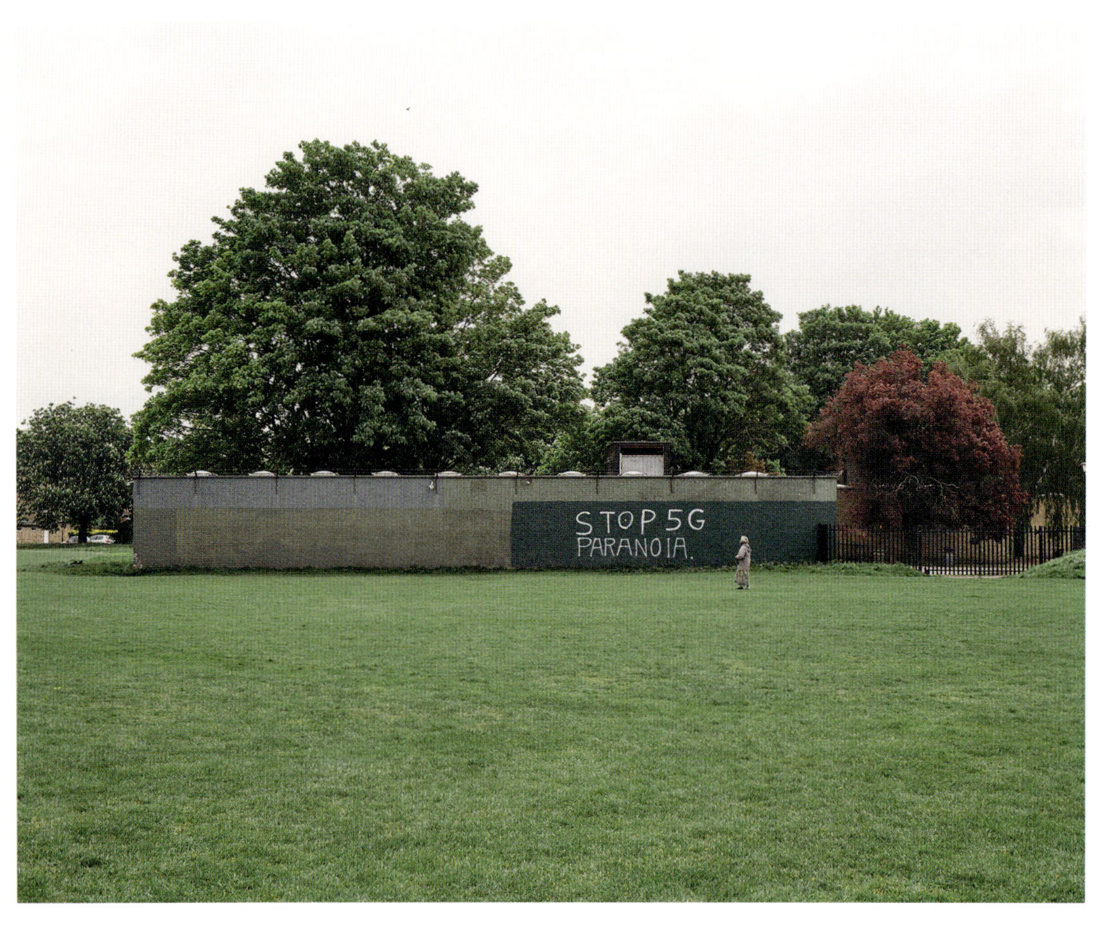



*'Stop 5G paranoia.', Wanstead Flats, 2020*

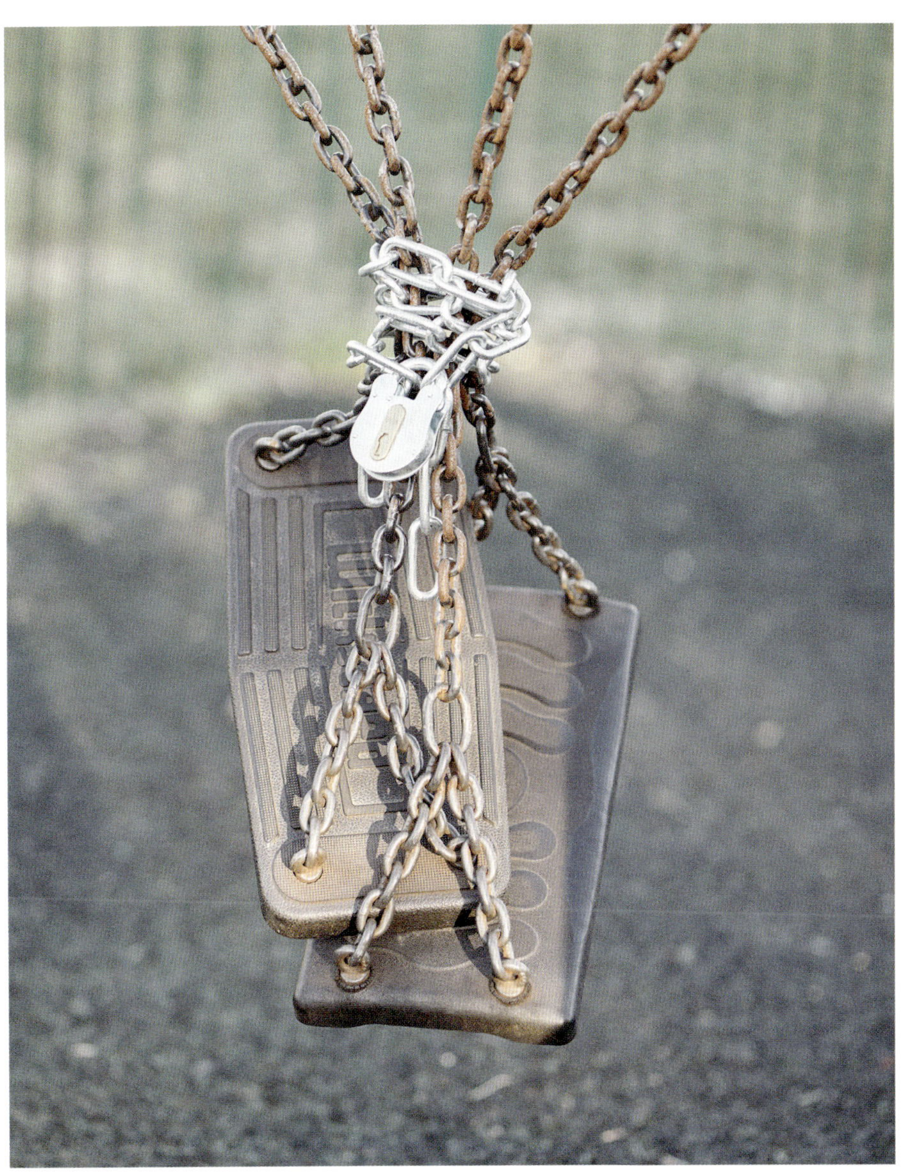

*Chained swings, Highams Park, 2020*

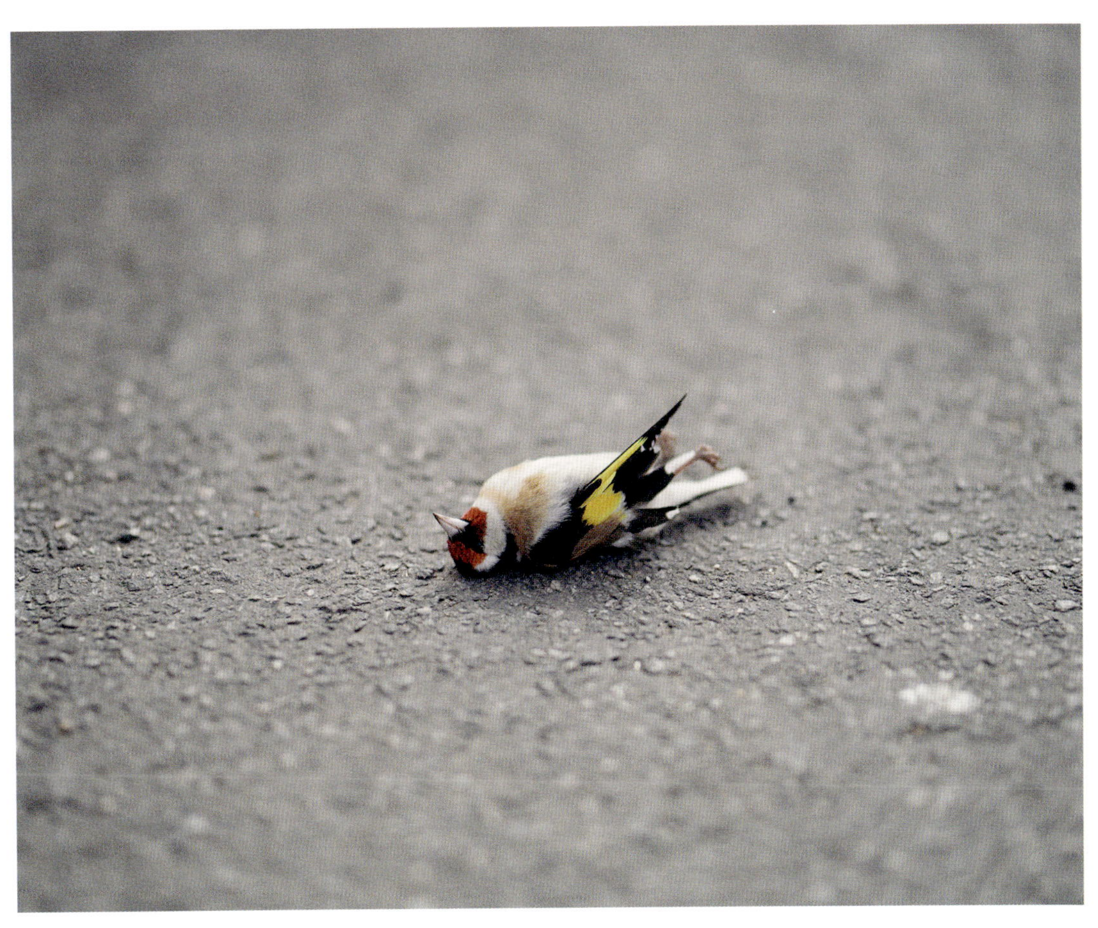

*Dead goldfinch, Hainault, 2020*

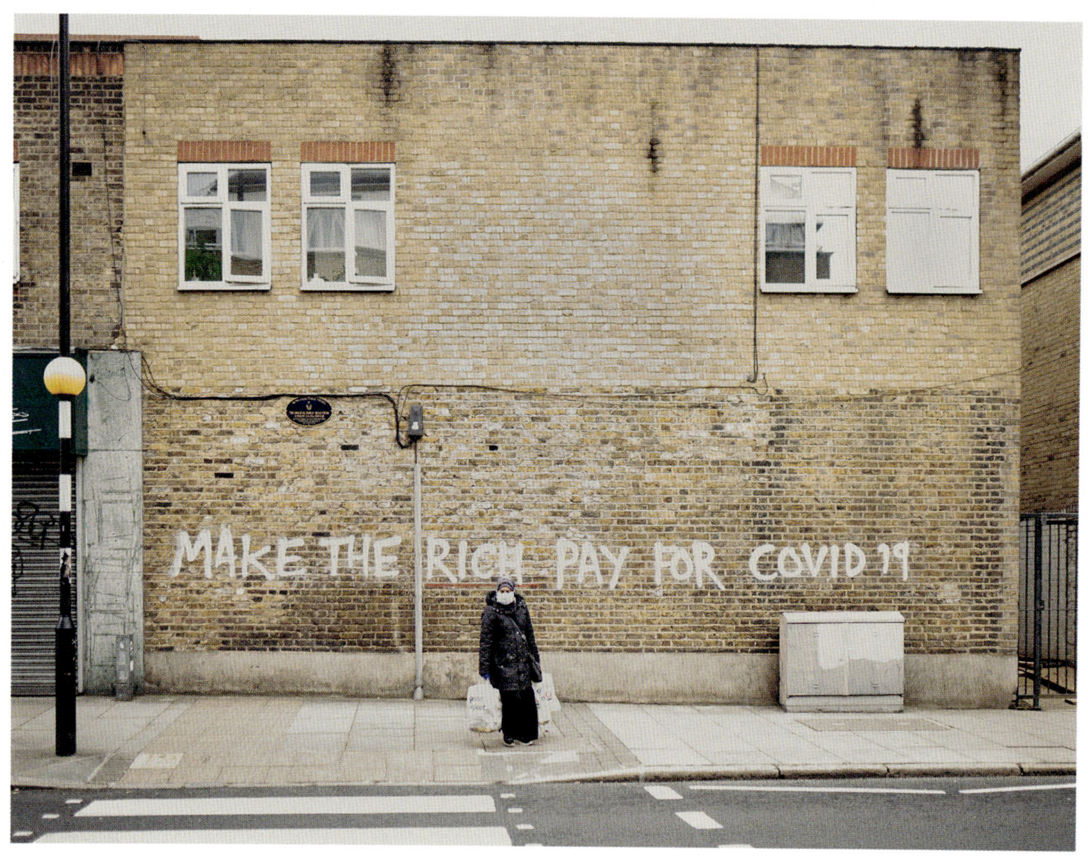


*'Make the rich pay for Covid 19', Roman Road Market, 2020*

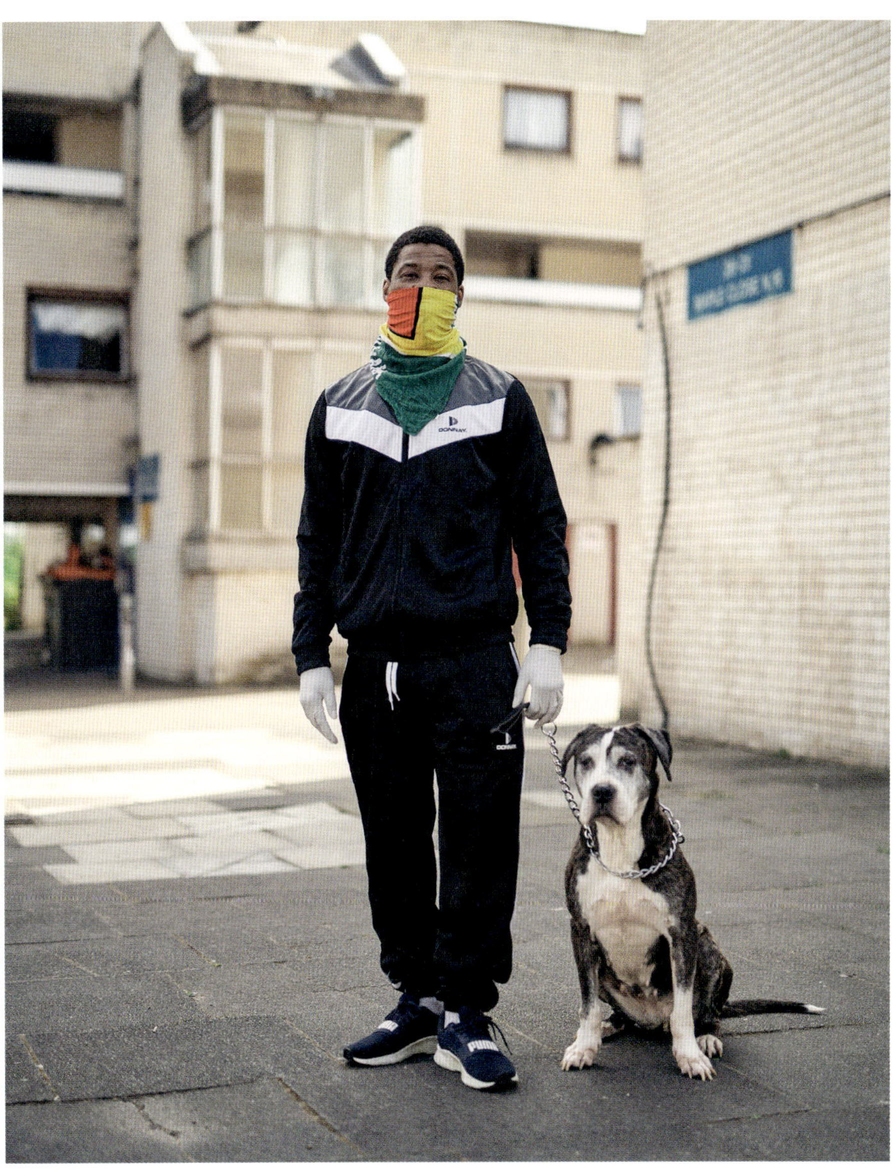

*Dog walker, Stamford Hill, 2020*

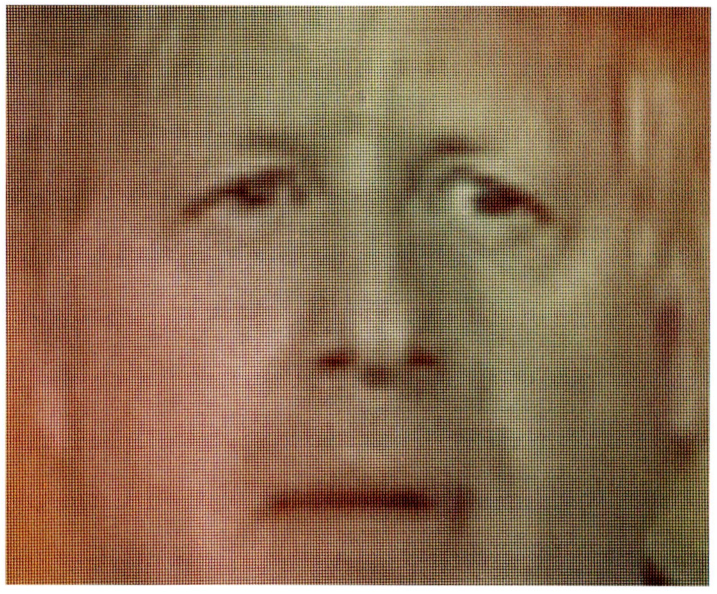

*Boris' degraded face, TV broadcast, 2020*

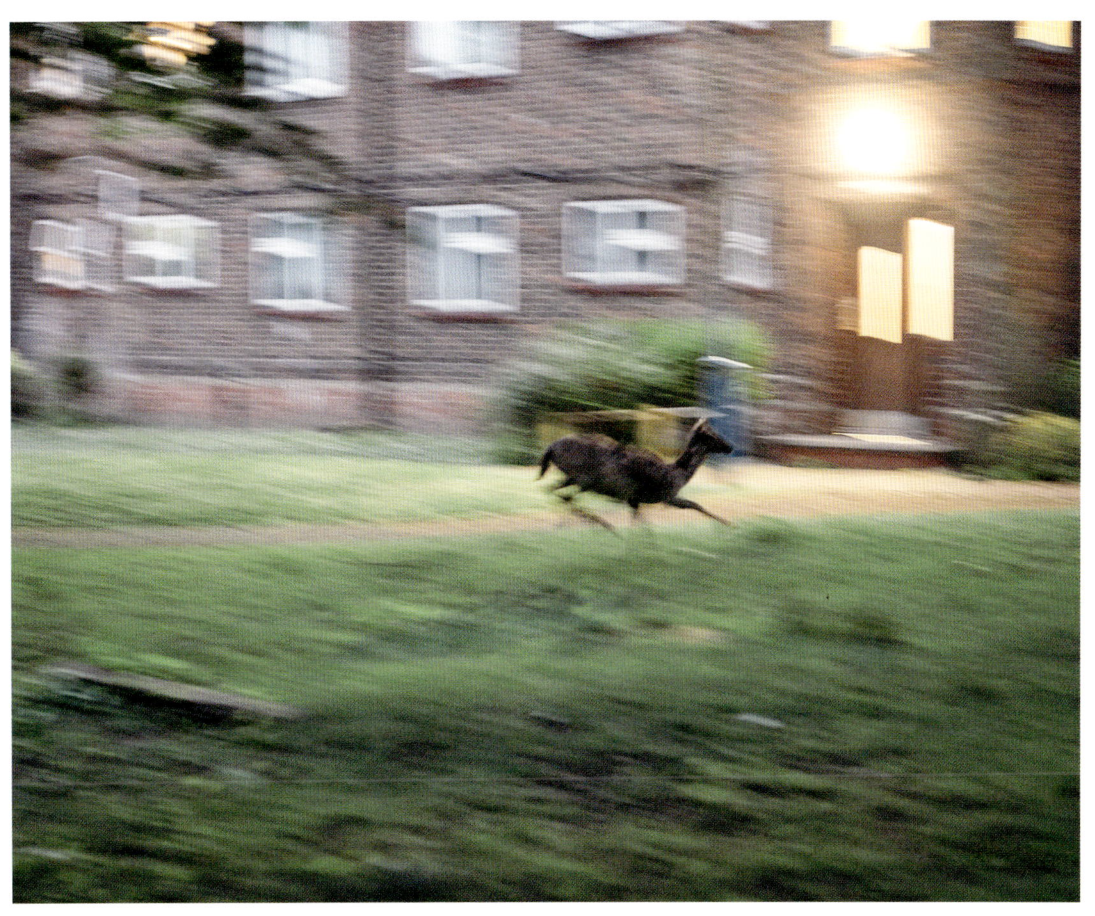

*Deer at dawn, Romford, 2020*

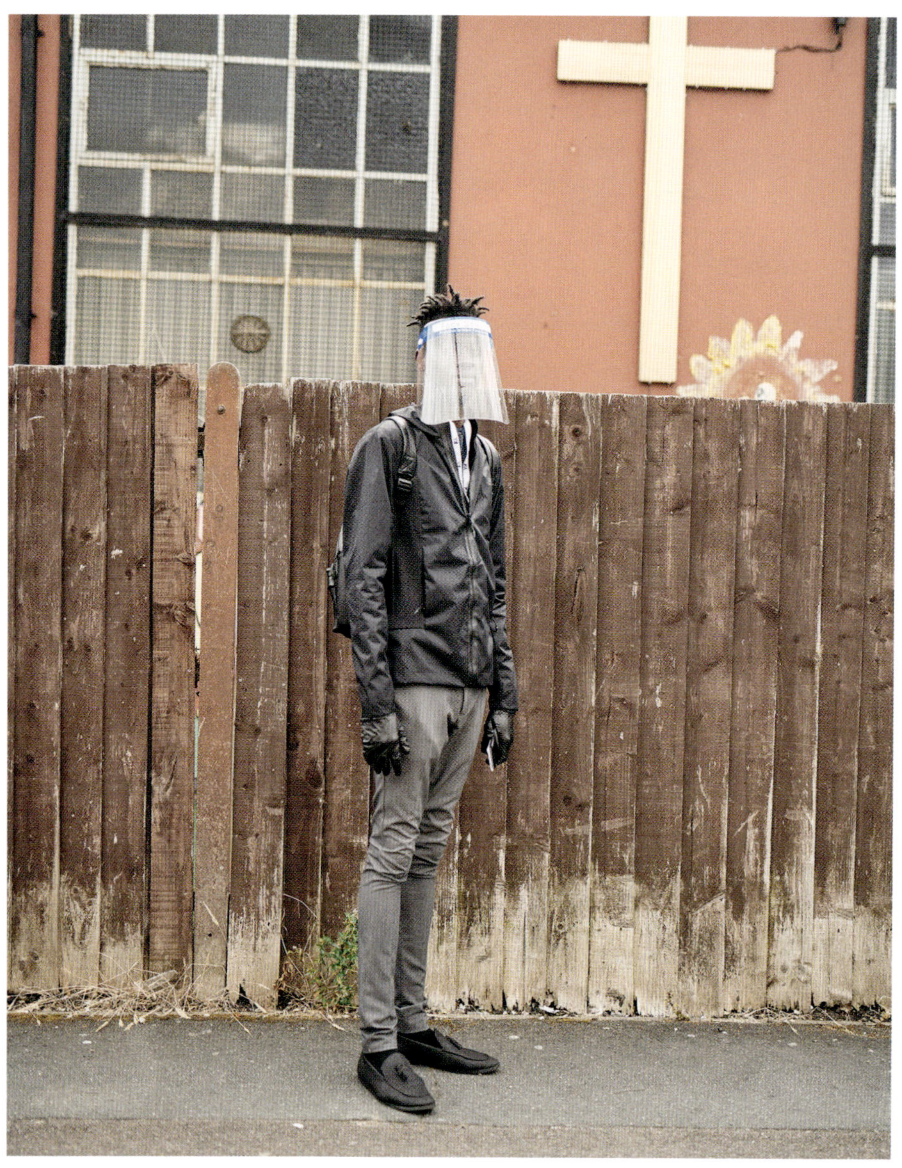

*Energy salesman, Leyton, 2020*

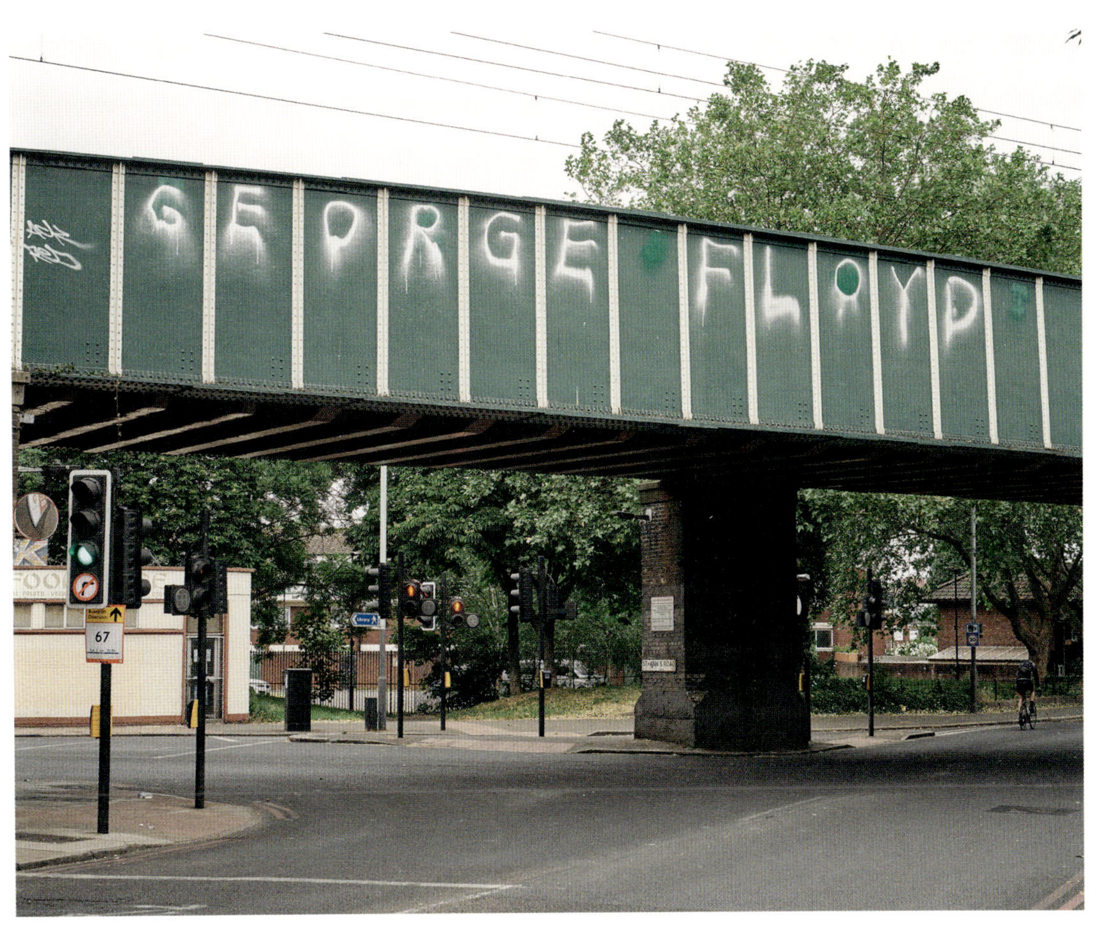


*'George Floyd', Seven Sisters, 2020*

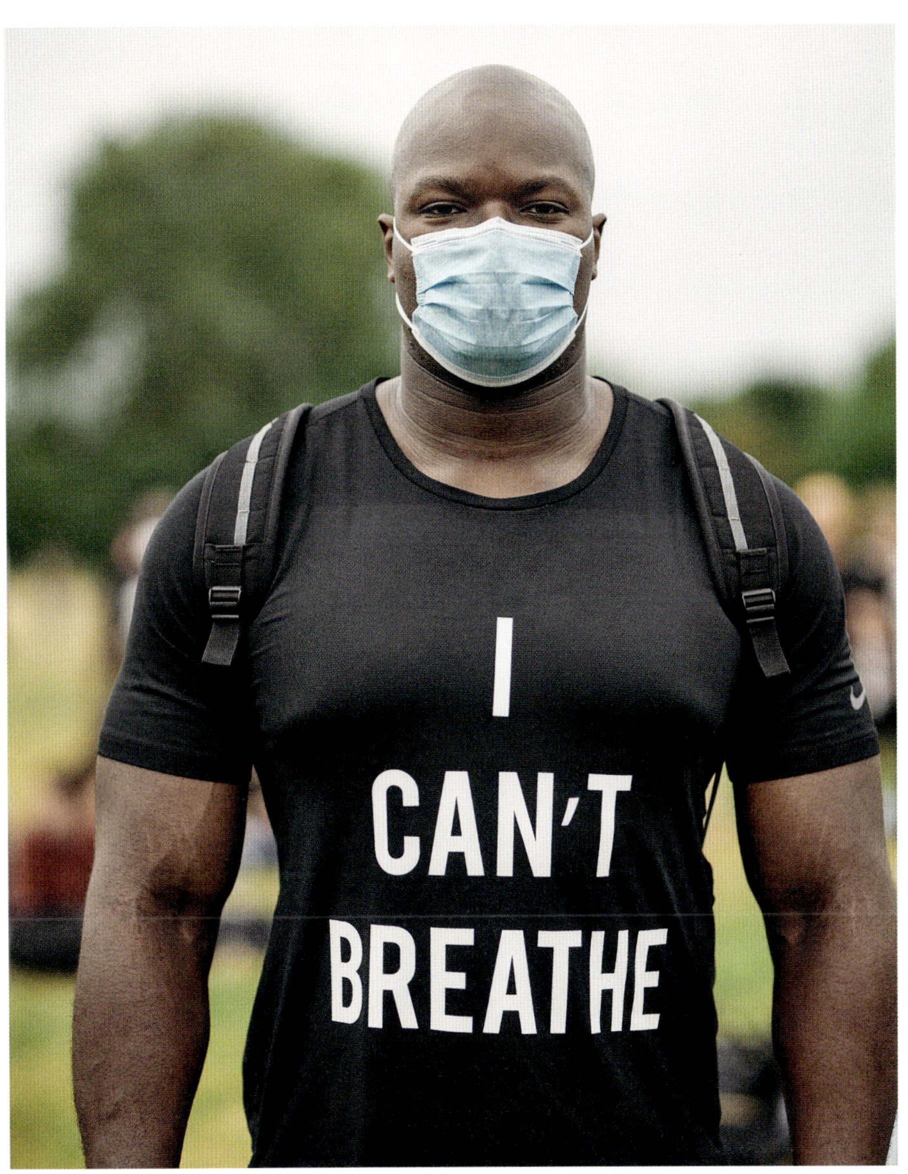

*Protest for George Floyd, Hyde Park, 2020*

*Lone plane, somewhere over east London, 2020*

# Chris Dorley-Brown
## *Deserted London*

'Photographers thrive on any change from the normal, and when an event like the pandemic lands on your doorstep it is almost what you have been waiting for,' says Chris Dorley-Brown. 'The word "surreal" has been overused, but the lockdown has been like a scene from a disaster film, especially in the West End. It really concentrates the mind because you realise: this is never going to happen again.'

If photographs are said to immortalise their subjects, Dorley-Brown's images certainly document the city as it might never be seen again. A long-time chronicler of urban life, Dorley-Brown casts London in an extraordinary light in this cinematic series. His moody skies and dream-like sunlight render the city a strangely purified version of itself; its streets and squares as pristine and uninhabited as an architect's visualisation. Somewhere between apocalyptic and utopian, unnerving and idyllic, the project prompts us to wonder: can these visions really be the same London we know?

By framing the pandemic in such carefully constructed images, Dorley-Brown uses photography as a way of unravelling the city's historic fabric and bringing its ghosts back to life. 'The pandemic stripped away all the extra baggage, the years you've spent in the city. All that suddenly disappears, and you're left with just a place, which has a history. All those things – the statues and the buildings and the things you never noticed before – suddenly move into sharp focus and you consider what they mean. Even though there are no people in my pictures, these places are very human: they have been constructed and mythologised and contextualised by people's aspirations and dreams.'

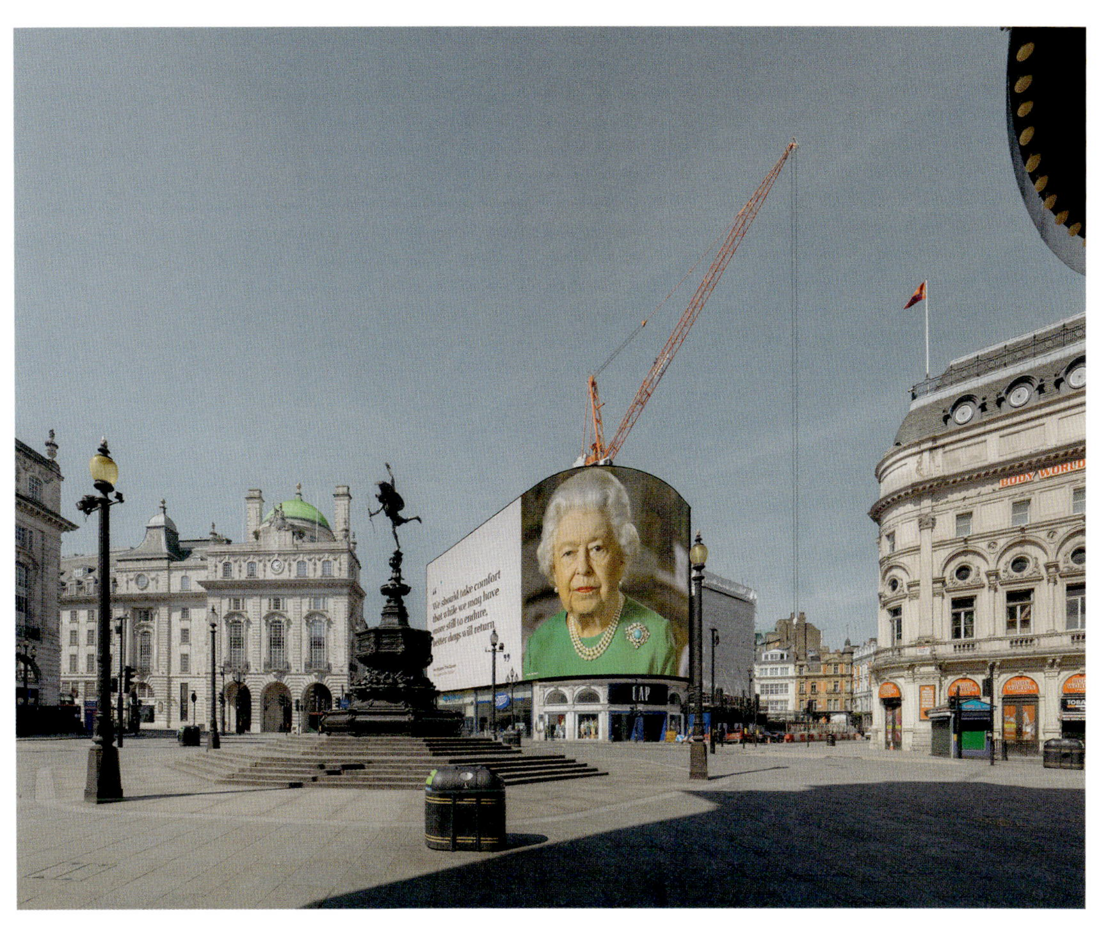



*Piccadilly Circus, Tuesday 7 April 2020*

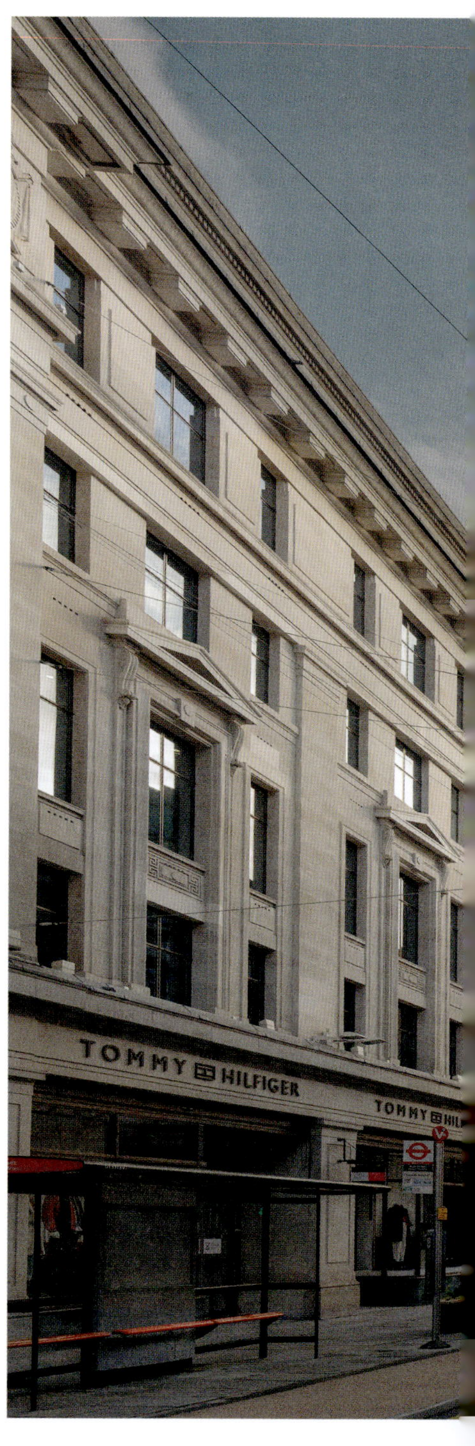

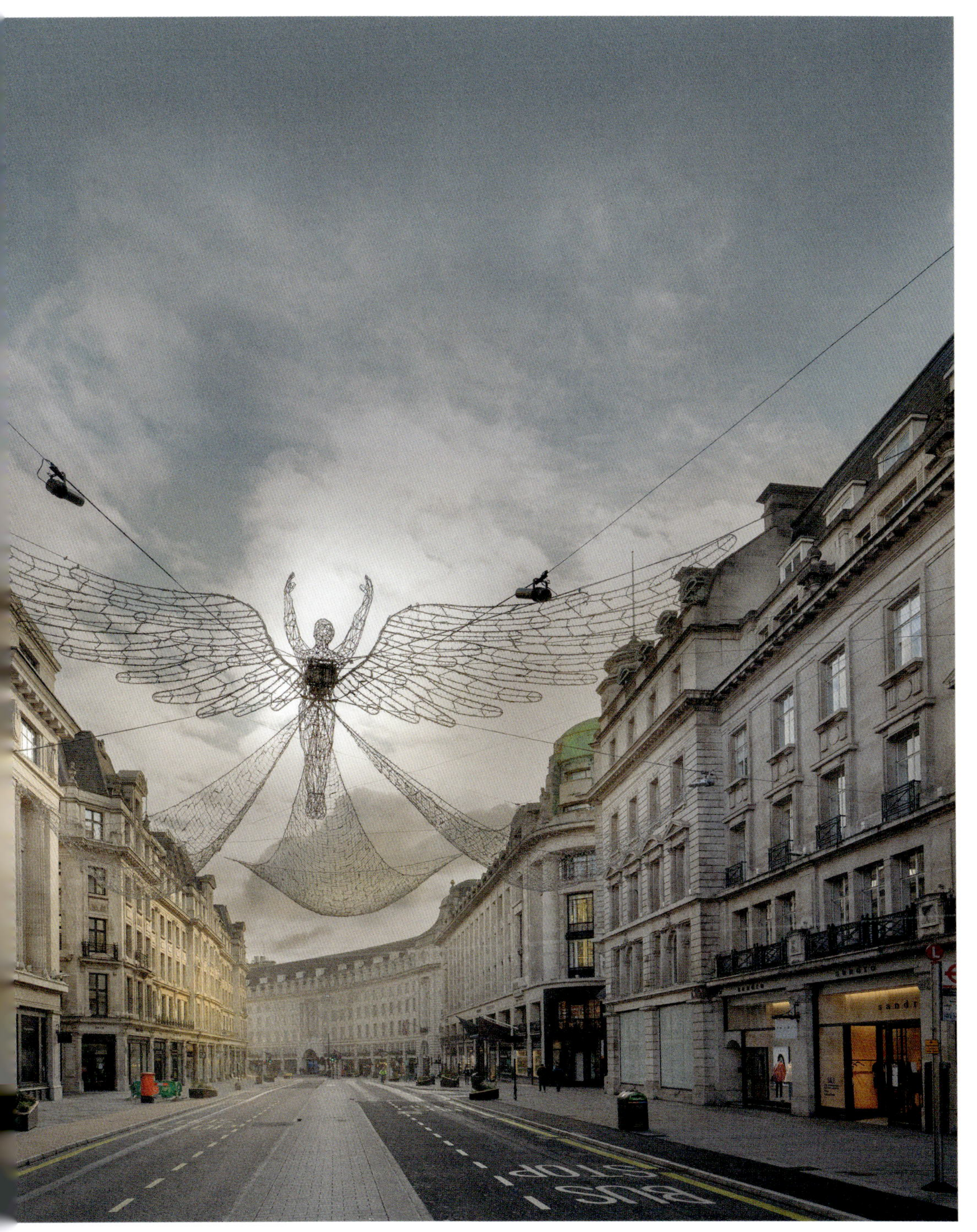

*Regent Street, Friday 8 January 2021*

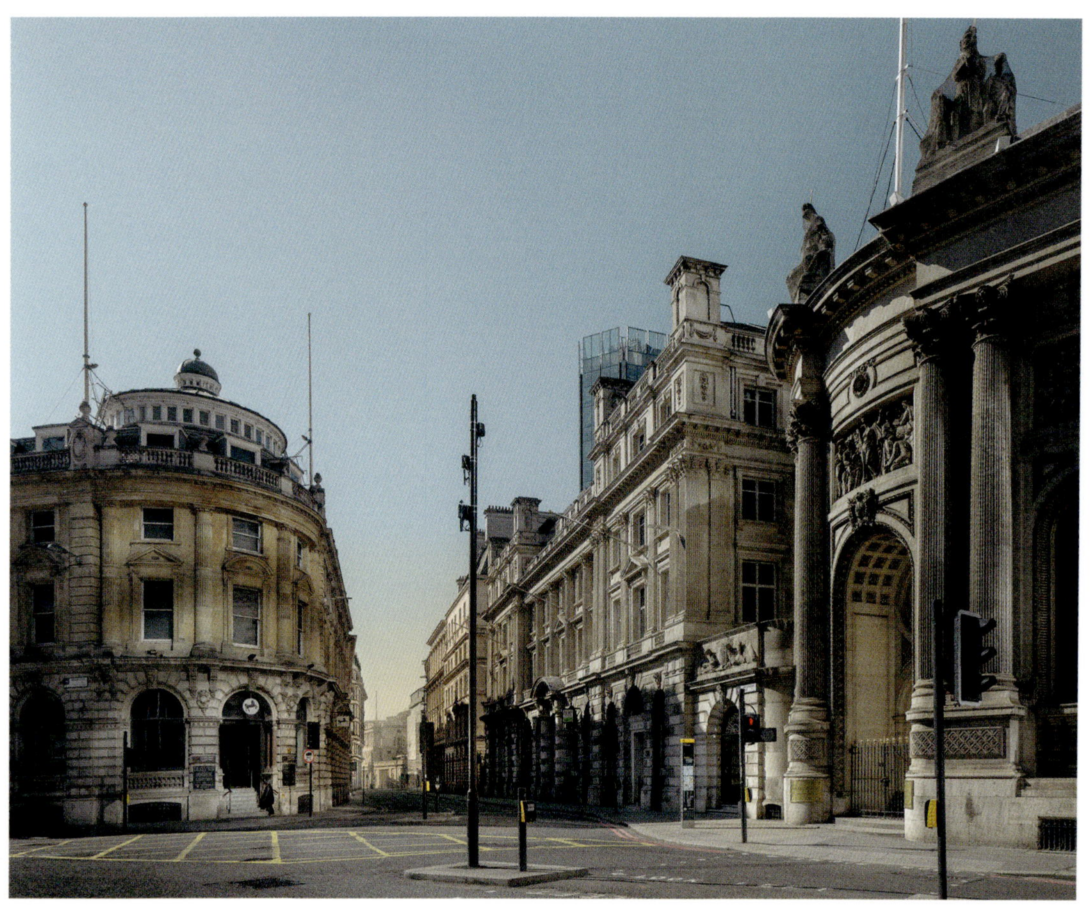

*Threadneedle Street, Monday 30 March 2020*

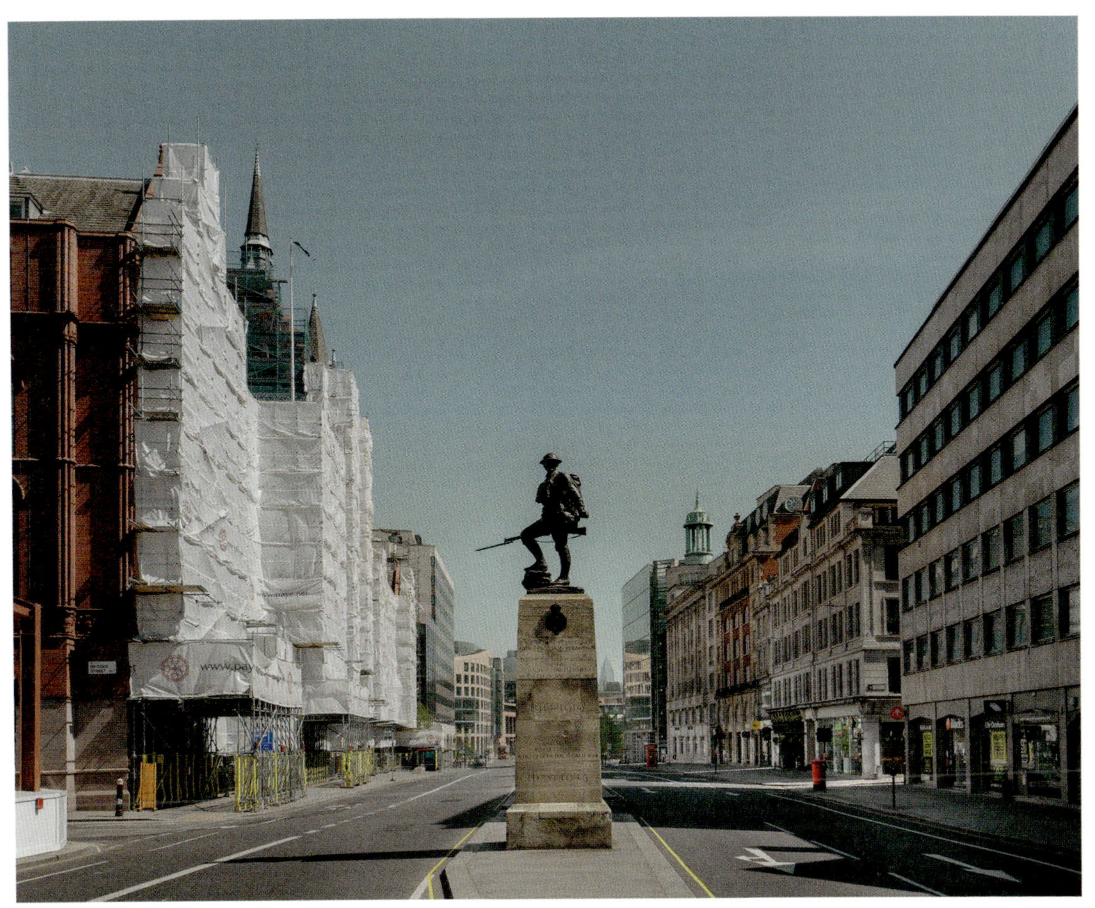

Royal Fusiliers War Memorial, *Tuesday 21 April 2020*

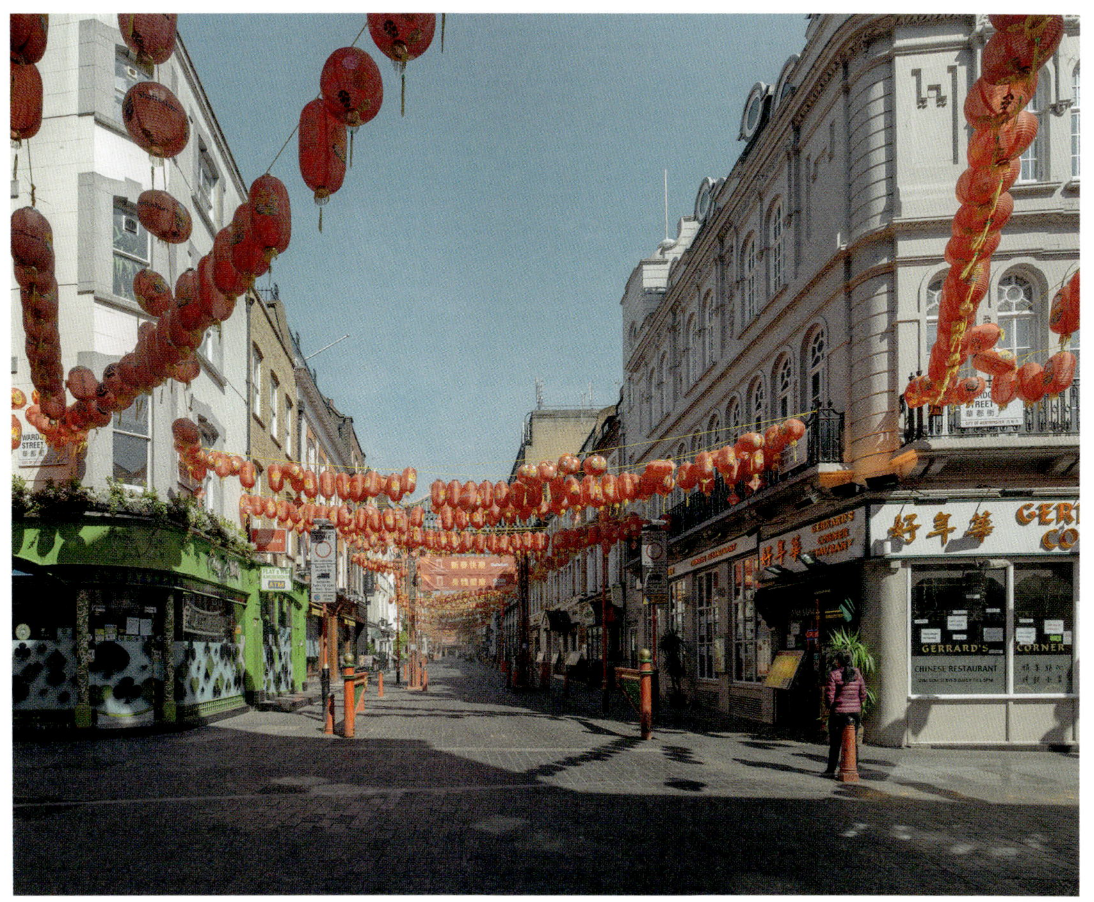

*Gerrard Street, Wednesday 15 April 2020*

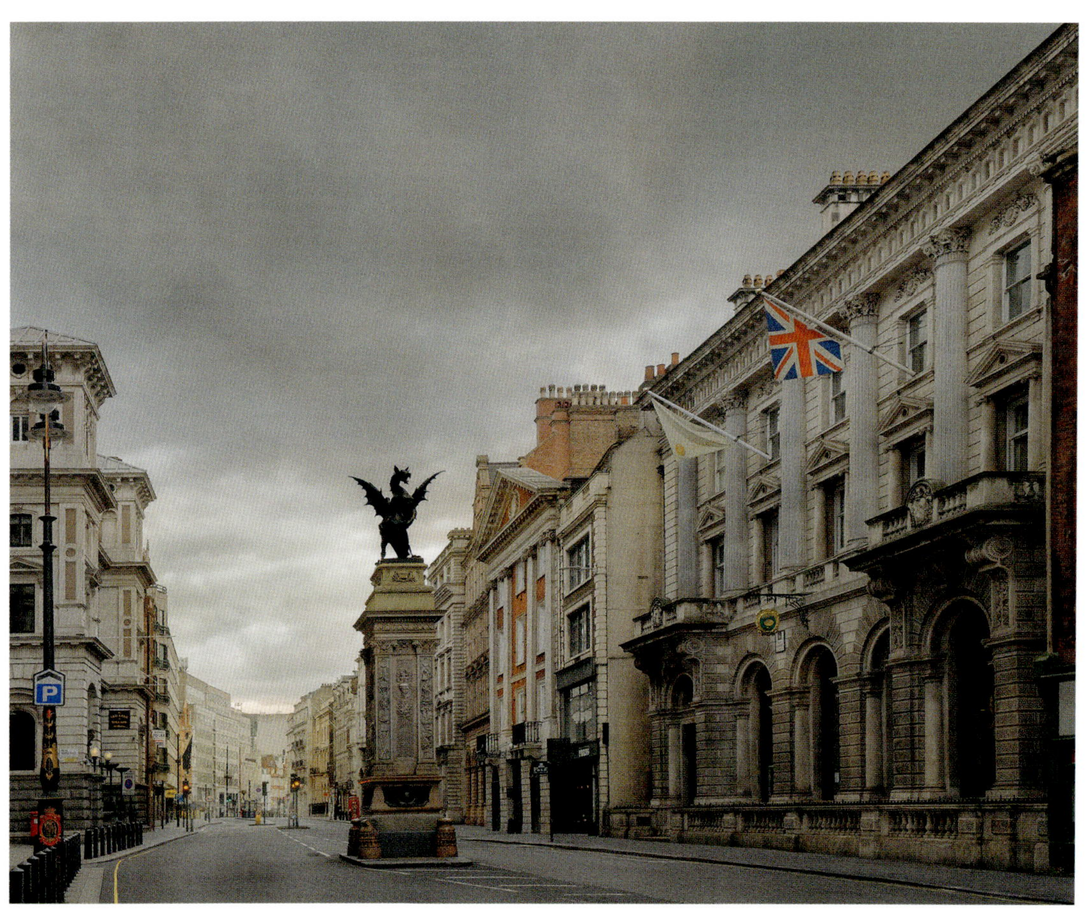

*Fleet Street, Friday 3 April 2020*

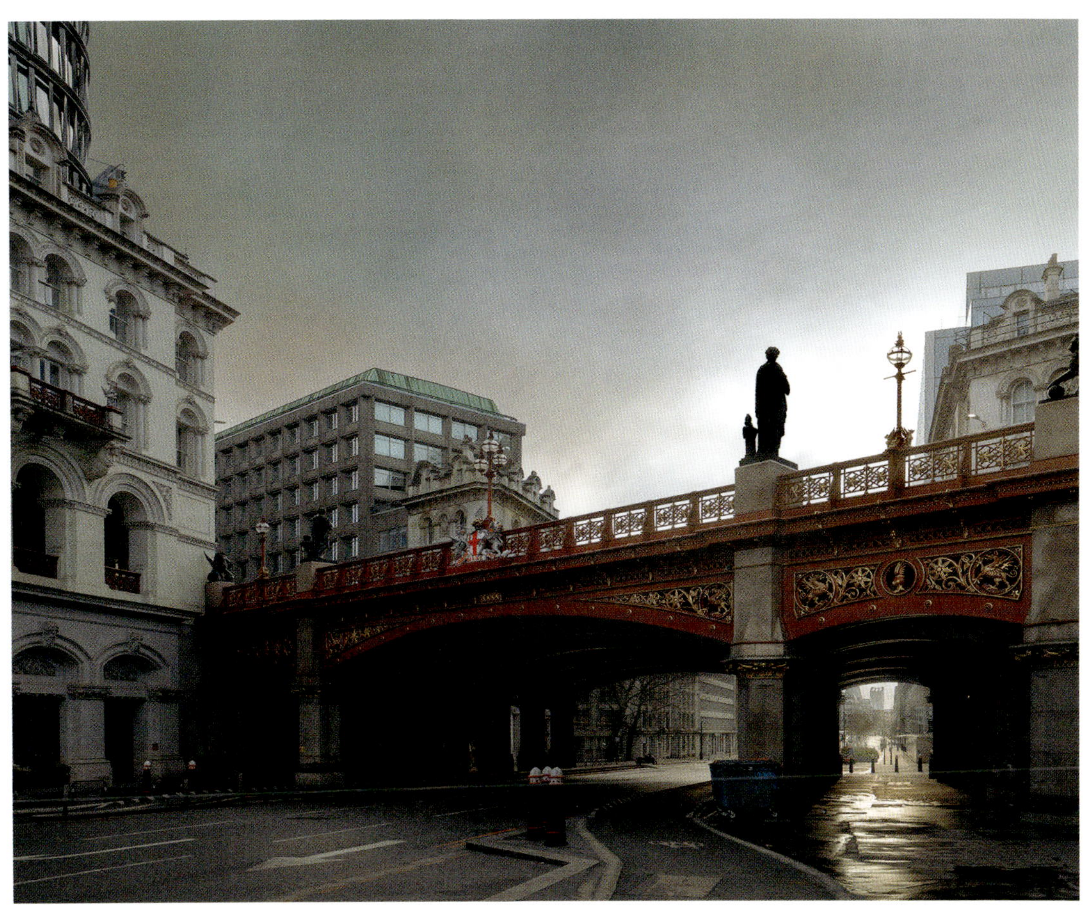

*Holborn Viaduct, Wednesday 6 January 2021*

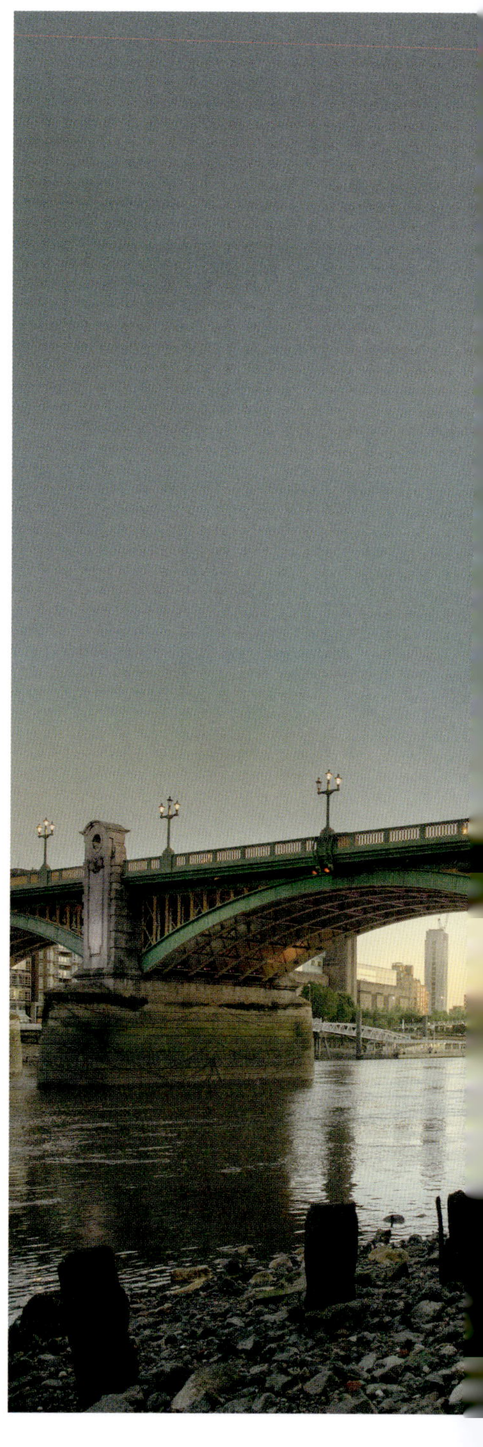

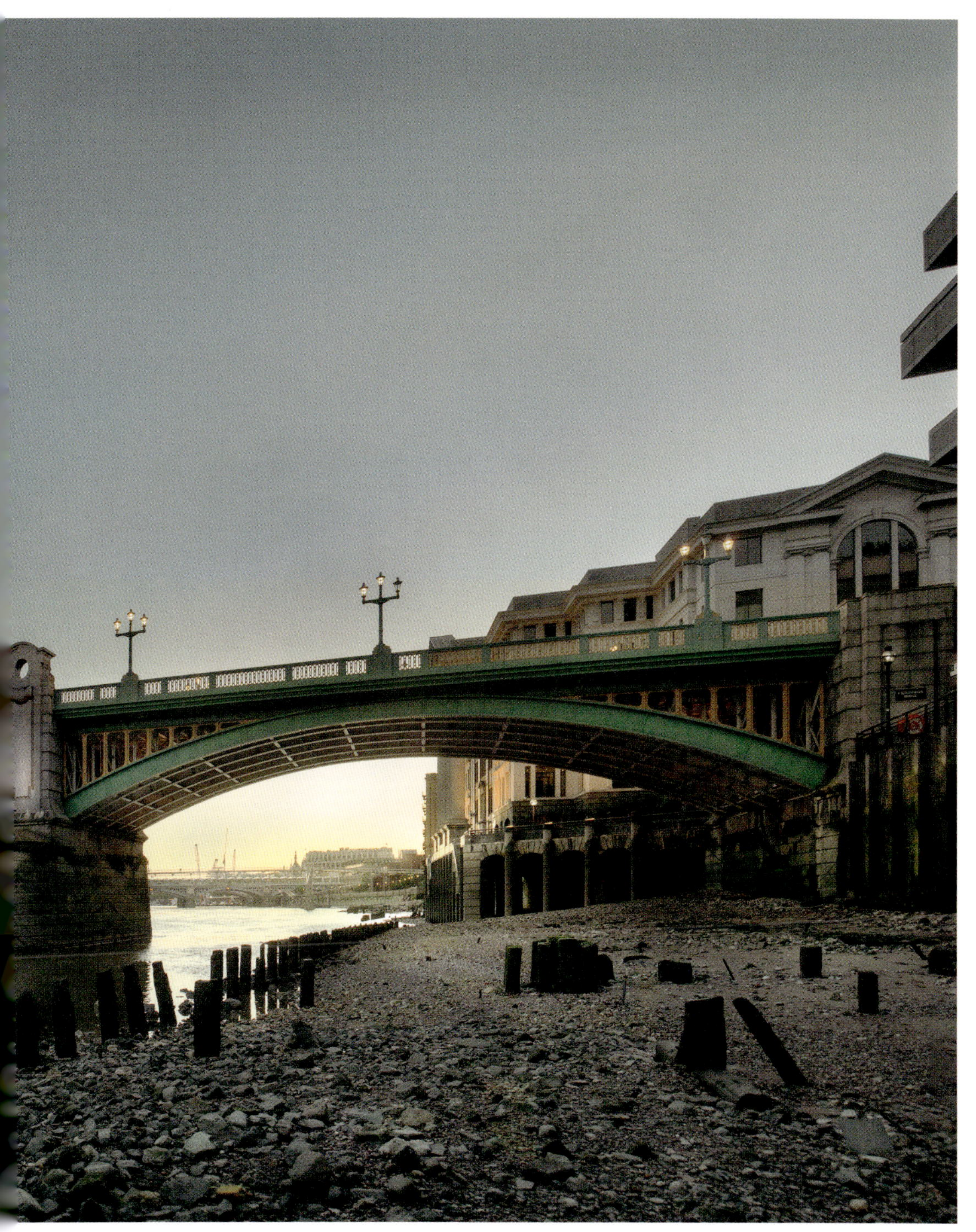

*Southwark Bridge, Sunday 21 June 2020*

# Lydia Goldblatt
## *Fugue*

Personal, lyrical and profoundly tender, Lydia Goldblatt's project *Fugue* contemplates themes of mothering, intimacy and alienation in the context of the pandemic. The series began when Goldblatt picked up her camera to photograph the scattering of her mother's ashes, just days before the first lockdown. It traces a confluence of emotions and events as she grappled with the state of absence caused by her mother's death while finding herself completely absorbed by the care of two young children. Through photography, Goldblatt found a way to express her experience of love and loss, anxiety and dissociation in enigmatic images that visualise the simultaneous mundanity and poetry of everyday home life, at a remove from a world that seemed to be collapsing in on itself.

Shooting on an analogue camera, Goldblatt found it both fitting and freeing to not instantaneously be able to see the images she was creating: 'There was this intangibility and lack of access and lack of visibility around it that was a very good metaphor for everything. The act of photographing and the knowledge that I was making something was a real saving grace for me. It helped me to be aware and to be present, and – as much as I could within the constraints of my situation – to reflect.' The immediacy and intuition of Goldblatt's images of her family and close surroundings communicate things that are difficult to grasp in words – emotions that run beneath the surface, and psychological processes happening unconsciously. In this way, *Fugue* echoes the rhythms of not only Goldblatt's own experiences, but of the state of transition that everyone existed in through the pandemic.

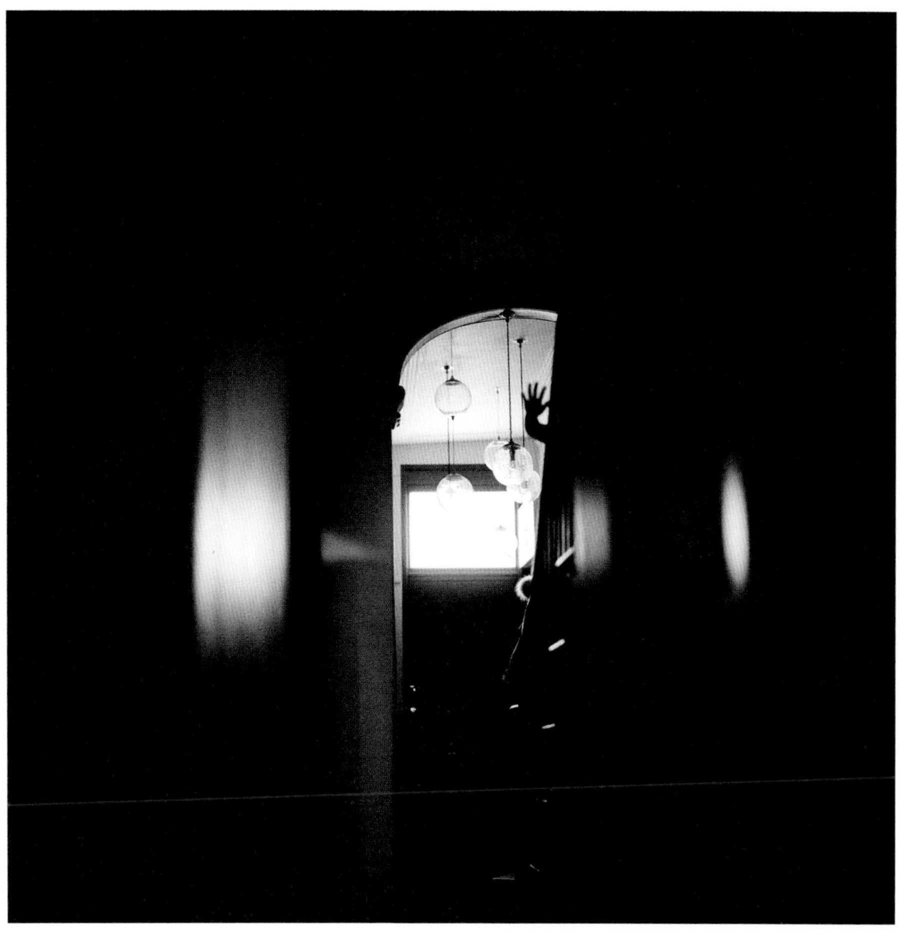

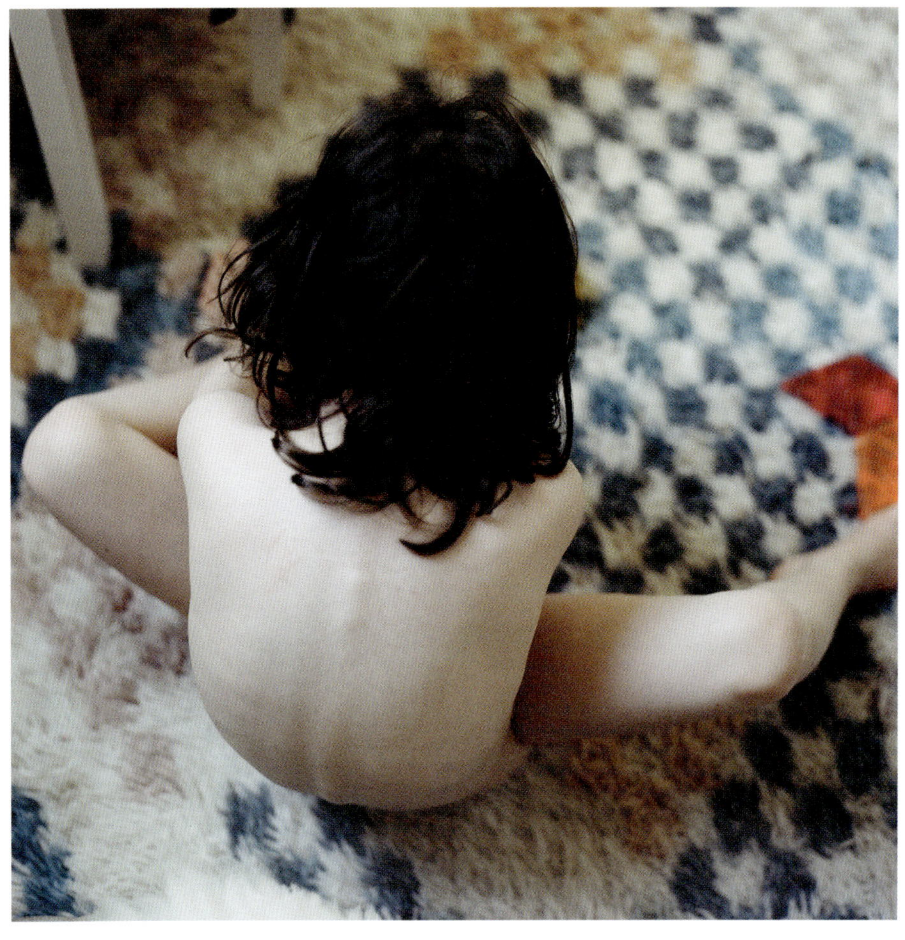

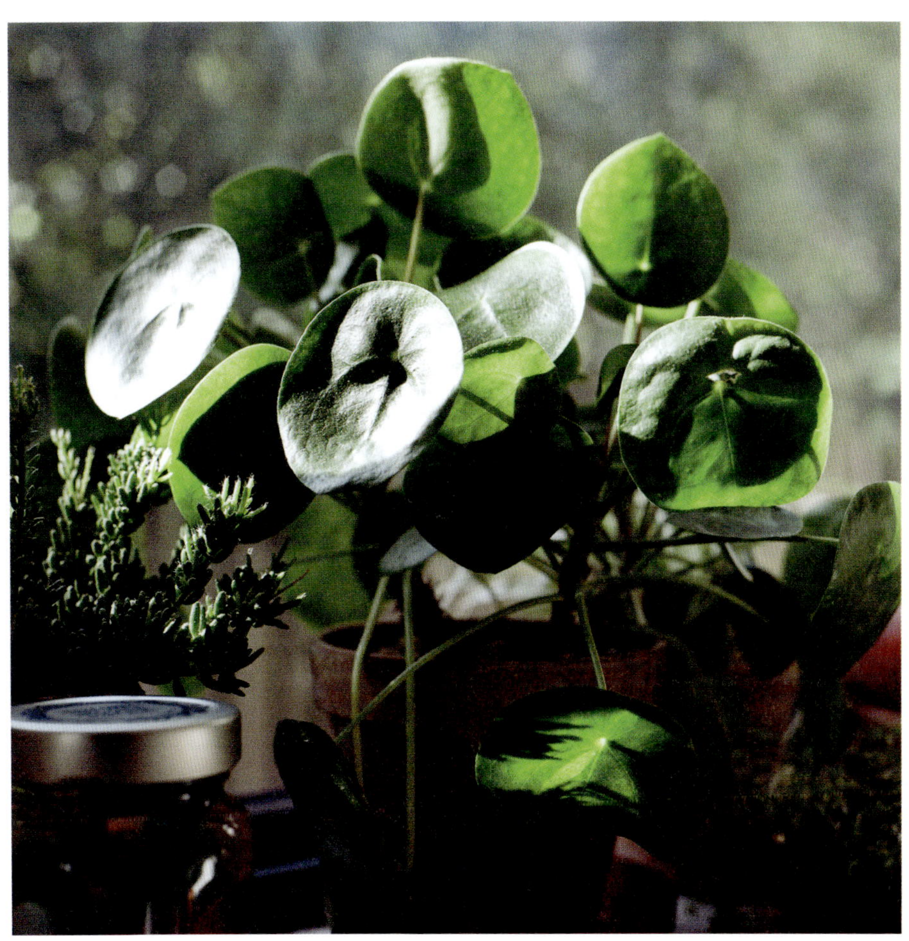

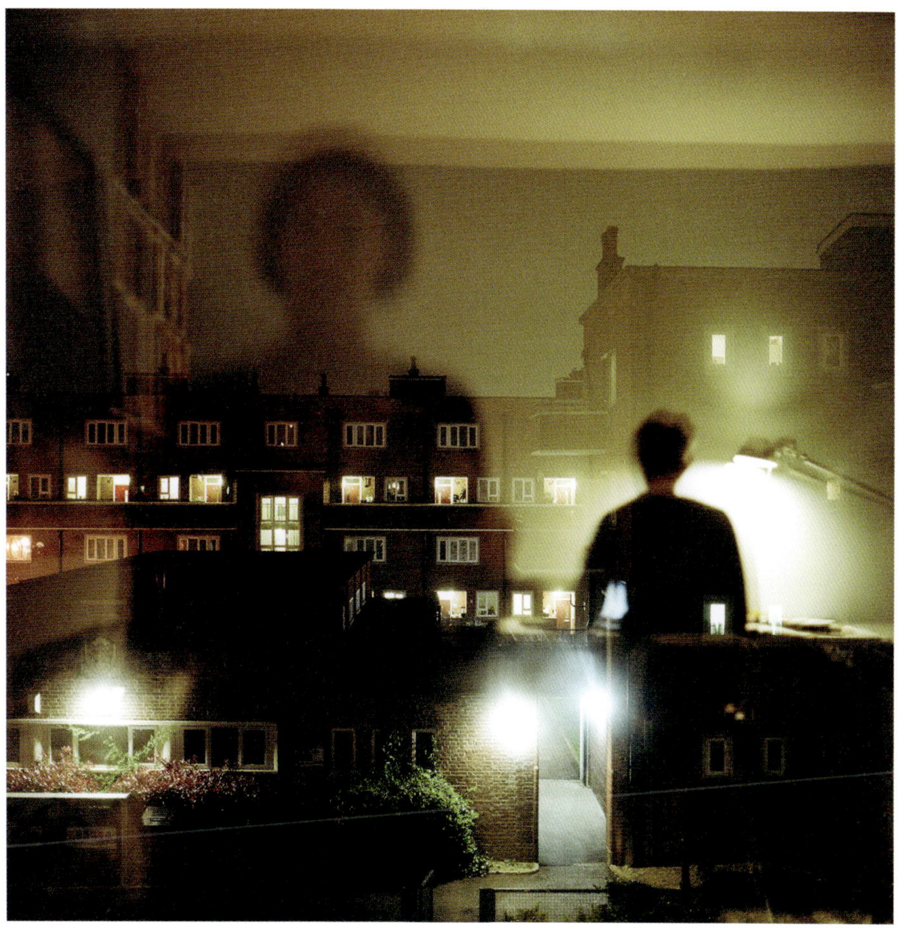

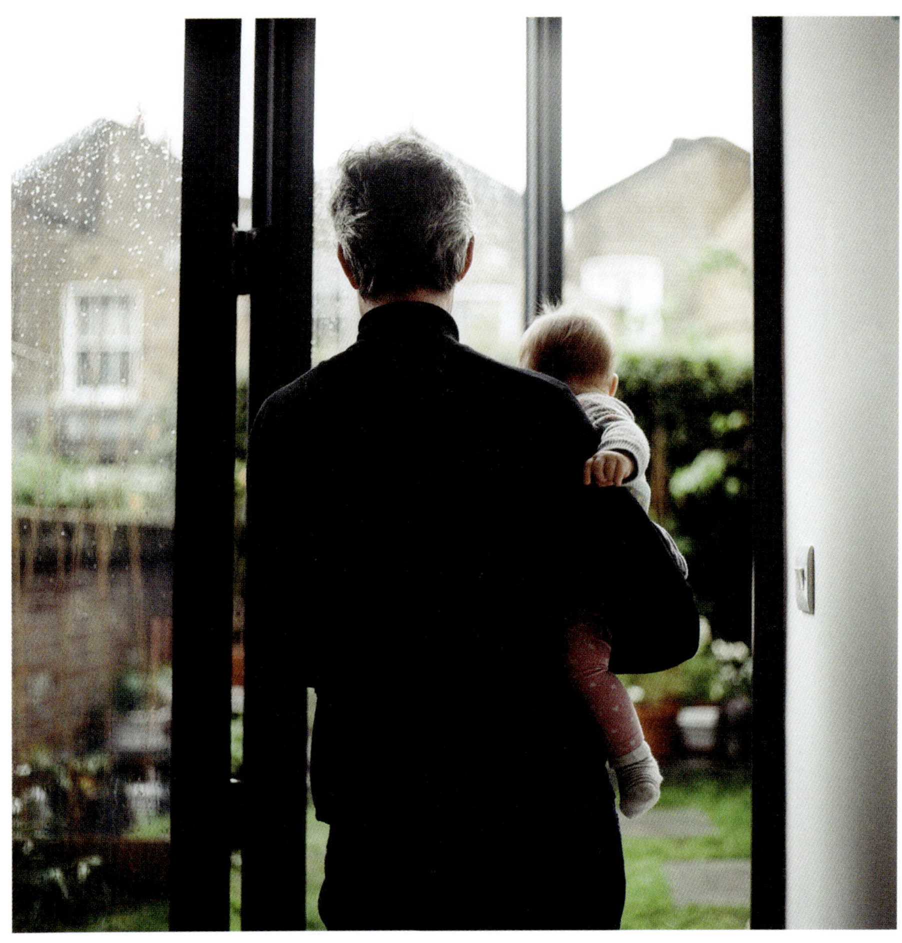

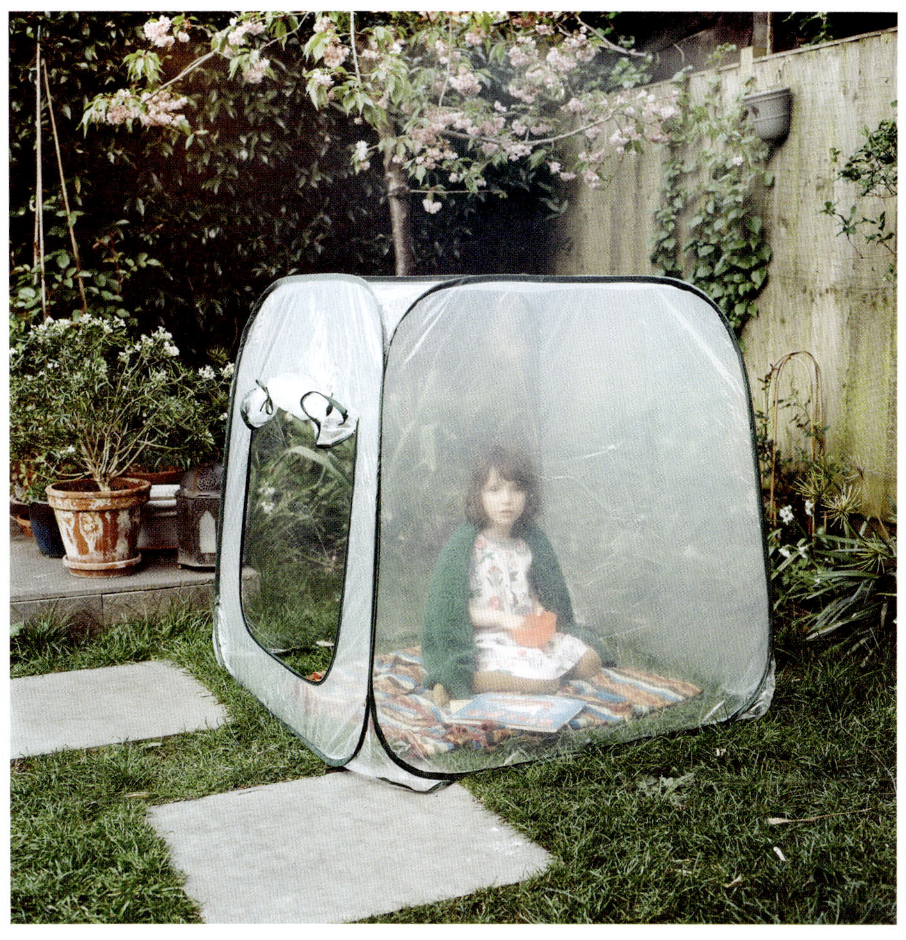

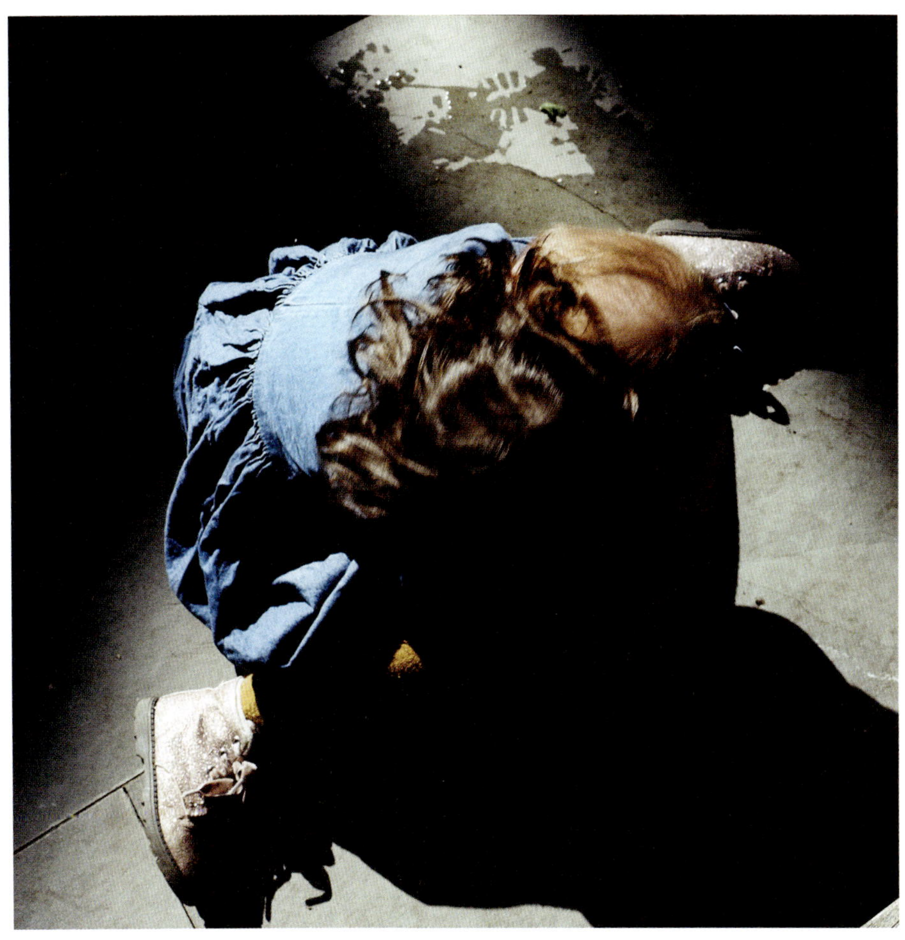

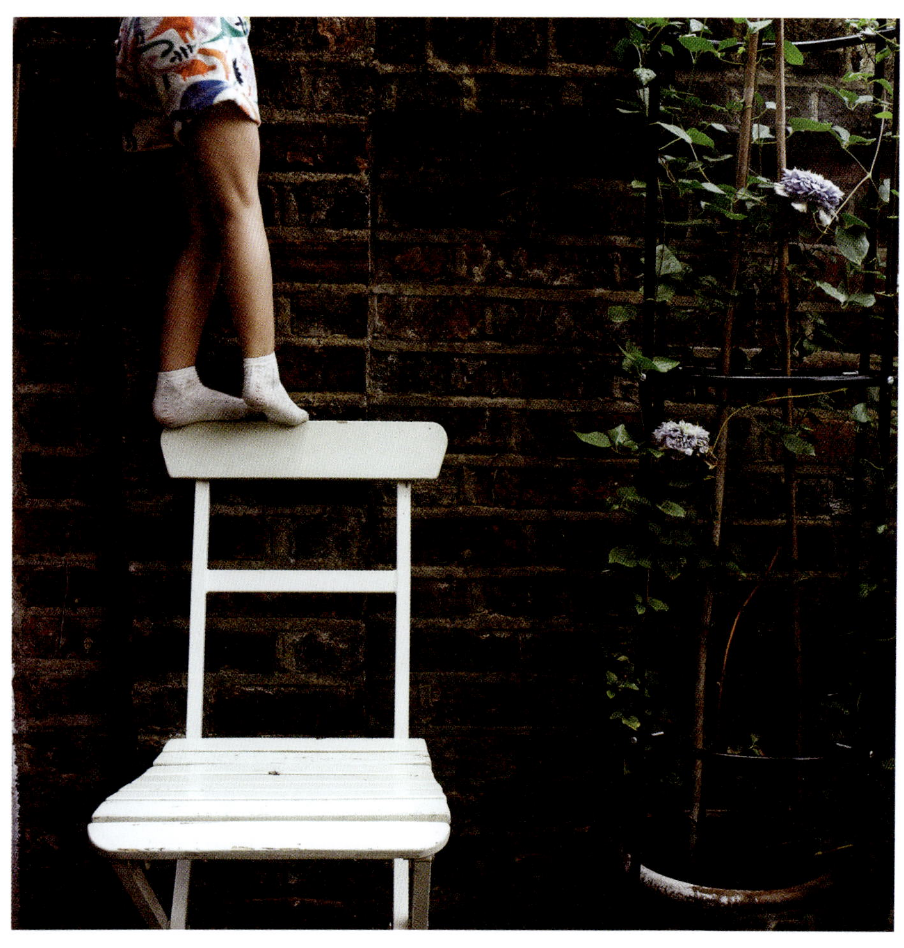

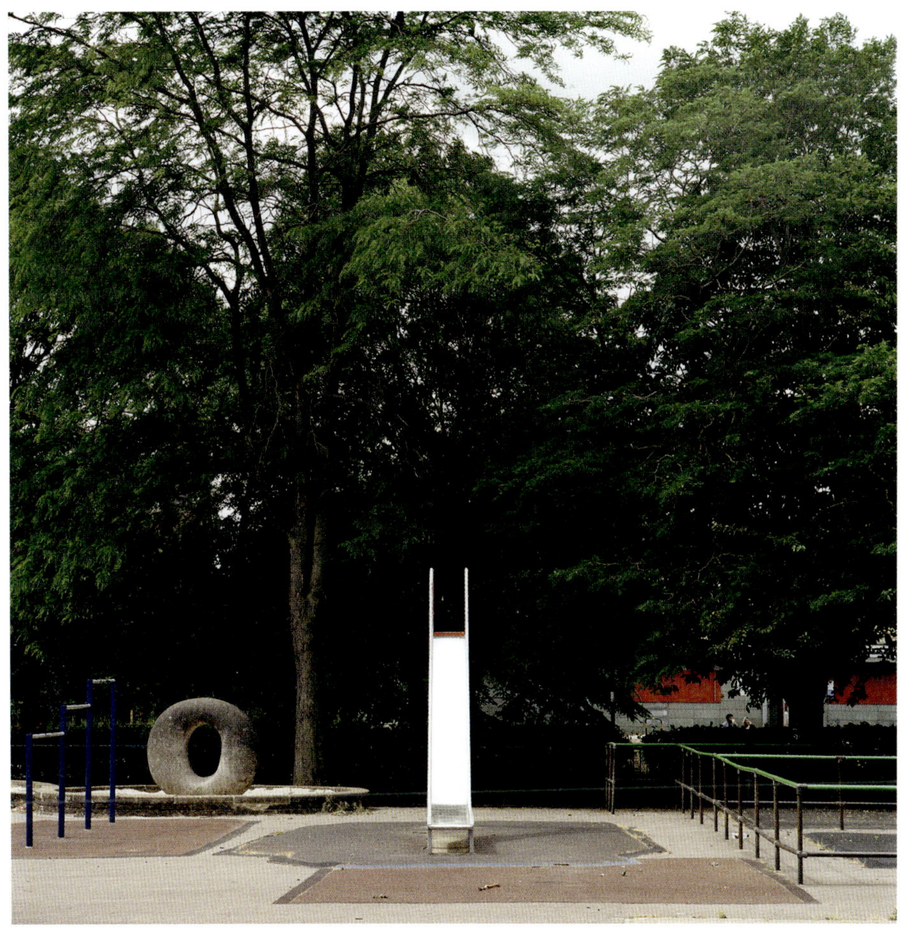

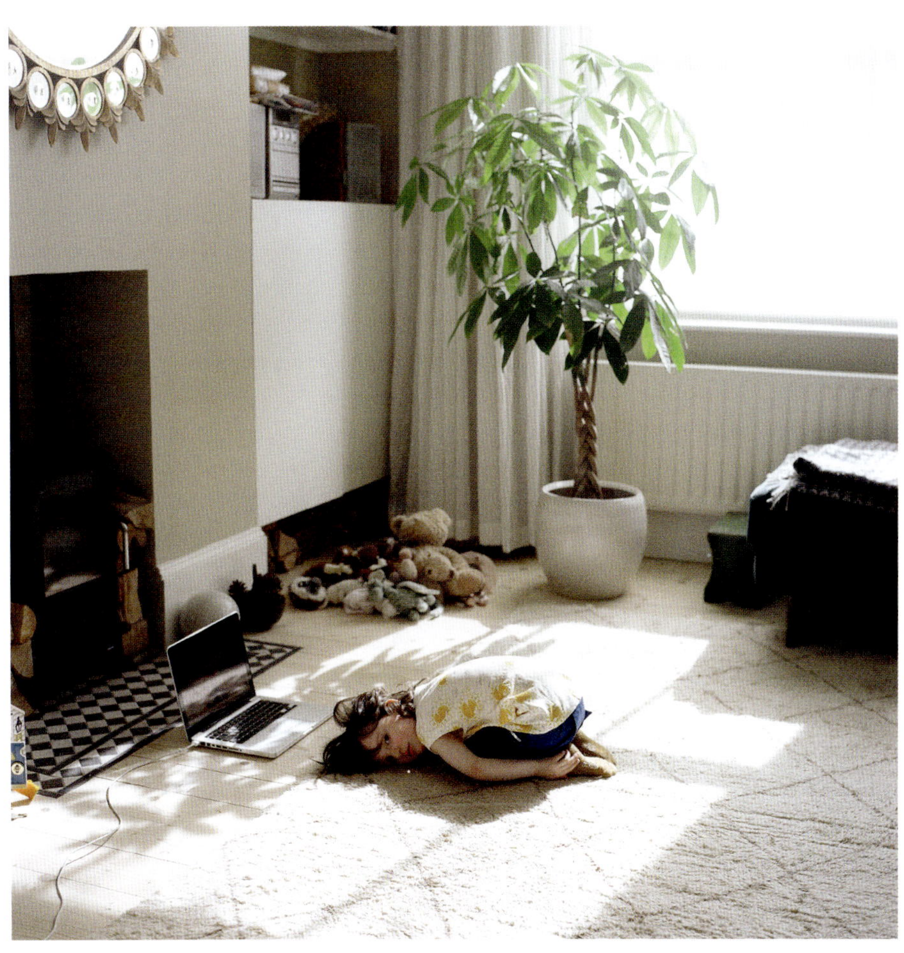

# Giles Duley
## *Inside the Red Zone*

Usually active in conflict zones and areas of humanitarian crisis, throughout May 2020 photojournalist Giles Duley instead documented the NHS response to Covid-19 across three London hospitals. As one of few photographers given access to intensive care units in the UK at a time when the virus was still poorly understood and healthcare services were close to being overwhelmed, Duley's images uniquely capture the harsh realities of this public health crisis. Echoing the language of war photography, these eye-opening photos make for difficult viewing; they render visible the struggle between life and death that was taking place in hospitals but remained largely hidden from public view.

'A Covid-19 intensive care unit is brutal: the stark environment, the physical strains, the knowledge that some patients won't survive,' writes Duley. 'Yet despite all this, what I found in these units is the greatest of humanity. The staff went about their work with professionalism and focus. They are the strongest of teams, all supporting each other and, most movingly, they treat their patients with such compassion and dignity.' Duley's sensitive documentation owes much to his work in conflict zones and his own experiences in a London ICU following an accident in 2011, when he stepped on an IED in Afghanistan. 'Some of the staff I was working with [during the pandemic] were responsible for saving my life. Indeed, it was they who asked me to come and document the hospitals during this unprecedented time.' For Duley, being on the wards in the midst of the pandemic 'was a stark reminder of the fragility of life, of how close I was to losing mine, of the heartbreaks and loss being felt across the country.'

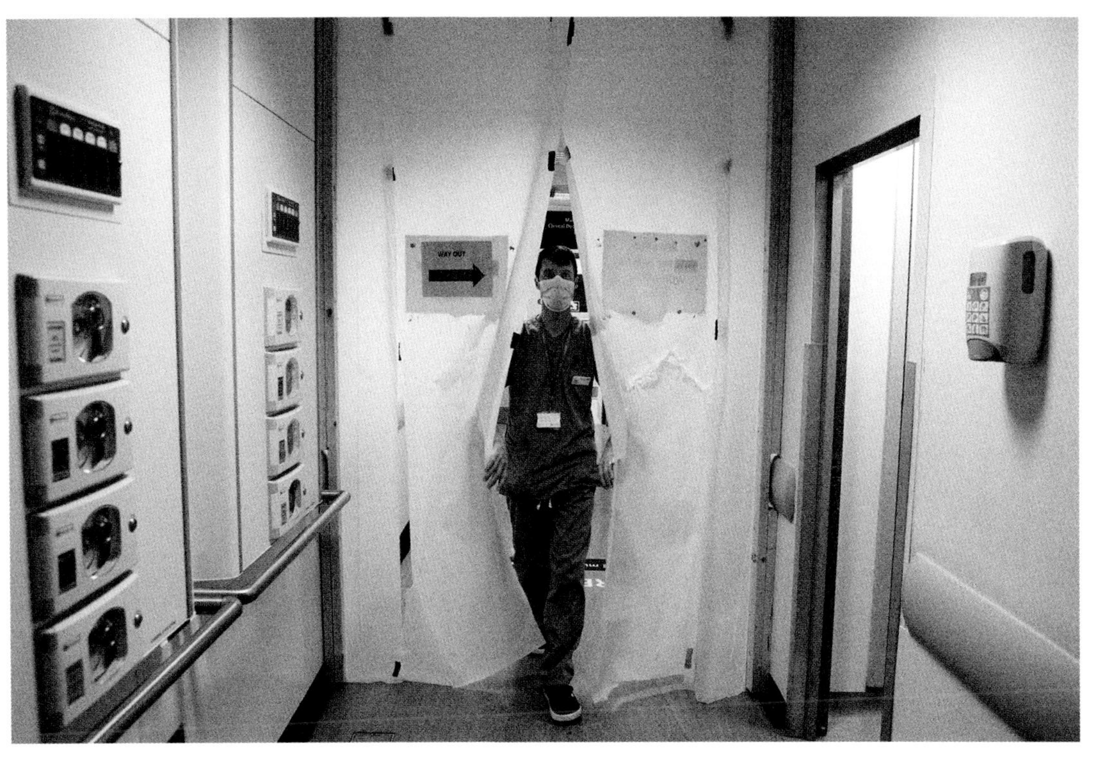



*Emergency technical assistant João Carlos Ruivo Alves steps
into the 'red zone' (for patients who have tested positive for Covid-19)
at Charing Cross Hospital's A&E department.*

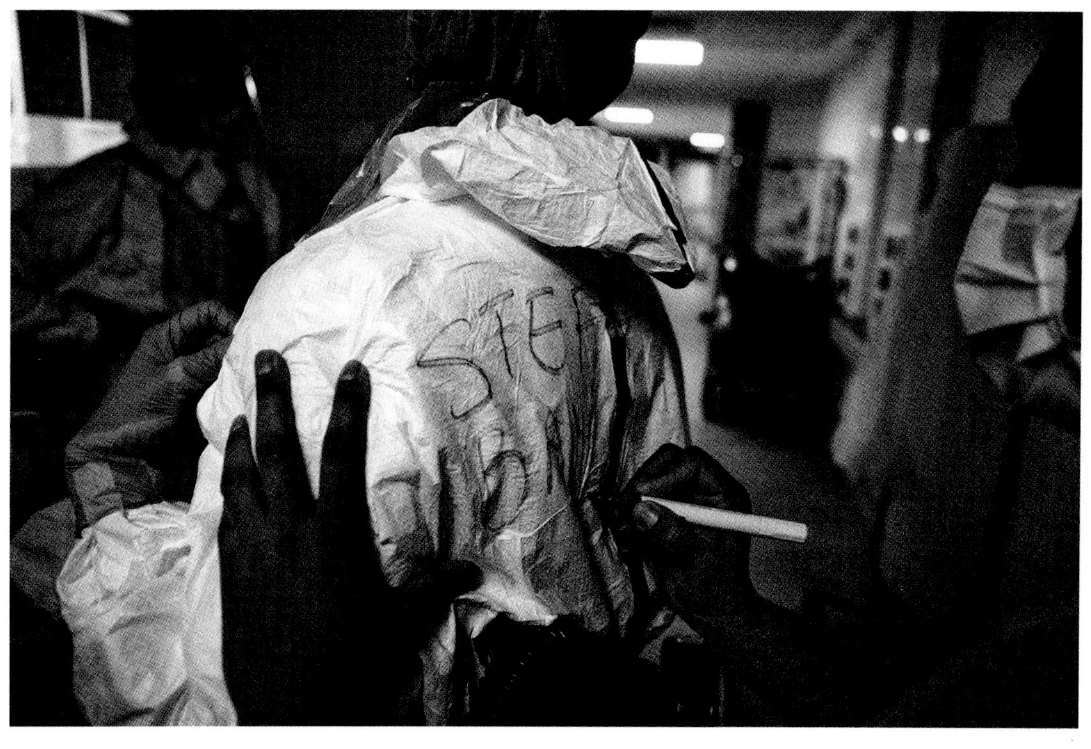

*A colleague writes Stefania Nodari's name on her back at St Mary's Hospital.*
*In full PPE, it's virtually impossible for hospital staff to recognise one another and,*
*for patients, it can be disturbing to not see carers' faces.*

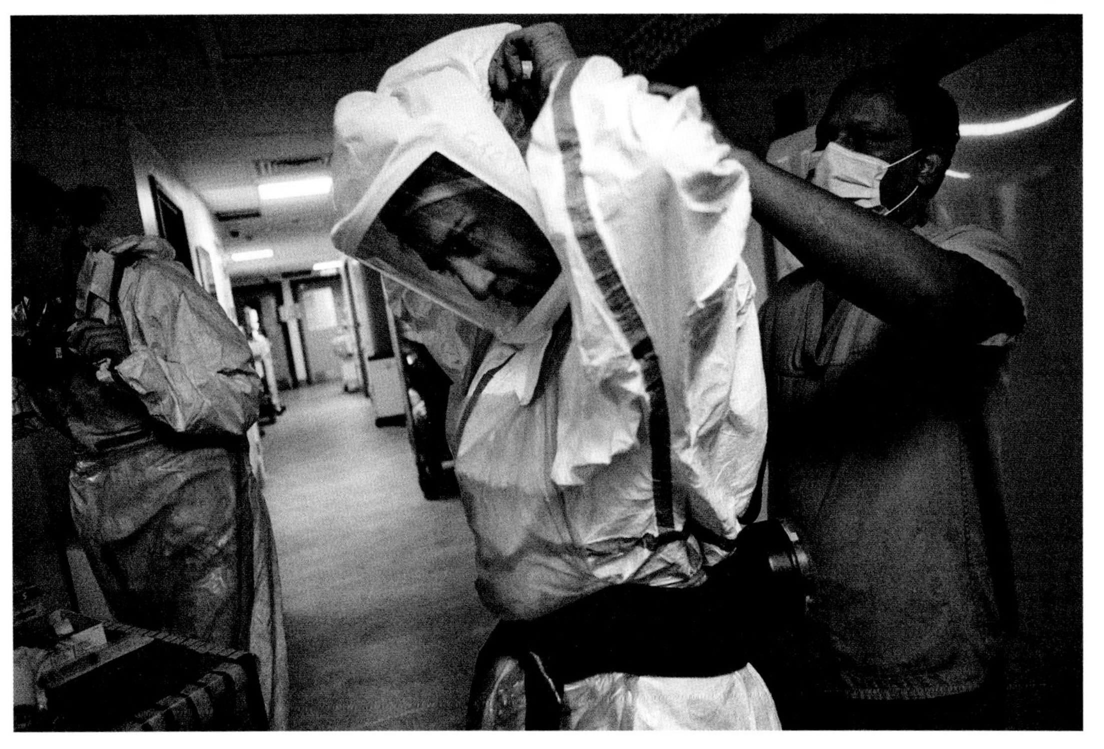

*Stefania Nodari, a paediatric ICU nurse at St Mary's Hospital,*
*dons PPE ahead of her shift.*

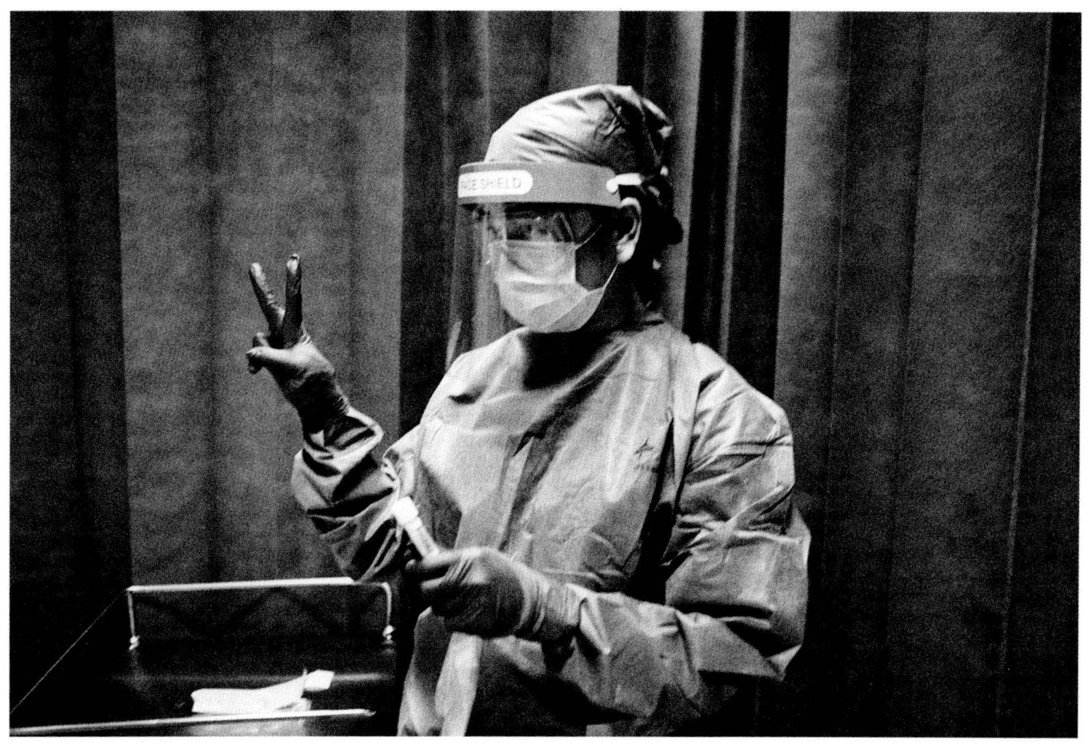


*In Charing Cross Hospital's A&E department, staff nurse Mhelody M. Castillo
prepares a patient for a swab test that will determine if they have Covid-19.*

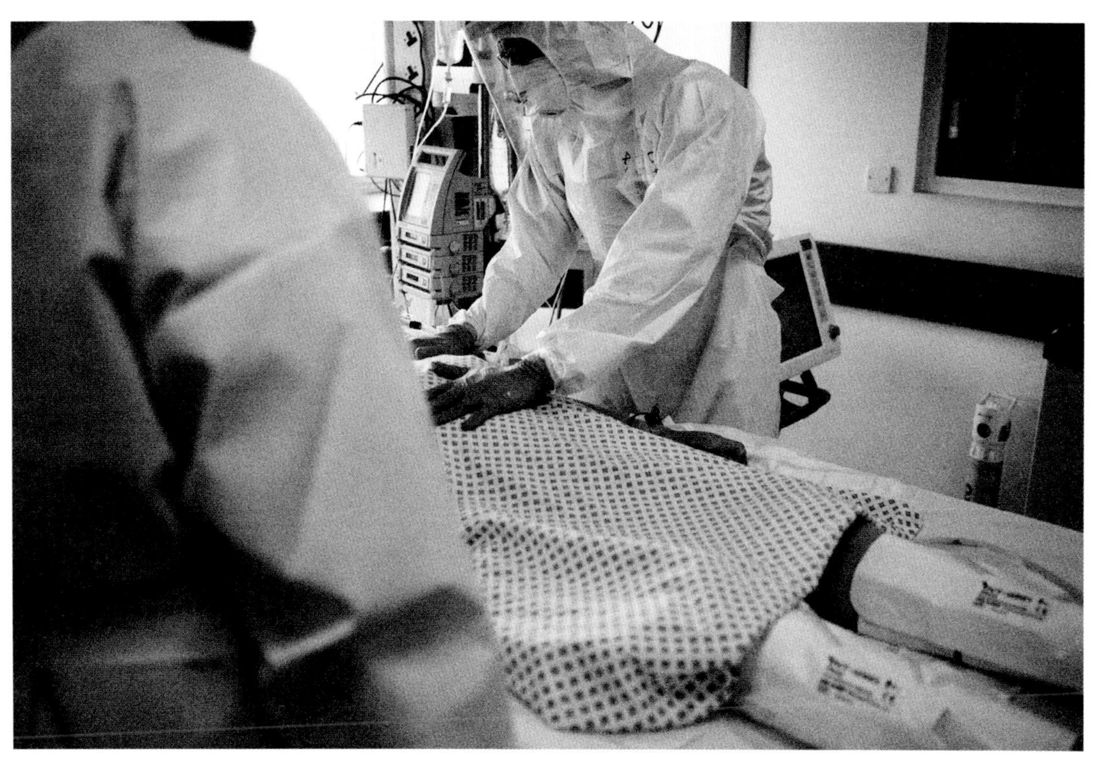

*Dr Ahmed ElHaddad examines a patient on the ICU of St Mary's Hospital.*

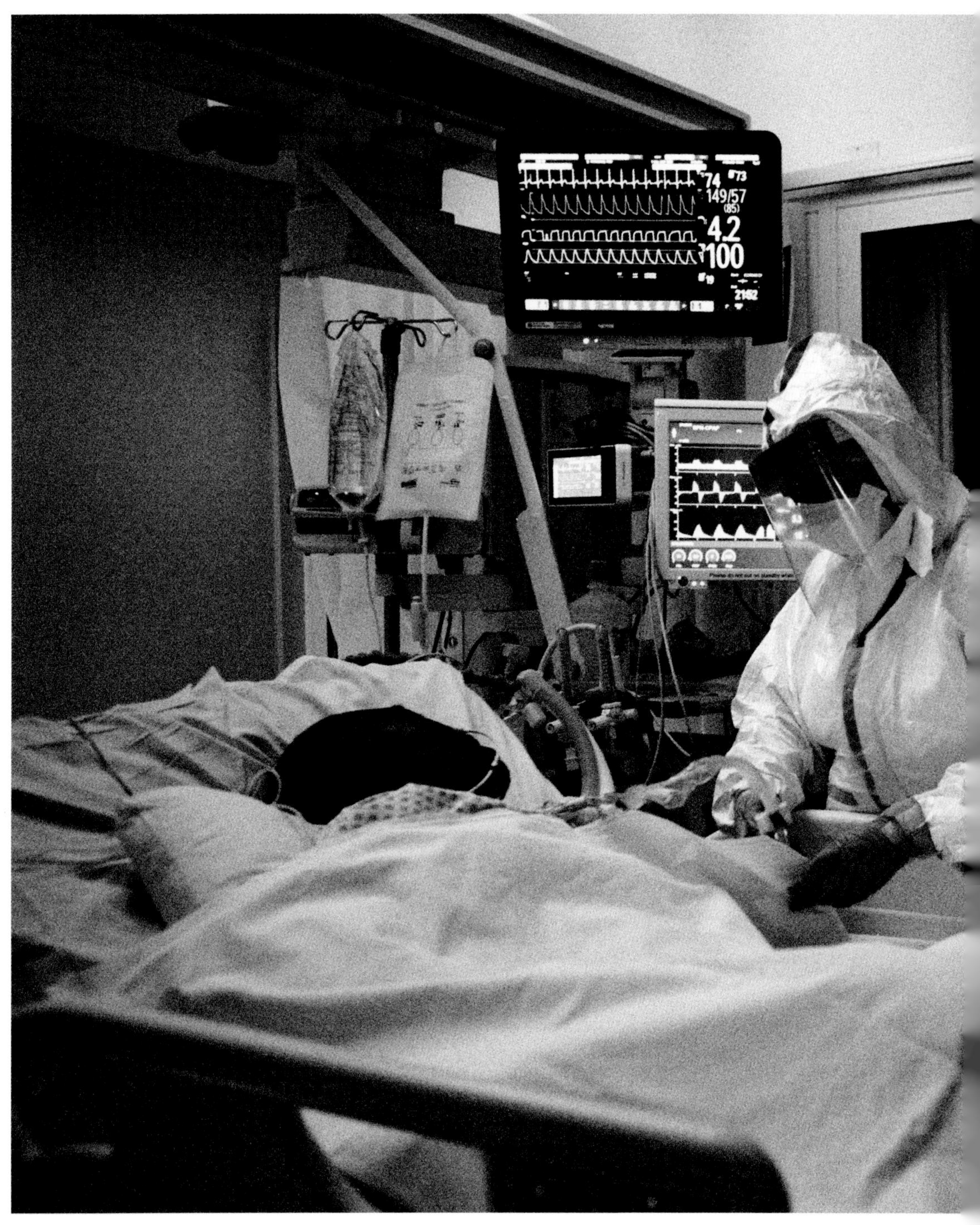

*The night shift on St Mary's Hospital's paediatric ICU, which is being used to provide extra beds for adult Covid-19 patients.*

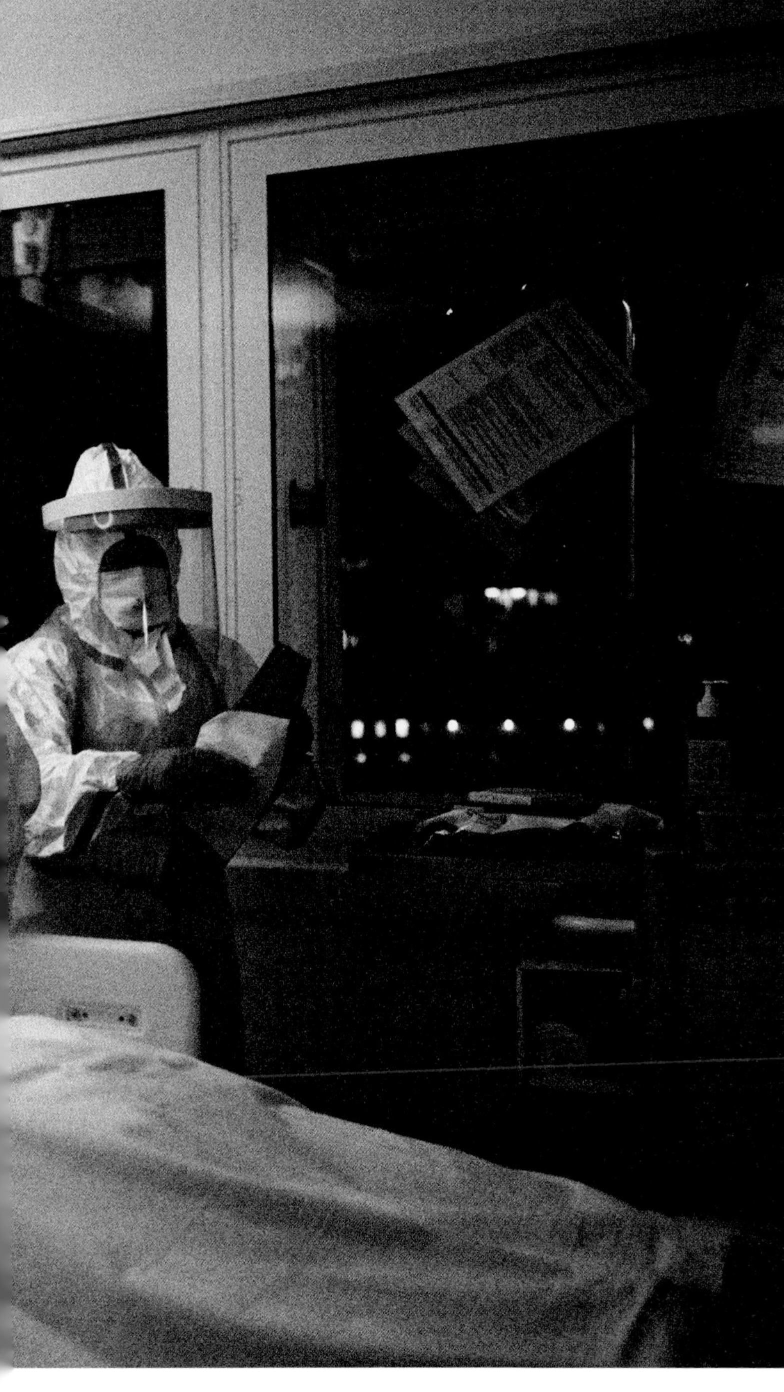

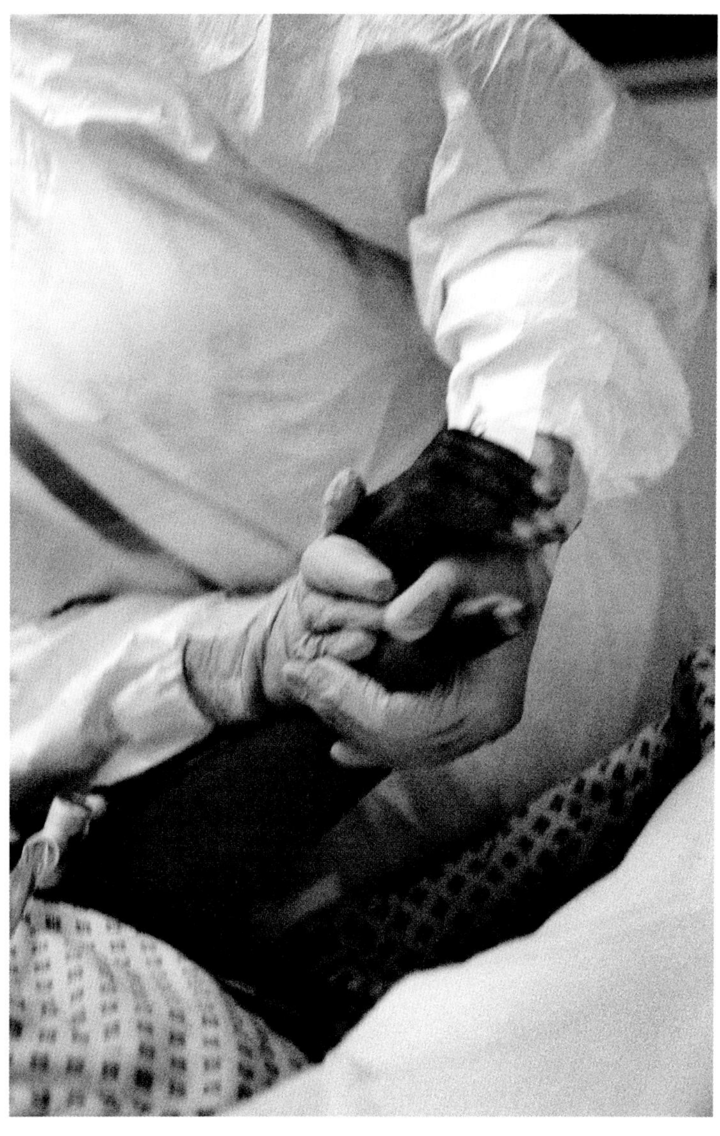

*Dr Sabeena Qureshi holds the hand of an adult patient using a ventilator on the paediatric ICU of St Mary's Hospital.*

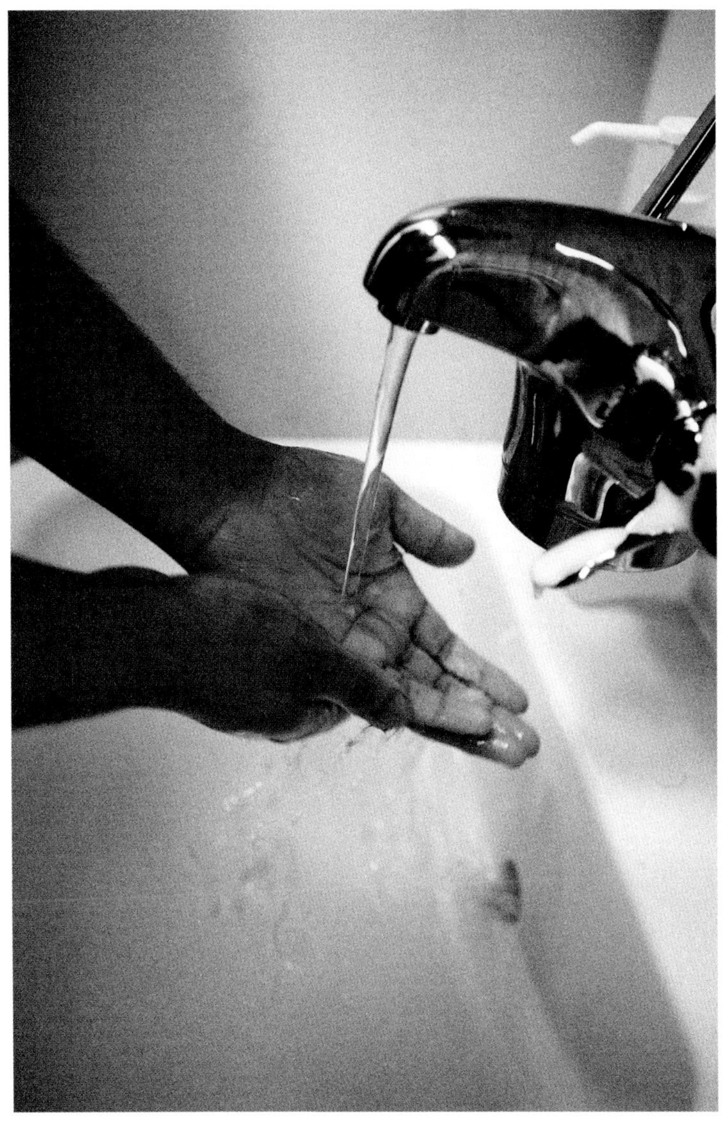

*Dr Ahmed ElHaddad washes his hands after a shift
on St Mary's Hospital's ICU.*

# Olivia Harris
## *Days on Repeat*

Shot between Tottenham and Tower Hamlets, Olivia Harris' intensely
chromatic images of lockdown humorously capture Londoners in
their attempts to make the most of an exceptionally warm spring. While
the pandemic unfolded around her and the news covered nothing but
Covid, Harris set off on her bike to document generally private Londoners
now exposing themselves on porches and doorsteps in a way that
reminded her of Mediterranean culture. 'It's a time capsule of that very
first lockdown,' says Harris. 'There was a real feeling of camaraderie
and coming together, and it felt so special and unique in a way that the
subsequent lockdowns didn't.'

Her use of an off-camera flash to enhance the already bright sunlight
resulted in deeply saturated, dazzling images that make you feel the
heat of the sun. For Harris, they match the dreaminess of an oddly magical
moment that soon dissipated, but will no doubt be remembered in years
to come. 'It is often the hard moments that form us, and that we get
our strength from. It is something that excites me, weirdly, seeing how
people deal with these quite difficult moments. When everything is
upended, there are opportunities and unique things that can happen.'

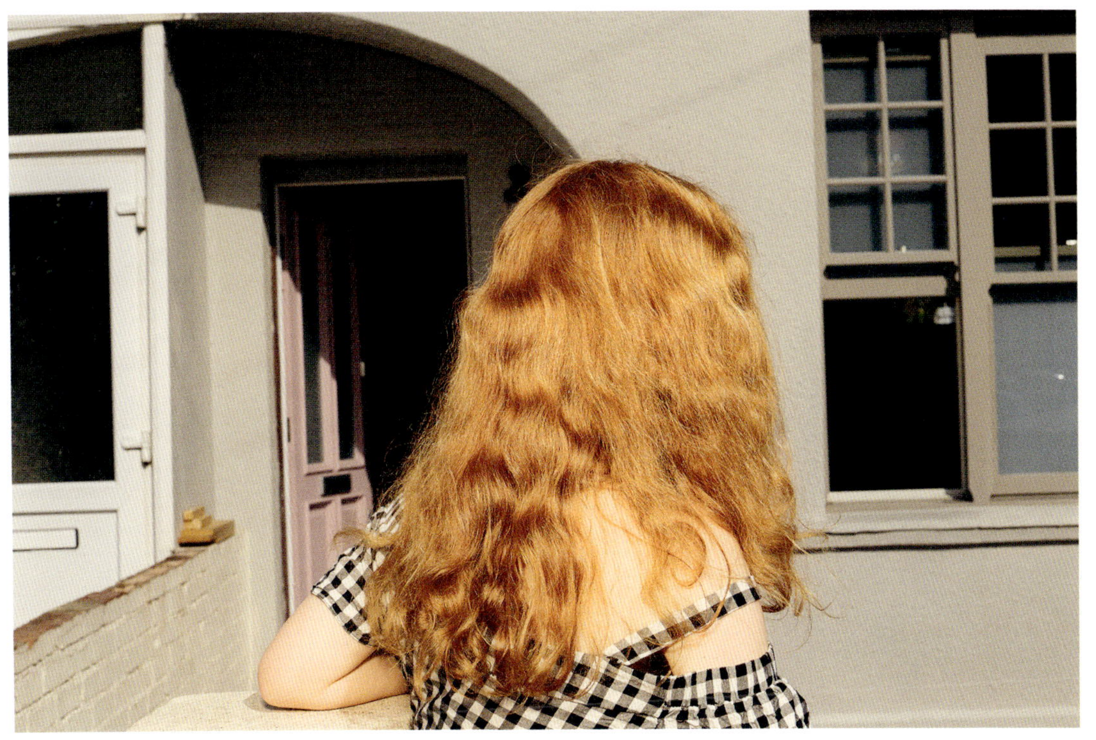

*Agnes, 9, has been off school for eight weeks. 'I'm bored.*
*I want to see my friends again.'*

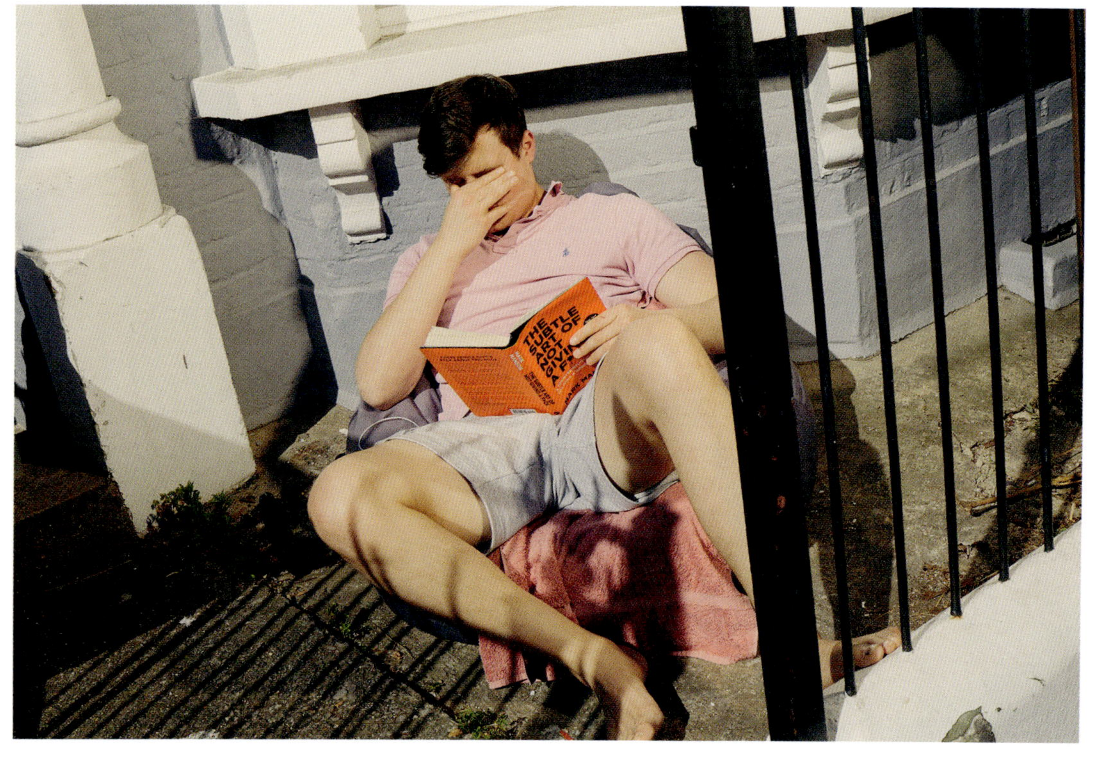

*Olly works in finance and lives with three other men. 'The biggest argument we had was on day three. It was about toast.'*

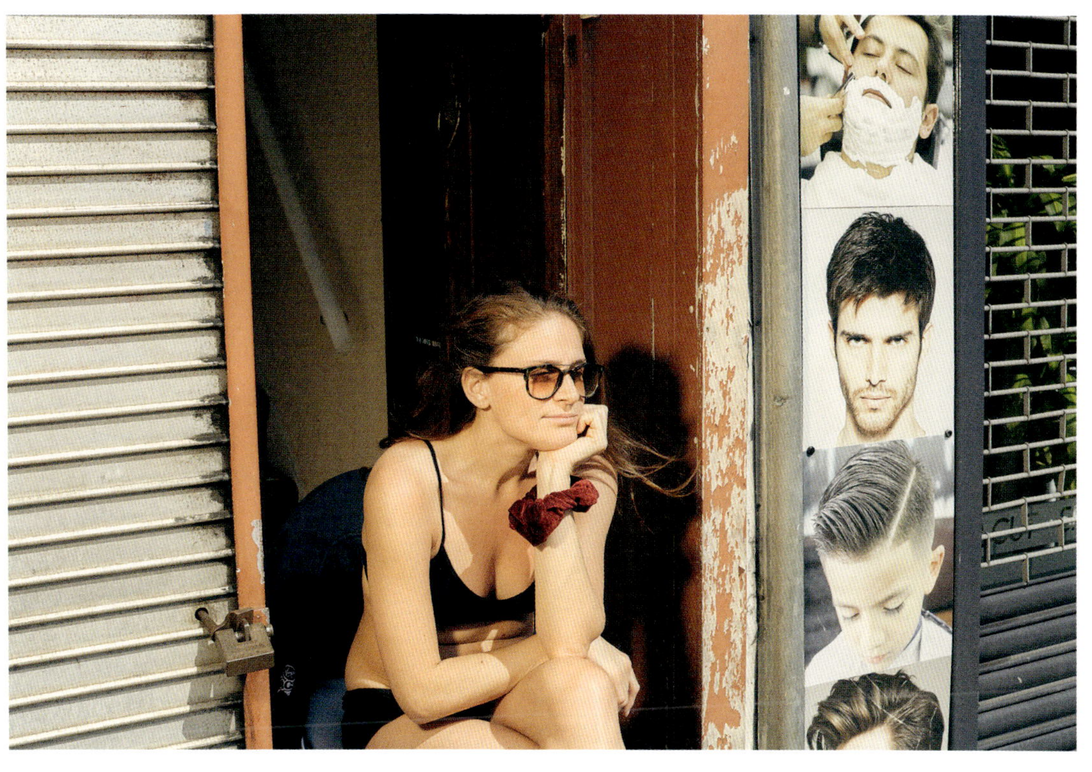

*Valeria is a gym manager. 'I always try to get some sun,*
*even if I can't go further than my front door.'*

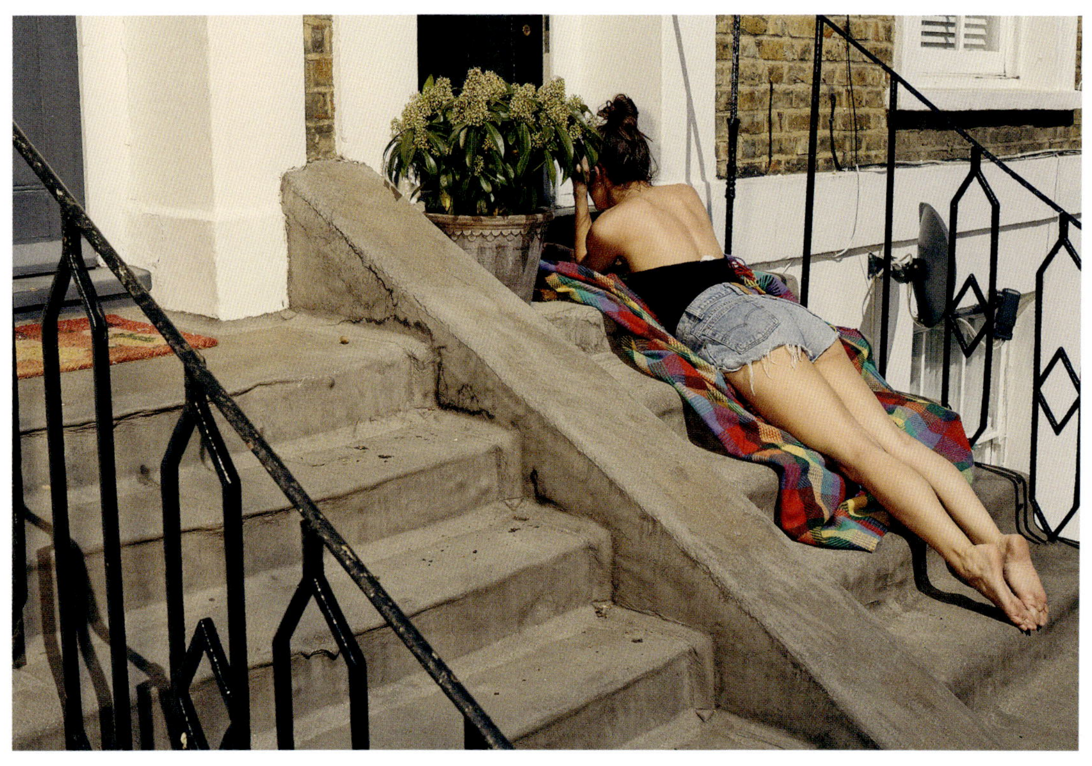

*Alexandra, a lawyer, is working from home.*
*'I don't want to sit in the park, but this feels okay.'*

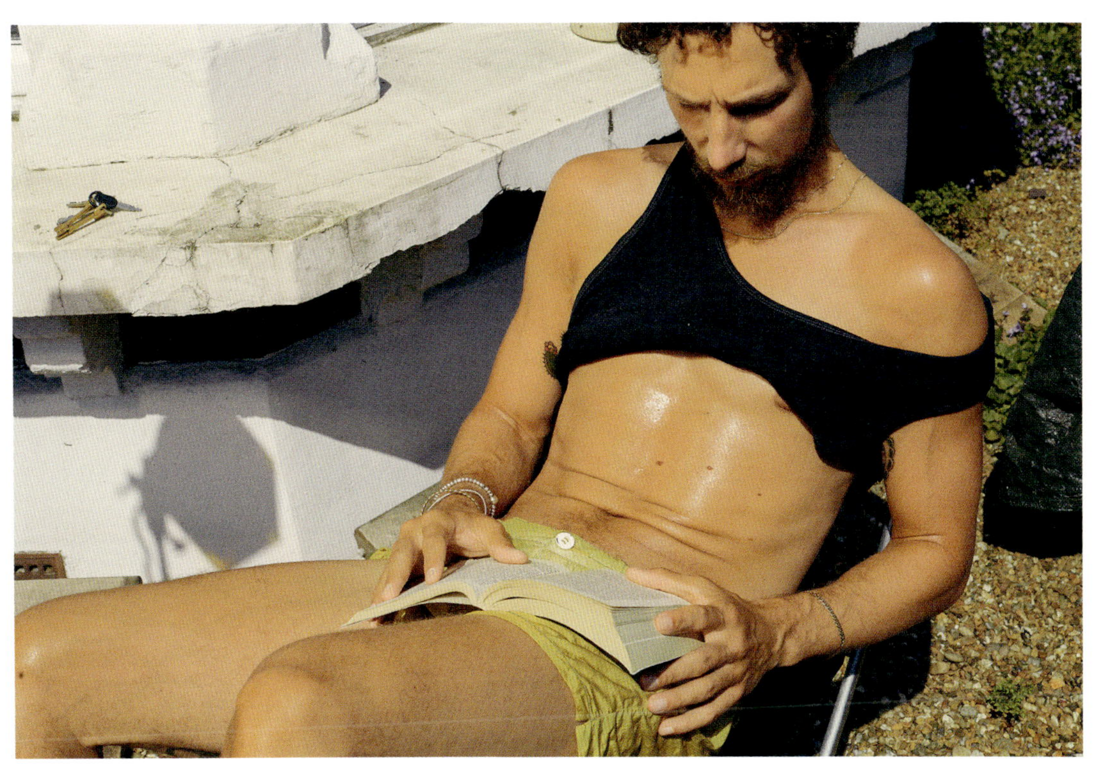

*Giacomo has been furloughed from his job in fashion. 'My girlfriend*
*thinks I'm a bit ridiculous, but this is the only way I can go out.'*

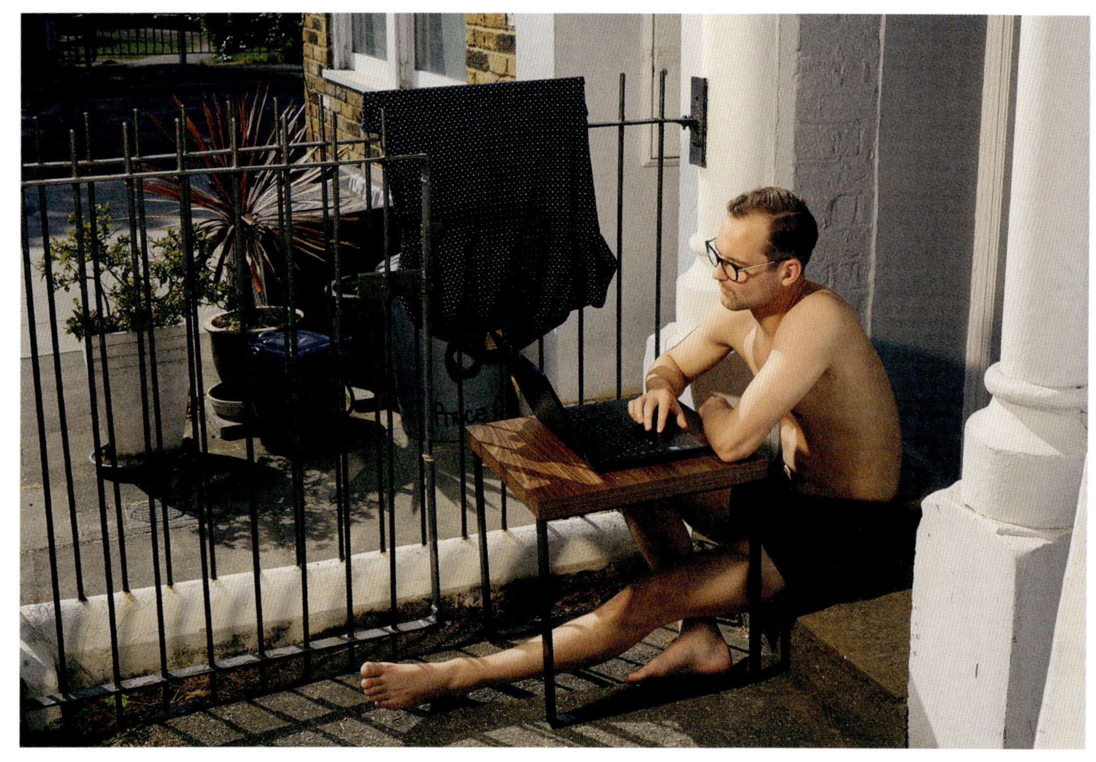

*Peter works as an asset manager. 'Lockdown has been a*
*combination of work, Xbox and a lot of quizzing.'*

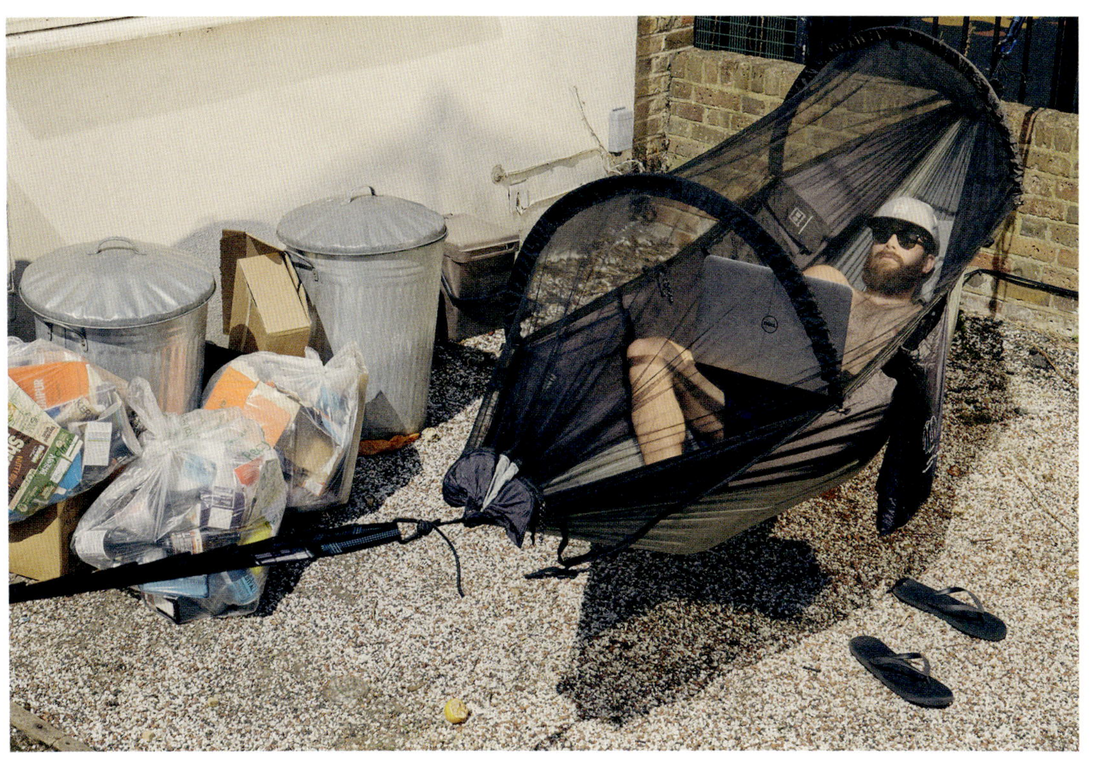

*Davide, a furloughed physio, is trying his new hammock.*
*'I was going to Epping Forest but now this is the best I can do.'*

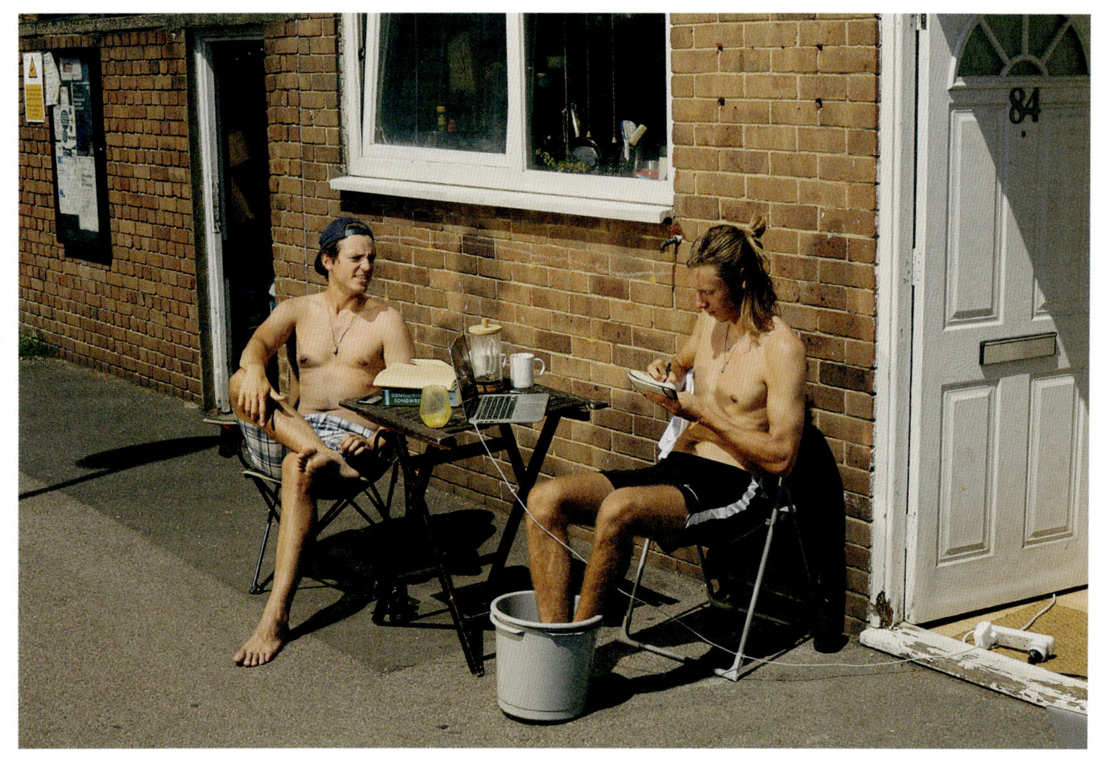

*Jonas is an account manager, Charlie works in education.*
*'Normally I'm surrounded by people. Not being validated by*
*that has been tough.' – Charlie (right)*

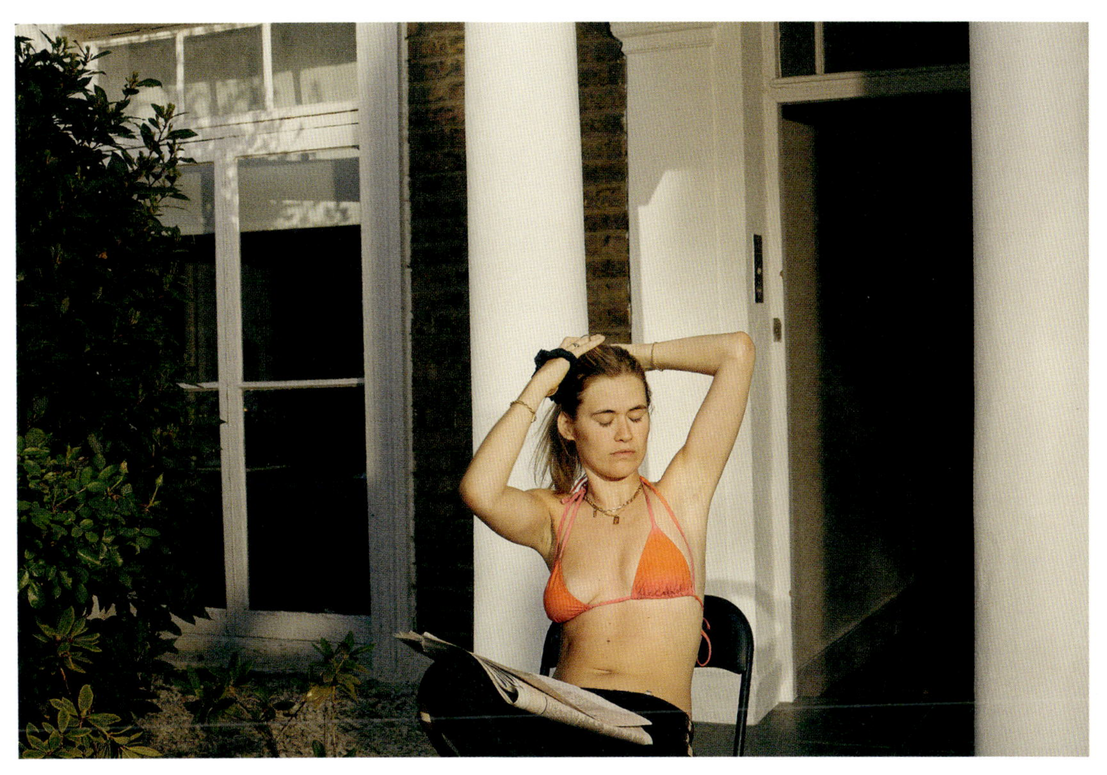

*Gabriela works in fashion – for Burberry.*

# Peter Dench
## *Tale of the Tape*

How do you prevent the spread of a highly contagious virus in a metropolis like London? Judging from Peter Dench's photographs, the answer was tape, tape and yet more tape. London's landmarks and its benches, buses, bannisters and bins are shown entangled in a web of red-and-white plastic warning the public against touching or stopping. Tickled by the sudden appearance of this tape everywhere in the early days of lockdown, when only one hour of exercise a day was allowed, Dench captured the whole of central London as one big danger zone. 'The tape was a visual signifier to encourage Londoners to keep moving,' he says. 'It appeared overnight – there was an escalation of it, and then an abandonment. I just had to go with the visual chaos of it. It did seem a little ramshackle... After a few days I'd go back to the same place and see the tape had been appropriated mischievously, tied around the breasts of a statue and such things.'

Hastily put in place but soon disintegrating or discarded, it is tempting to read an analogy into the ubiquity of this ultimately pointless tape: a blundering government that struggled to get the spread of the virus under control. For Dench, there is an irony too in the extensive use of planet-polluting plastic during a crisis caused by environmental destruction: 'I wonder what happened to all that tape. Months later I would still find shreds of it under an ice-cream kiosk. It's probably floating down the Thames now. Or was it ever collected? Was there an evening when it was all removed and swept up? I'll never know, and that mystery will always be an empty place in my heart!'

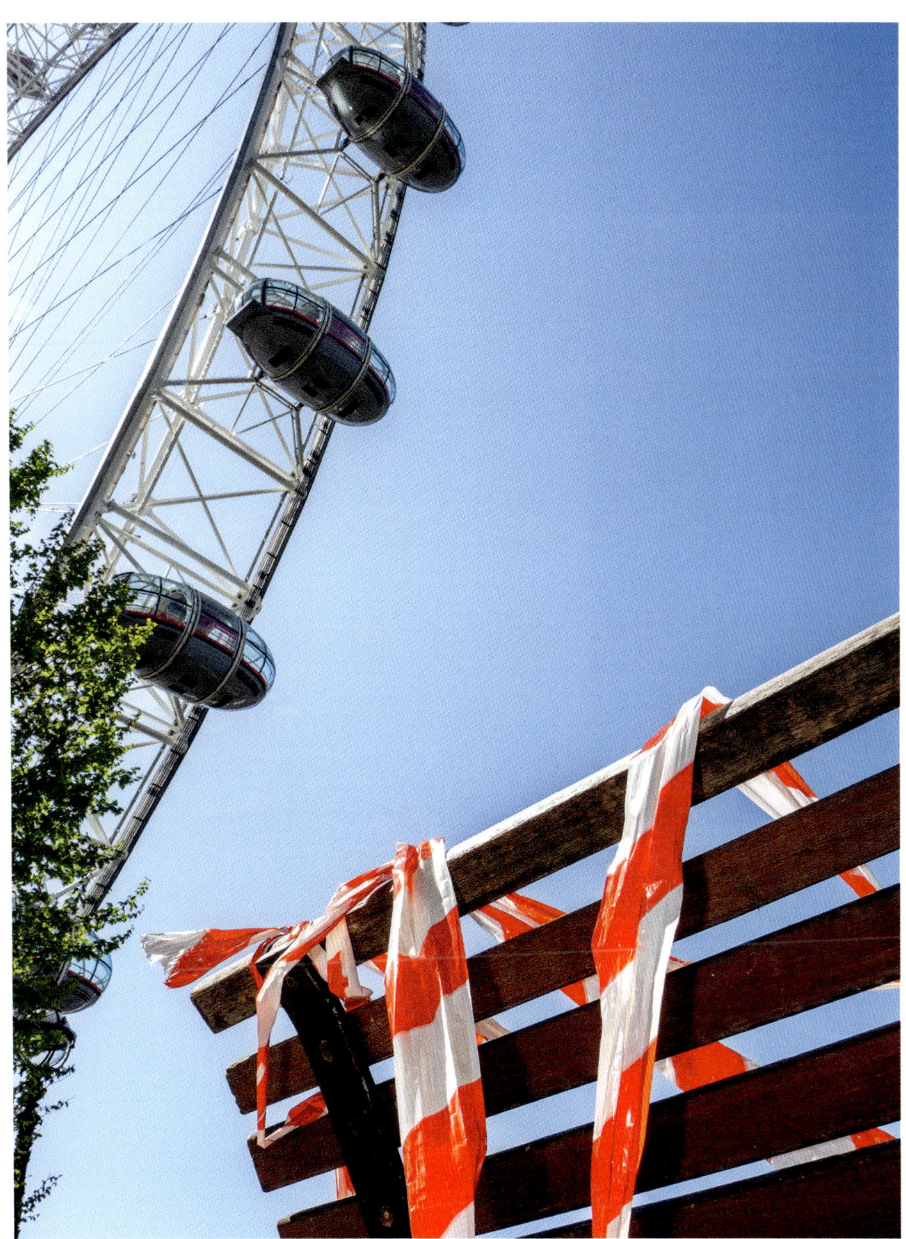

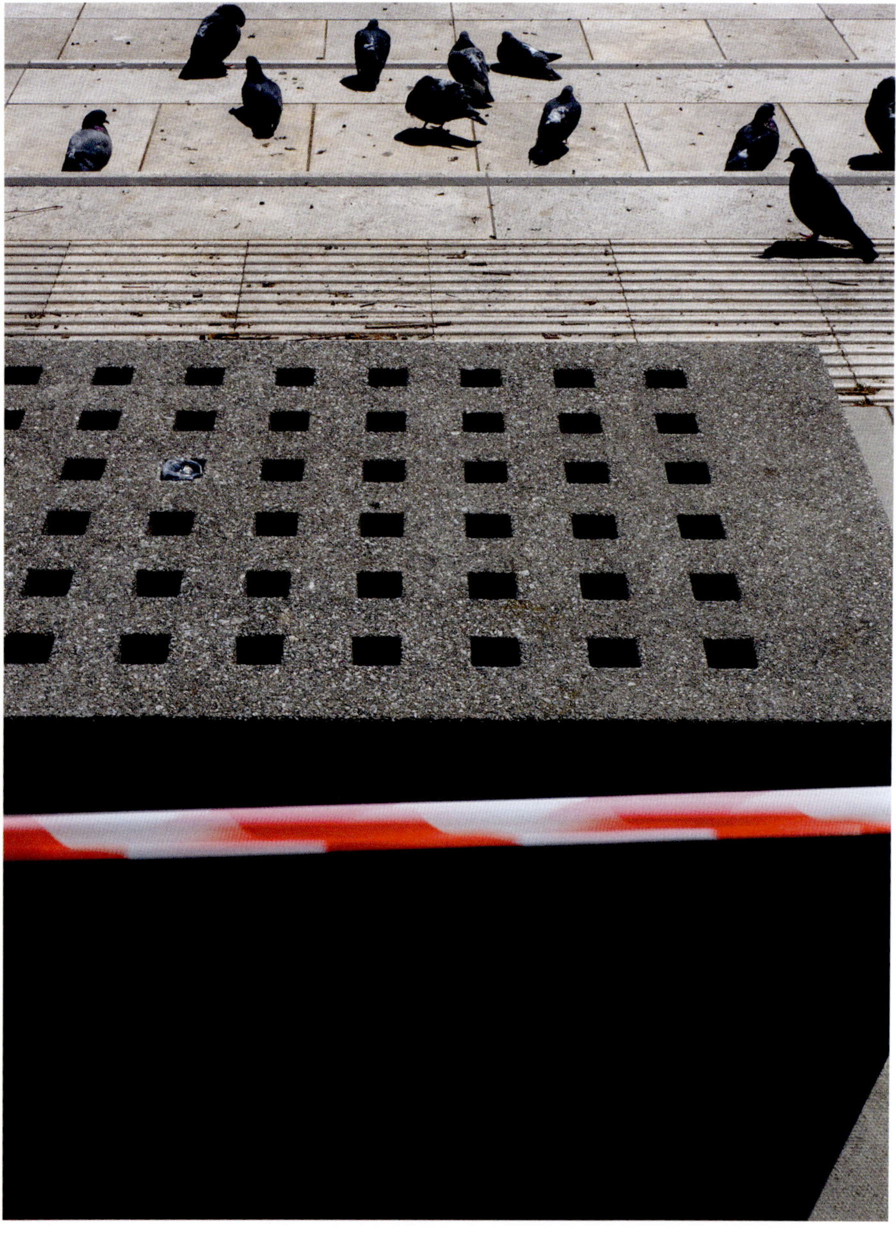

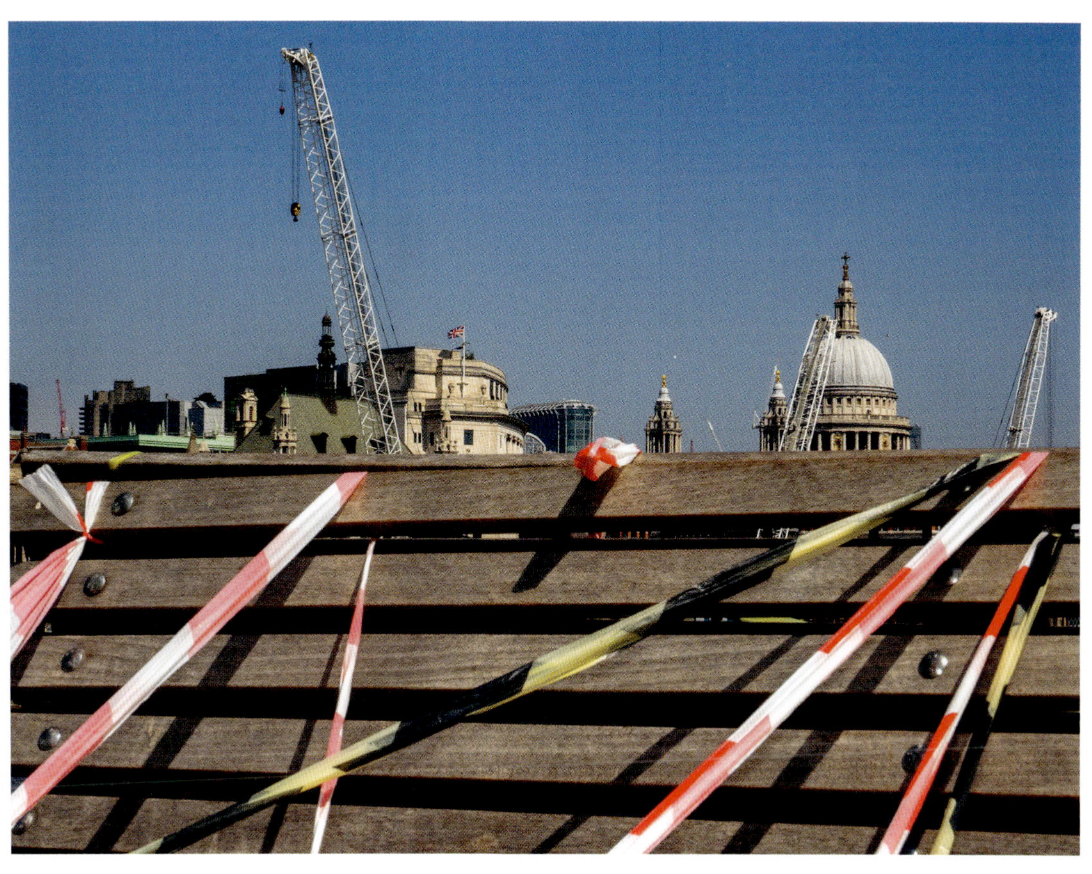

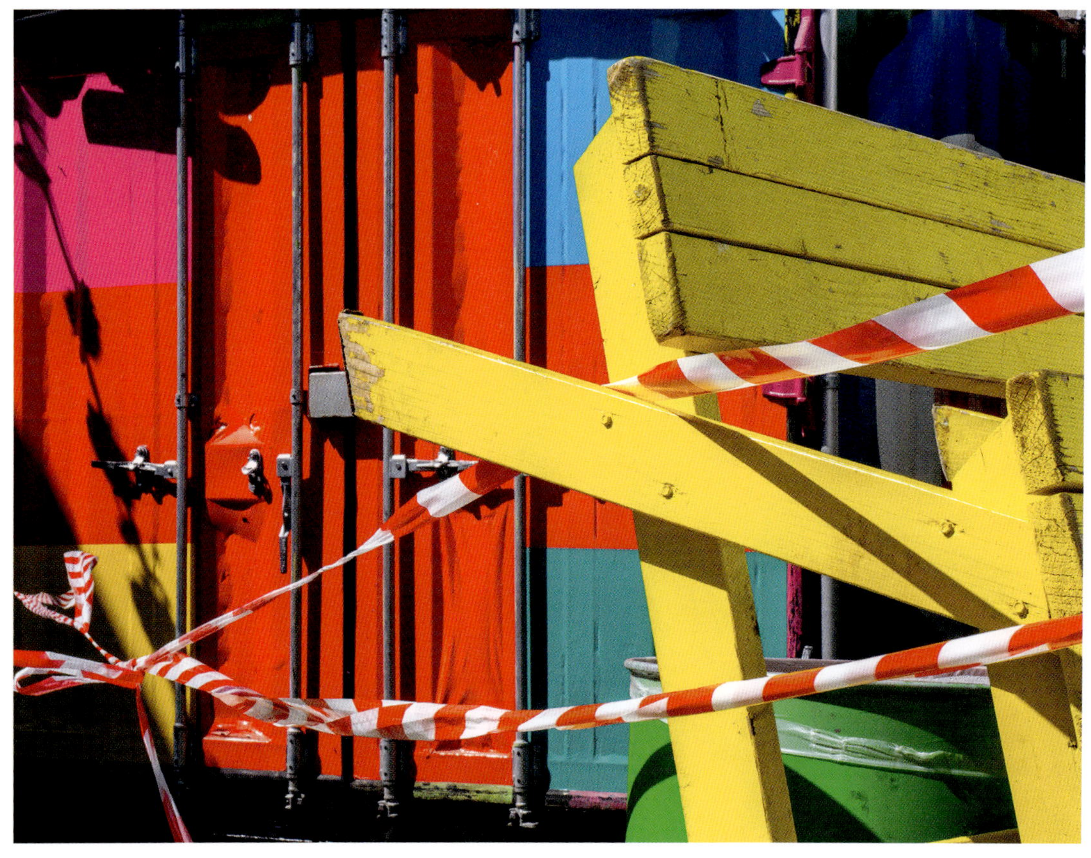

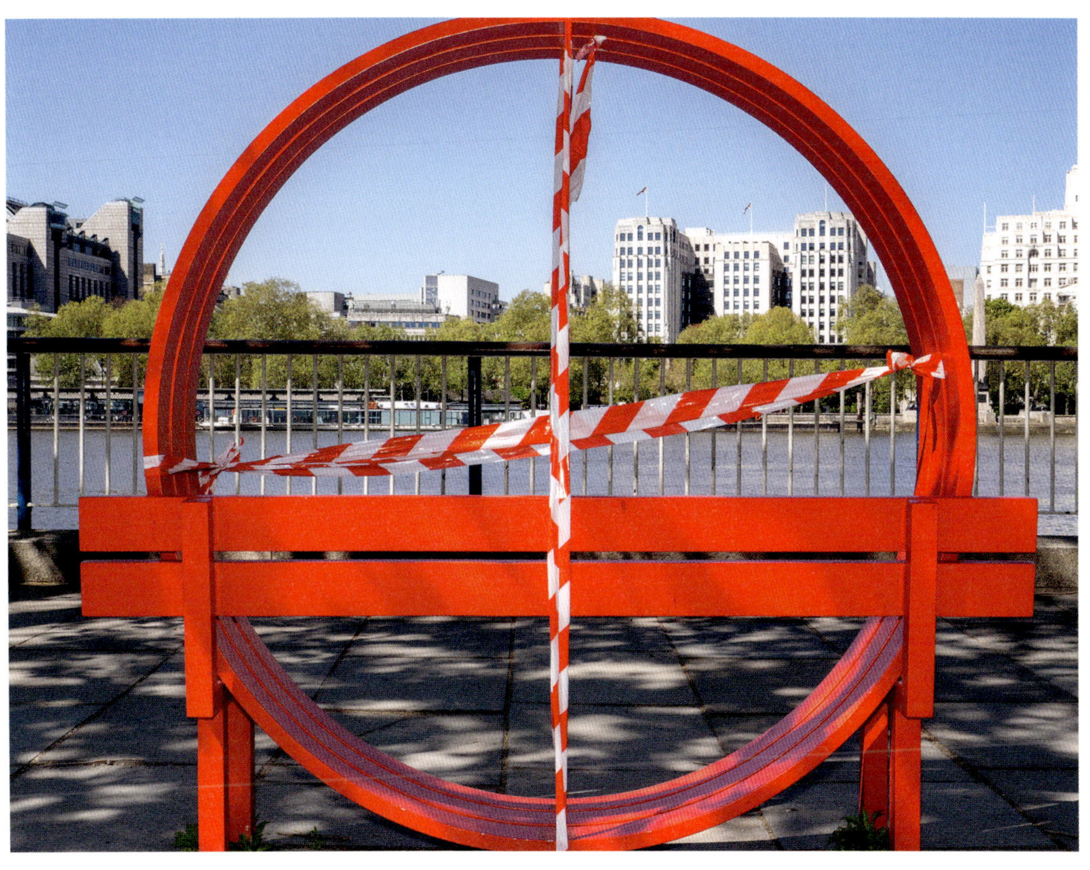

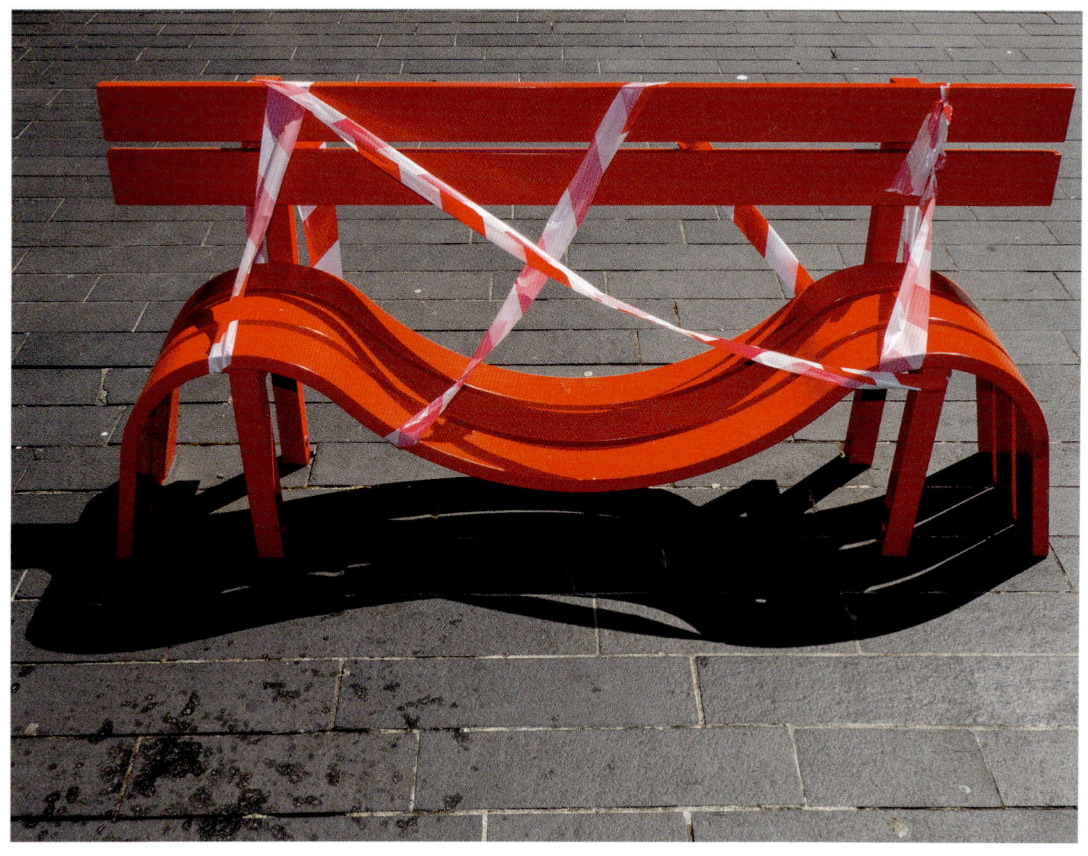

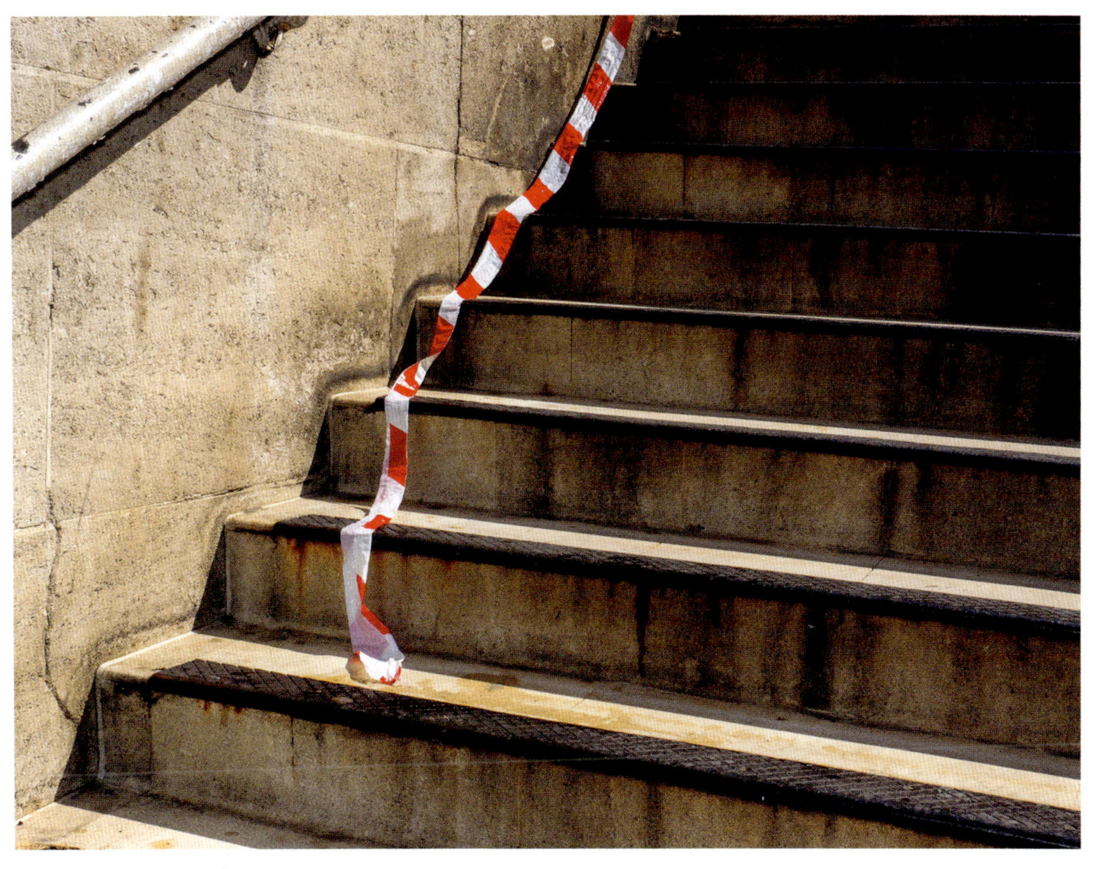

# Grey Hutton
## *The Ties That Bind*

During the first weeks and months of lockdown, Hackney resident Grey Hutton began to document the myriad community support networks, charities and volunteer organisations that popped up in his neighbourhood. Through his observation of food distribution hubs, mental health support services, baby banks, ambulance workers and more, Hutton realised just how badly his borough had been hit by the pandemic. Hackney is one of London's most diverse areas, but also one of its most disadvantaged, with high levels of unemployment, food shortages, crime, housing struggles and health issues. Having recently returned to his hometown after living in Germany, Hutton found the scenes of lockdown eye-opening: 'Child poverty in Hackney is at 35 percent. I never realised the scale of it all, and how badly people were impacted. It was really difficult to see how families that were living so close to me were struggling.'

The project evolved organically over the following year as Hutton recorded the extraordinary compassion, resilience and solidarity with which these support networks were run, often with few resources and by local volunteers. The project shows how they became indispensable lifelines for a great number of people. Deeply touched by the individuals, stories and struggles that entered his field of vision, Hutton found himself becoming part of the community. First and foremost, he wanted to depict the incredible positivity and resourcefulness of these informal networks: 'These organisations are not government bodies, they are literally just your community; your neighbours; a person who is living down the road. It brings home the importance of these organisations and how reliant so many of these families are on them.' In the face of so much adversity, 'they really are holding certain communities together.'

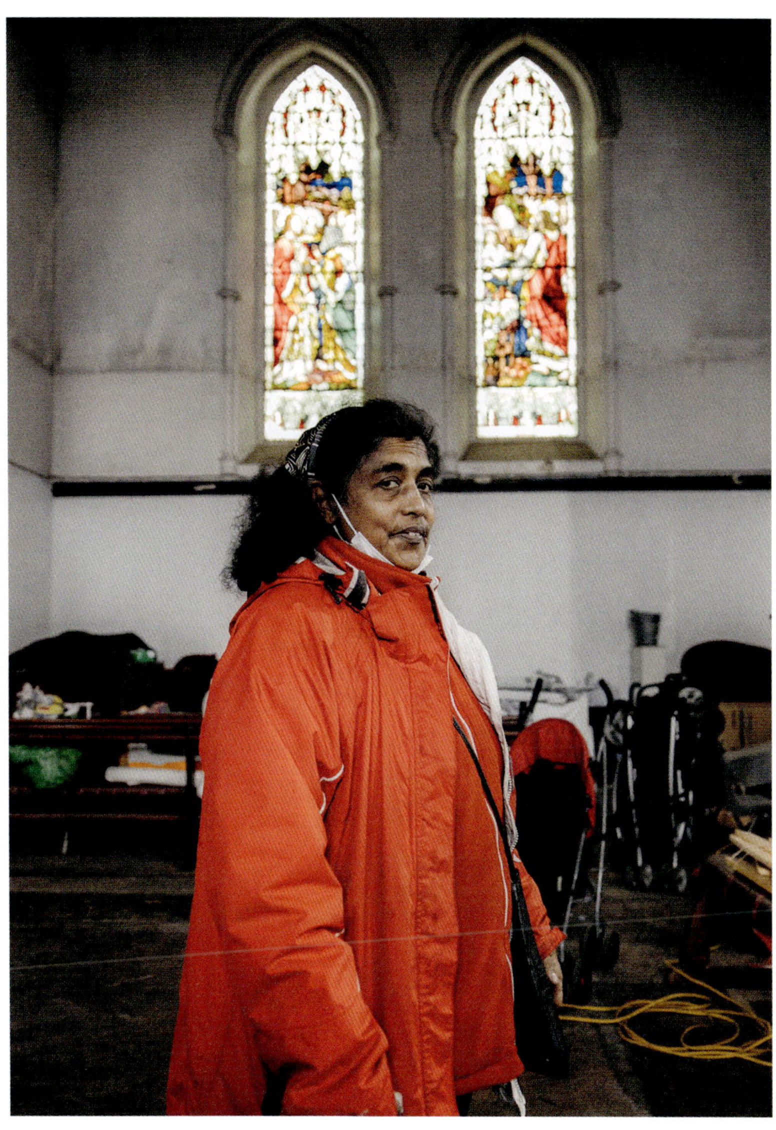

*Paediatric nurse Beautine Wester in Clapton Community Seventh-day Adventist Church, where she set up the E5 Baby Bank. Over the pandemic, she has seen a shocking increase in the number of local families who cannot afford basic essential items, including clothing, food and nappies. 21 October 2020.*

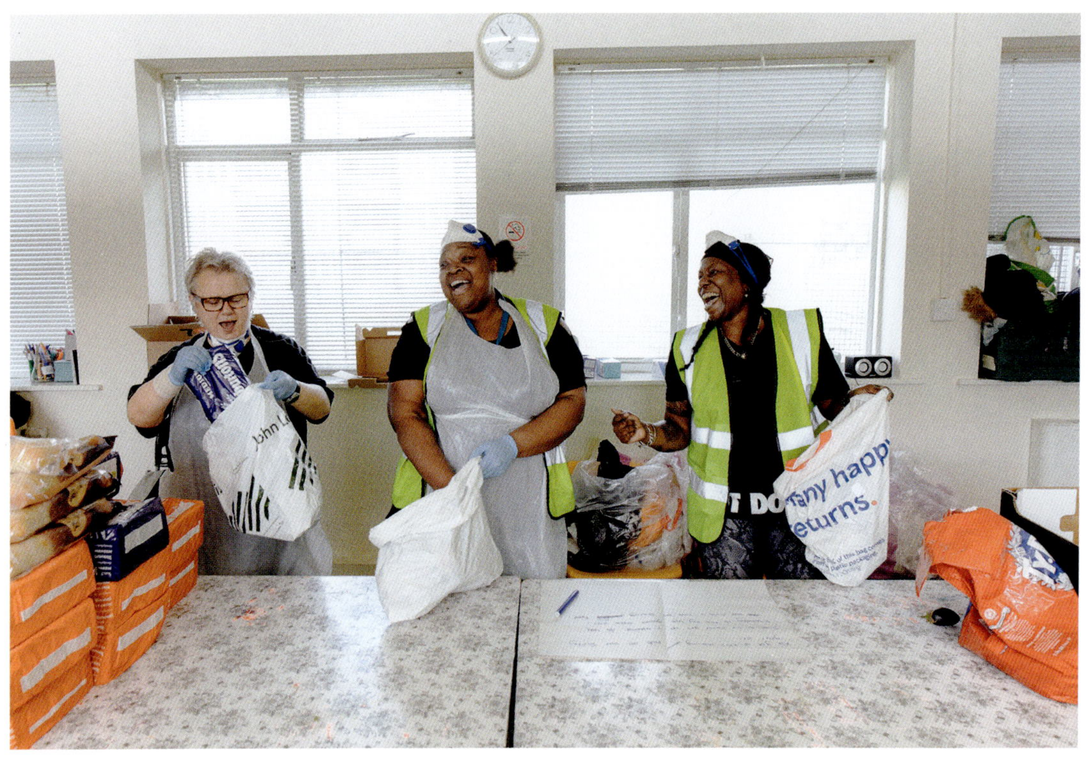

*Ziggy Noonan, Carletta Gordon and Michelle Dornelly, members of the Hackney-based non-profit Children with Voices, sing along to Whitney Houston as they pack bags at the Wilton Estate Community Food Hub. Since lockdown, demand at the Hub has grown exponentially. 6 April 2020.*

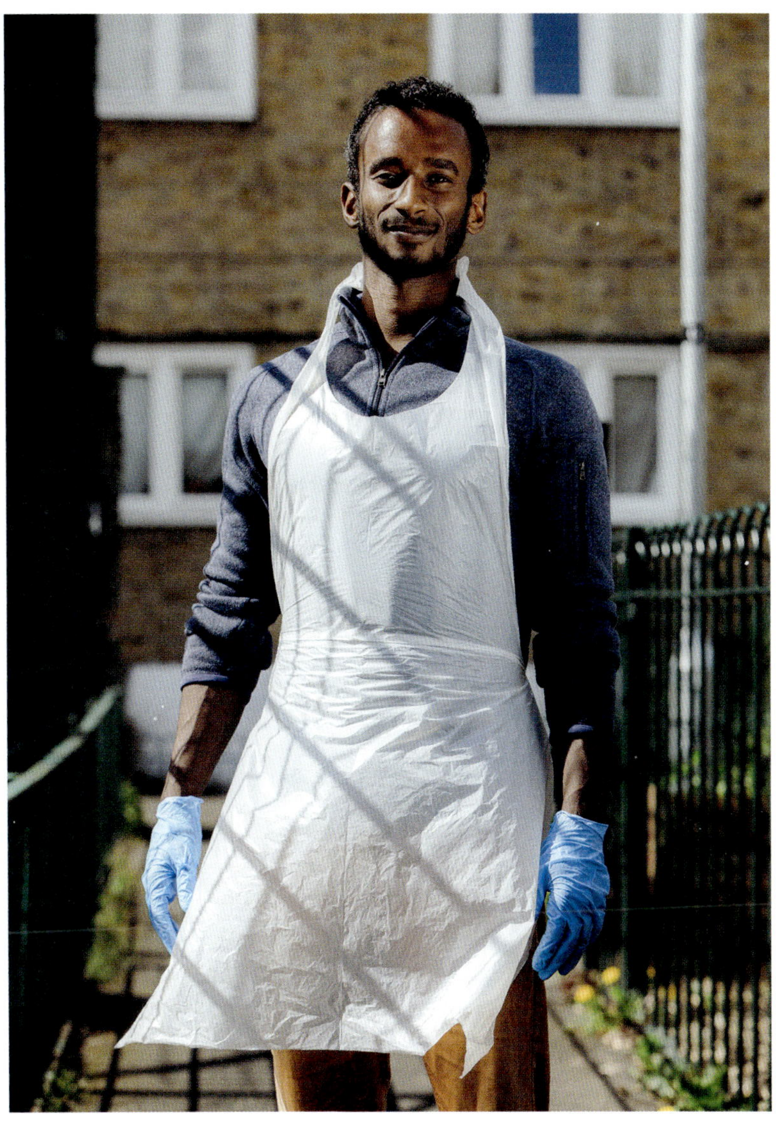

*Sami Ayad on his first day volunteering at Children with Voices' Community Food Hub. Born in Sudan but raised in Brazil, he is now studying for a PhD in the UK. He recently moved into an apartment overlooking the Food Hub, and came down to lend a hand. 6 April 2020.*

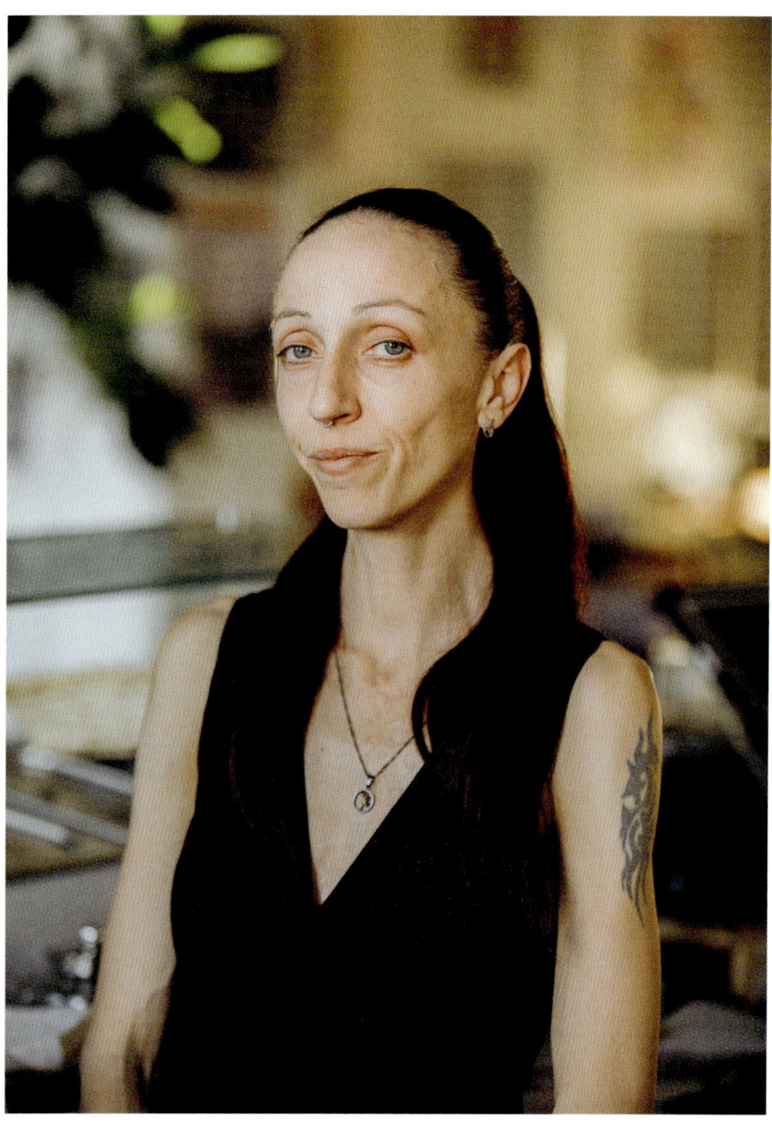

*Agnes works as a chef at Ridley Road Social Club in Hackney. The restaurant had only been open for five months when the pandemic hit, so they pivoted to running a subsistence kitchen providing healthy meals for a small cost, as well as letting a local homeless charity prepare food using their facilities. 6 April 2020.*

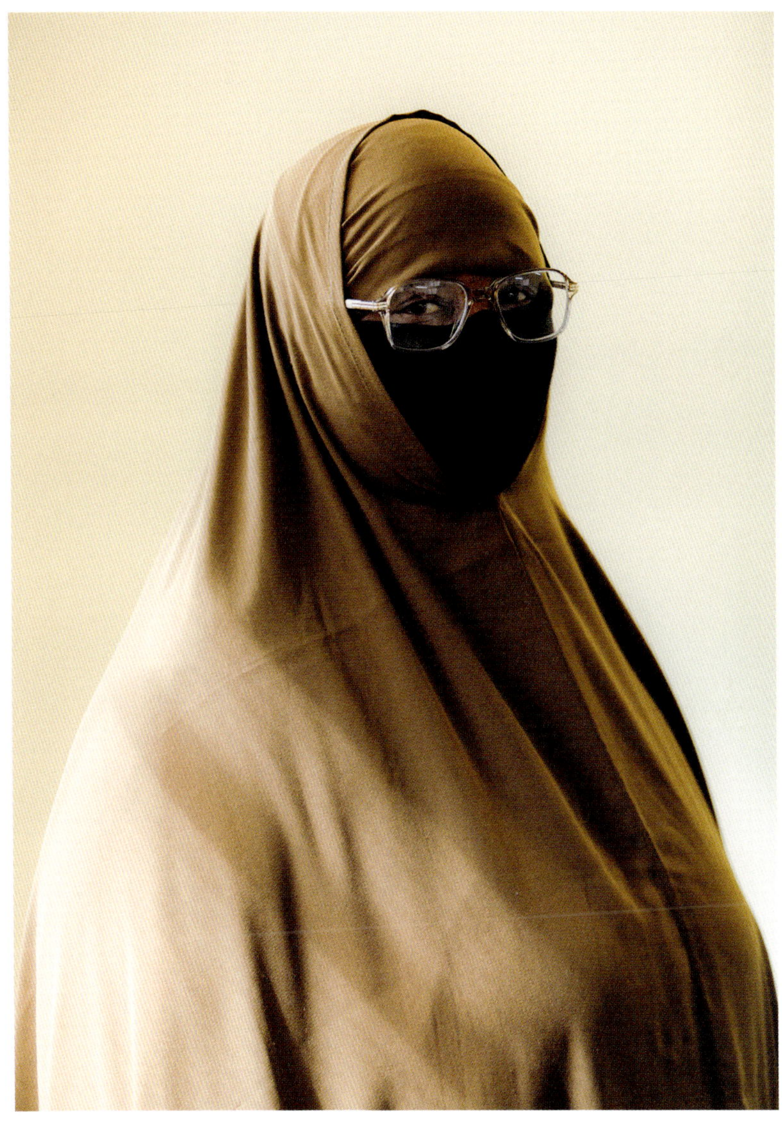

*Sahra Adan in Banister House Community Hall. Sahra is a Somali refugee who, together with her daughter Nimo, volunteers with the community support group Connecting All Communities to distribute food to local Hackney residents. 25 August 2020.*

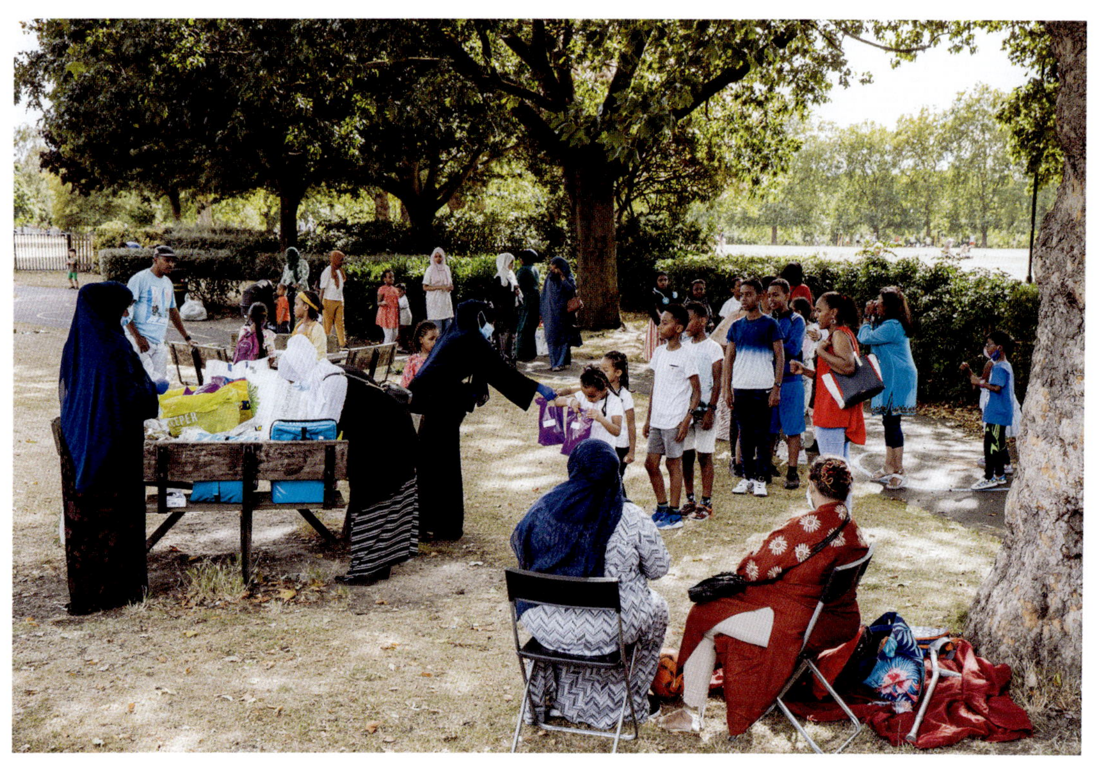

*Shukri Adan, founder of Connecting All Communities, and volunteers hand out free meals and bags filled with small gifts for Eid on Hackney Downs. 2 August 2020.*

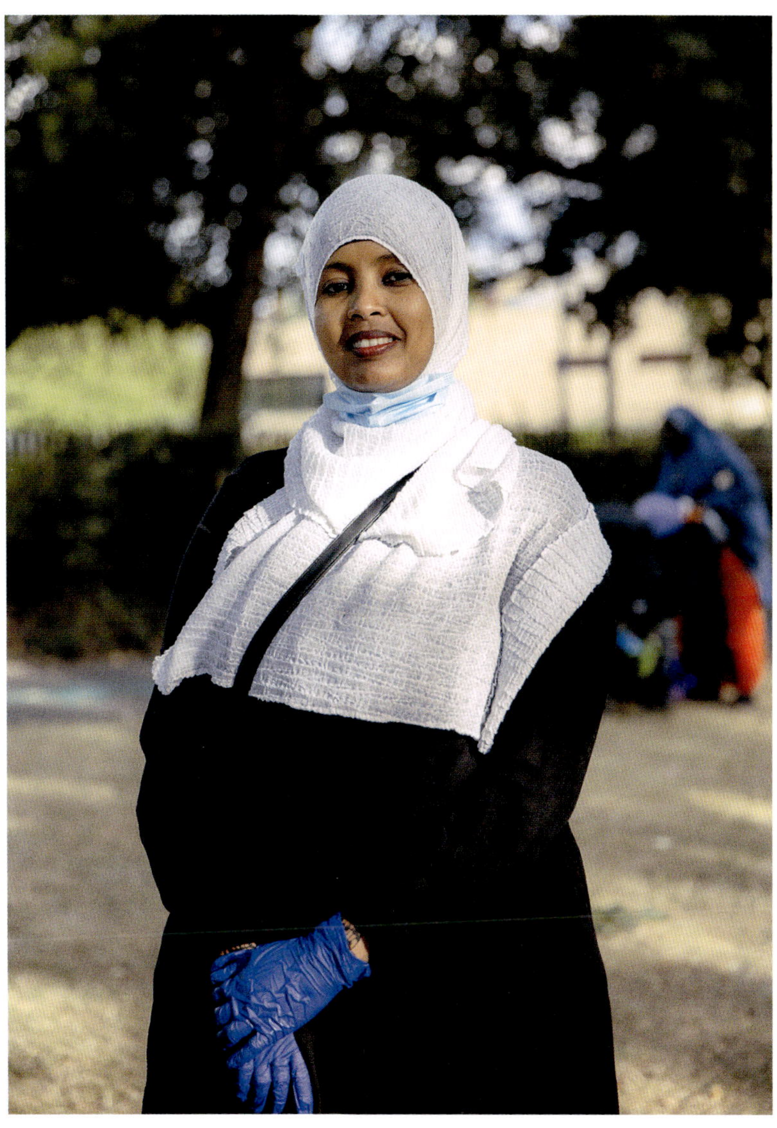

*Shukri Adan on Hackney Downs. With people unable to come together in large groups to celebrate Eid inside, due to social distancing guidelines, Connecting All Communities distributed meals and presents to families in the park instead. 2 August 2020.*

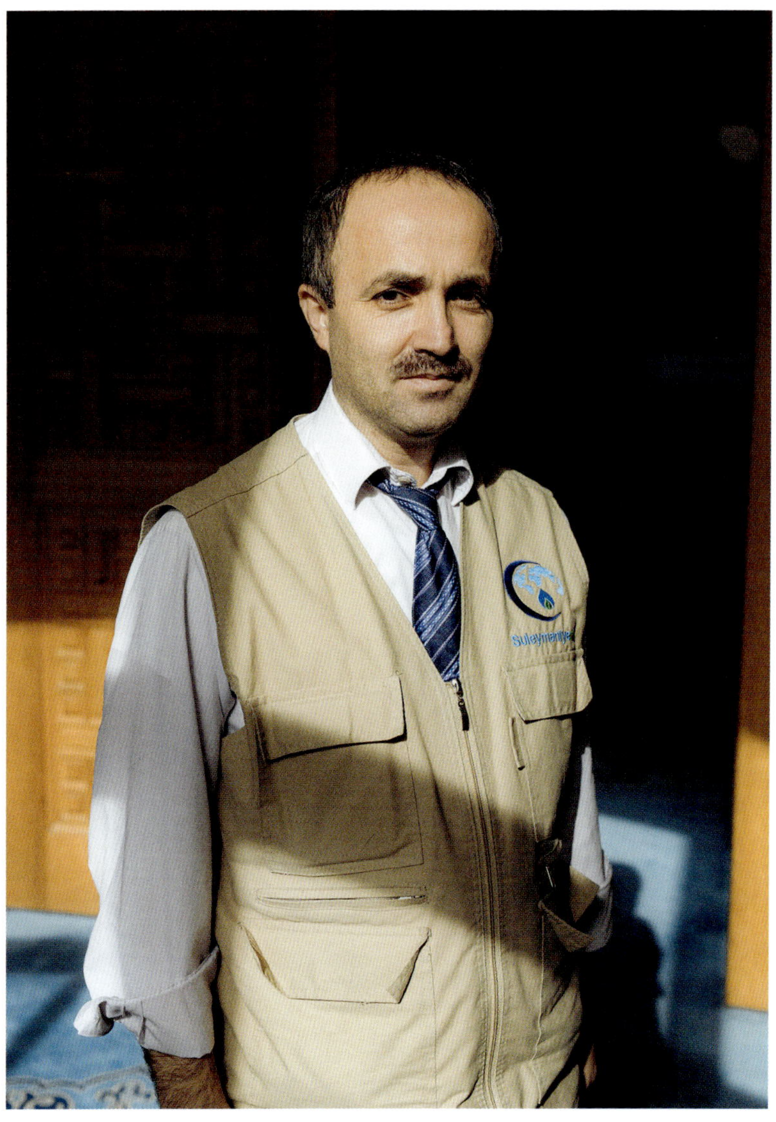

*Tunahan Bilir, a coordinator for Suleymaniye Aid, inside the Suleymaniye Mosque. Tunahan spearheaded a partnership with Haggerston Mutual Aid to cook and deliver thousands of meals to local families during Ramadan.*
*11 May 2020.*

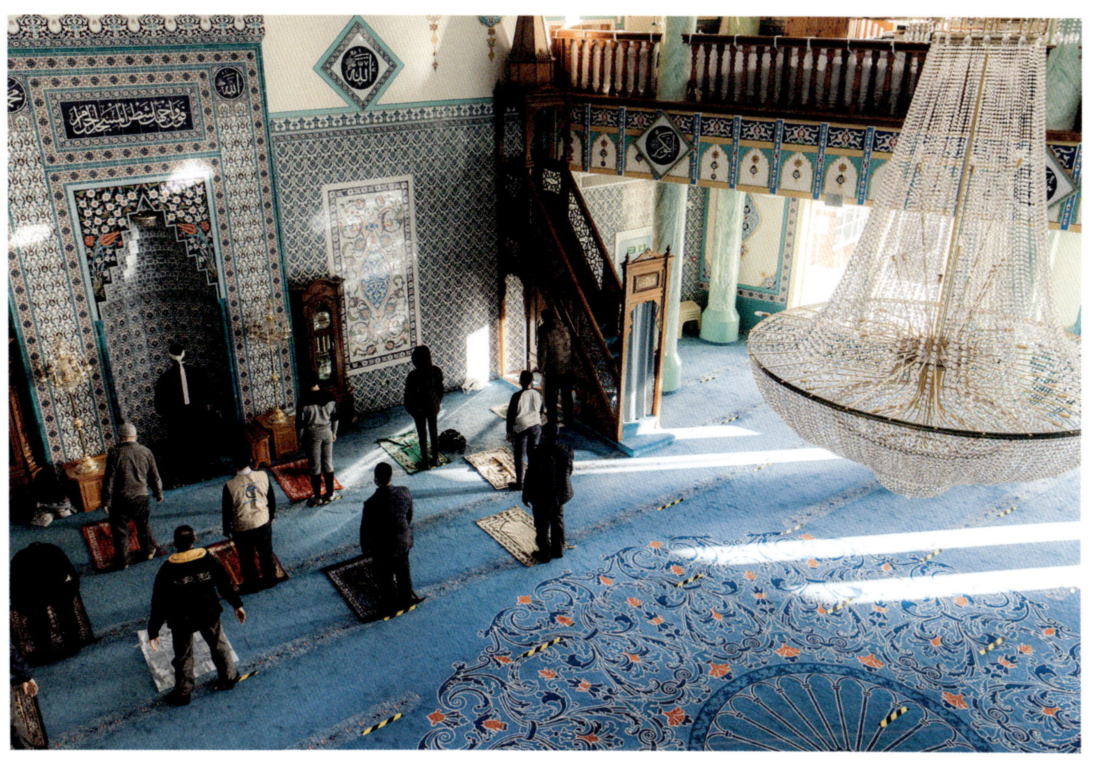

*On the eve of the second lockdown, a socially distanced congregation take part in last prayers before Hackney's Suleymaniye Mosque once again closes for public worship. 4 November 2020.*

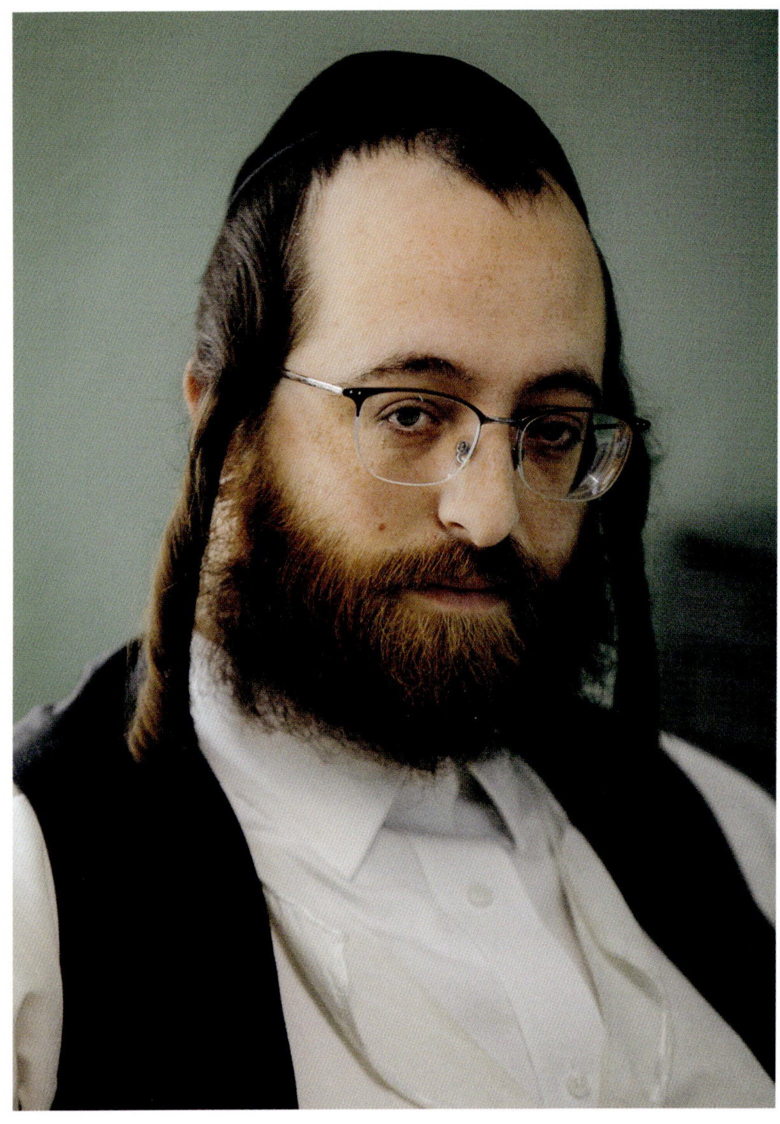

*Graphic designer Sam Friedman in his offices in Stamford Hill. Some members of the Orthodox Jewish community struggled to adapt to new public safety measures, so Sam started a physical distancing awareness campaign, putting notices in local magazines and on social media. 2 April 2020.*

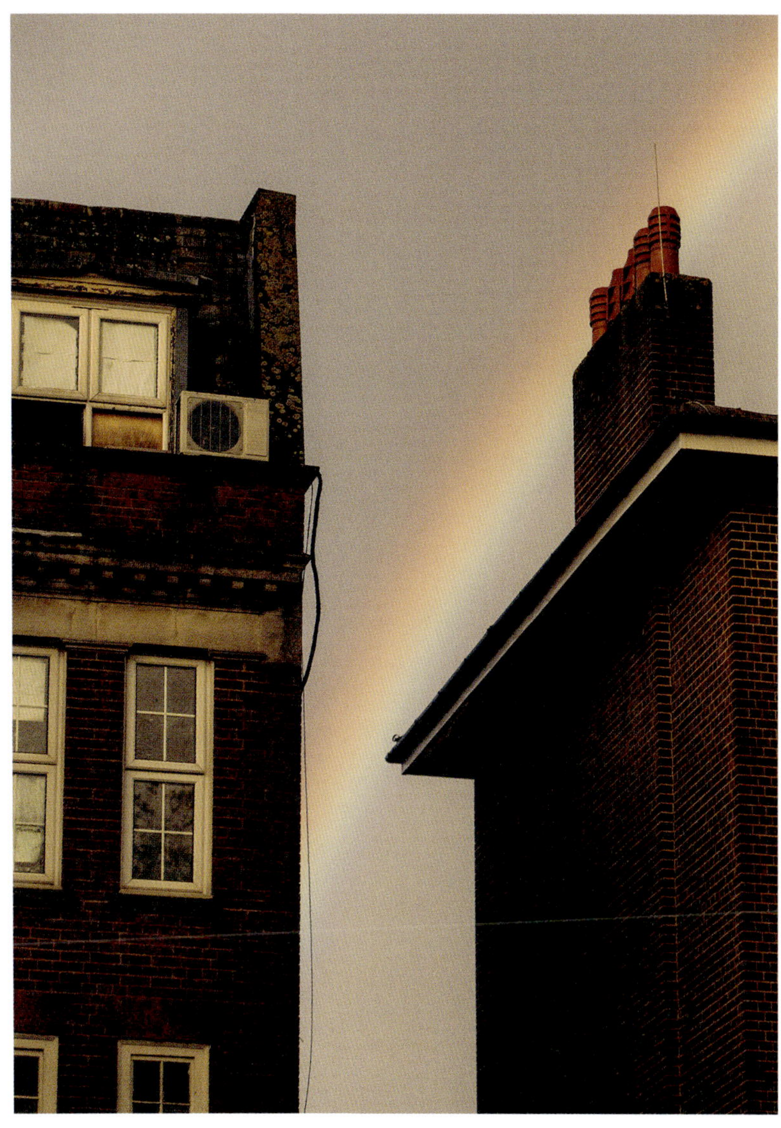

*On a Thursday evening in Stamford Hill, just before Clap for Carers begins,
a rainbow stretches across the sky as if in solidarity. 30 April 2020.*

# Will Hartley
## *While You Were Sleeping*

Dreamlike and melancholy, Will Hartley's diaristic series elevates
the mundanity of homebound life through stolen moments of everyday
beauty. The central character in this story is his partner Chiara, whose
presence emerges in closely cropped images of hands and ethereal
portraits. Wrapped up in personal experience, the highs and lows of
living together in close quarters at a time of extreme pressure and
intensity form the backbone to the project, amplified by a poem drawn
from Hartley's journal entries. 'I realised how anxious I was feeling and
instead of documenting the situation outside, I used photography as
a way of escapism,' says Hartley. 'I thought I would make a project about
the pandemic, but it became very internal: about me and my girlfriend.'

Hartley admits, 'like probably most couples, we've had some of
our biggest arguments during lockdown. There was a lot of beauty in it
but also a lot of frustration.' The intensity of these moods and emotions –
the tension and tenderness, intimacy and vulnerability – are expressed
in his play on dark and light in images that flit between subtle tones
of colour and high-contrast black and white. 'We'd go out for an hour
in the marshes and it tended to be when the light was just coming
down, just as the sun was setting. My girlfriend always says that I dream
too much, but when I was walking around the marshes, I felt like I was
walking in a painting. In this hyper-sensual world, I was constantly aware
of everything, like the tiniest little bug landing on my boot.'

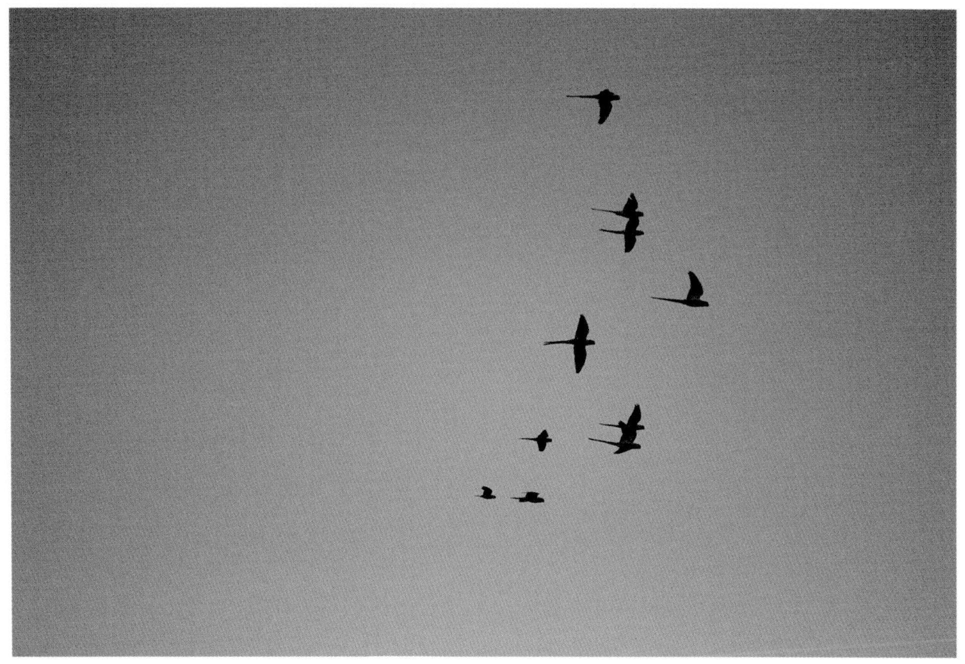

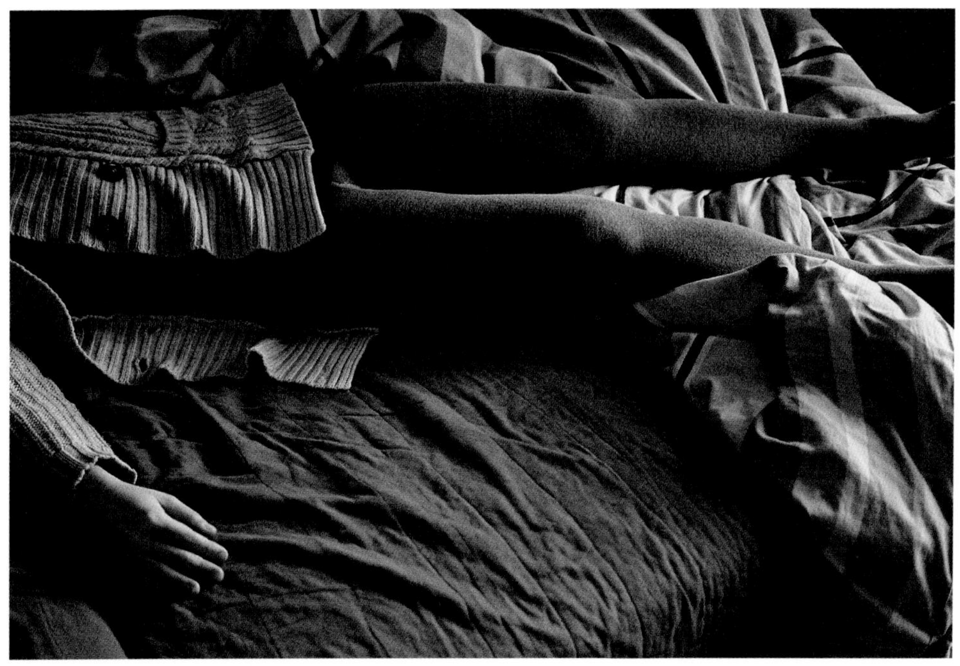

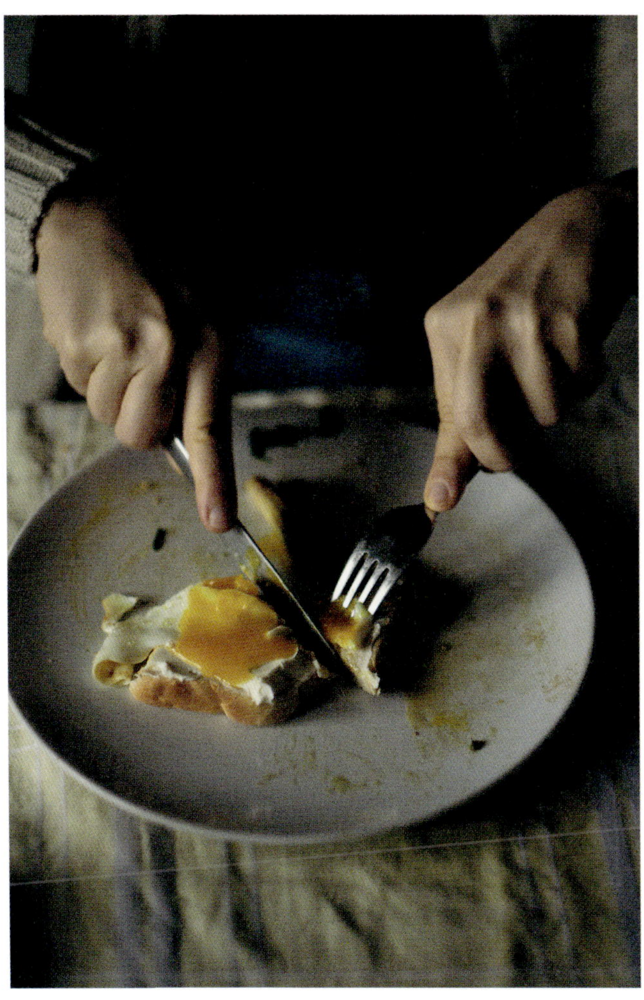

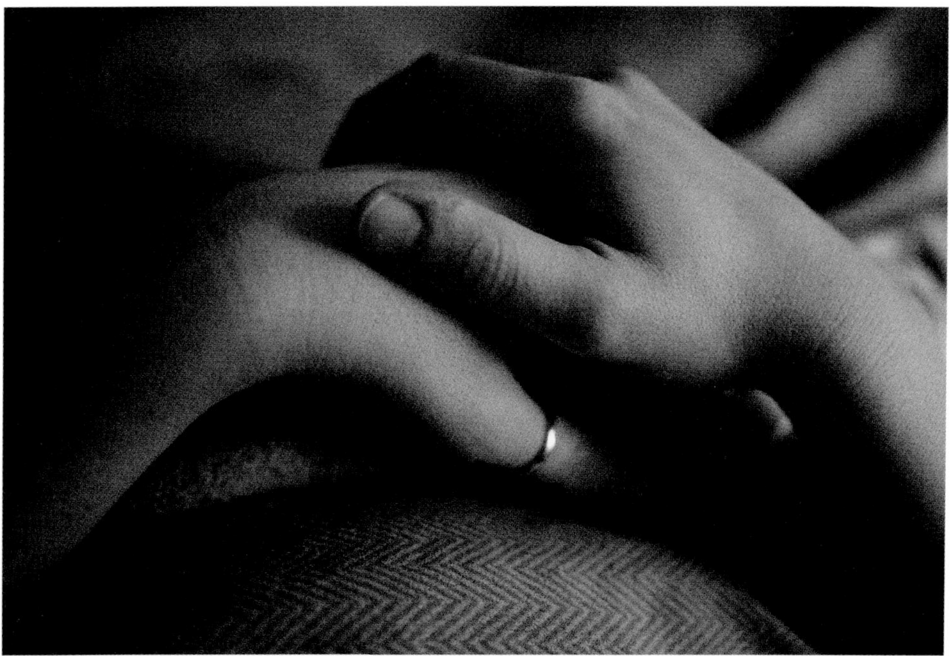

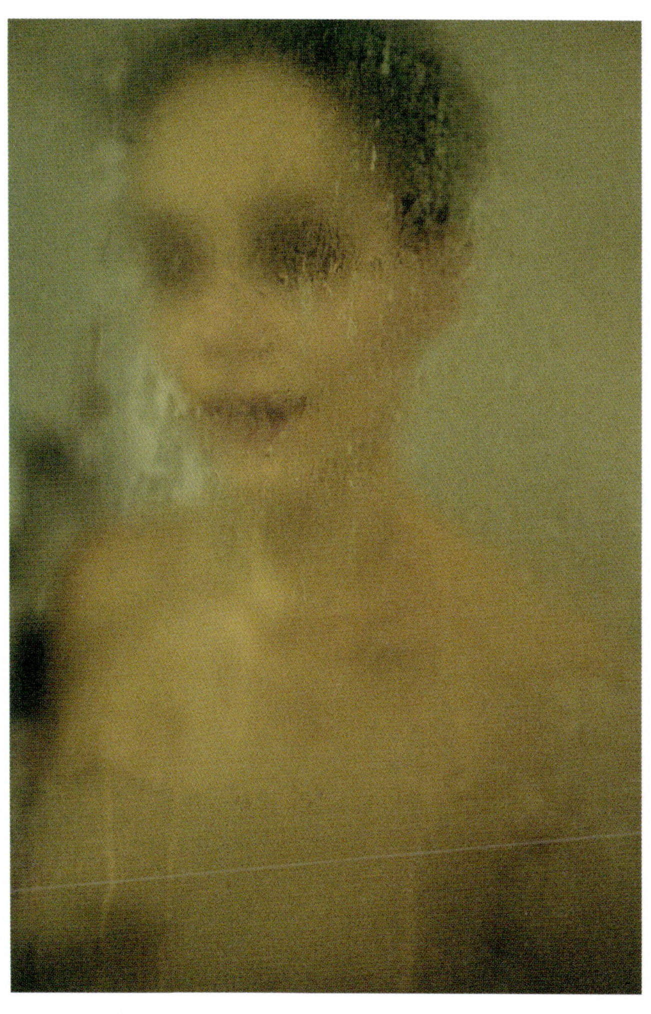

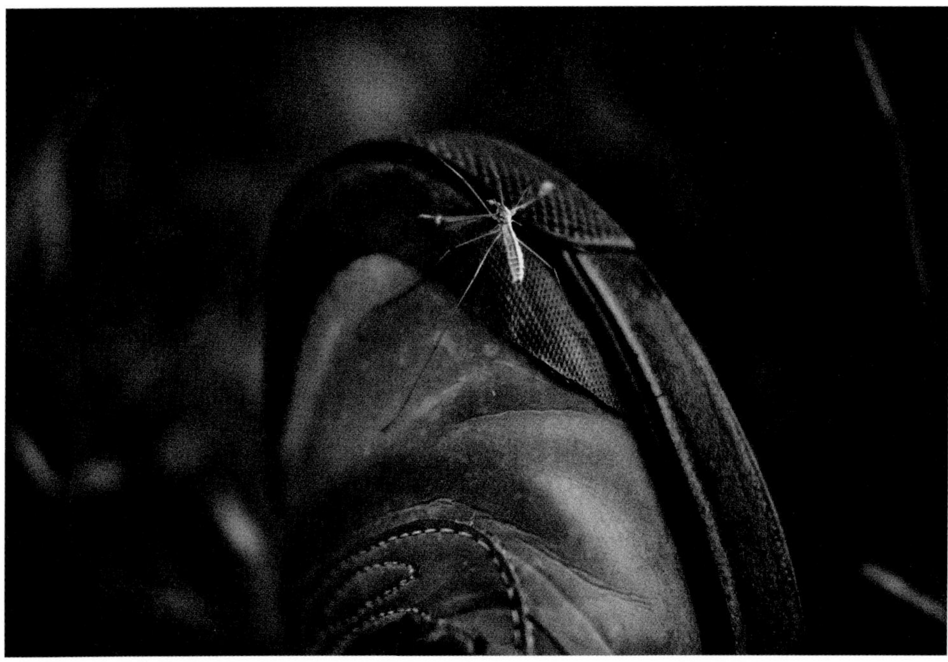

*It was raining heavily yesterday evening as the sun came down,*
*it created a soft orange haze throughout the apartment, making everything glow.*
*The light felt like it was physical, sitting inside the apartment with me,*
*making its way around the room.*

*I threw my camera on the sofa and walked outside, my heart pumping*
*        and my head spinning,*
*like someone had put a clamp around my head and they were squeezing it tight.*
*I slammed the door shut and sat on the balcony facing away from the house.*
*I breathed in slowly to try and calm down.*

*It's so quiet and peaceful, there are no cars around, or trains going past.*
*You can hear the birds, the nature, the stillness in the air.*

*She took her headphones off and gave me a hug, and said sorry,*
*she started to cry and I said I was sorry too.*
*She said I didn't need to be; 'I don't want to lose you.'*

*We headed out to the marshes, I hadn't noticed how beautiful the sunset*
*        was before the lockdown,*
*rich deep blues and purples fill the sky for a moment until the sun goes down,*
*and the moon takes over for the night.*

*– Will Hartley*

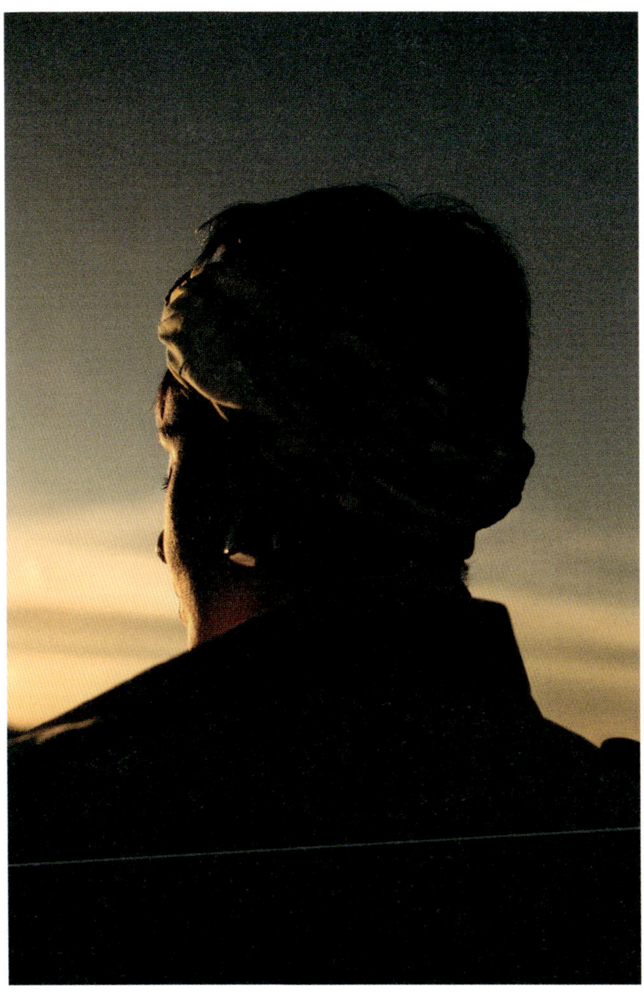

# Mimi Mollica
## *Moon City*

Mimi Mollica's project *Moon City* brings together two subjects hundreds of thousands of miles apart: the City of London and the moon. When the supermoon of April 2020 first compelled the photographer to gaze up from the balcony of his top-floor flat in Dalston, it marked the start of a fascination with these two mysterious, expansive phenomena during an extended period of confinement at home. 'I found myself creating a dialogue between the full moon and the close-ups of empty offices, left vacant because of the lockdown measures in London. They both influence our lives and the way our planet behaves; one follows the rules of nature and the other obeys the rules of the free market,' Mollica writes. Shooting on his iPhone through the lens of a telescope, Mollica tracked the daily metamorphoses of these two powerful forces that appeared simultaneously within close reach and infinitely distant.

The resulting project is a rumination on the play of light and dark that illuminates the moon's coarse surface and the City's sleek architecture against an ever-changing sky – one a generous muse, the other 'an empty capitalist machine, looking somewhere between film noir and *Blade Runner.*' Presented in diptychs, the spherical frames and semi-abstract compositions of Mollica's photographs produce an alienating vision of both a terrestrial and extra-terrestrial world. 'I felt it was like peeping through a keyhole and seeing an obscure system that preys on social inequality, dictating public policies to favour the market.' With his juxtapositions, Mollica aims to spotlight two crucial concerns brought to the fore during the pandemic: the concealed structures of global capitalism and the at-risk future of our planet.

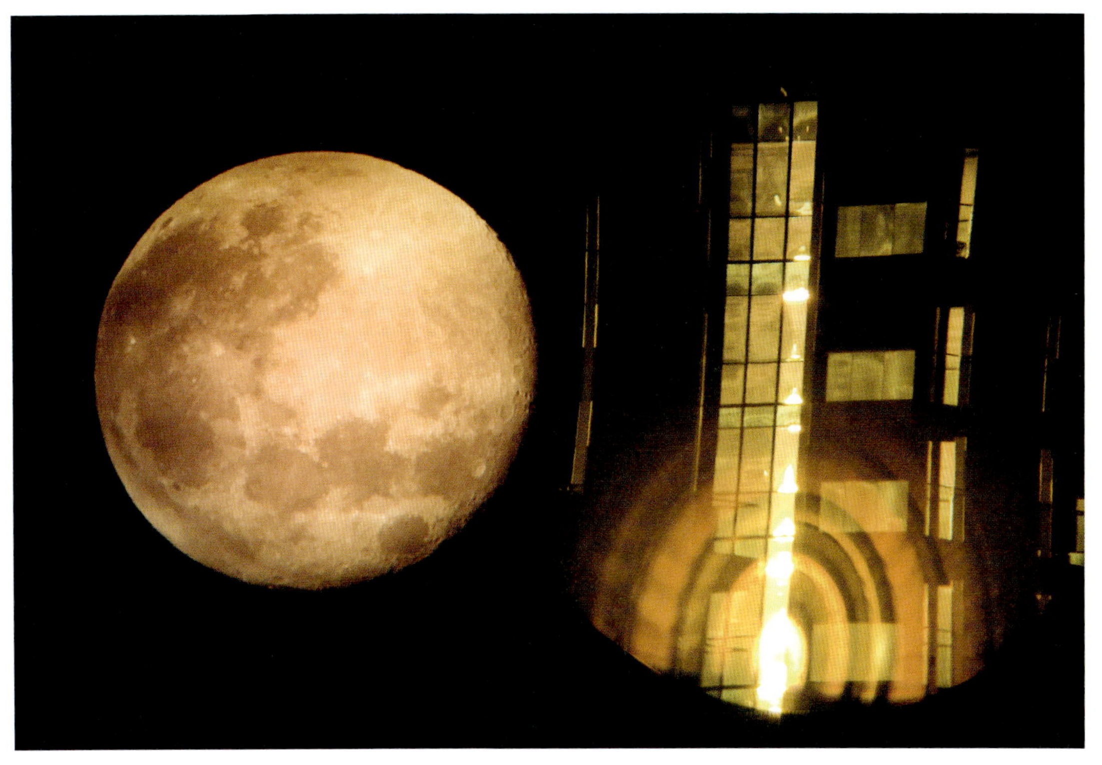

*22:43, 8 May 2020 / 20:04, 11 May 2020*

Mimi Mollica

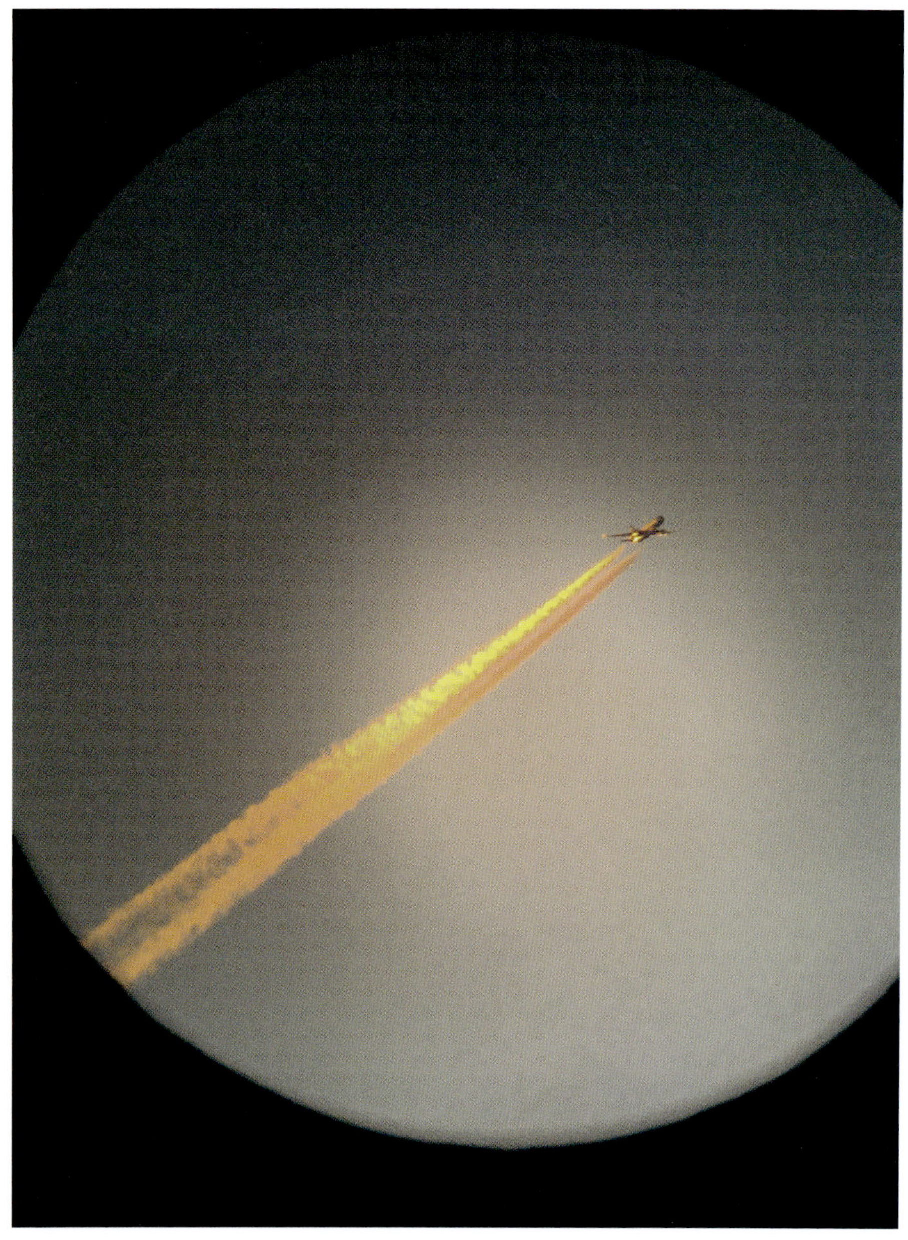

*20:46, 6 May 2020*

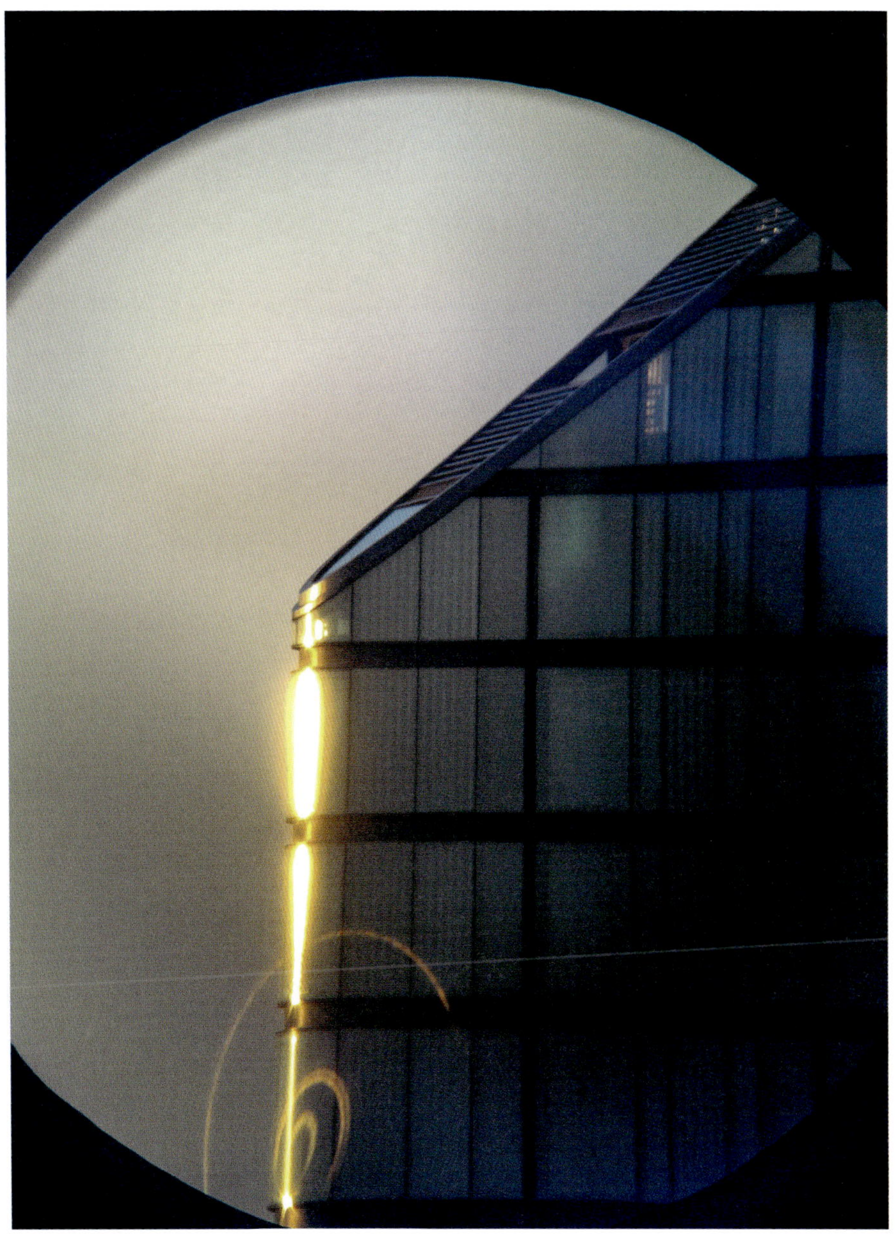

*20:08, 6 May 2020*

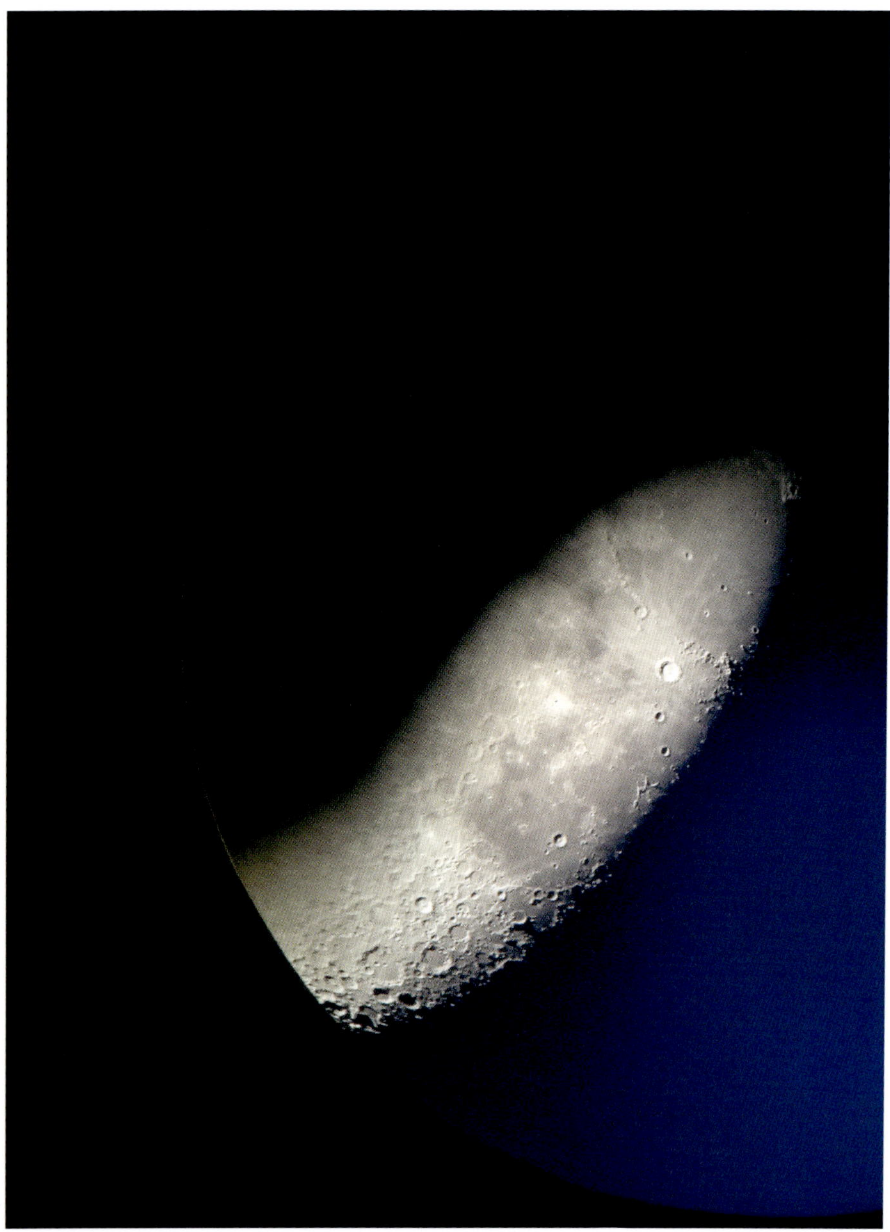

*20:41, 2 May 2020*

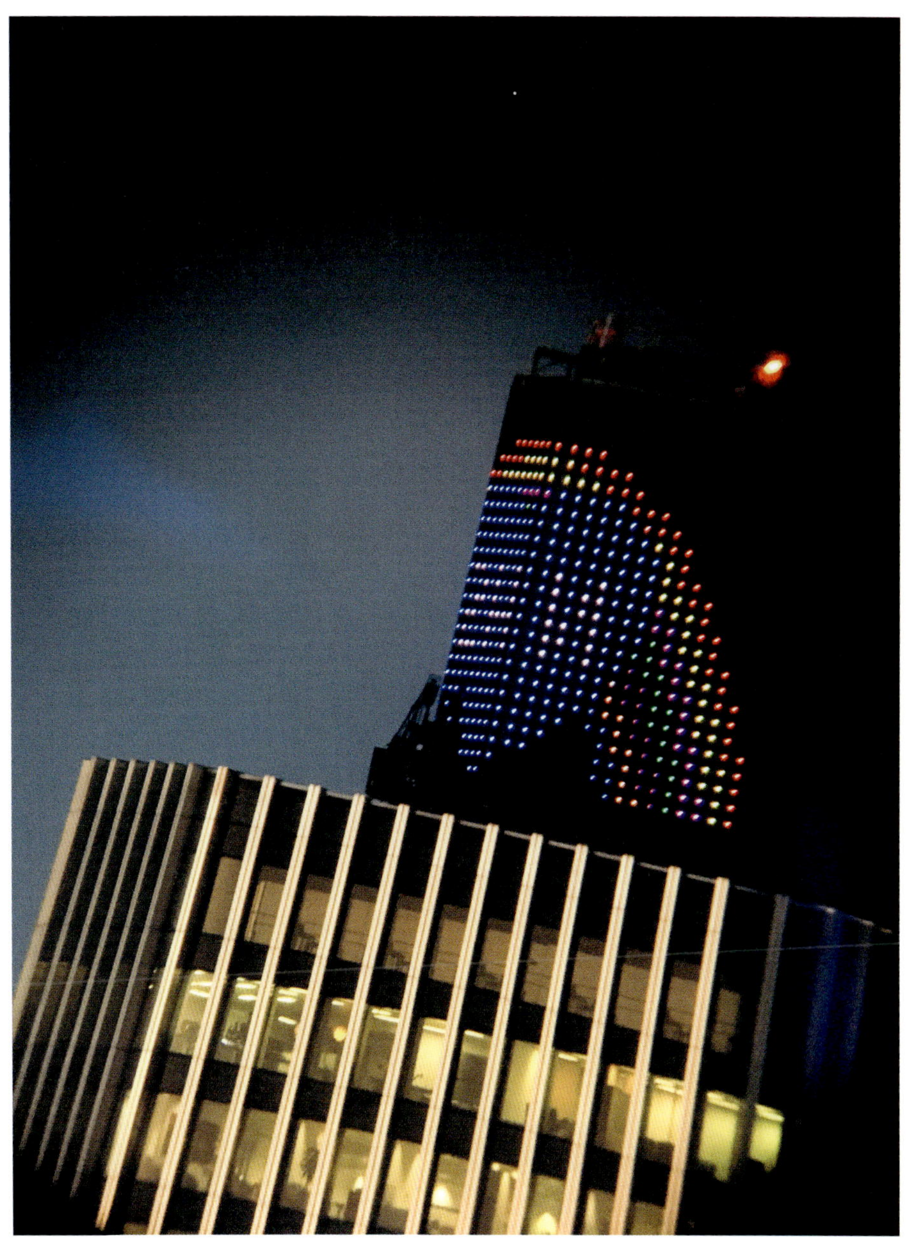

*20:25, 20 April 2020*

# Olivia Arthur
## *Small Changes*

A rotting banana, kids' toys, a zebra crossing, an unexceptional rectangle of blue-grey sky: the minutiae of existence take centre stage in Olivia Arthur's cumulative project *Small Changes.* As a member of the international co-operative Magnum Photos, Arthur usually shoots in faraway settings, travelling to places like India, Saudi Arabia and the US-Mexico border. When lockdown put a stop to all this movement, she found herself grounded in London. Confronted with the open-endedness of this new situation, she picked up her camera and began photographing repetitively around her home, as if counting down the days with each release of the shutter. Every morning, around 10 o'clock, she took pictures of objects or viewpoints from the same perspective, creating a set of daily, near identical photos that record the slow passing of time.

Starting on the first day of lockdown on 23 March 2020, Arthur produced nearly 500 miniature prints over 50 days, which she pinned onto her studio wall. In its repetition and continuity, the resulting grid reveals life as a perpetual cycle of scarcely noticeable change. But it also mirrors Arthur's own internal process of accepting the uncertainty of the pandemic – eventually finding elation in being fixed in one place with nowhere to go and no obligations to attend to. Writing at the time, she reflected: 'Initially there is no visible change but eventually the leaves start to come out on the trees, the flowers inside die, the girls' room gets messy but then gets clean again. We still don't know how long it will go on, but we take it a day at a time and are learning to be patient.'

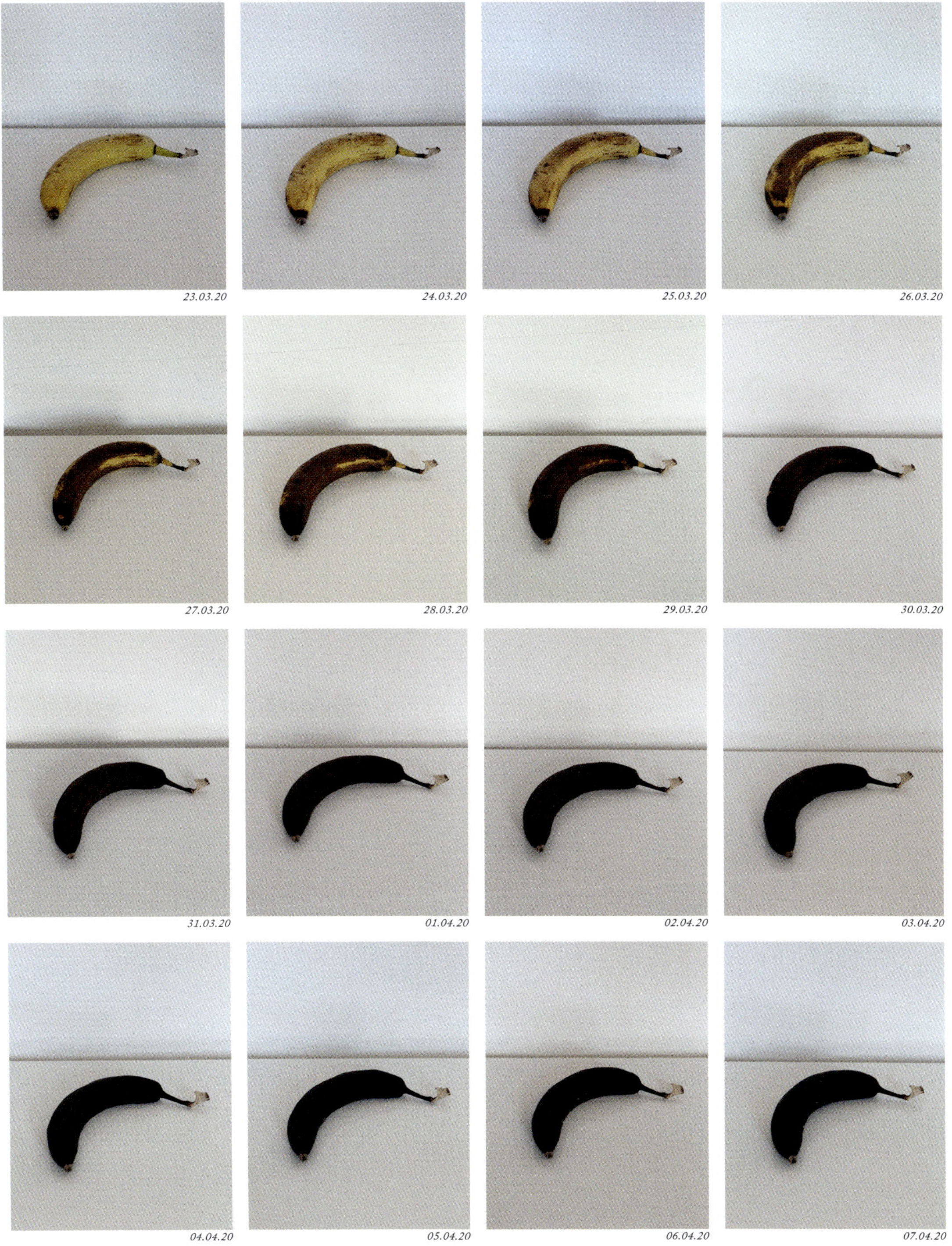


23.03.20
24.03.20
25.03.20
26.03.20
27.03.20
28.03.20
29.03.20
30.03.20
31.03.20
01.04.20
02.04.20
03.04.20
04.04.20
05.04.20
06.04.20
07.04.20

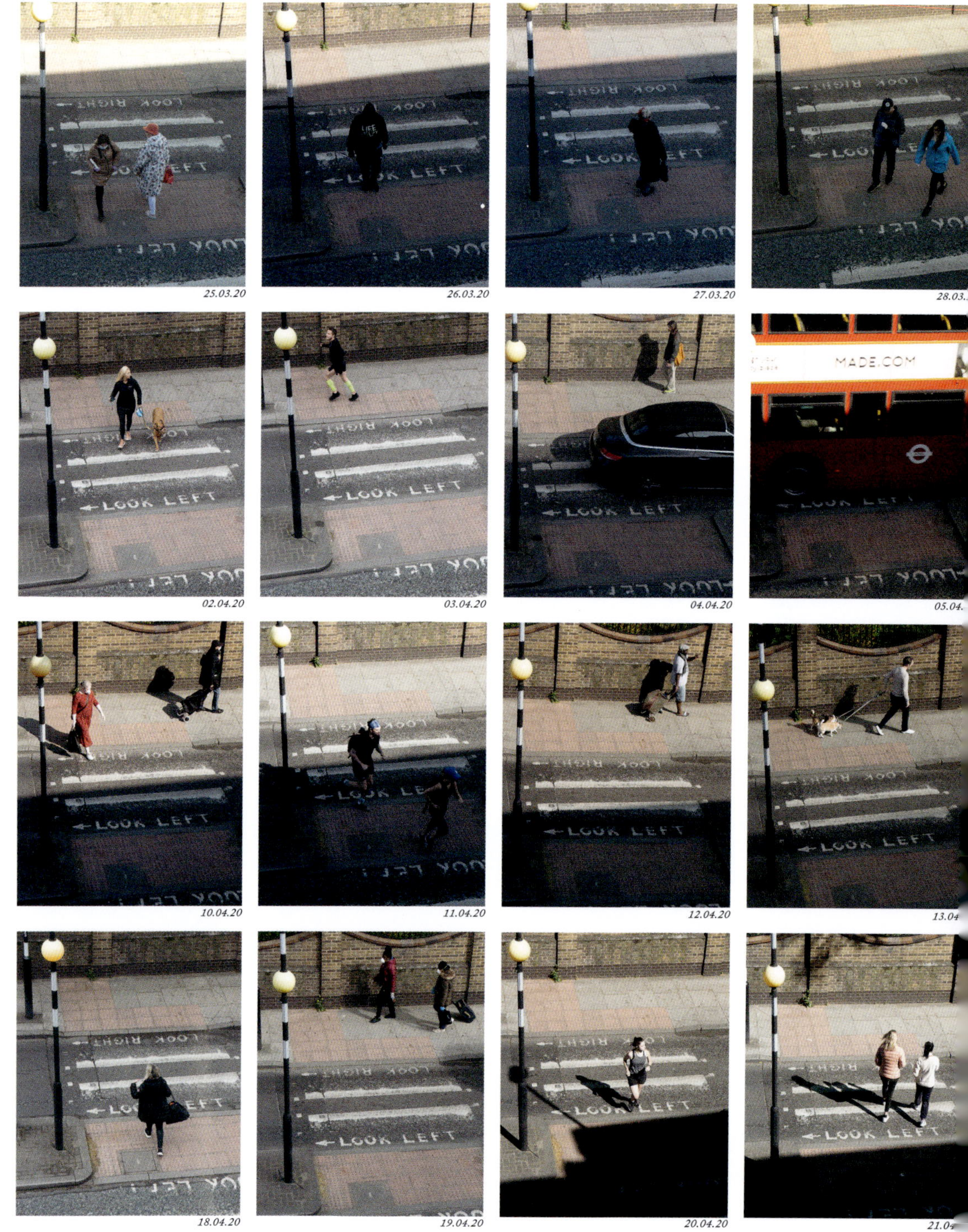
25.03.20
26.03.20
27.03.20
28.03..
02.04.20
03.04.20
04.04.20
05.04.
10.04.20
11.04.20
12.04.20
13.04
18.04.20
19.04.20
20.04.20
21.04

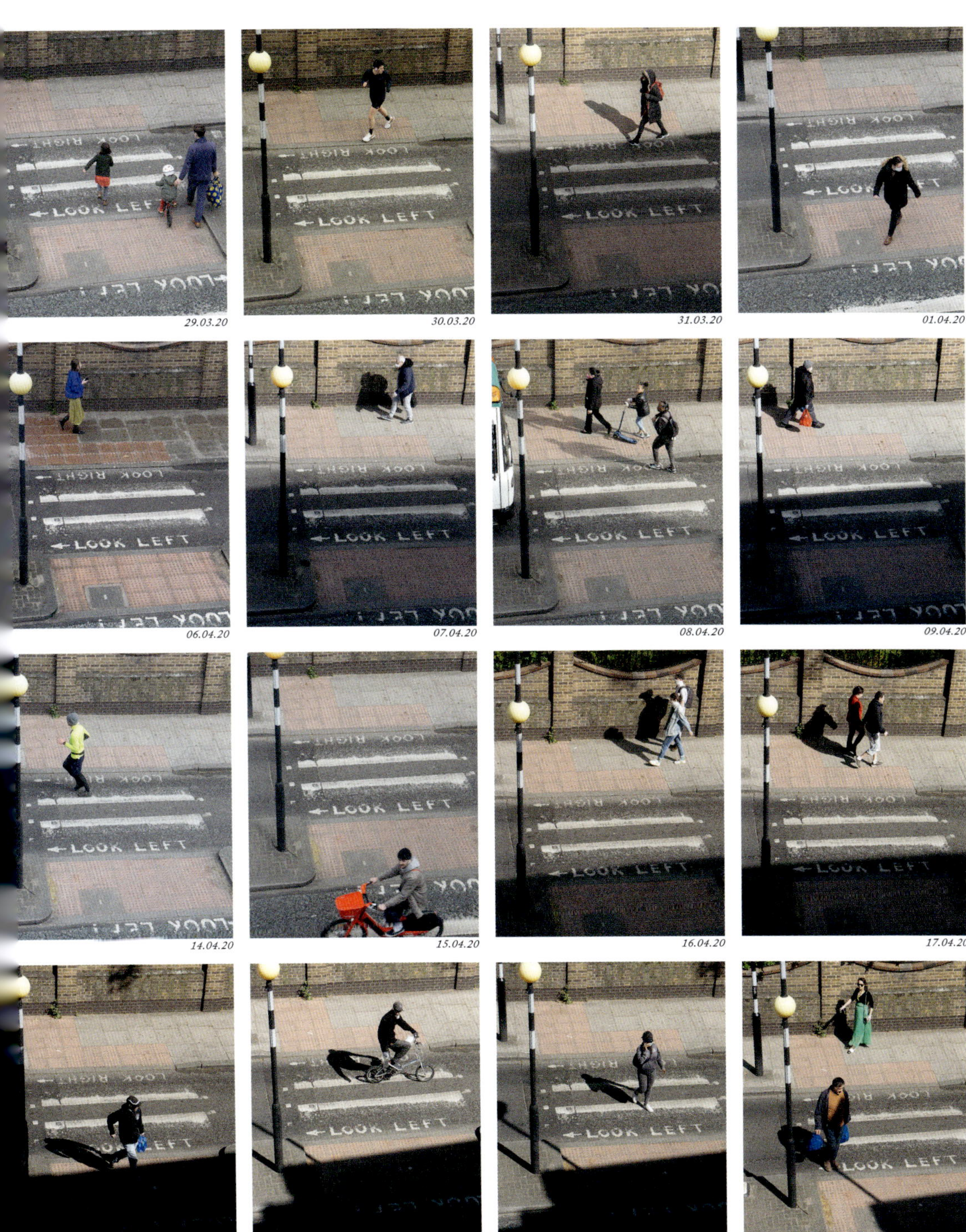

29.03.20    30.03.20    31.03.20    01.04.20

06.04.20    07.04.20    08.04.20    09.04.20

14.04.20    15.04.20    16.04.20    17.04.20

22.04.20    23.04.20    24.04.20    25.04.20

Olivia Arthur

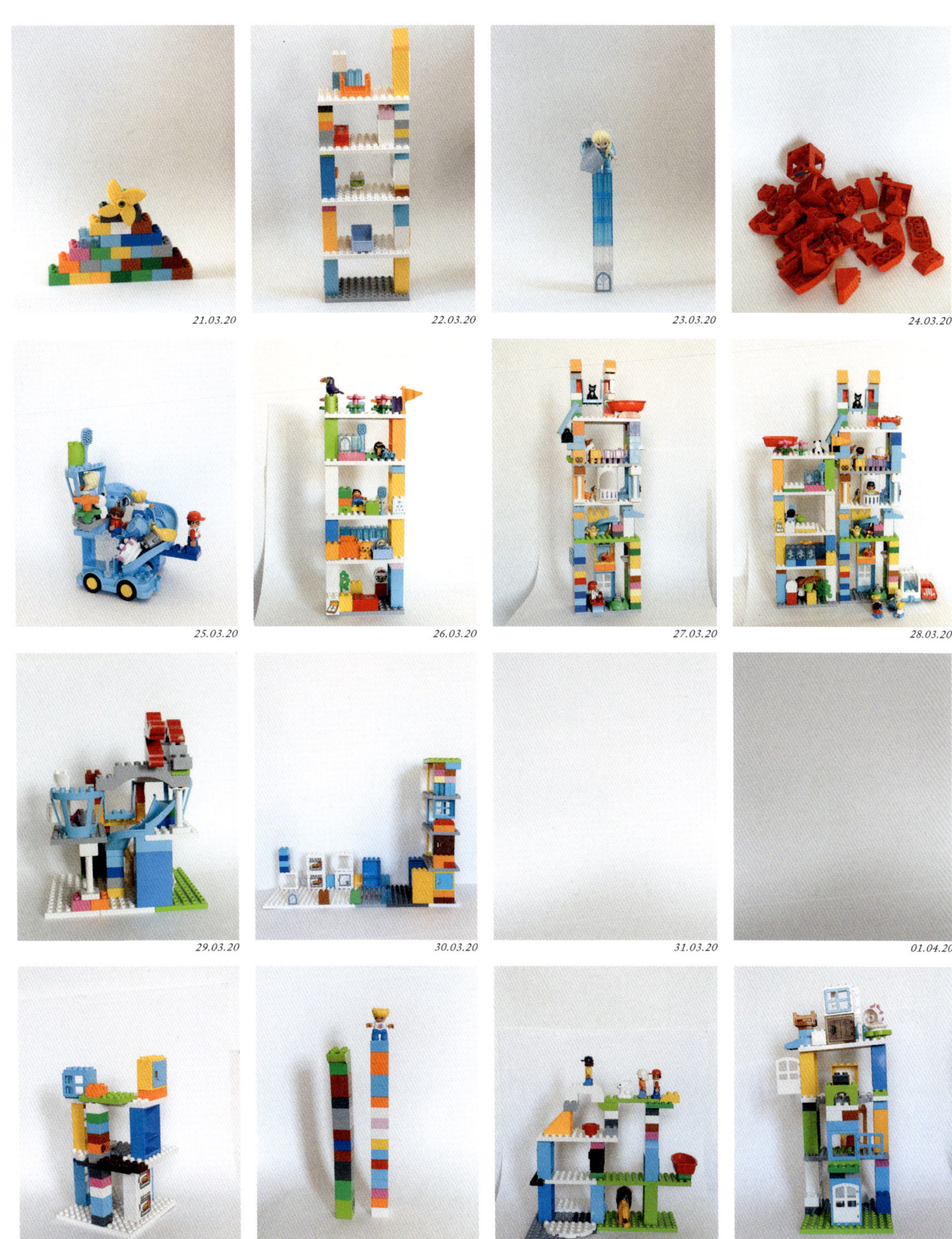

21.03.20

22.03.20

23.03.20

24.03.20

25.03.20

26.03.20

27.03.20

28.03.20

29.03.20

30.03.20

31.03.20

01.04.20

02.04.20

03.04.20

04.04.20

05.04.20

Olivia Arthur

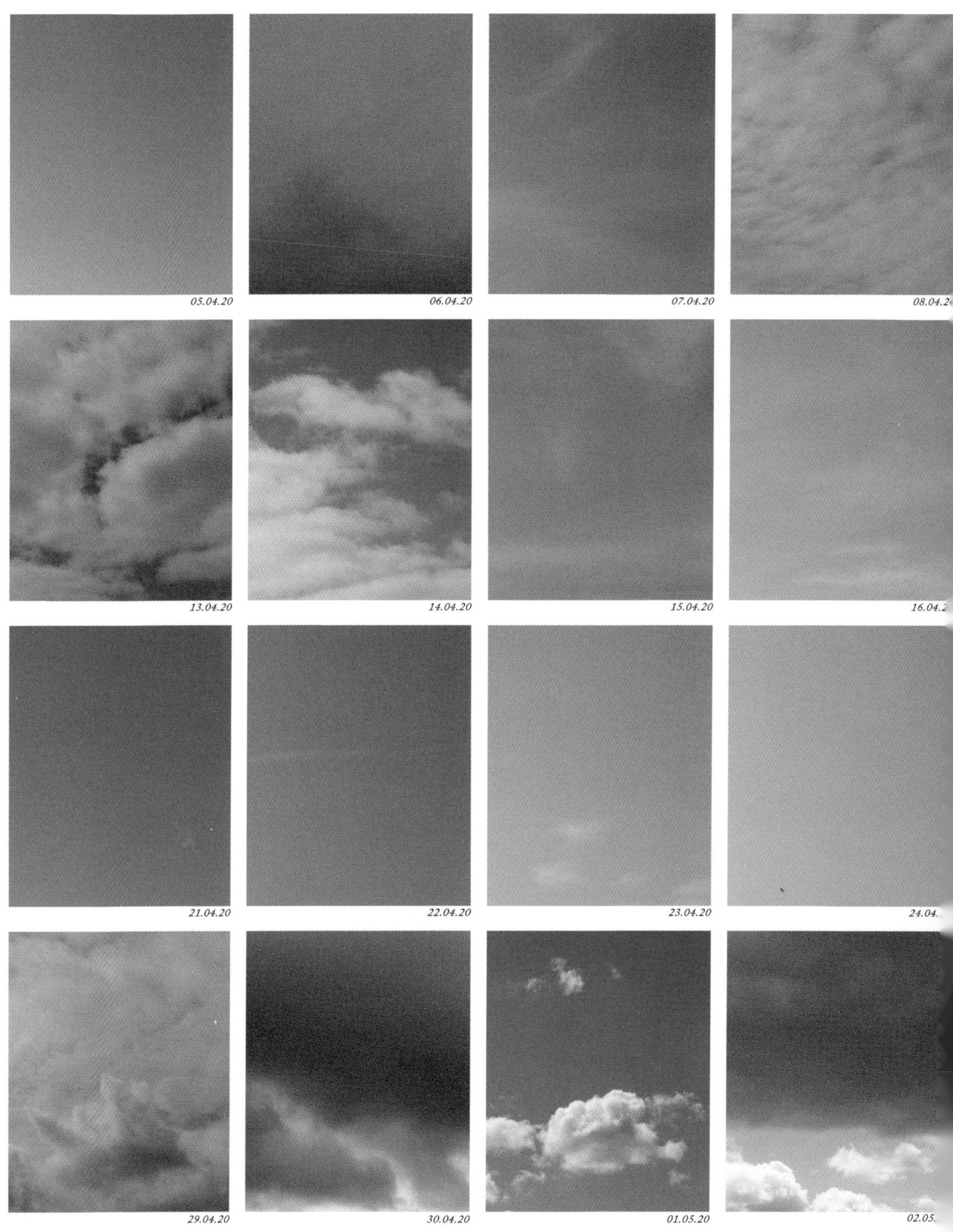

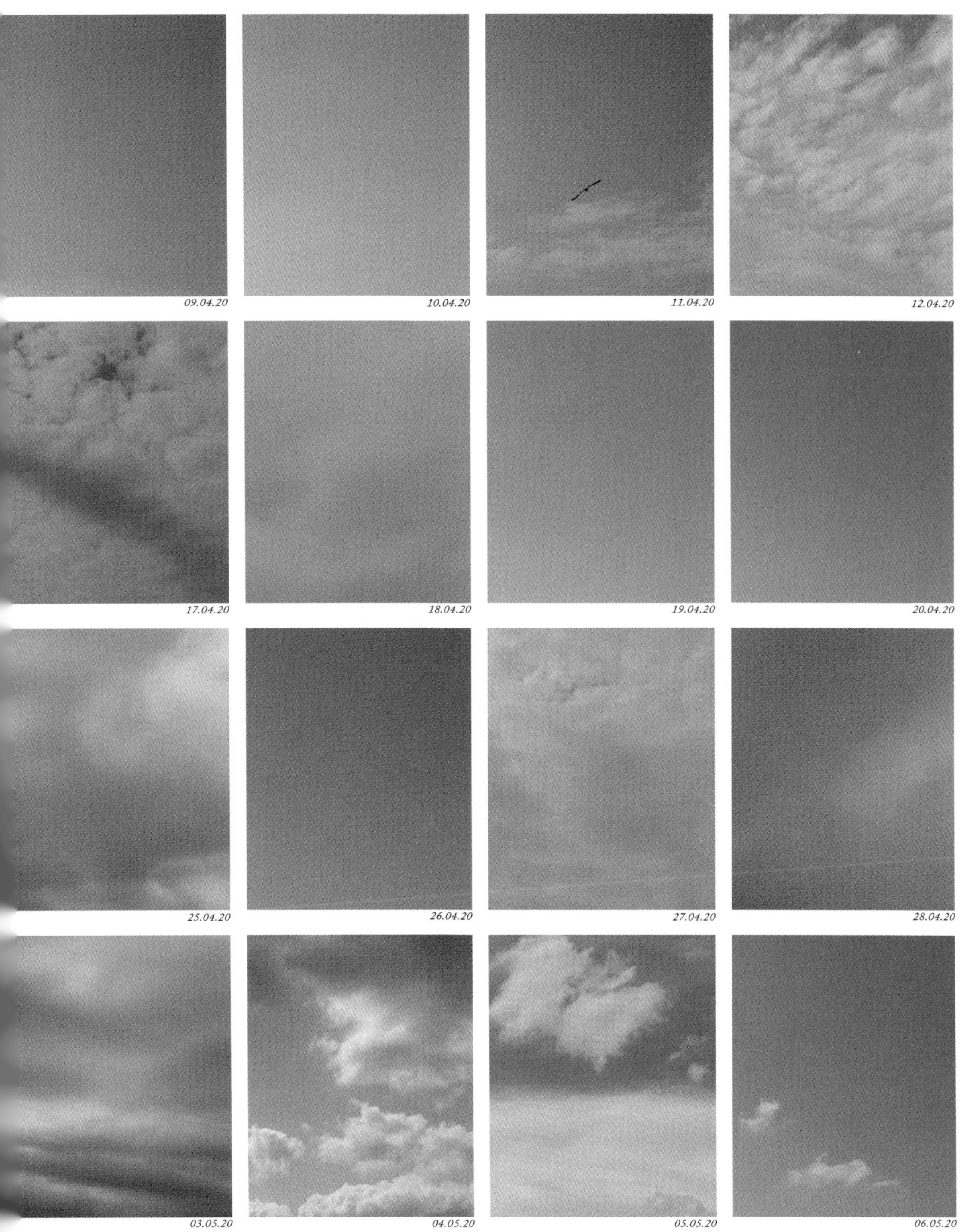

09.04.20 10.04.20 11.04.20 12.04.20
17.04.20 18.04.20 19.04.20 20.04.20
25.04.20 26.04.20 27.04.20 28.04.20
03.05.20 04.05.20 05.05.20 06.05.20

# Simon Norfolk
## *Lost Capital*

In these imposing panoramas, taken during the first lockdown, Simon Norfolk casts London as a post-apocalyptic city – one not too dissimilar from the imaginary ruins drawn by Romanticists Gustave Doré and Joseph Gandy. Seen through Norfolk's eyes, the pandemic-struck city is always more than it appears to be: devoid of signs of life, but richly textured with historic clues and traces. He uses the camera to scratch at the surface of what is visible, revealing the city's many underlying layers: 'I have always thought I am more of an archaeologist than a photographer. The places that interest me historically are almost like landslips – where the land has fallen away and suddenly you can see all these archaeological strata on top of each other. All kind of stacked up and waiting to be excavated. London for me is like that.'

The project began as an exploration of sites of past plagues and epidemics in London, but it soon became a broader rumination on the capital's architecture. 'I thought I knew those landscapes so intimately – I have lived here forever. But when you remove all of the chaotic, attention-grabbing stuff of the people and the buses and the trucks, I realised how little I knew about the theatre, about the stage settings of these things. You get a real sense of how London is a grand design: a designed imperial landscape.' In Norfolk's words, *Lost Capital* reminds us that 'this microscopic virus has made proud fools of us all. It has shown us to be ultimately powerless and our investments misguided and empty. All our dreams and schemes and the protections that insulate us from the world were found to be as tough as wet cardboard.'

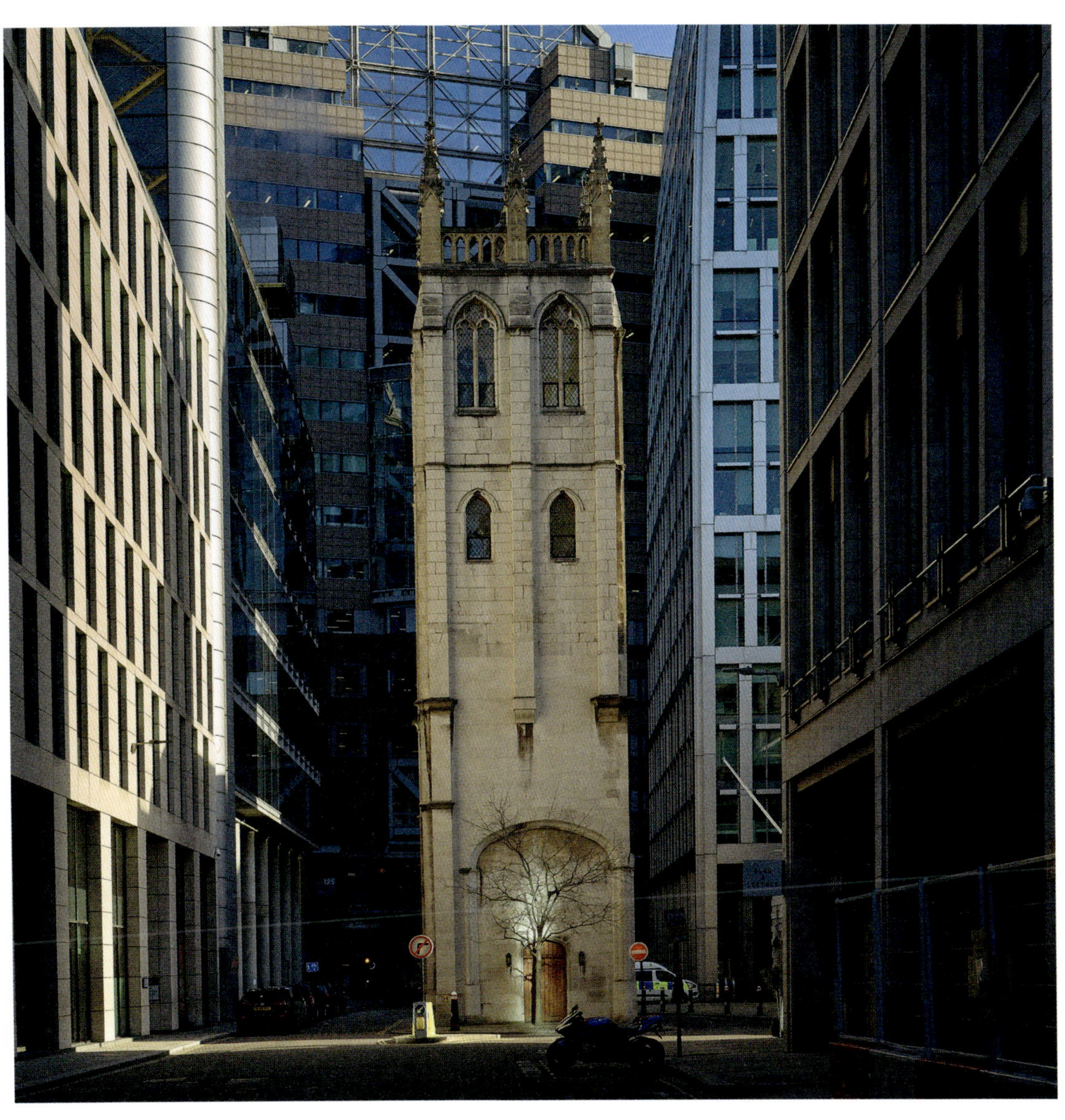

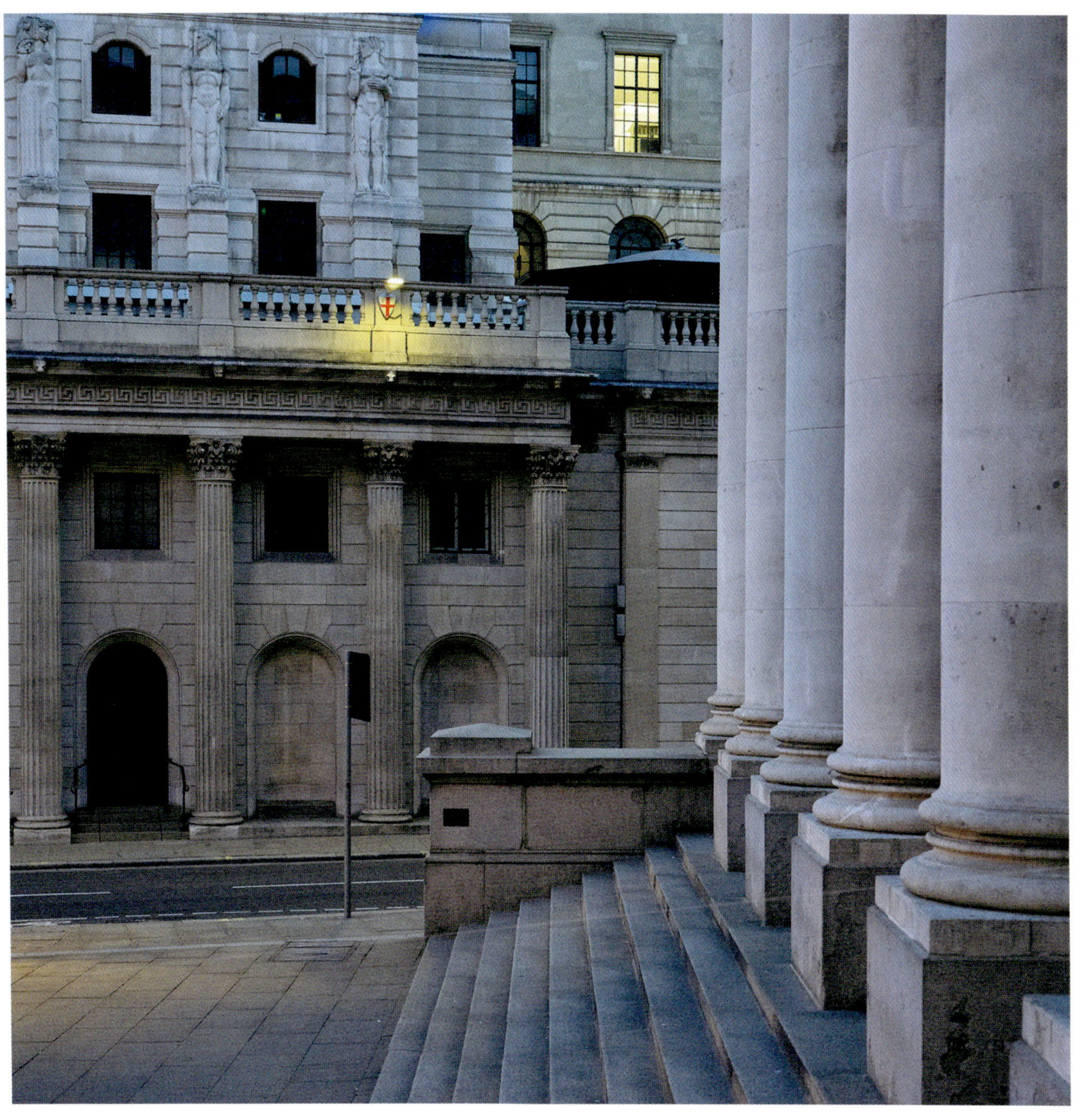

Simon Norfolk

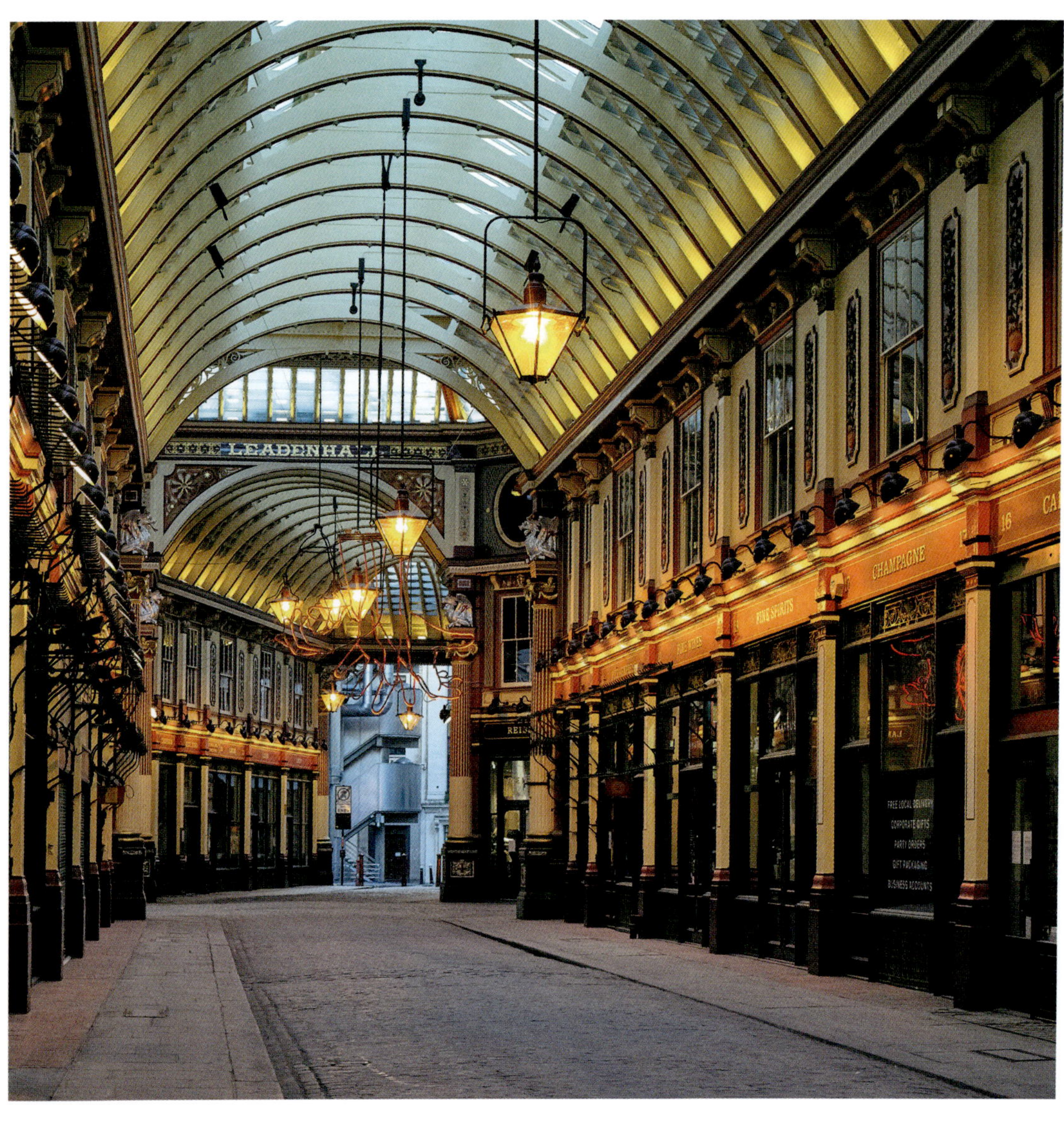

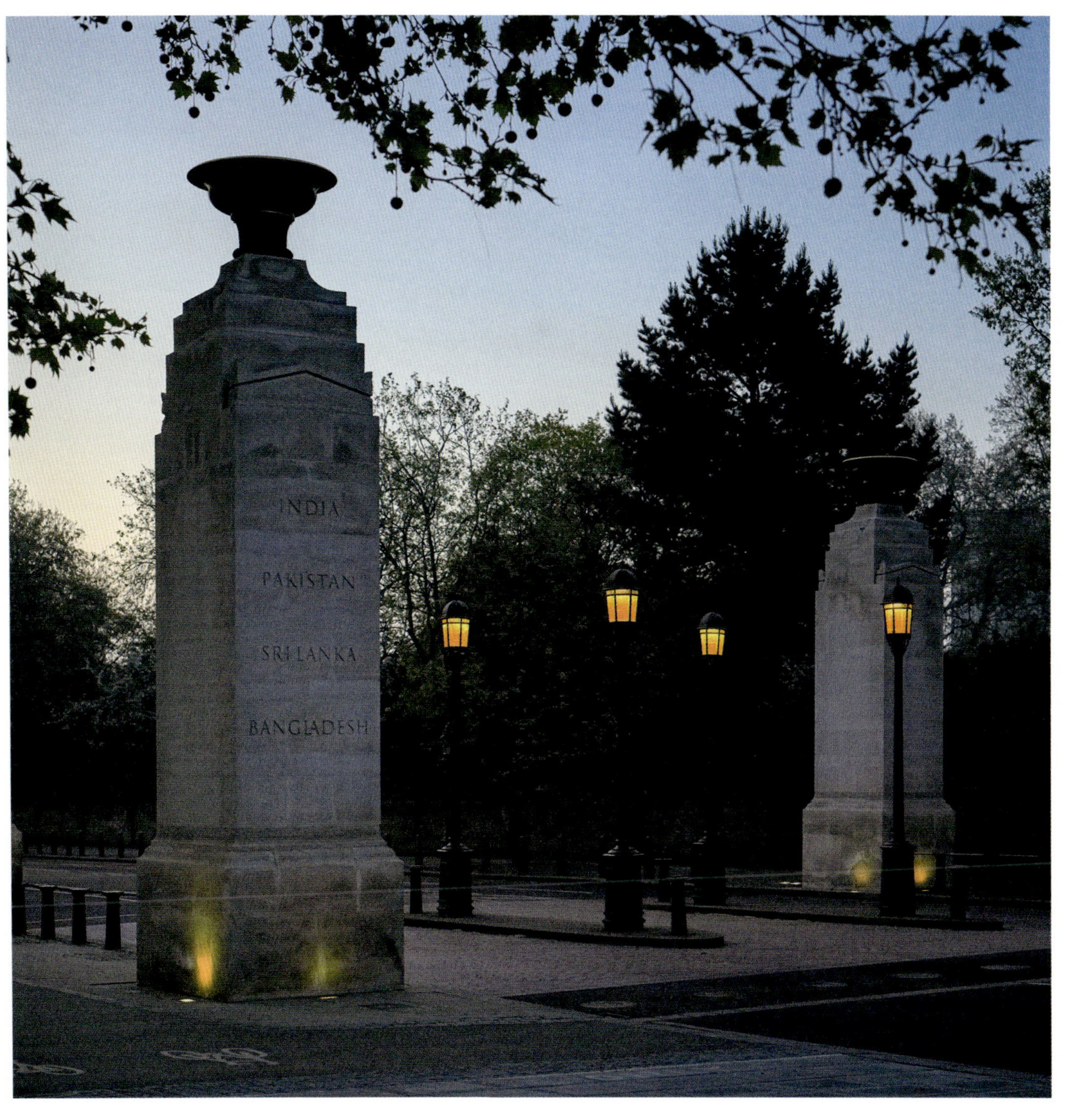


INDIA

PAKISTAN

SRI LANKA

BANGLADESH

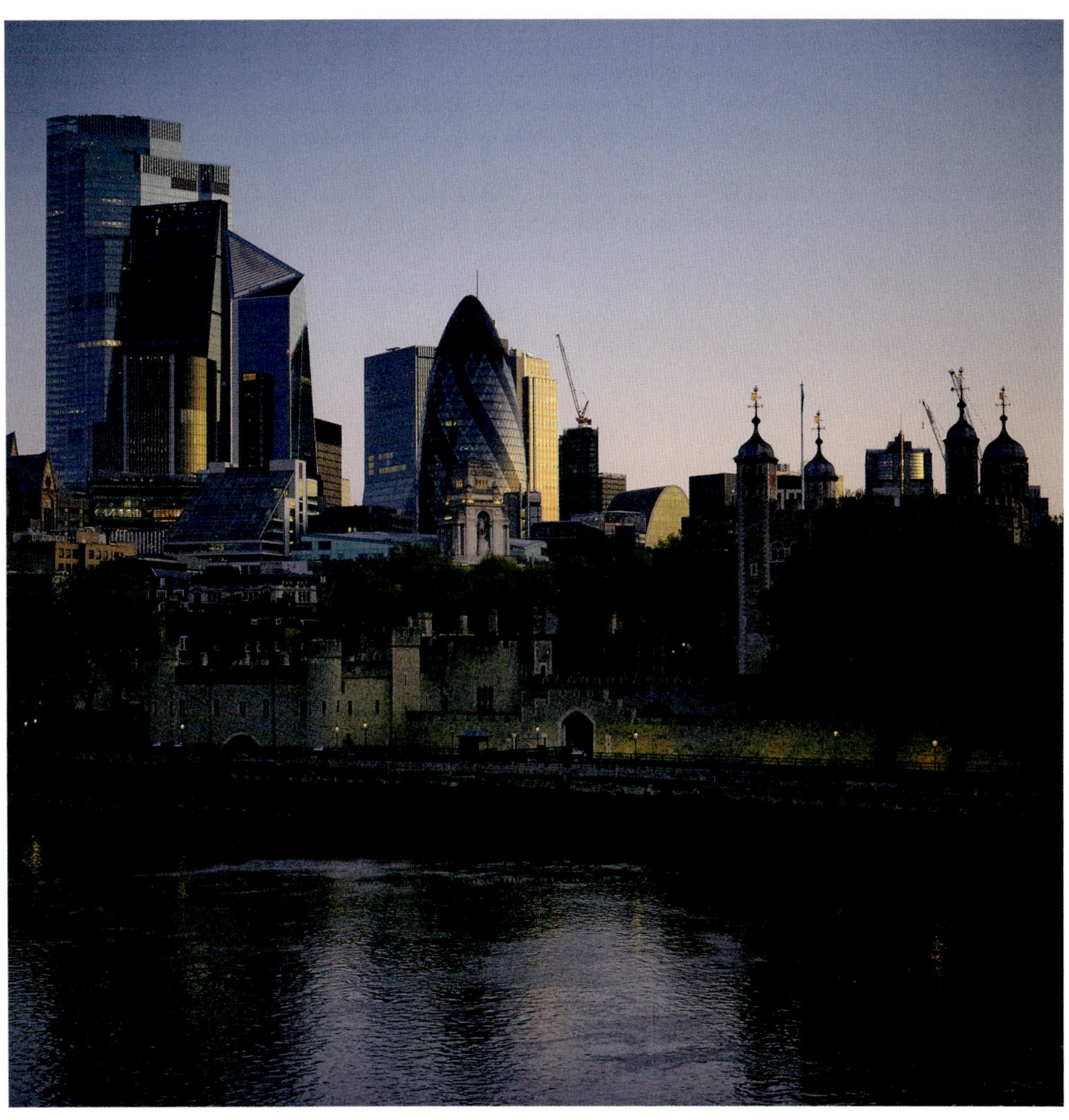

# Andy Sewell
## *Food Banks*

Angered by a year of governmental failure in managing the pandemic, Andy Sewell began a series of photographs in response to the long queues outside his local food bank. He turned his camera away from the lines of people – not wanting to photograph those in a situation perhaps already loaded with stress and shame – and focused it instead on the interiors of the (often religious) spaces providing help and support to a community let down by the system. Overwhelmed by the scale of need in the midst of the pandemic, Sewell remembers the disheartening experience of entering a food bank in Bethnal Green: 'St Matthew's is this cavernous Georgian church that has been rebuilt after being bombed in the war and there were all these bags in the pews lined up like a congregation. It was quite devastating to see, walking into that quiet space and knowing that each of those bags represented a family.'

Sewell brought his photographs together in triptychs. Not quite seamlessly sewn together, they reference both the traditional design of a church altarpiece and the disjointedness of the pandemic – a crisis of such magnitude that it cannot be fully contained within the frame. Society's increasing reliance on food banks, Sewell points out, was worsened by the pandemic but caused by a decade of austerity politics. He hopes that 'people who look at these pictures feel a sense of anger at the scale and shame of our politics that makes this kind of thing necessary in the fifth wealthiest nation in the world.' At the same time, 'there is also something beautiful in these spaces and the acts of people wanting to try to make things a bit better for those who are having a tough time.'

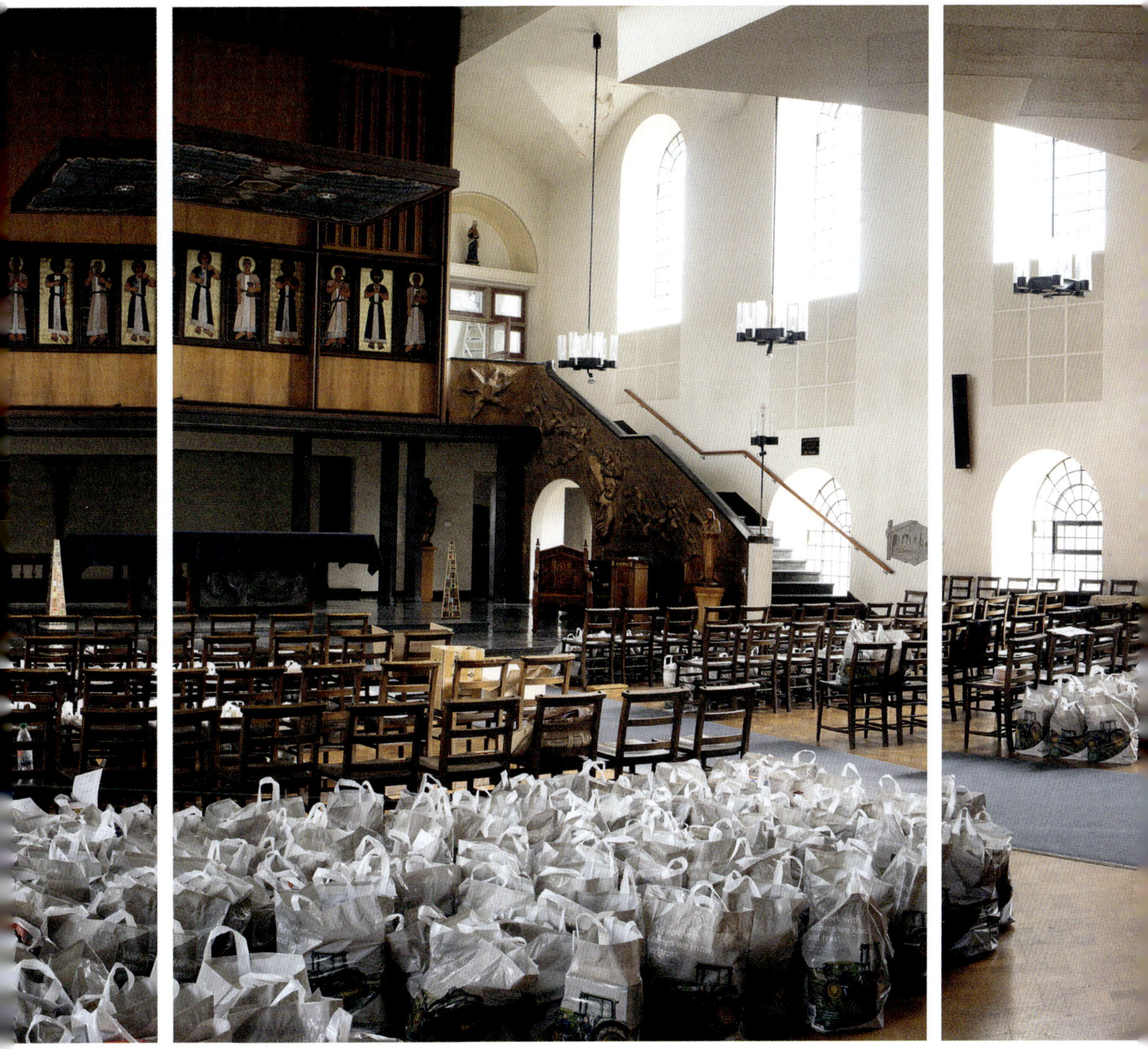

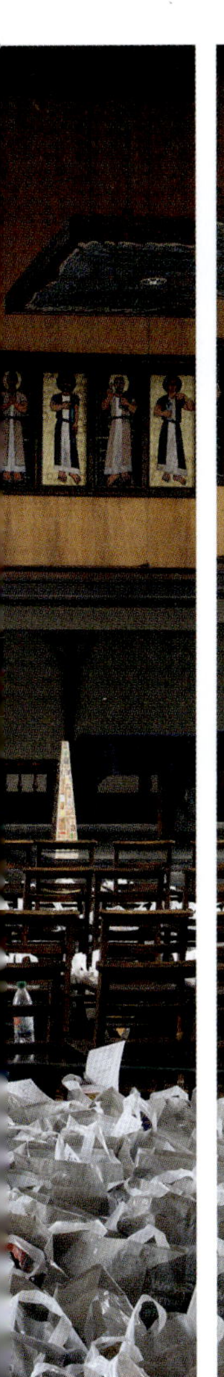
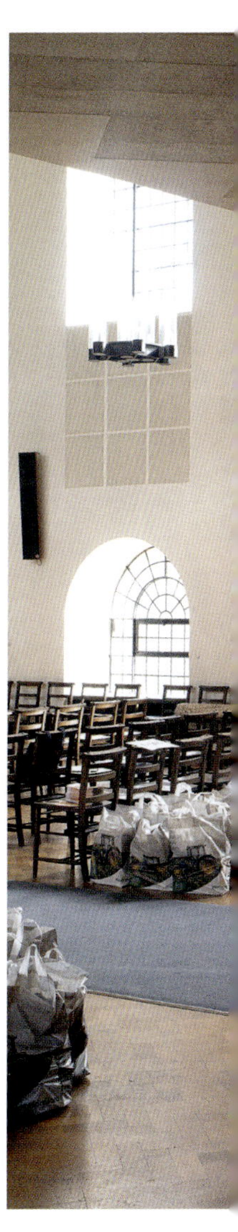

*St Matthew's Church, Bethnal Green, February 2021*

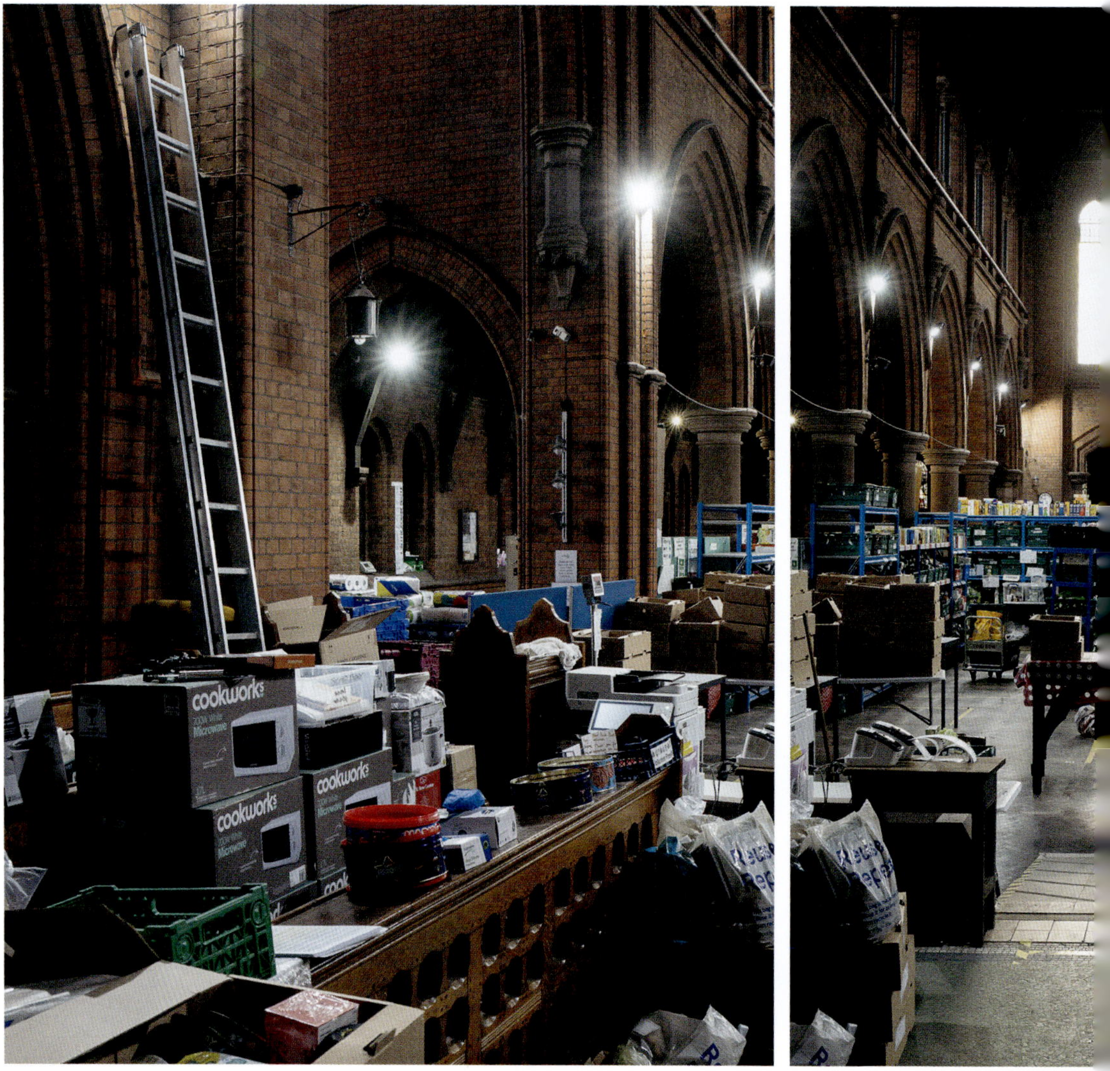

Andy Sewell

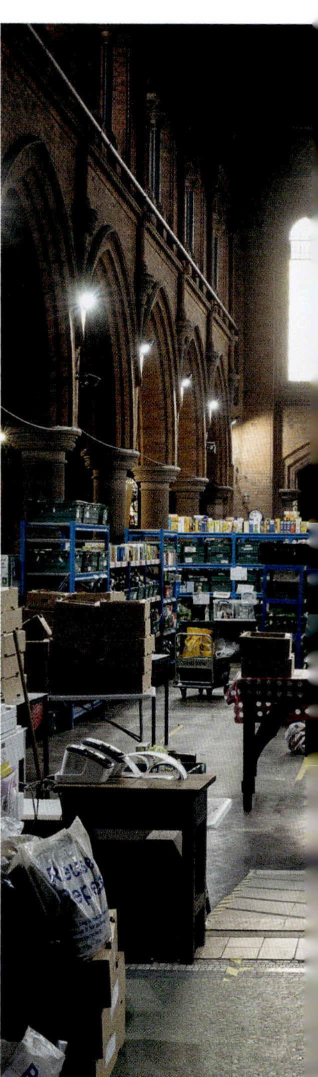

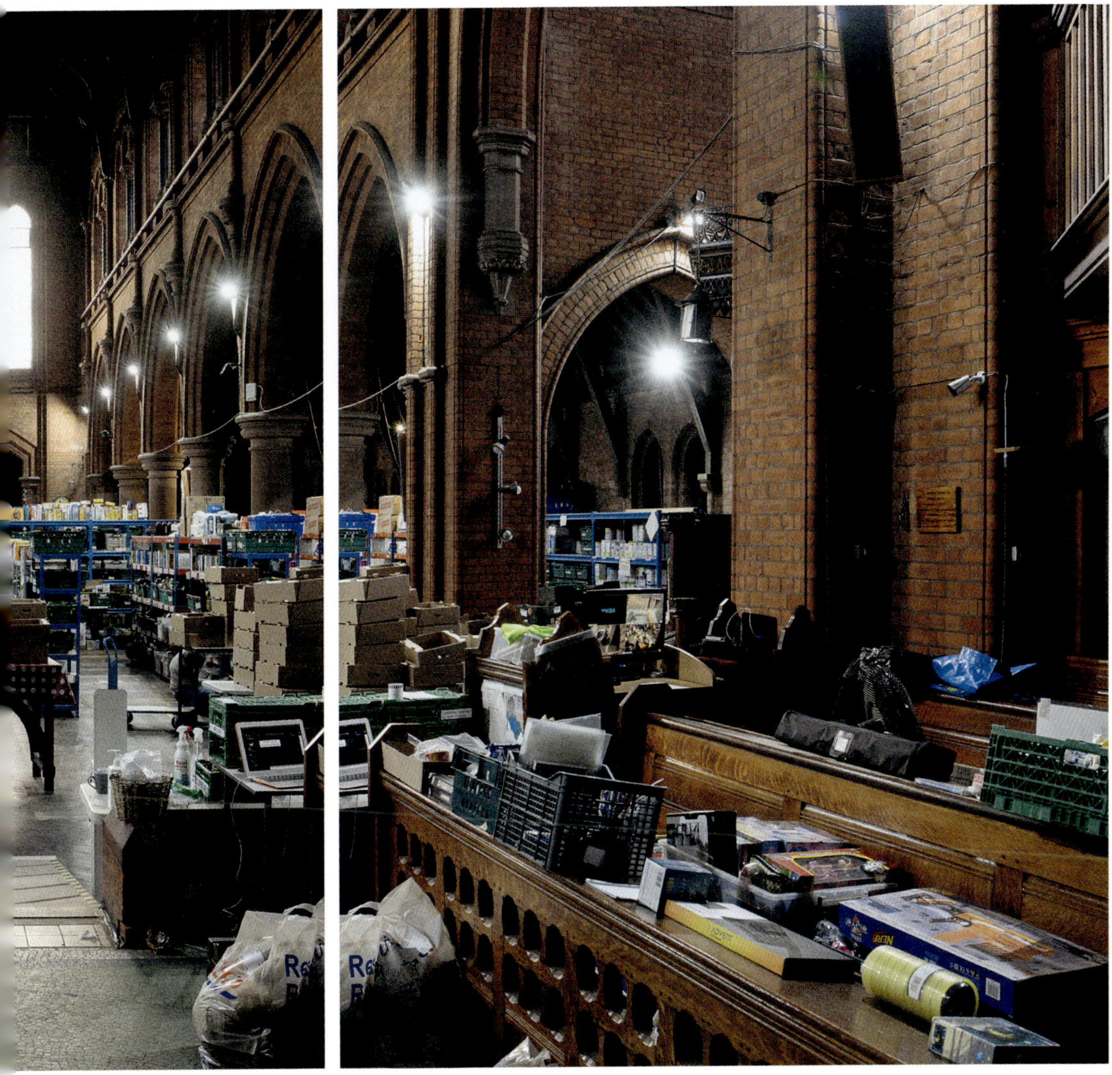

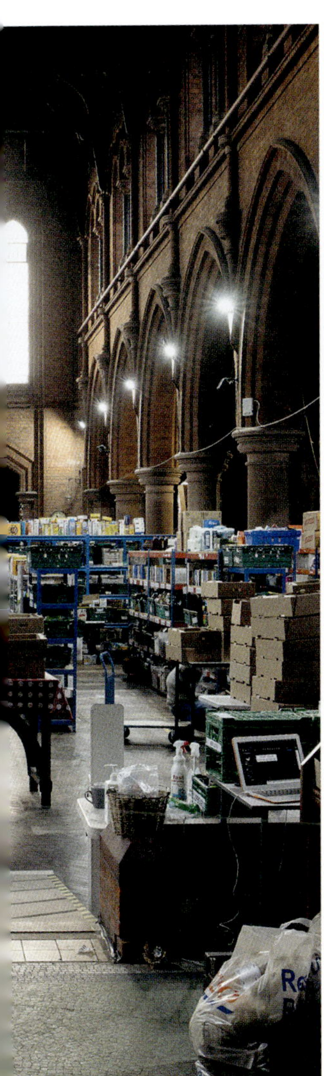

*St Margaret the Queen Church, Streatham, February 2021*

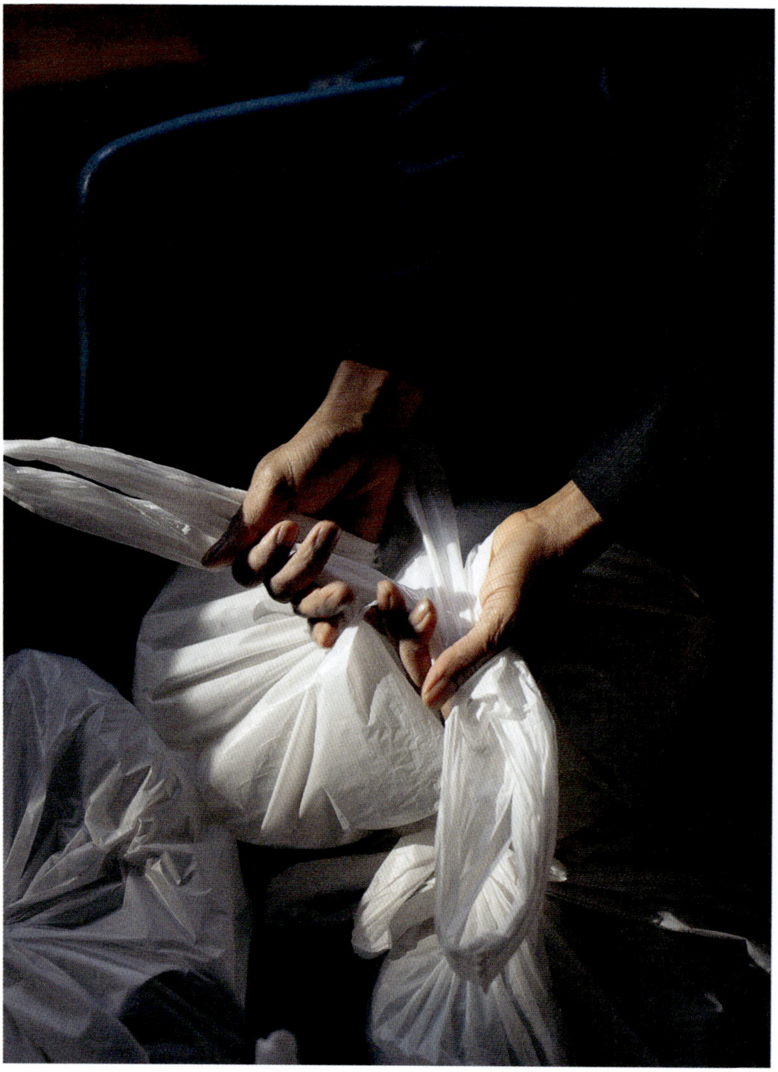

Andy Sewell

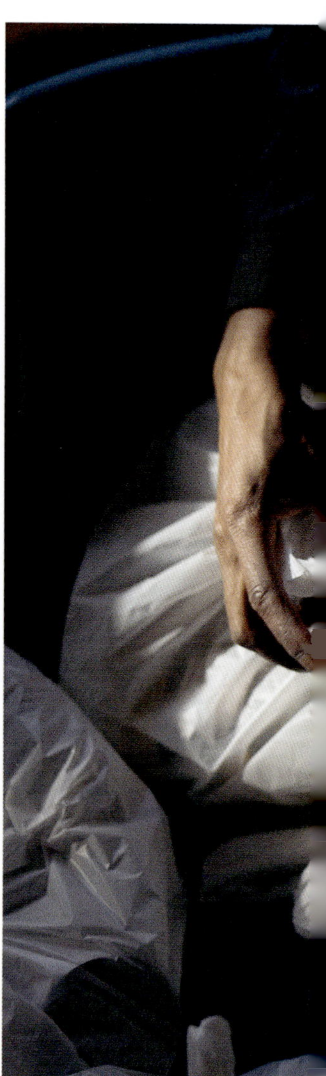

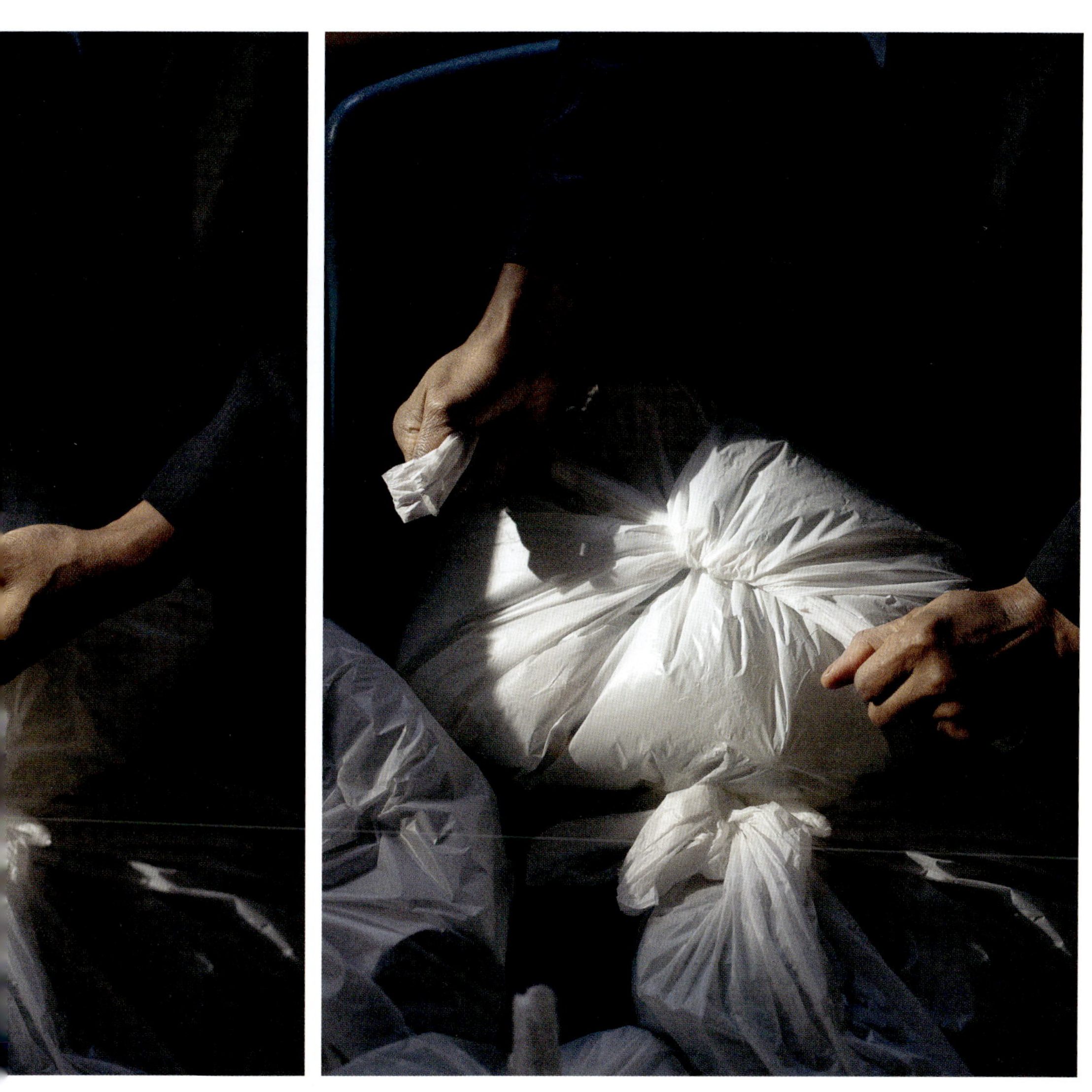

*Christ Apostolic Church, Hackney, February 2021*

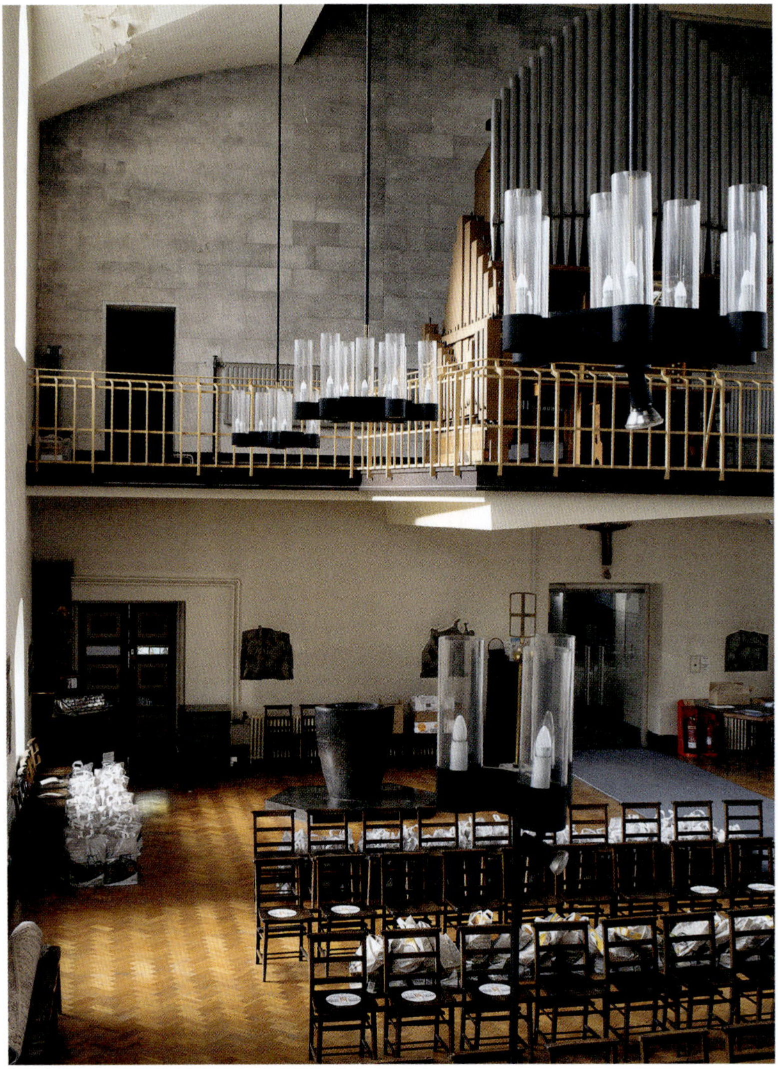

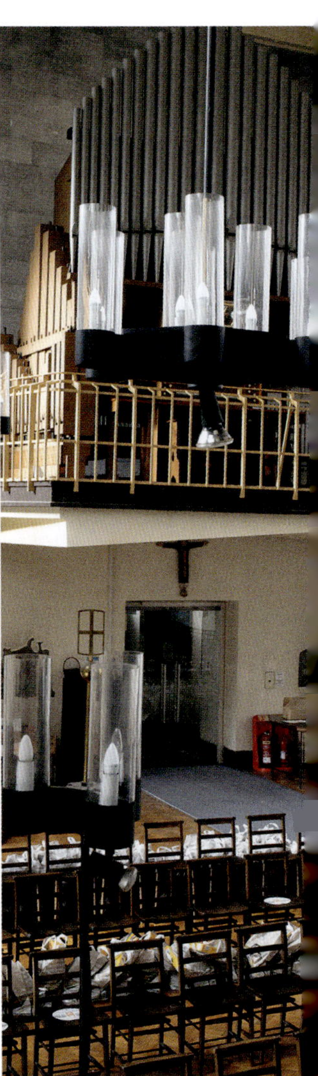

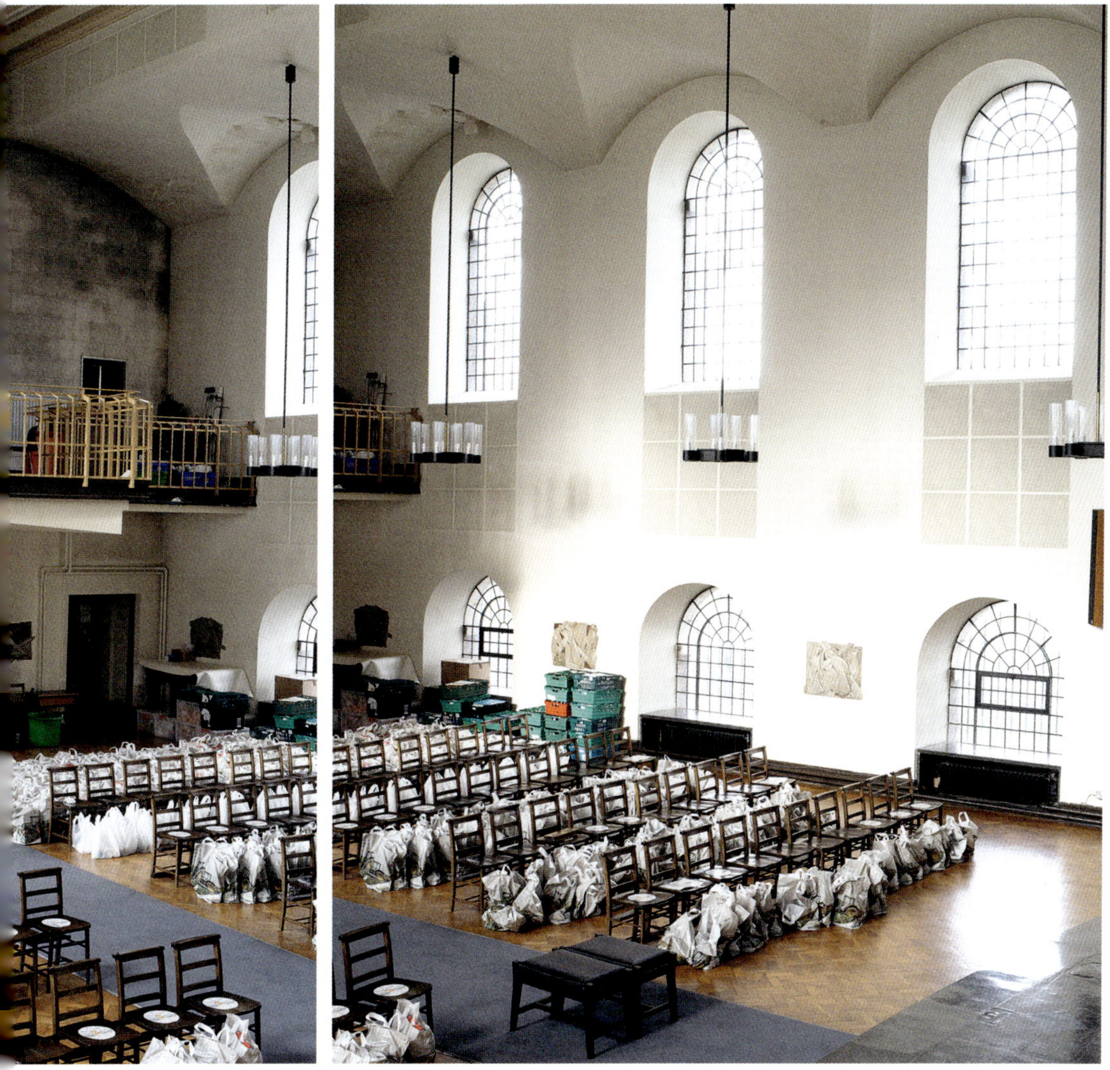

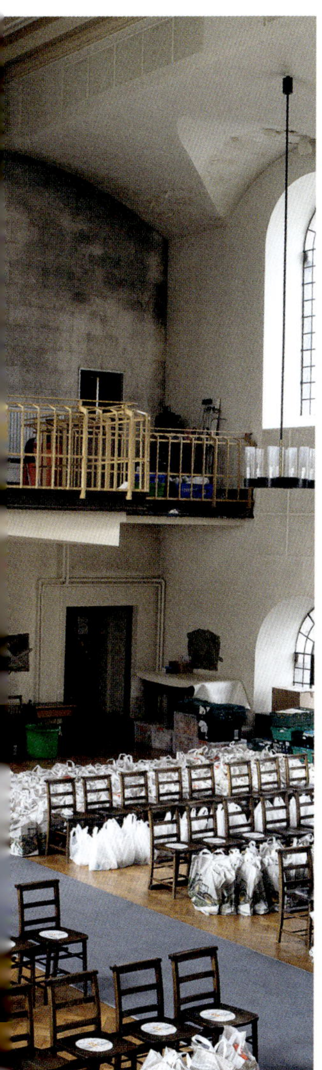

*St Matthew's Church, Bethnal Green, February 2021*

# Joanna Vestey
## *Custodians for Covid*

When social distancing measures forced museums, concert venues, cinemas and theatres to close their doors or limit access, the consequences for box office sales, revenues and jobs were catastrophic. In the UK, as many as 70 percent of workers in the cultural sector were furloughed under the government's job retention scheme, followed by mass redundancies that hit those on zero-hour contracts and in front-of-house roles hardest. Joanna Vestey embarked on her *Custodians for Covid* series in June 2020 as a fundraising initiative for the performing arts, selling prints of her imposing architectural photographs and donating the money to the iconic London theatres and performance spaces depicted.

Drawn in by the splendour of the majestic structures in Vestey's images – their intricate ornamental details and lush materials – it is easy to overlook the solitary custodians who quietly occupy them. Usually unobserved in their work behind the scenes, guardians, managers and keyholders continued to be tasked with the care and stewardship of empty venues throughout the lockdowns. Here, their lone forms among a sea of unoccupied seats make us confront the absence of hundreds of bodies usually present. 'The custodians I encountered were a real reflection of the breadth of people involved in theatre,' says Vestey, 'from a security guard to a director going in every day to flush the loos to someone who had been opening the theatre every night for the past 25 years – they were all totally unsure of what was going to happen next.' Given the financial hardship and uncertainty many performing arts spaces will face in a post-pandemic world, it is yet to be seen if all of them will be restored back to life.

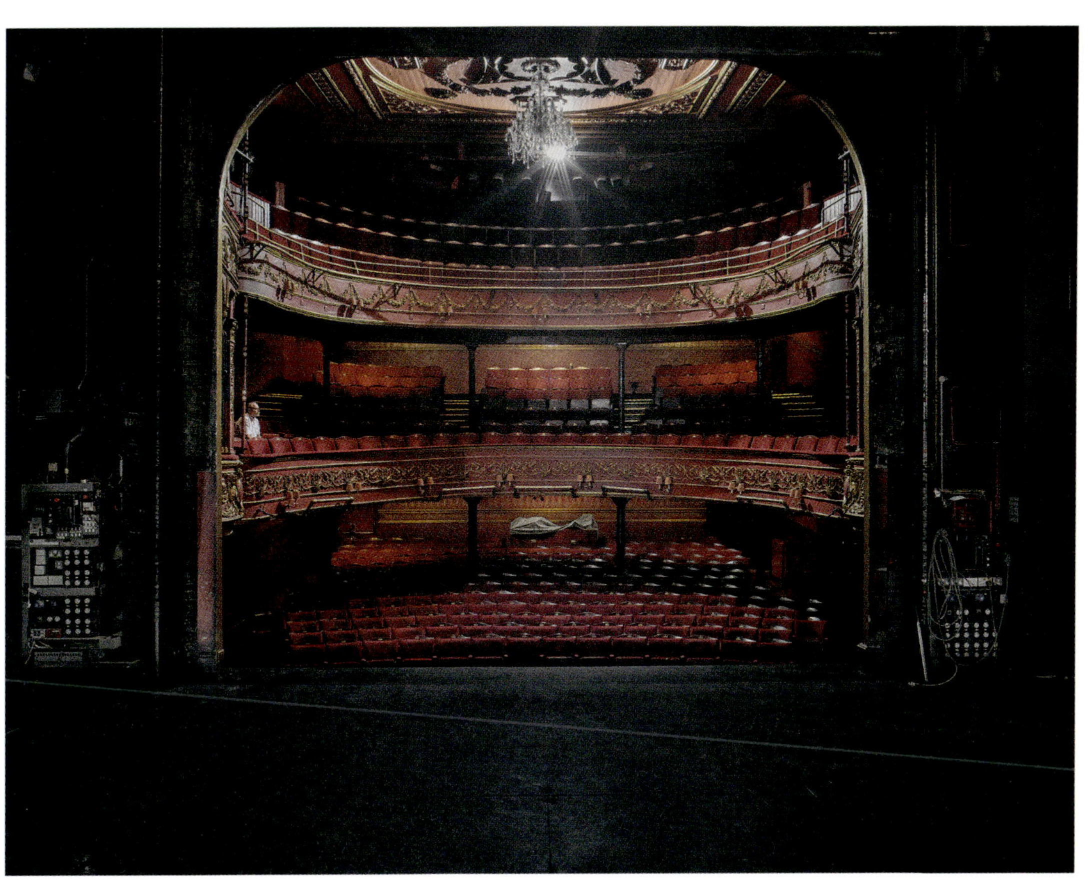

*Graeme Bright, Building and Facilities Manager,*
*Theatre Royal Stratford East, June 2020*

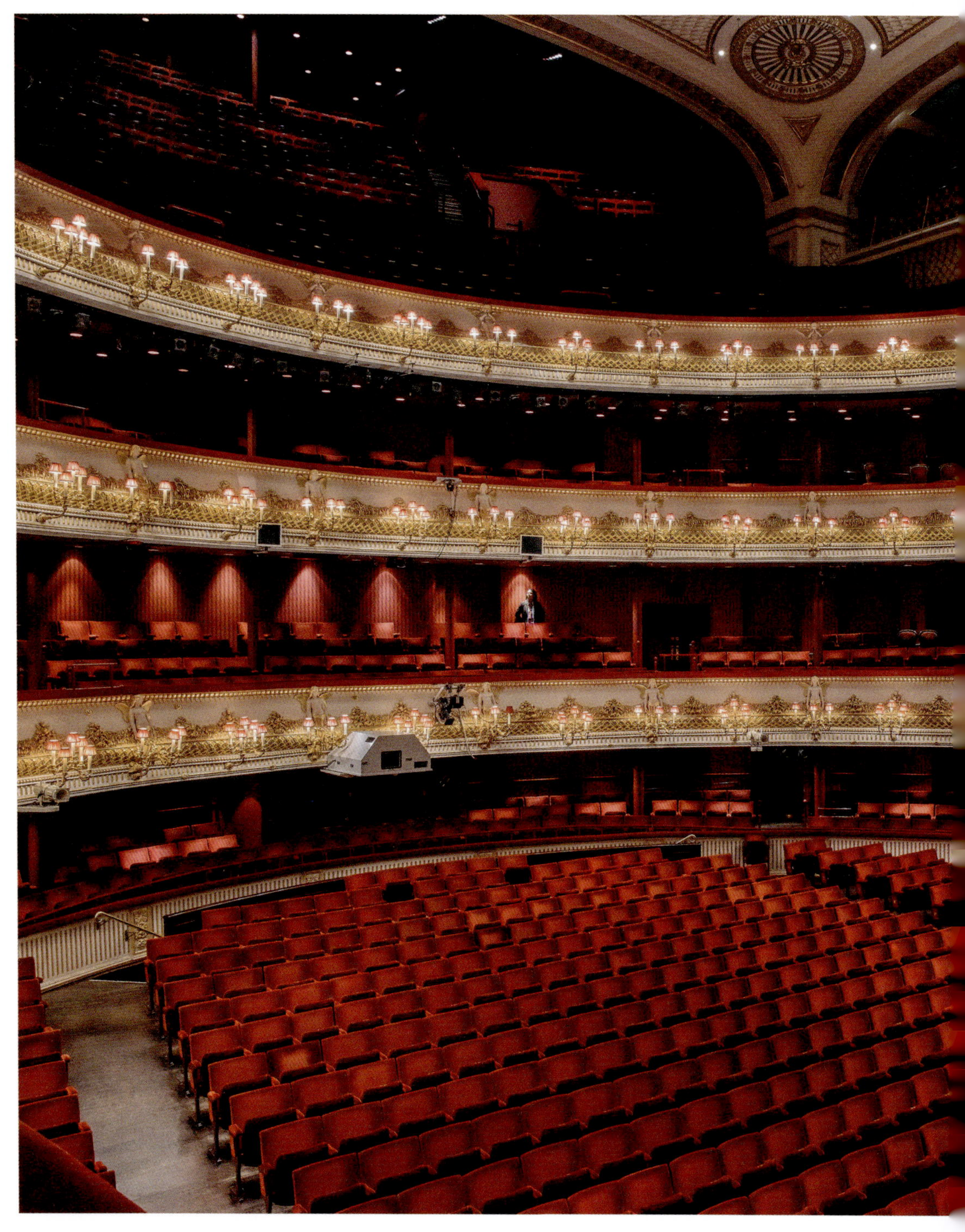

*Amina L'Bini, Security Supervisor, Royal Opera House, June 2020*

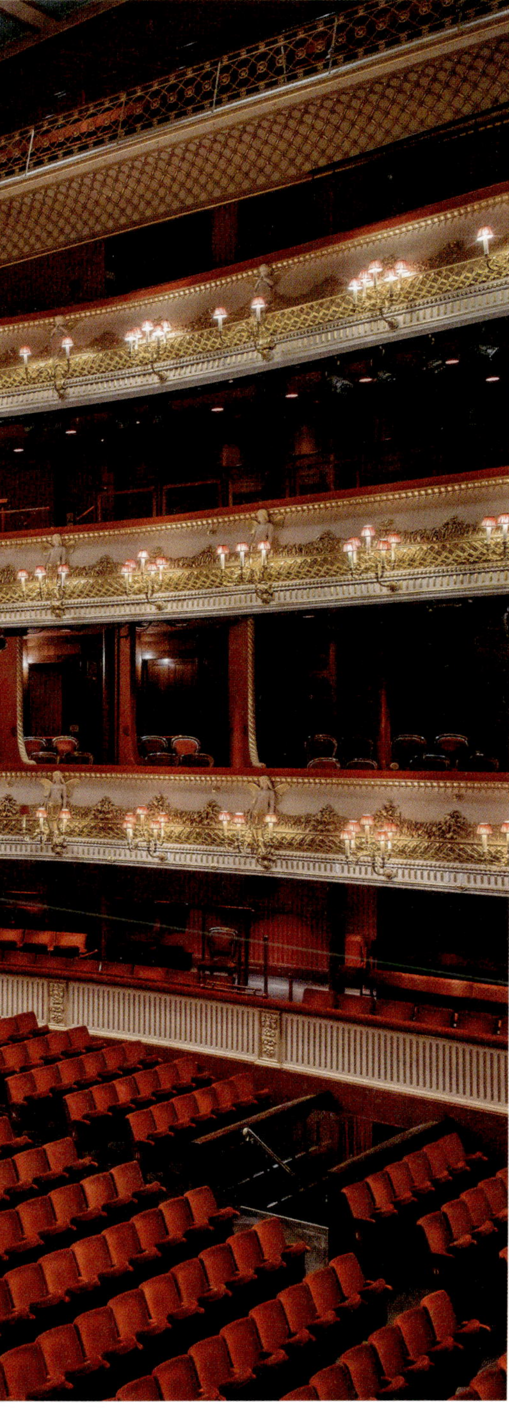

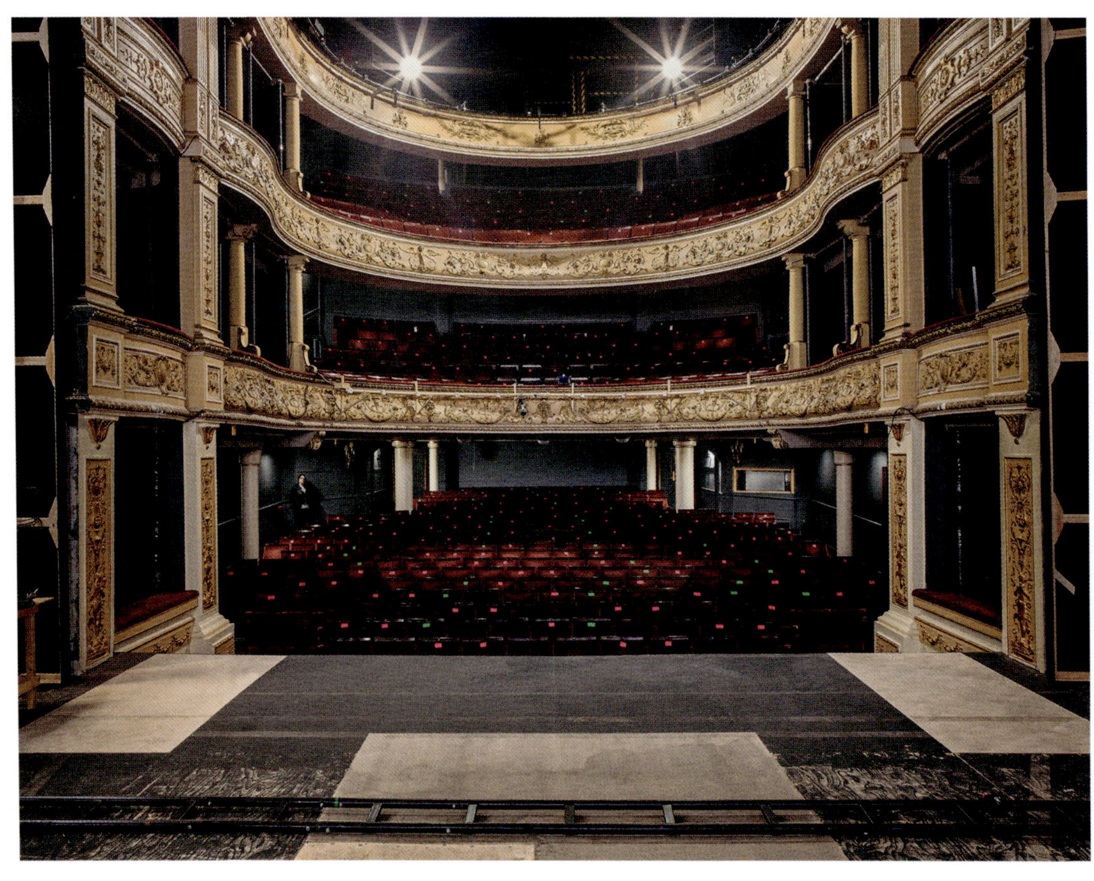

*Grace Christie, General Manager,*
*The Duke of York's Theatre, December 2020*

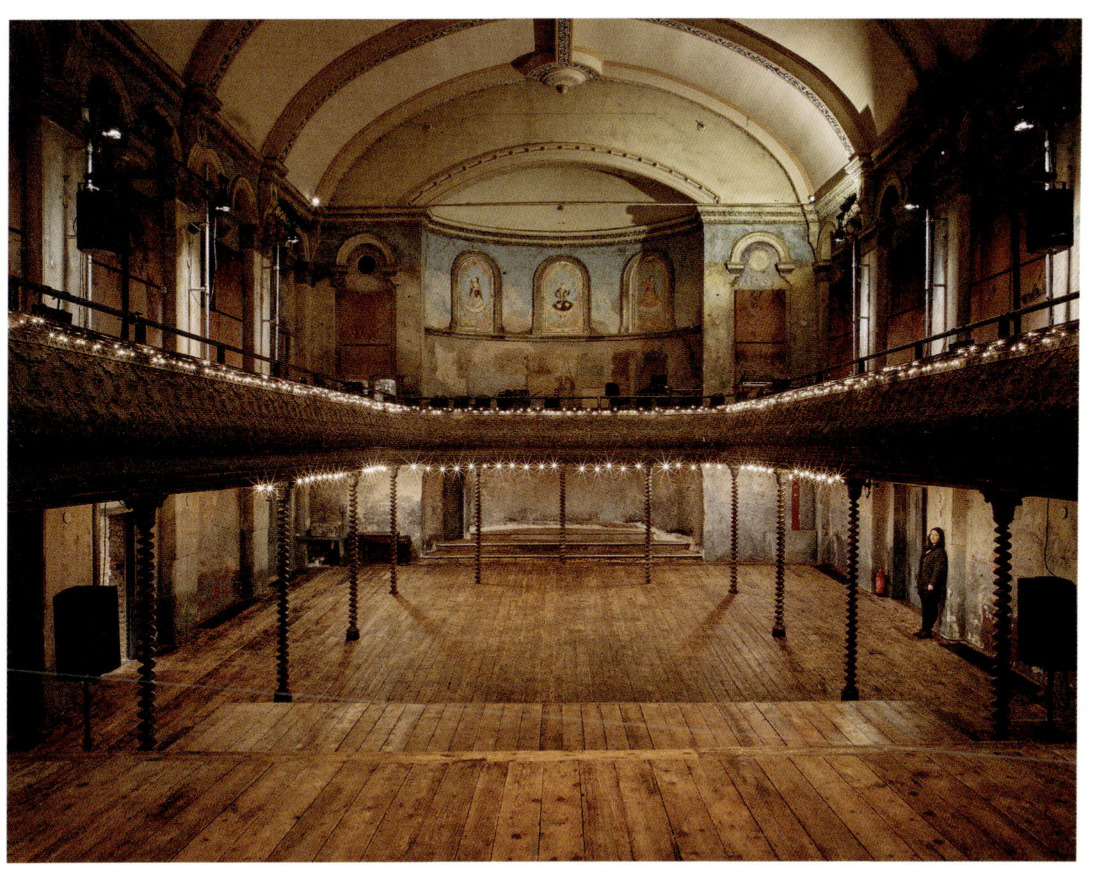

*Kate Mullan, Head of Commercial Services and Operations,*
*Wilton's Music Hall, December 2020*

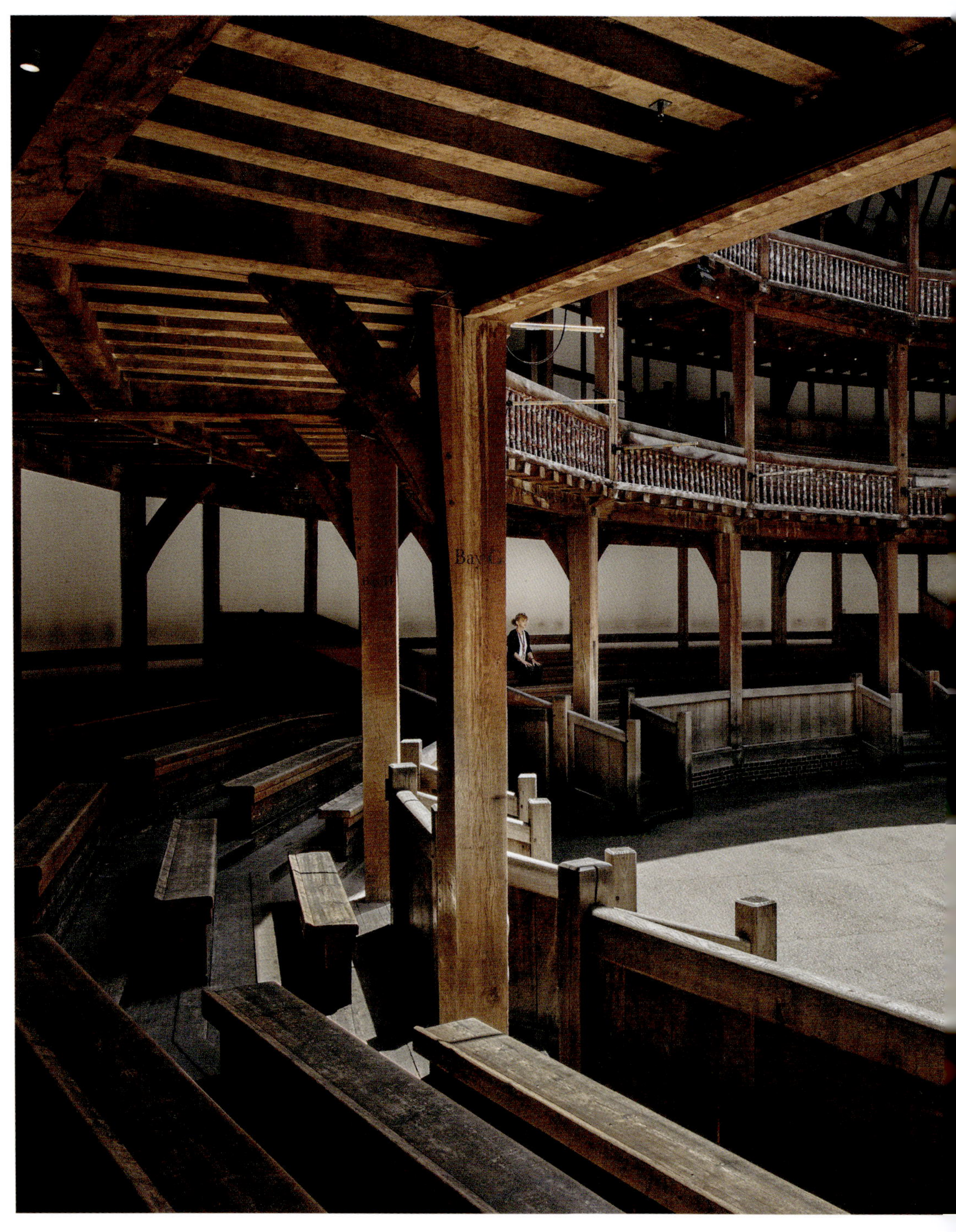

*Deborah McGhee, Head of Building Operations, Shakespeare's Globe, June 2020*

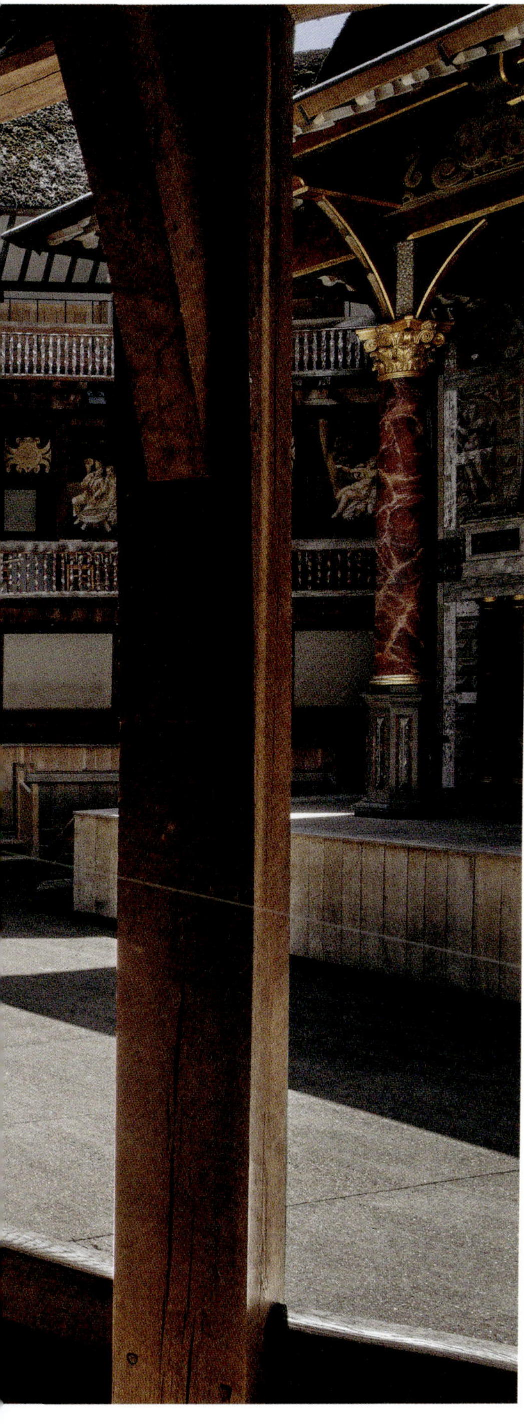

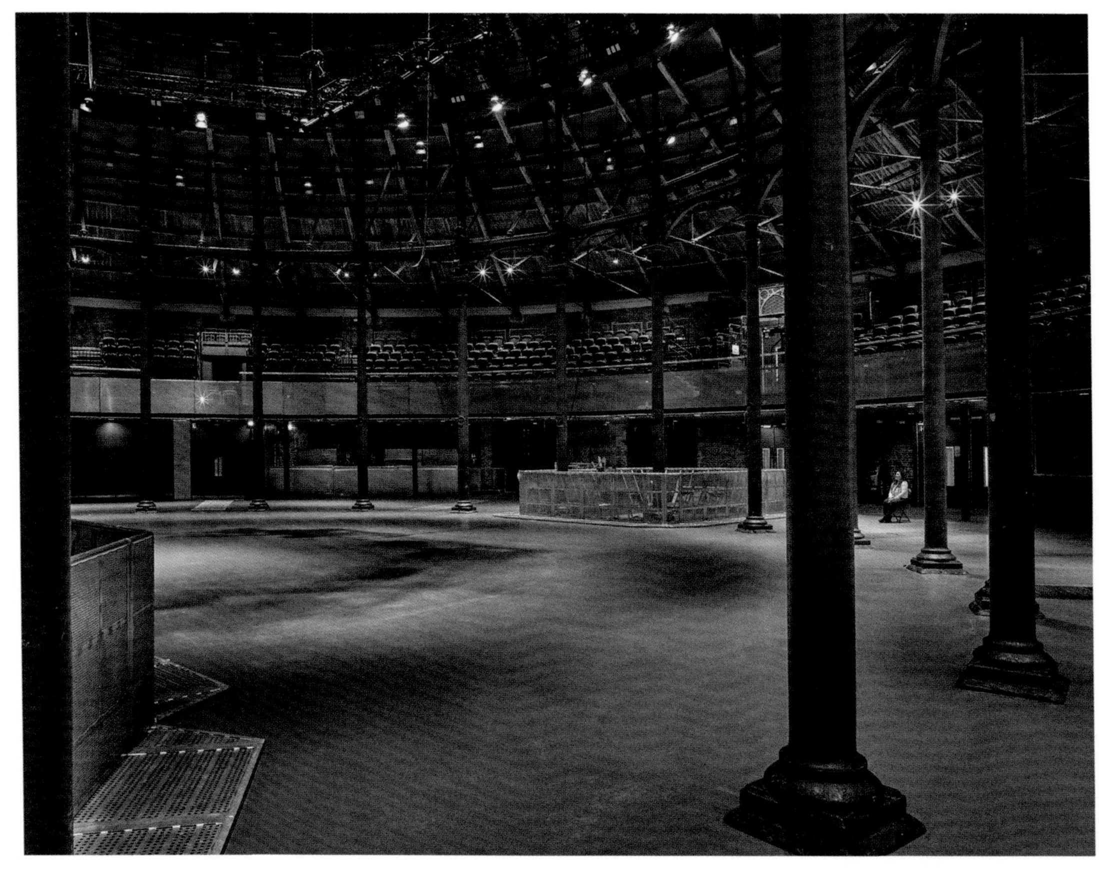

*Denise Stracey, member of Showsec Security team,*
*Roundhouse, June 2020*

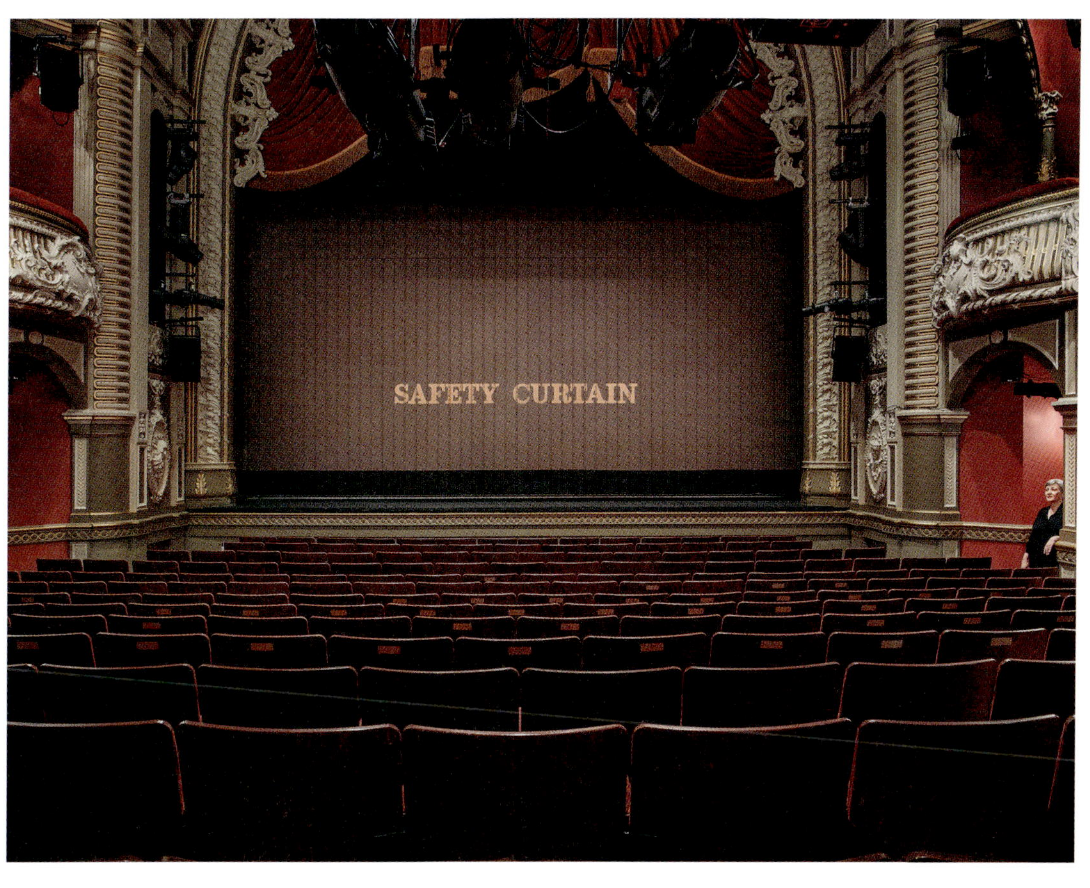


*Sian Alexander, Executive Director,*
*Lyric Hammersmith Theatre, June 2020*

# Jemima Yong
## *Field*

On 30 March 2020, soon after the first nationwide lockdown was announced, performance maker and photographer Jemima Yong responded to a creative prompt from a friend by capturing an image of the small patch of green outside her south east London flat. That first photograph marked the start of a four-month-long observation of this inconspicuous corner of shared space from the vantage point of her seventh-floor window, at a time when exercise and outdoor activities were strictly limited.

'I began to photograph the activity on the field in black and white to abstract the images, drawing attention first to textures, lines, shapes, gestures, and then to the space and its meaning,' writes Yong. 'As I made more photographs, a visual pattern began to emerge of people alone together, energetic and active because of – or in spite of – their solitude. I am drawn to the ways in which photography can capture the intangible: relationships, atmosphere, the essence of things. I seek out the spaces in between people that evoke a sense of story.' With her razor-sharp bird's-eye view, Yong conveys an overpowering sense of solitude and distance in these stark images; her own isolated self perpetually removed from the figures adrift on the field below in what feels like a moment out of time.

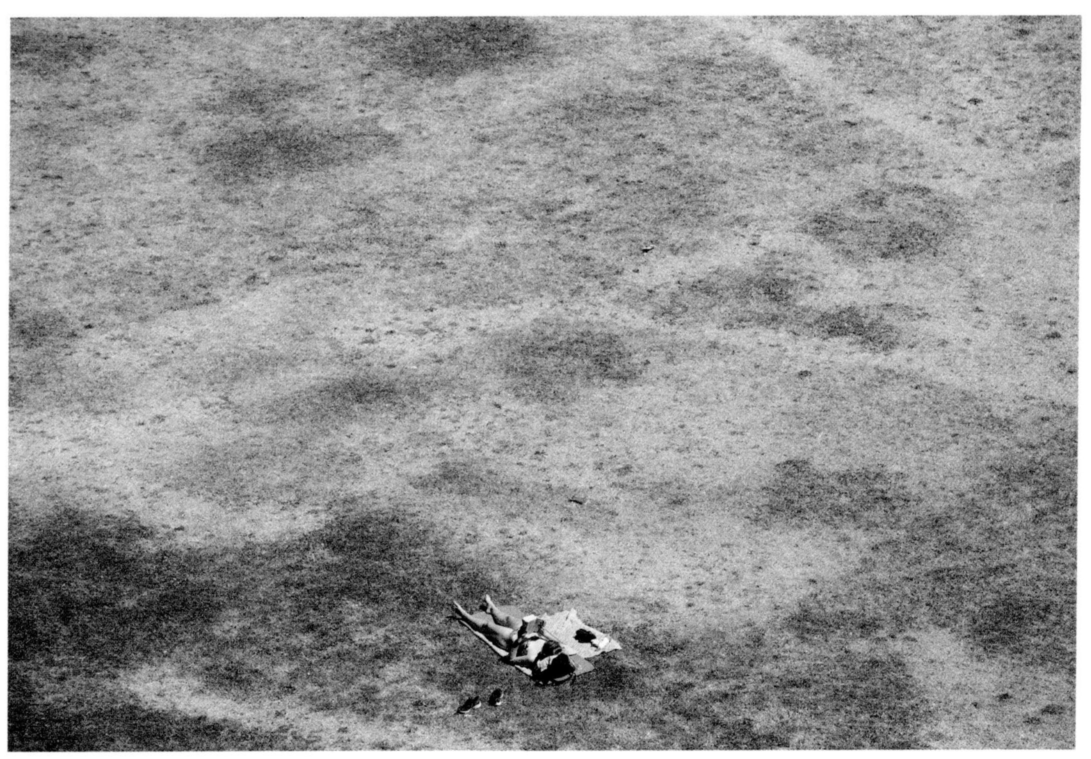

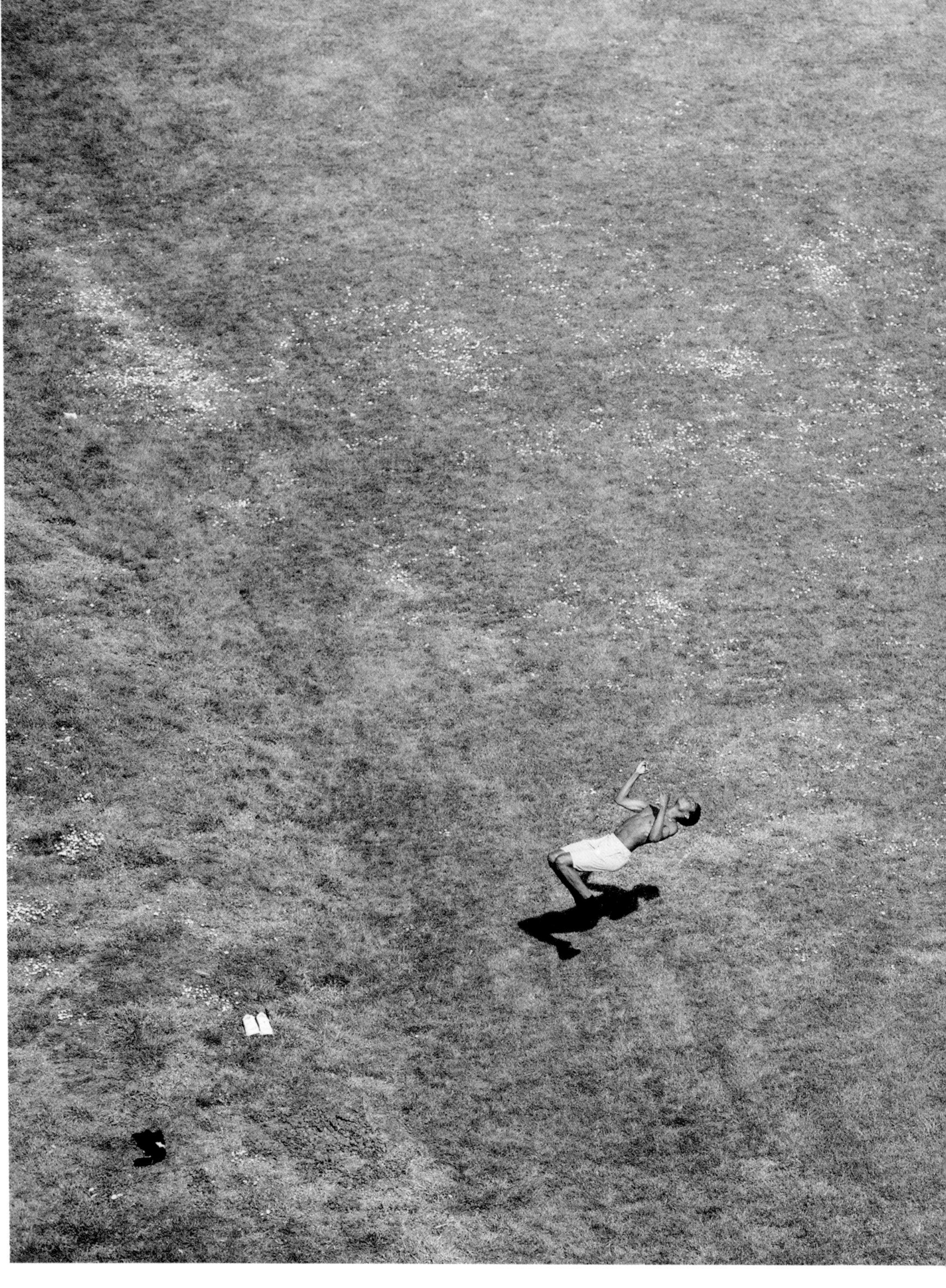

Jemima Yong

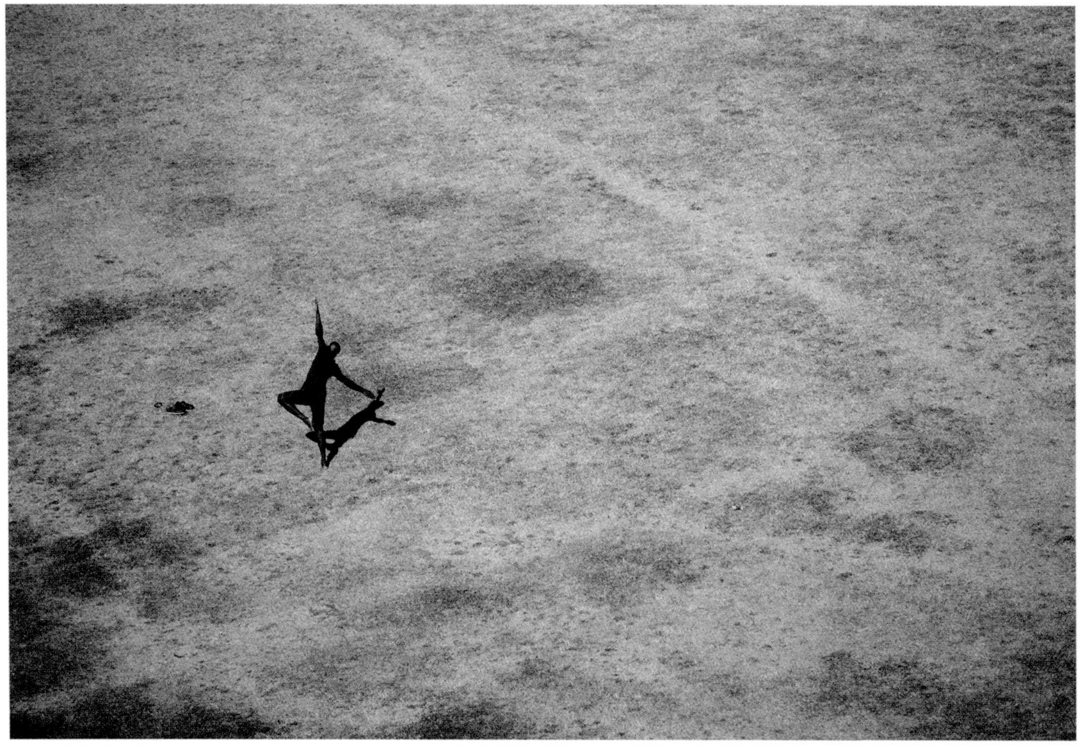

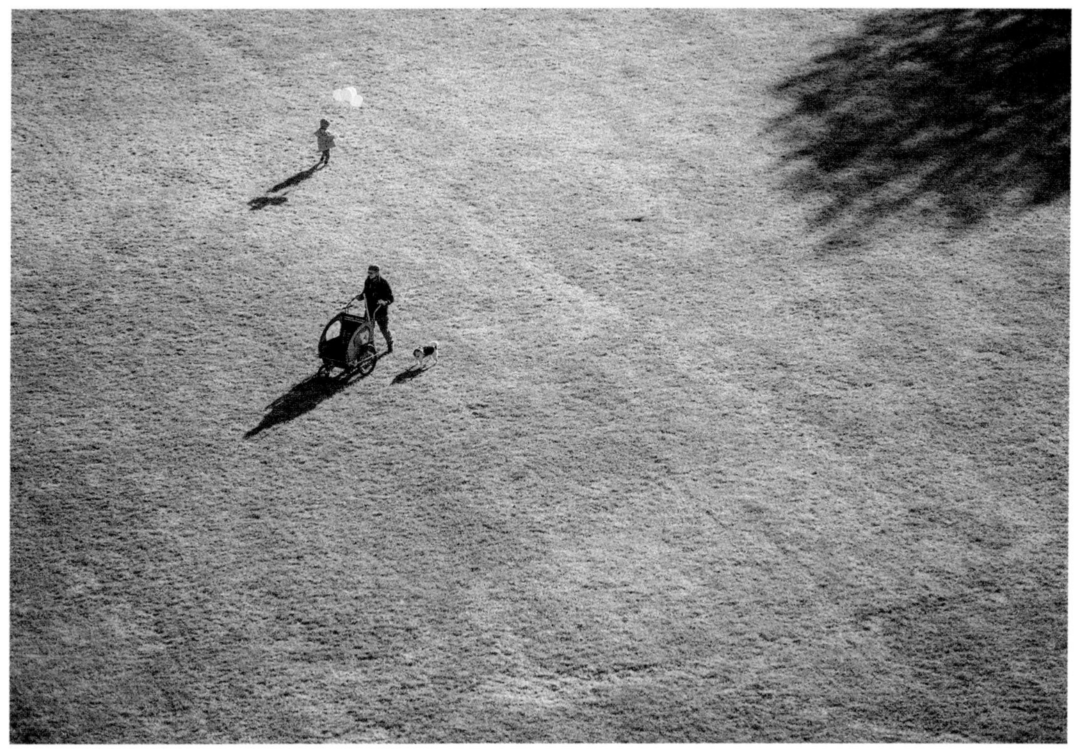

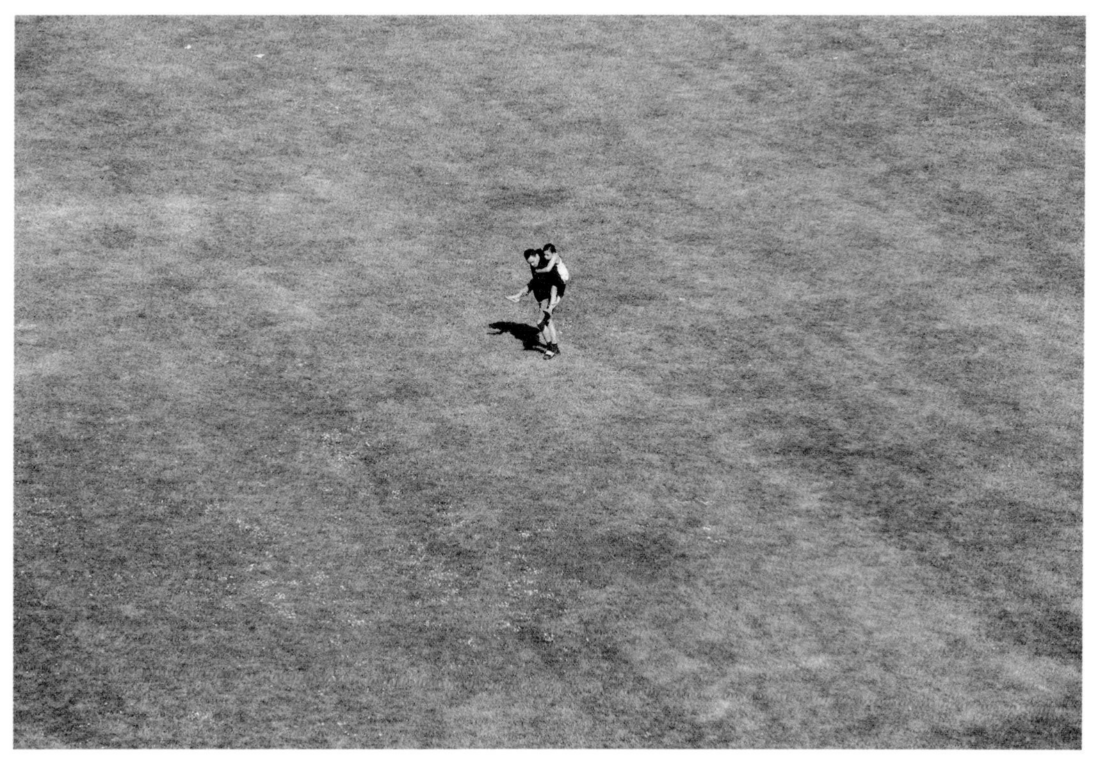

# Hannah Starkey
## *Empty City*

For Hannah Starkey, the first coronavirus lockdown came at the tail-end of her residency with the Guildhall Art Gallery in the City of London, where she was photographing women who work in the (still) male-dominated space of the Square Mile. Starkey's practice has long revolved around the question of what it means to be represented as a woman in today's world; when lockdown happened, she focused her particular gaze onto the urban fabric of the suddenly empty City. On its abandoned streets she encountered only key workers, security guards, people who were homeless and a score of (mostly male) photographers in search of good camera angles. Wandering among this cast of characters in the deserted cityscape of one of the most highly surveilled areas of London, Starkey happily embodied the figure of a modern-day *flâneuse*, on the look-out for impressions that scratched at the surface of everyday urban reality.

In her record of the project, Starkey wrote: 'I'm now starved of human interaction. I realise I photograph the way I do because it's not buildings but people that make up my landscapes. My City of just a few weeks ago is simply no longer here. Though the place has not fallen silent: the buildings still whirr with computers, busy with phantom operators who have no need for the City's pavements. I surprise myself with how sad the abandonment makes me feel.' In her take on the City, Starkey's sense of estrangement and illusion is translated into a series of carefully constructed window reflections, mirages and spectral visions that flirt with ideas of absence and presence, visibility and invisibility.

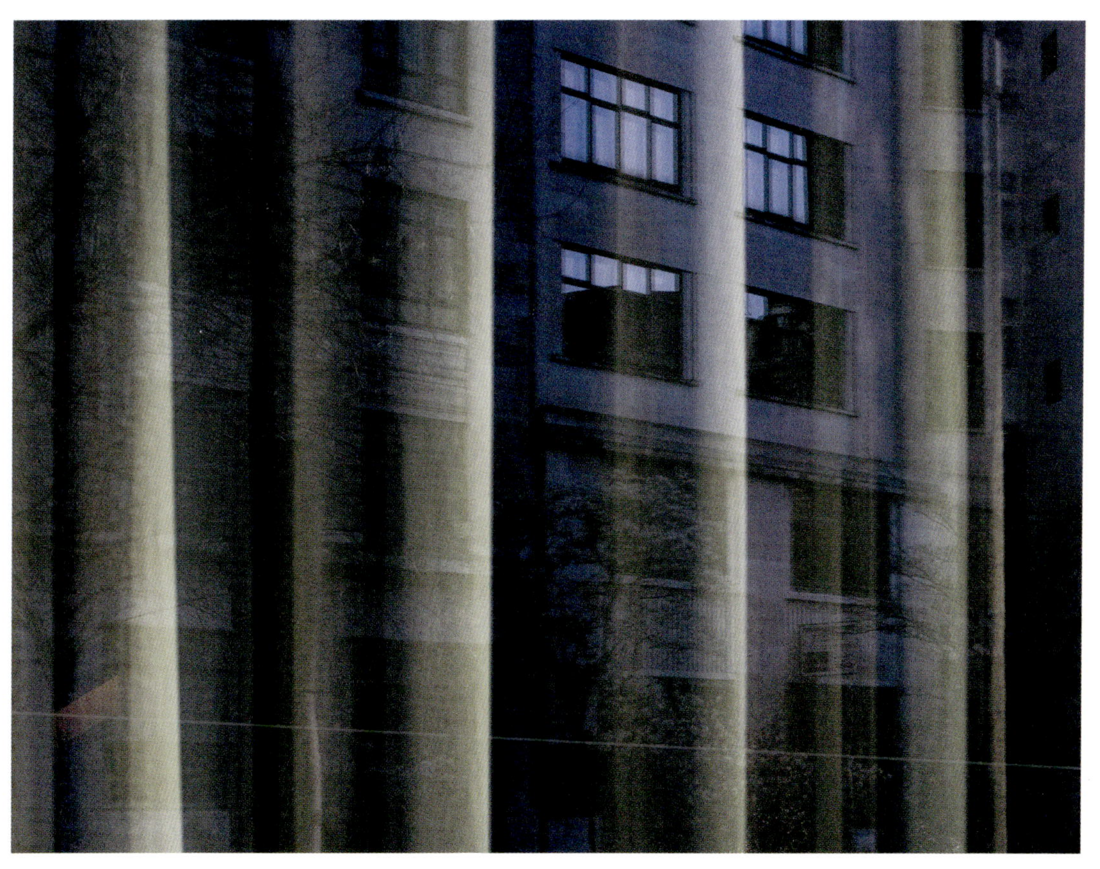

*Fenchurch Avenue*

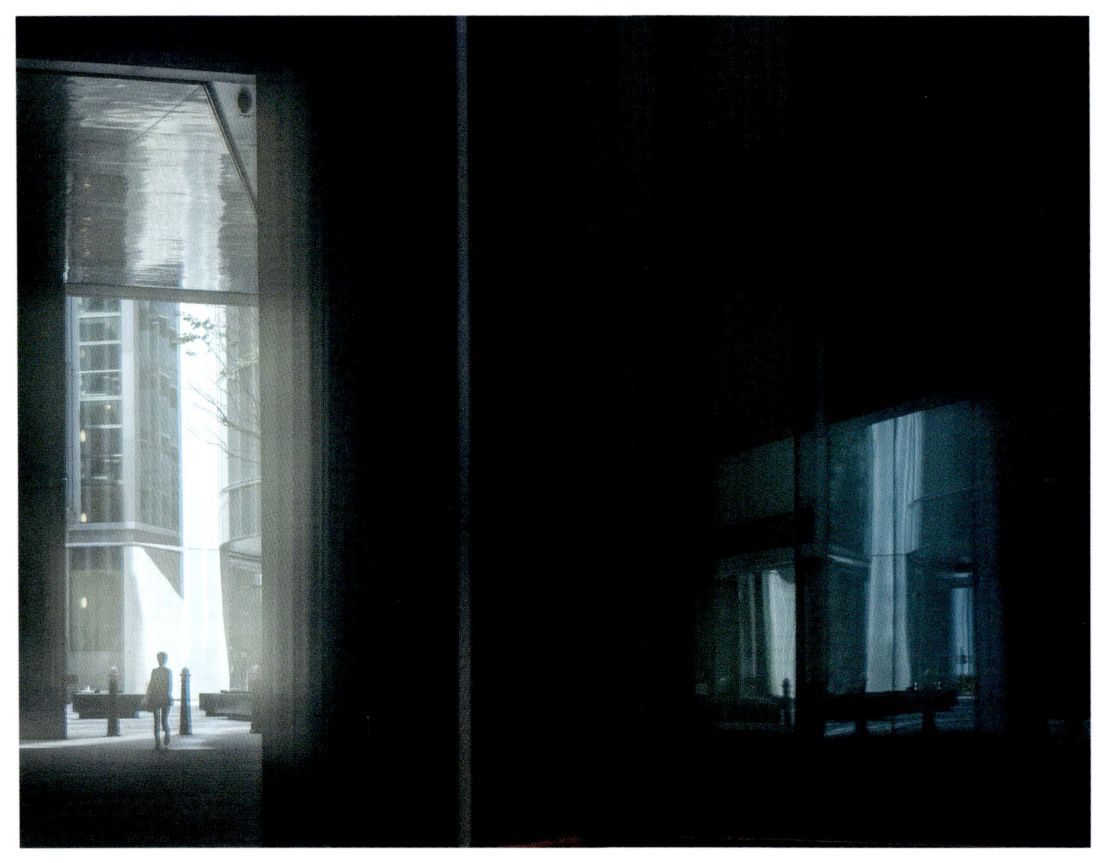

*Fenchurch Street*

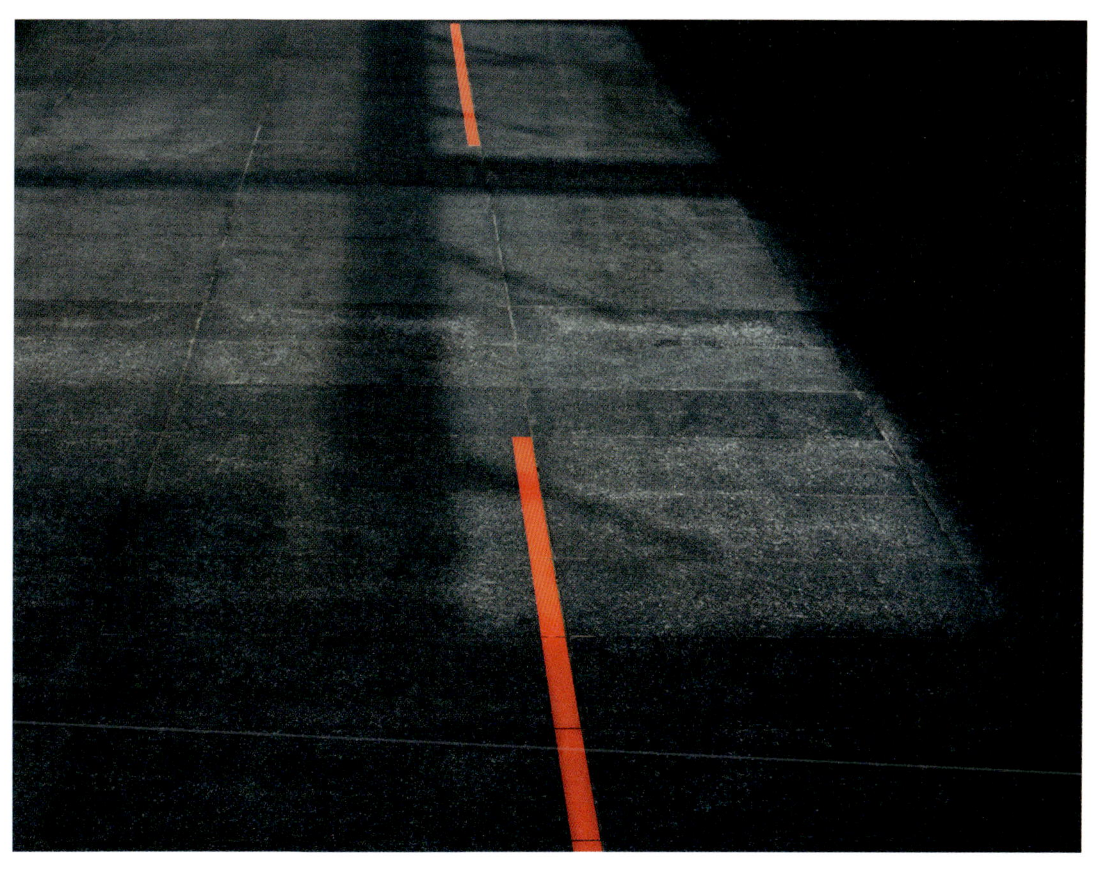

*Spitalfields Market*

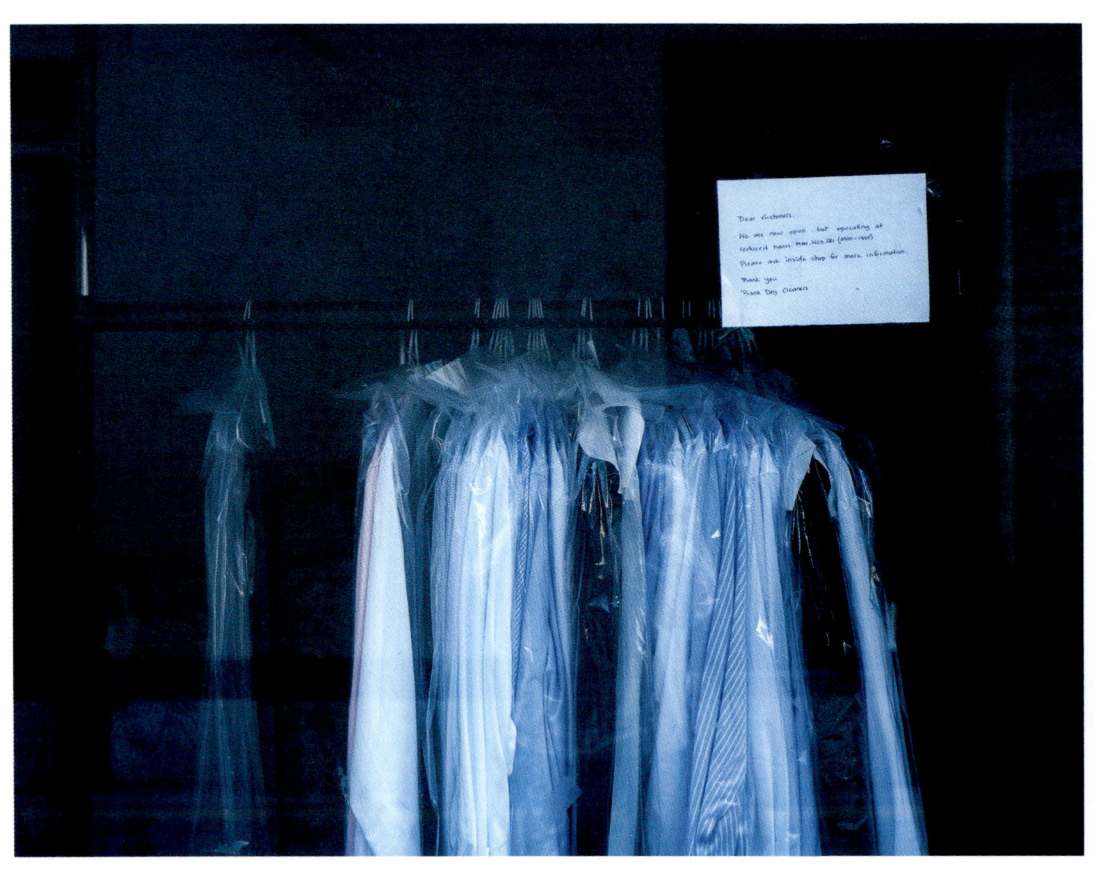


*Throgmorton Street*

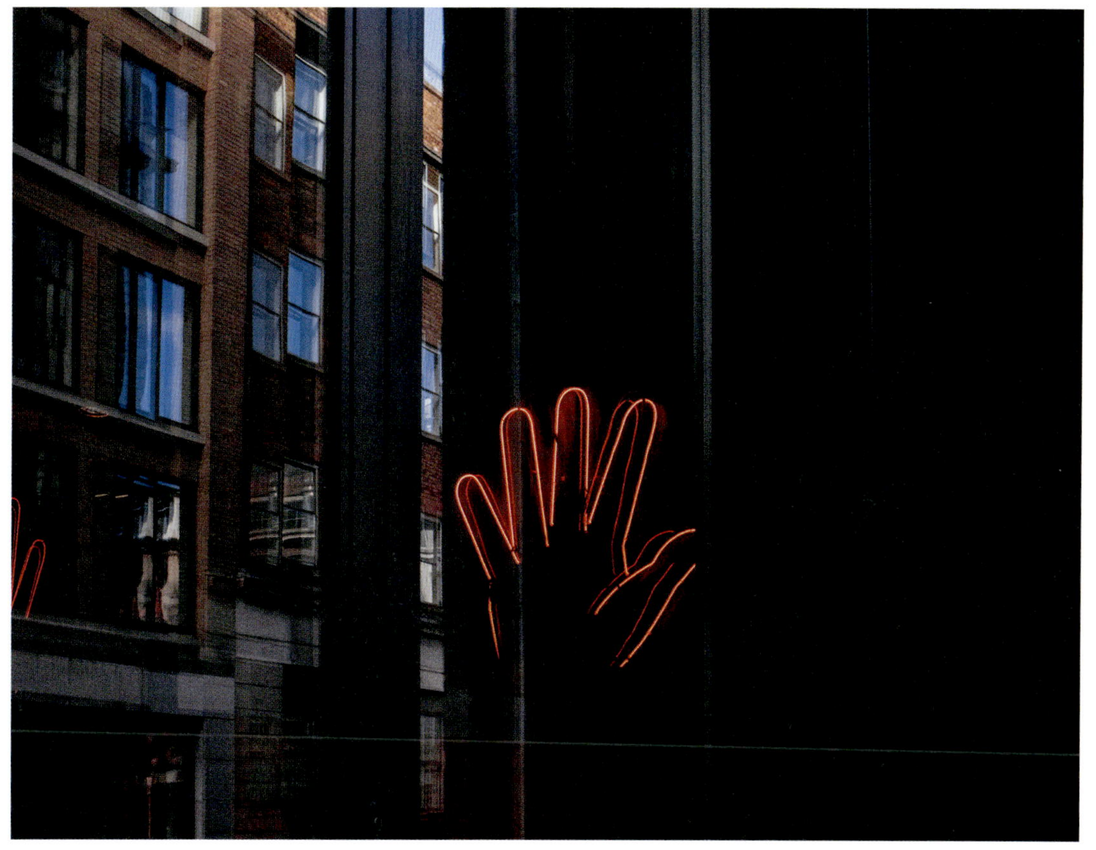

*Finsbury Avenue*

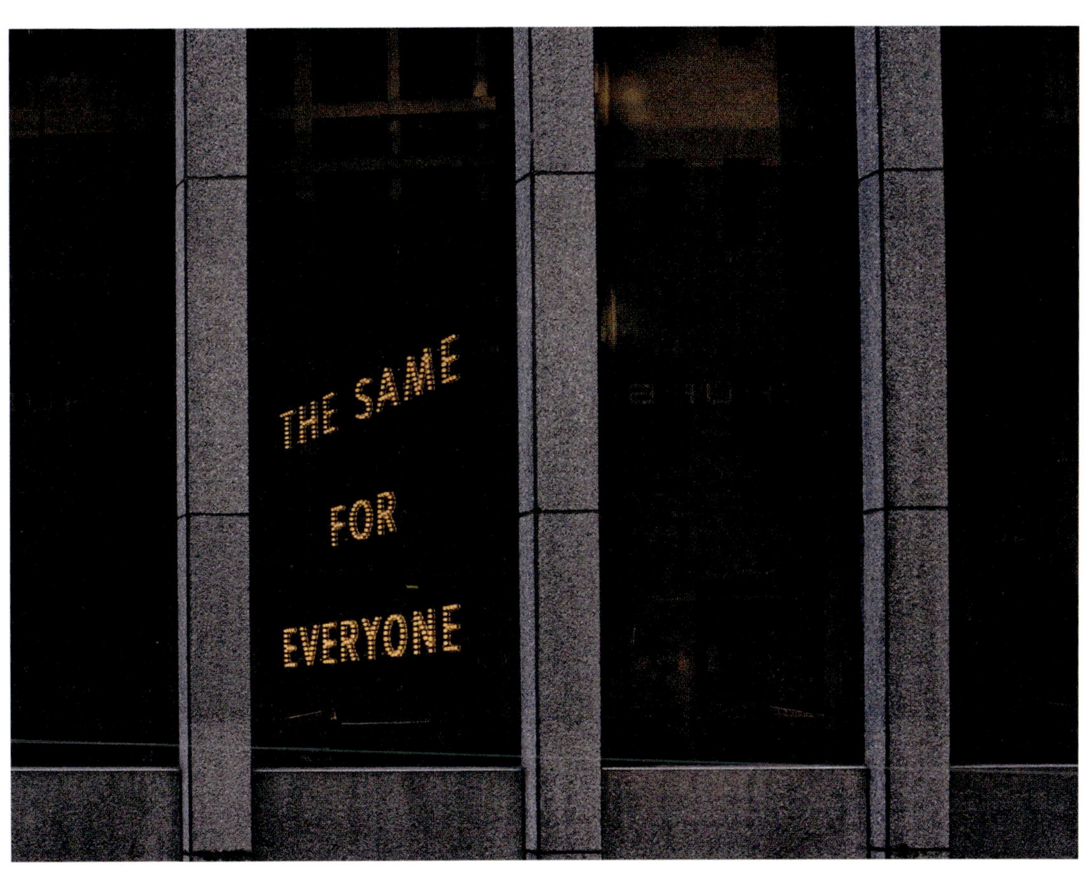


*Cunard Place*

# Morgana Secco
## *Growing Up in Quarantine*

With schools closed and nowhere to go, for most parents lockdown meant being cooped up inside with the family – looking after their children around the clock and substituting the role of teacher at home – while also often maintaining a job. For family photographer Morgana Secco, the pandemic arrived just as she was about to return to work from maternity leave. Lockdown vetoed the possibility of her picking up her usual business, so she turned her camera to her own family instead. With her husband now at home, she was no longer always holding the baby: 'I could have a space to think about photography again. It was a moment at which my daughter started walking, talking and interacting with us more, and it was the first time I was experiencing that with my own kid. Everything she did at the time was new for me, I could see life from her perspective and see how she was discovering the world.'

In *Growing Up in Quarantine*, we follow Secco's daughter Alice, the playful protagonist of this story, through those precious moments of early life. Secco's pictures reveal the madness, humour, love and affection that permeate the experience of being stuck inside as a family. 'After a while we started to feel like we were missing out on things, but in the beginning we gained a lot from the opportunity to be together all the time. It was a happy time for my husband to be home every day and to see our daughter growing up. Taking these photos ended up helping me to frame those moments. From tension, we went to lightness and joy.'

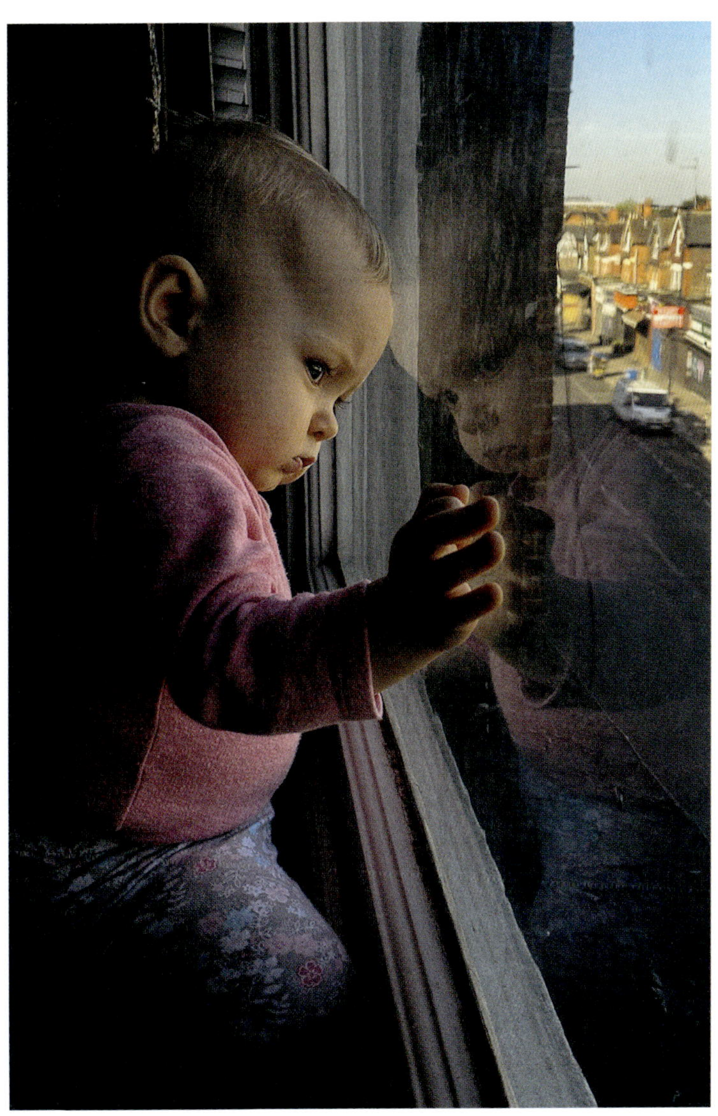

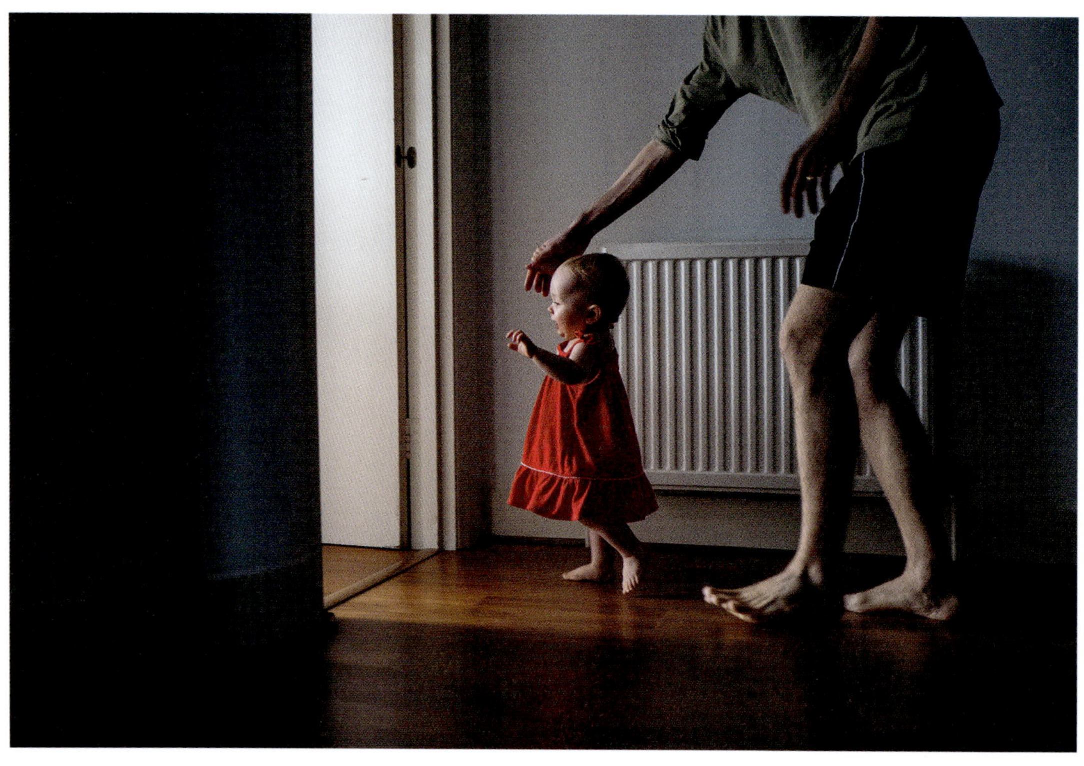

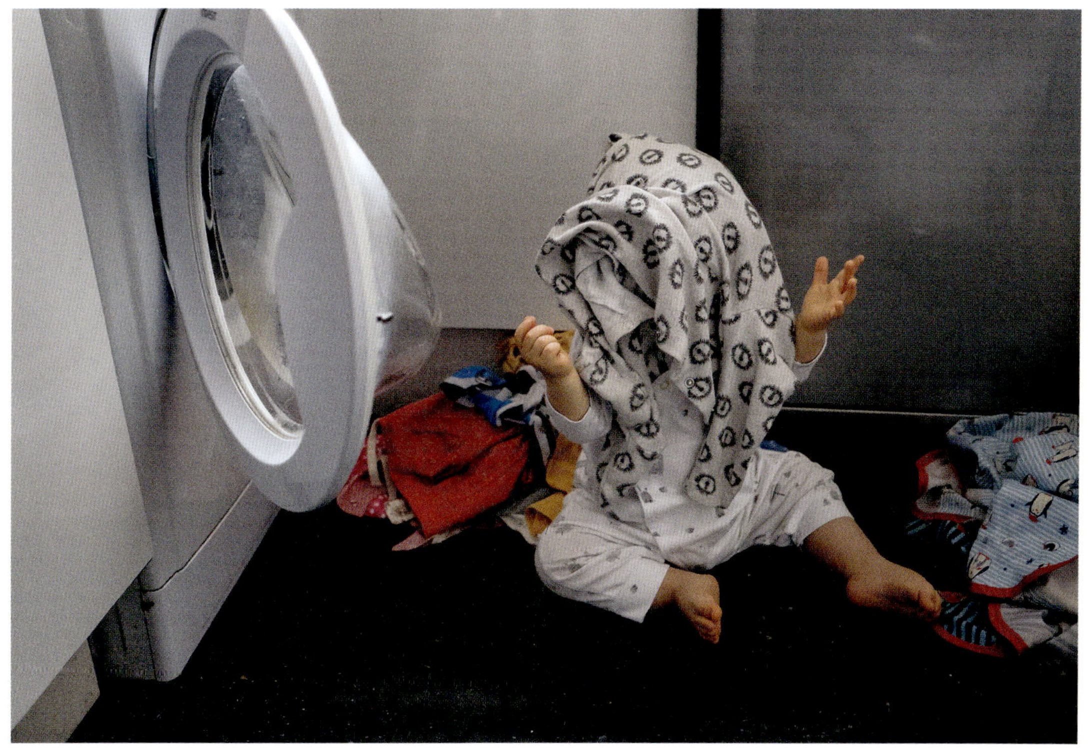

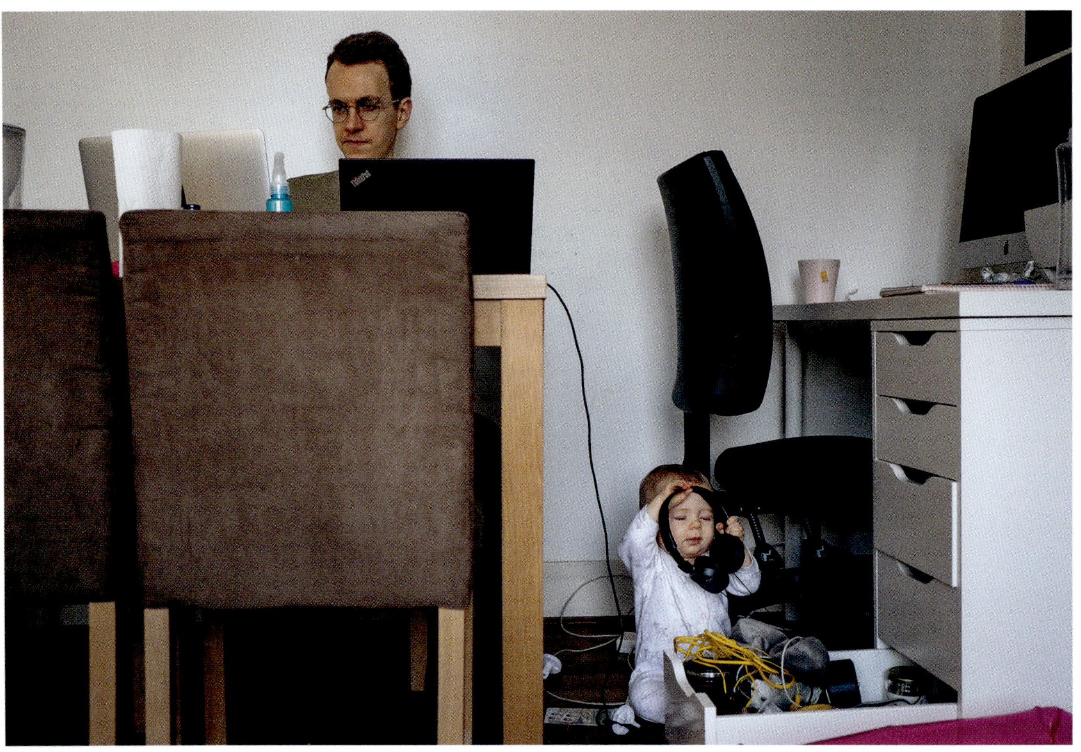

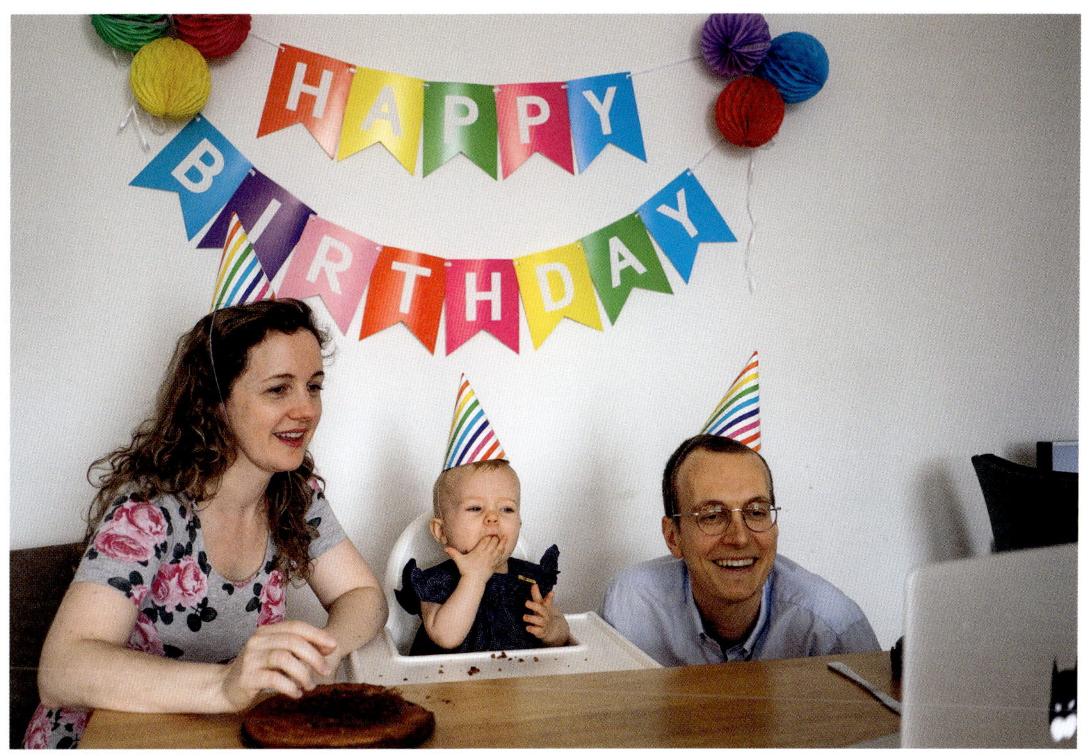

Morgana Secco

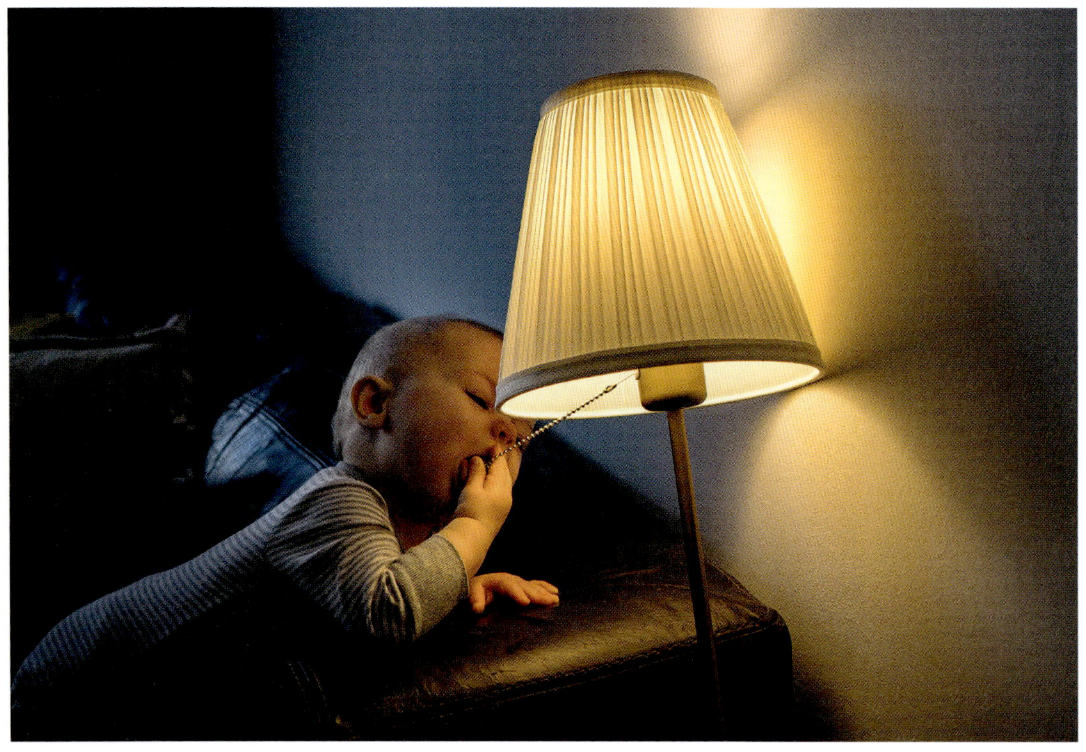

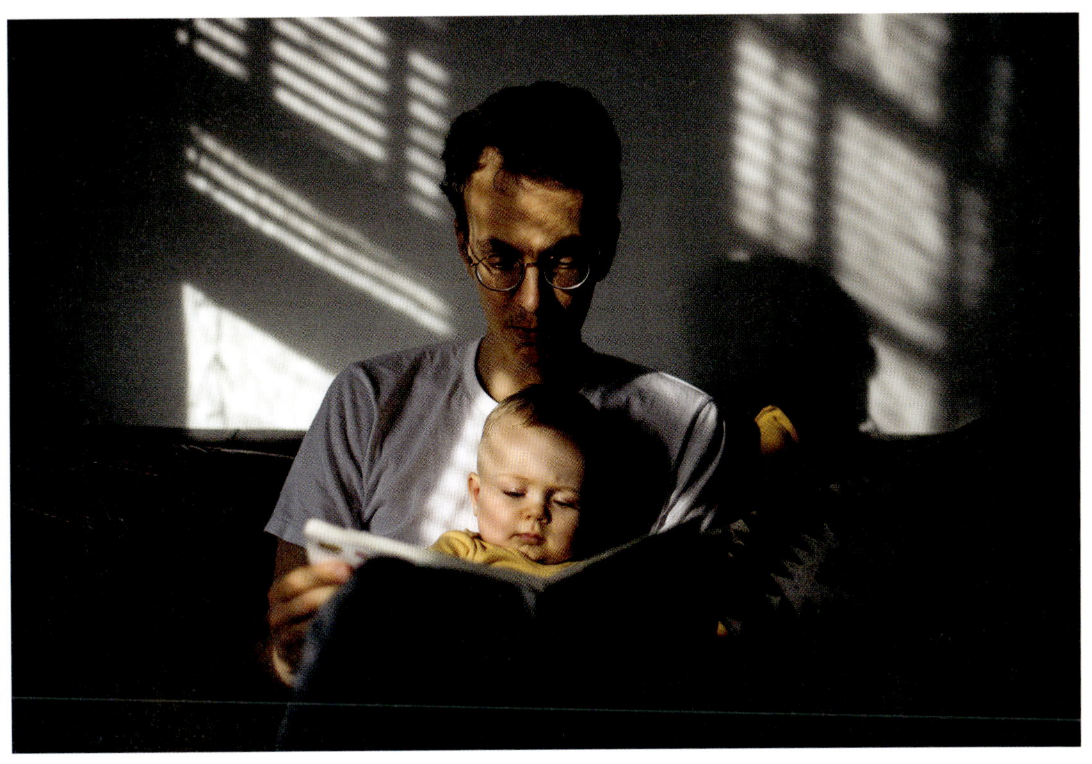

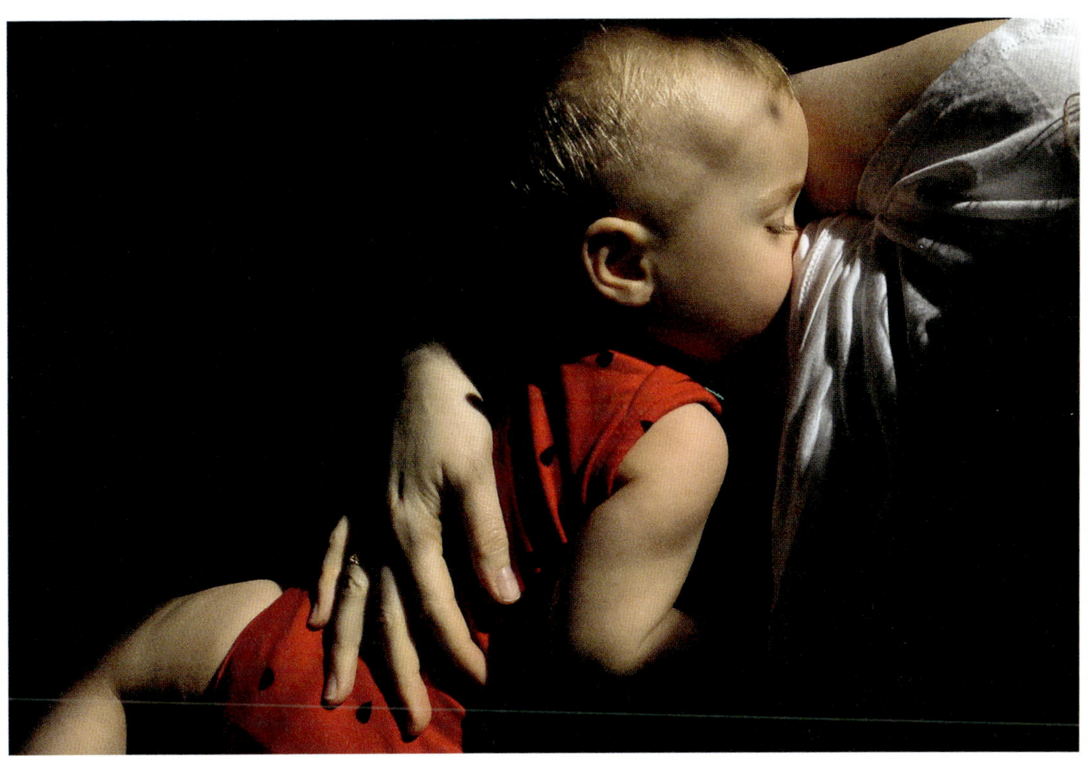

# Christian Sinibaldi
## *Evering Road*

When the first lockdown began, Christian Sinibaldi noticed a sudden openness among his neighbours on Hackney's mile-long Evering Road; they relinquished their usually well-protected sense of personal privacy to make the most of their front gardens and communal spaces. He writes: 'I've lived here for more than eight years, without ever truly knowing those around me. Lockdown presented a unique opportunity. I couldn't do my usual work, but I could turn my camera to my own community.' From March to May 2020, Sinibaldi chronicled life on his leafy street, where Victorian terraces are interspersed with low-rise social housing blocks. Posting a picture a day on Instagram, Sinibaldi's project became a platform for residents to connect with one another in a perfect microcosm of London life, where people of all ages, ethnicities and social backgrounds live side by side.

Through his encounters with both recent arrivals and families who had called the road home for decades, Sinibaldi discovered the history of the area – from Blitz bombsites and Windrush-generation blues parties to squatters, ravers and a new wave of hipsters. 'At first, the project was mostly for my personal sanity, but in talking to the people of Evering Road I began to uncover a consoling web of human stories, small gestures and common threads. I've had the privilege of listening to a wide variety of stories across the generations – from the struggle of millennials to the anxiety of people in their 80s. Whatever our age or background, we share so many of the same joys and fears. Despite the huge range of voices, what emerged most from the many people I spoke to was our collective humanity.'

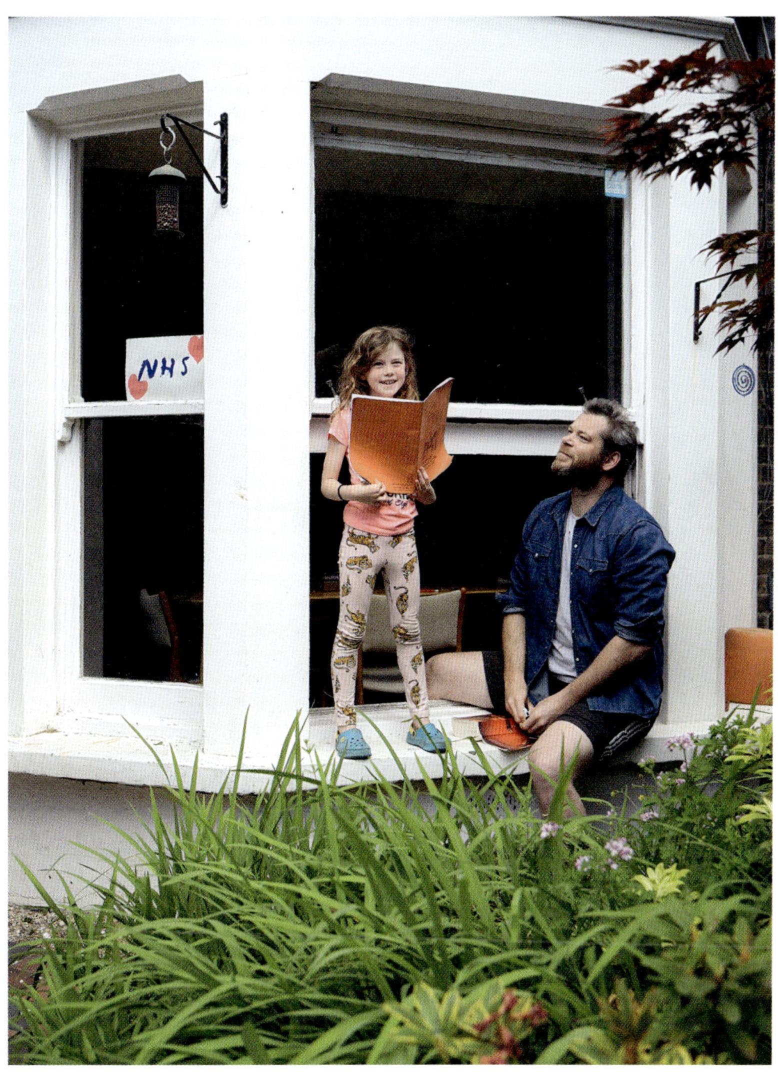



*Ben and Ivy. 'Homeschool can be good or bad, depending on my mood. But mostly it's been great. We do PE lessons and cooking and baking. I'm reading* Harry Potter *and I get dressed in my Hogwarts uniform. We do magic lessons instead sometimes and pretend Daddy is a wizard. That's much more fun than maths. It's nice to spend more time with my parents but I also really miss school and my friends.' – Ivy (left)*

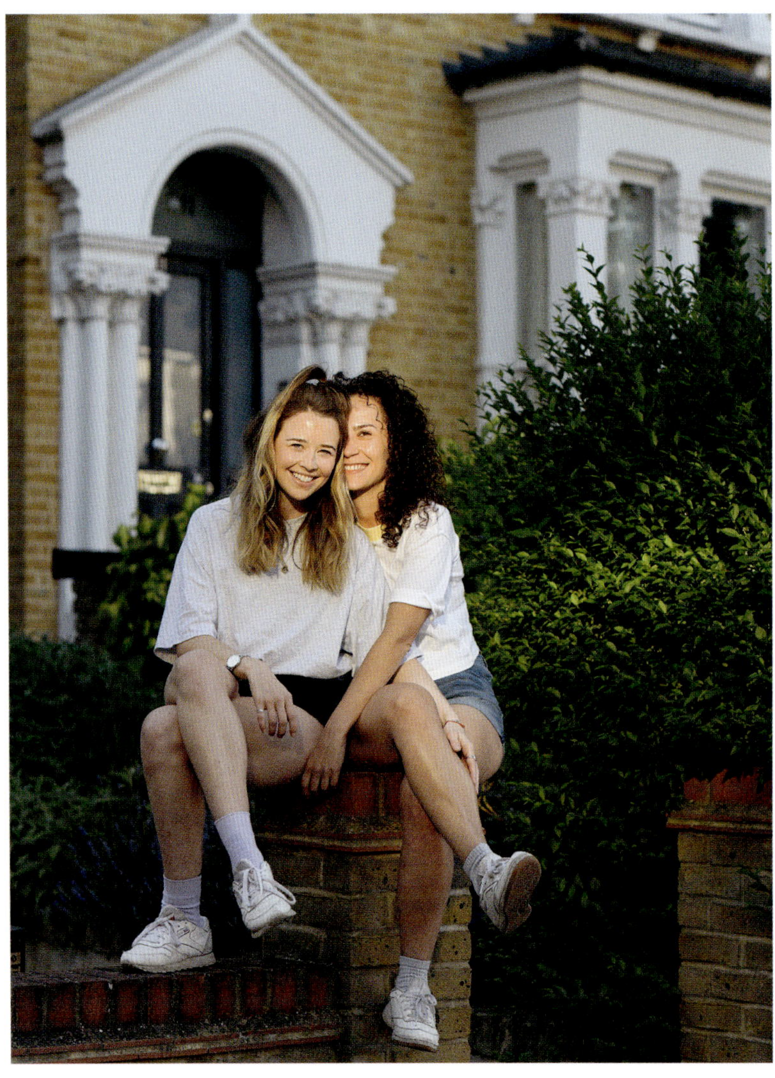

*Emma and Grace. 'I'm really trying to embrace the positives of lockdown. We're so used to being go, go, go all the time: hectic work schedules, plans most evenings and every weekend. Sometimes it feels like we don't have time to breathe or take time for ourselves. So it's been refreshing to just slow down, recharge and enjoy each other's company.' – Grace (left)*

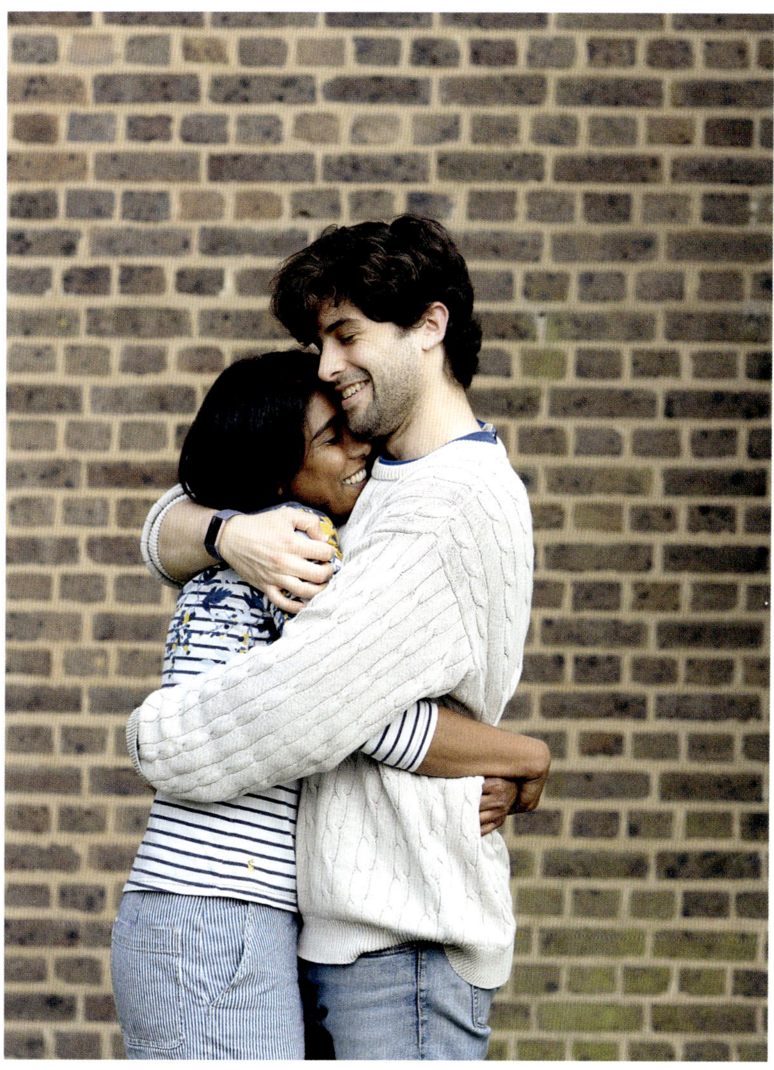

*Sam and Roberto. 'I'm originally from India and Roberto is from the States. We met at uni and bought our first flat in 2015, marrying the following year. Ever since we've embraced what we think of as the "Hackney spirit". Lots of people here are from different walks of life. The class division feels much more blurred than in many places. One of the few good things about this situation is that it's brought people closer together.' – Sam (left)*

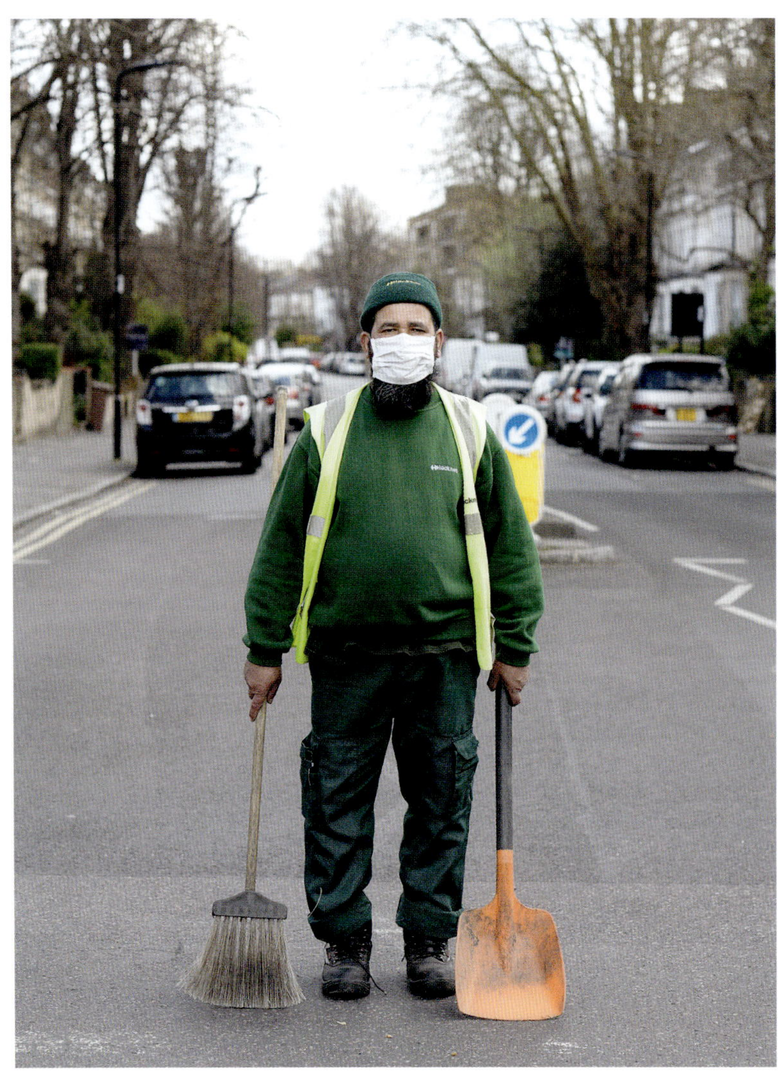

*Mohammed. 'I moved from India to the UK ten years ago. Within two months I was employed by the council and have been taking care of Evering Road ever since.'*

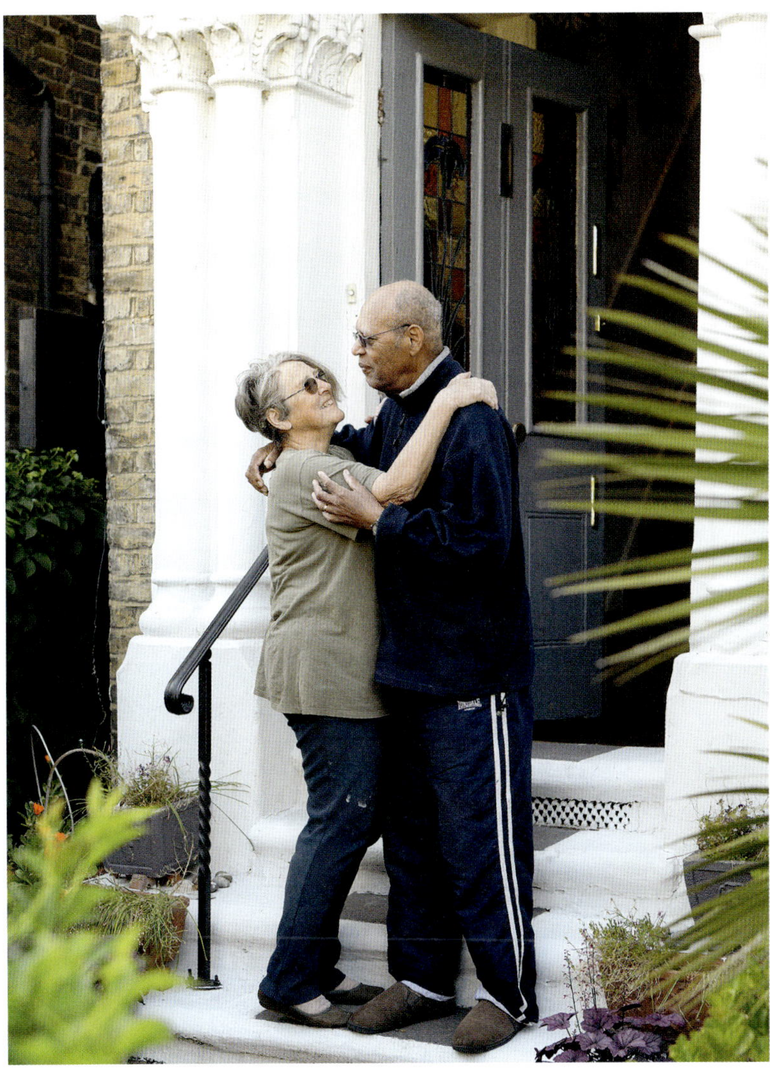

*Celia and Neil. 'We moved to the road in 1985. Neil came to the UK in 1963 from Trinidad, bringing with him a deep passion for music and a carnival vibe. In the past we held many word-of-mouth "blues parties". They would start at 11pm and go on all night long. Hackney was very different back then in many ways. It was a very working class area with a lot of grassroots culture, as well as feminist activities and radical literature projects, many of which we were involved with. It is still a fairly diverse area, and still full of creative people.' – Celia (left)*

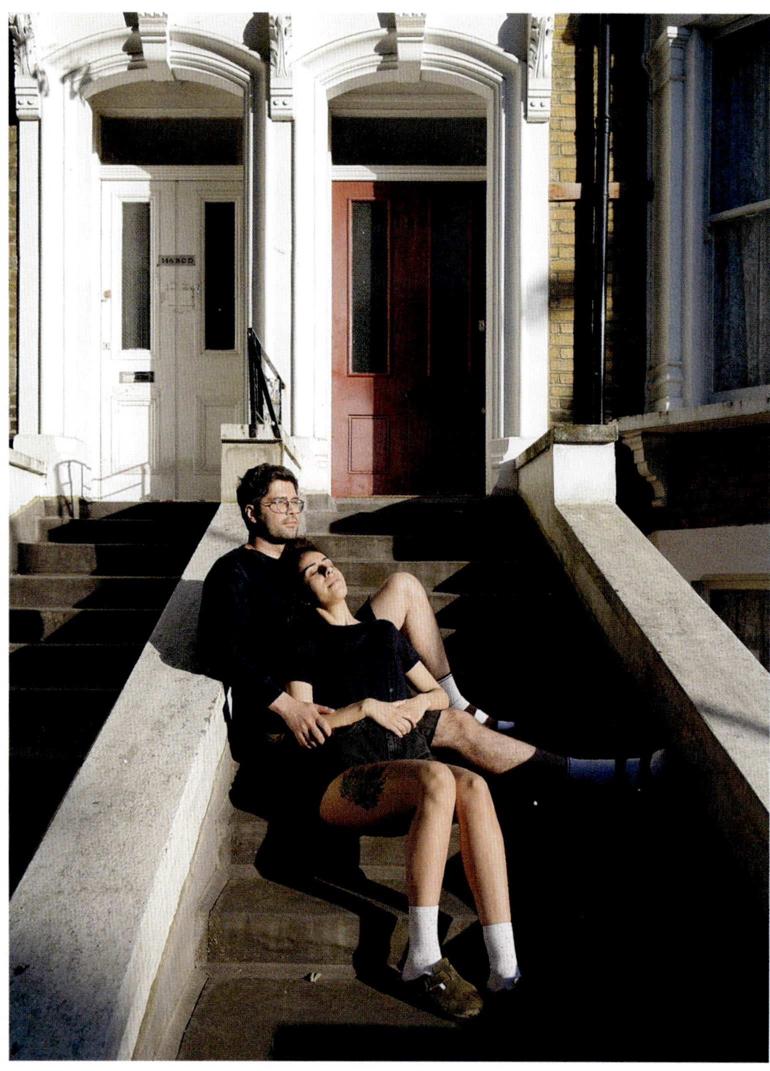

*Meyla and Eser. 'We've been married for three years. The lockdown has helped us as a couple. Eser became less stressed due to the lack of commuting for work. I feel happier because I am at home and feel safe. In Turkey, like in many Mediterranean places, sitting outside and talking to passers-by is very common. So this is something we really appreciate about this specific time. I enjoy sitting on our front steps "people watching" because it grounds me and makes me feel a part of something.' – Meyla (right)*

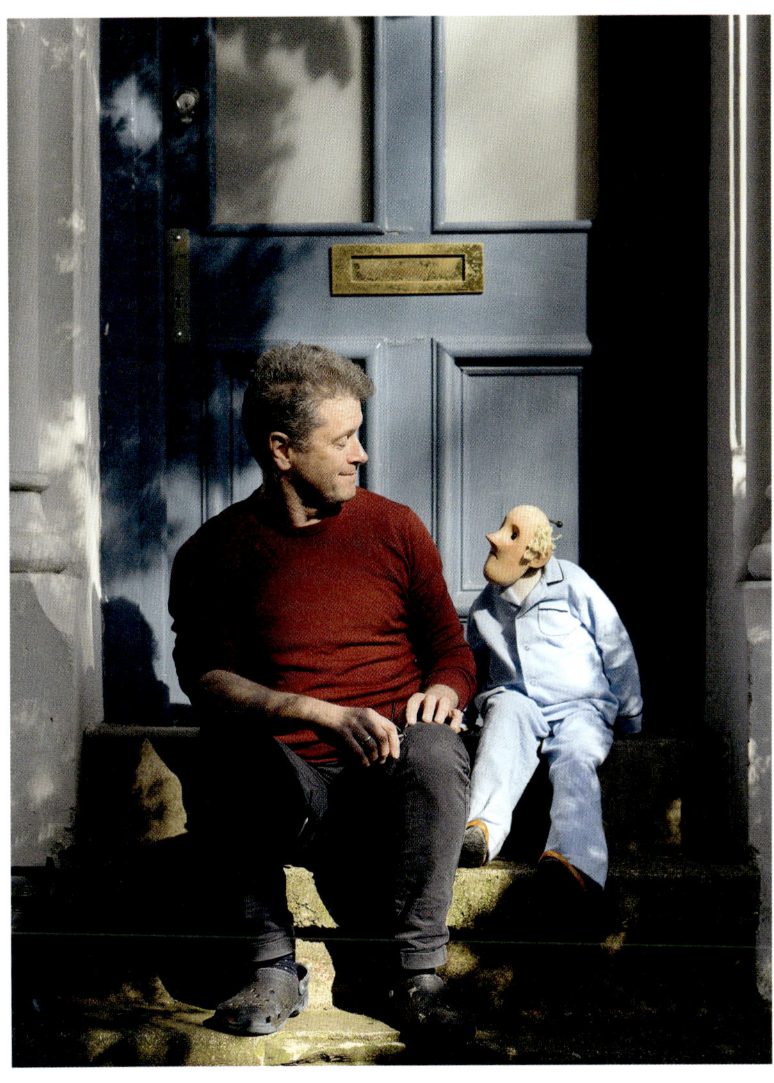

*Peter with 'Dad'. 'I've lived on Evering for 13 years and in Hackney since 1984. I create my*
*puppets in the attic of the house. My latest show is an adaptation of the nonsense poem*
The Dong with the Luminous Nose *by Edward Lear. It's a heartfelt expression of my own*
*feelings of isolation and loneliness. The themes are so apt for the current moment. "Dad"*
*is the main character.'*

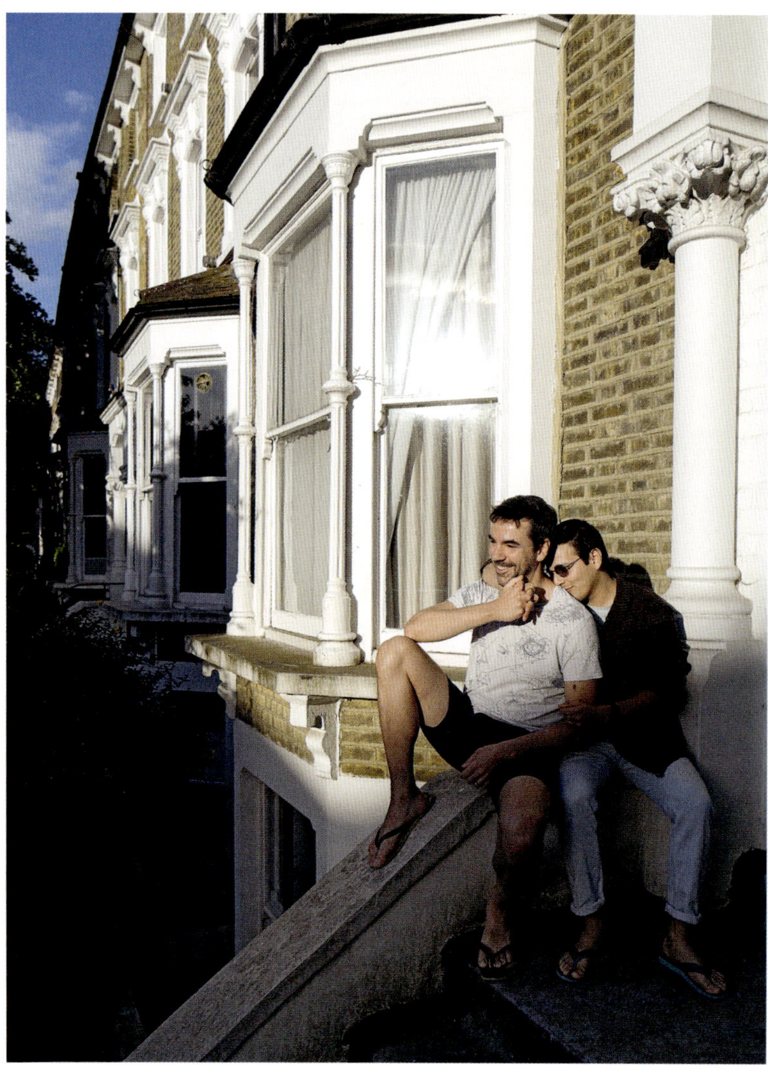

*Vini and Vincente. 'We've been married for four years, together for six. We met one evening at The Joiners Arms on Hackney Road. We got married at Pub on the Park in London Fields, and have been living on Evering Road ever since. As a gay couple and as foreigners, we feel accepted, safe and at home here in Hackney. We love the road for its beauty and our neighbours. Many of us are now making greater efforts to greet each other on the street and get to know each other.' – Vini (left)*

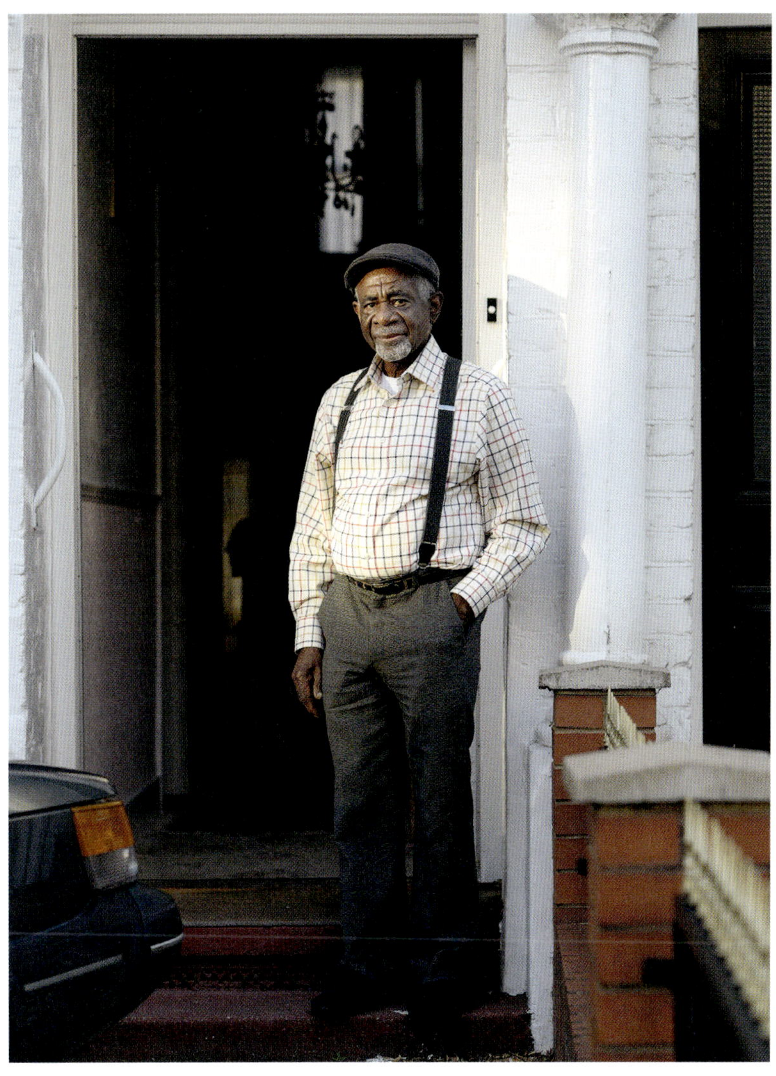

*Mr Danny.* 'I think I'm the oldest resident of Evering Road. I've lived in this house since 1960. It was derelict when I bought it, the only place I could afford. It took me many years to refurbish the place and I did everything myself, from the front door to the staircase. I was a French polisher by trade, which is a very skilled job. I came from Jamaica as a part of the Windrush generation. It took my neighbours ten years to even say hello. Back then the place was very different and not very inclusive. So we've come a long way.'

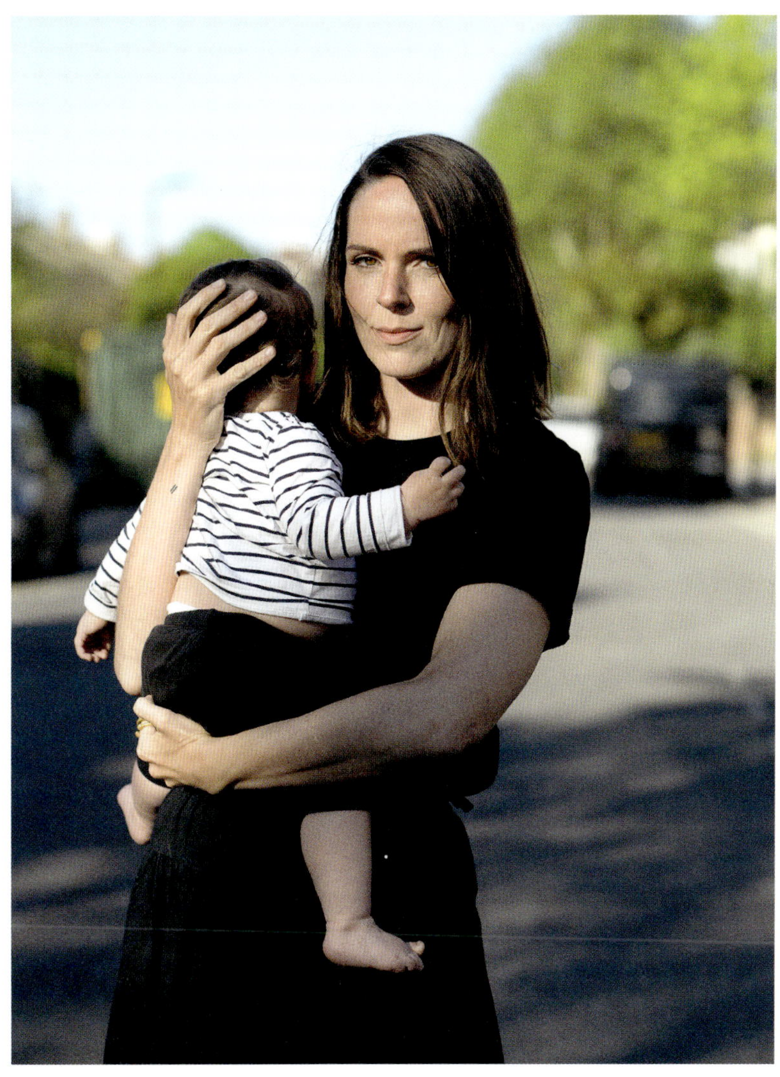

*Kate and Rita. 'It's been just over a month so far of lockdown. I think it's amazing how a situation like this, outside any of our experience, soon becomes normalised. We adapt so quickly. But while this ability to accept things can be a strength, I do worry that it might prevent us from asking the right questions. Yes, the ways in which communities are coming together to support one another is inspiring and worth celebrating, but it mustn't stop us from demanding answers from those responsible.' – Kate*

# Sophia Evans
## *River Lea*

After months of isolation, the sunny weather of late spring and summer 2020 drove many locked-down Londoners out of doors. In east London, people flocked to the River Lea at Hackney Marshes, which transformed from a quiet pocket of urban nature into a jam-packed tropical paradise. Local photographer Sophia Evans captured the sun-loving crowds – many of whom were Latin American – on the verdant banks of the river in scenes of euphoria and wild abandon that reveal a shared desire for release and reconnection in a dark and difficult time.

'It was just such a dream,' says Evans. 'Sometimes I would get up at six in the morning and go there, just to hear birdsong and watch the light bounce off the water. You could spend any time of day there and that place was rocking, but in the afternoon on a hot day it was crowded. Salsa music everywhere, and you'd see parakeets fly by in a flash of green. In May, elderflower was dripping almost into the water and there were little purple wildflowers everywhere along the riverbanks. It was just so exotic to me that I sometimes wondered if I imagined it.'

Yet despite the River Lea's enchanting features, many have warned that it is one of the most polluted waterways in the UK, and that the traces left behind by the crowds pose a serious risk to the area's protected wildlife. For Evans, however, the project shows that the pandemic was not just a period of suffering and death, but also of bliss and joy – although, after a year of strict limits on physical contact, seeing such close proximity of exposed bodies may still trigger some unease.

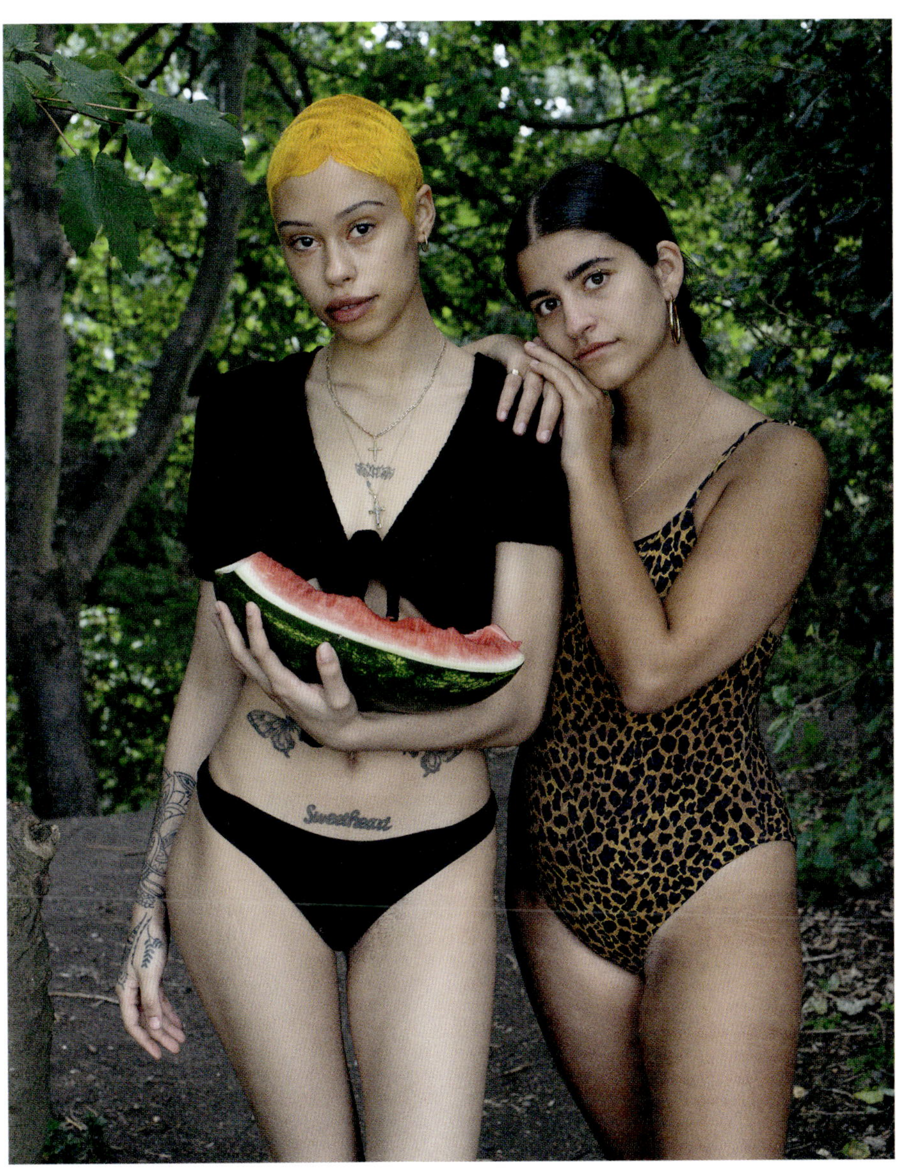

*Jennifer and Leonor with bitten-into watermelon, July 2020*

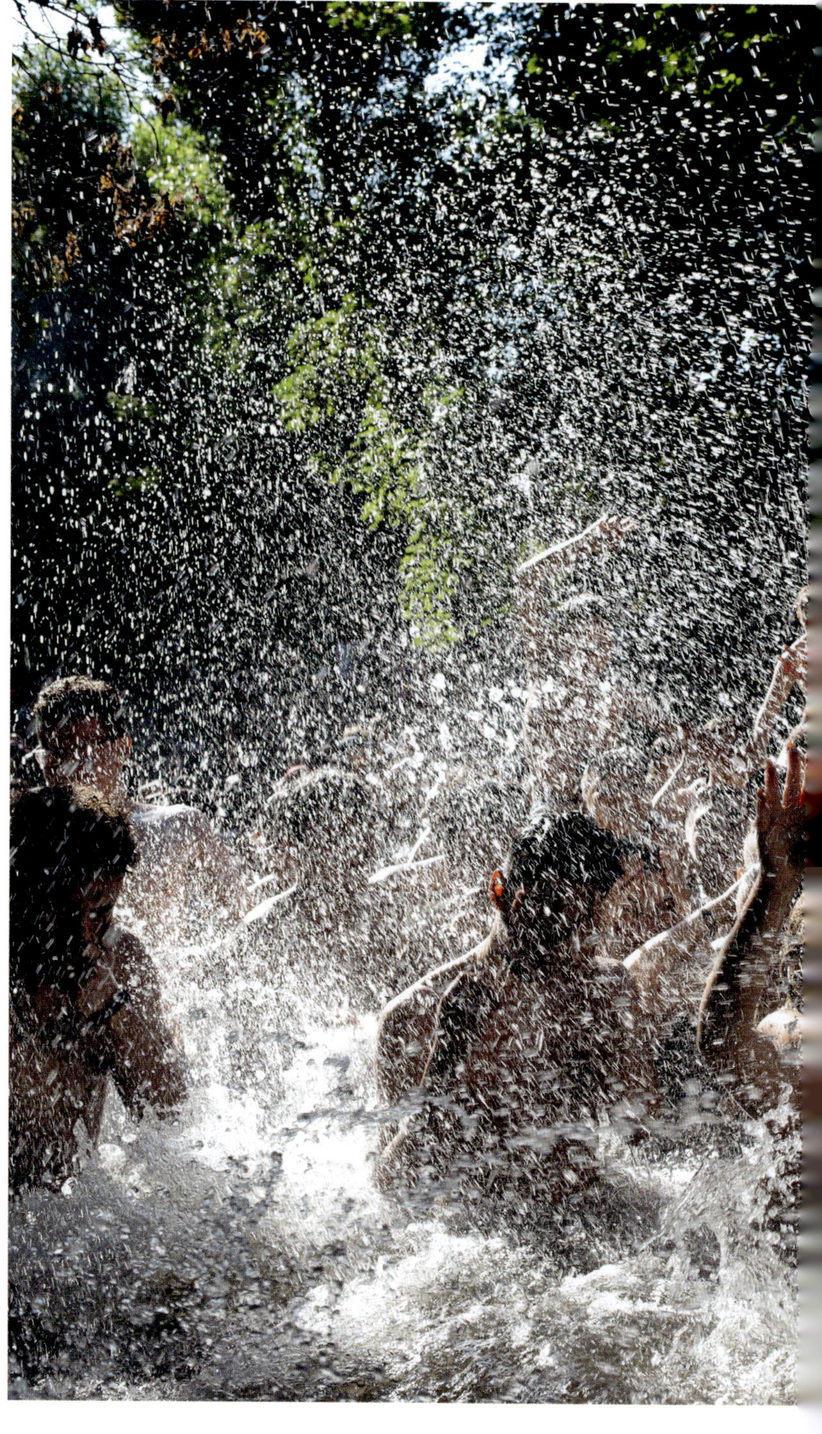

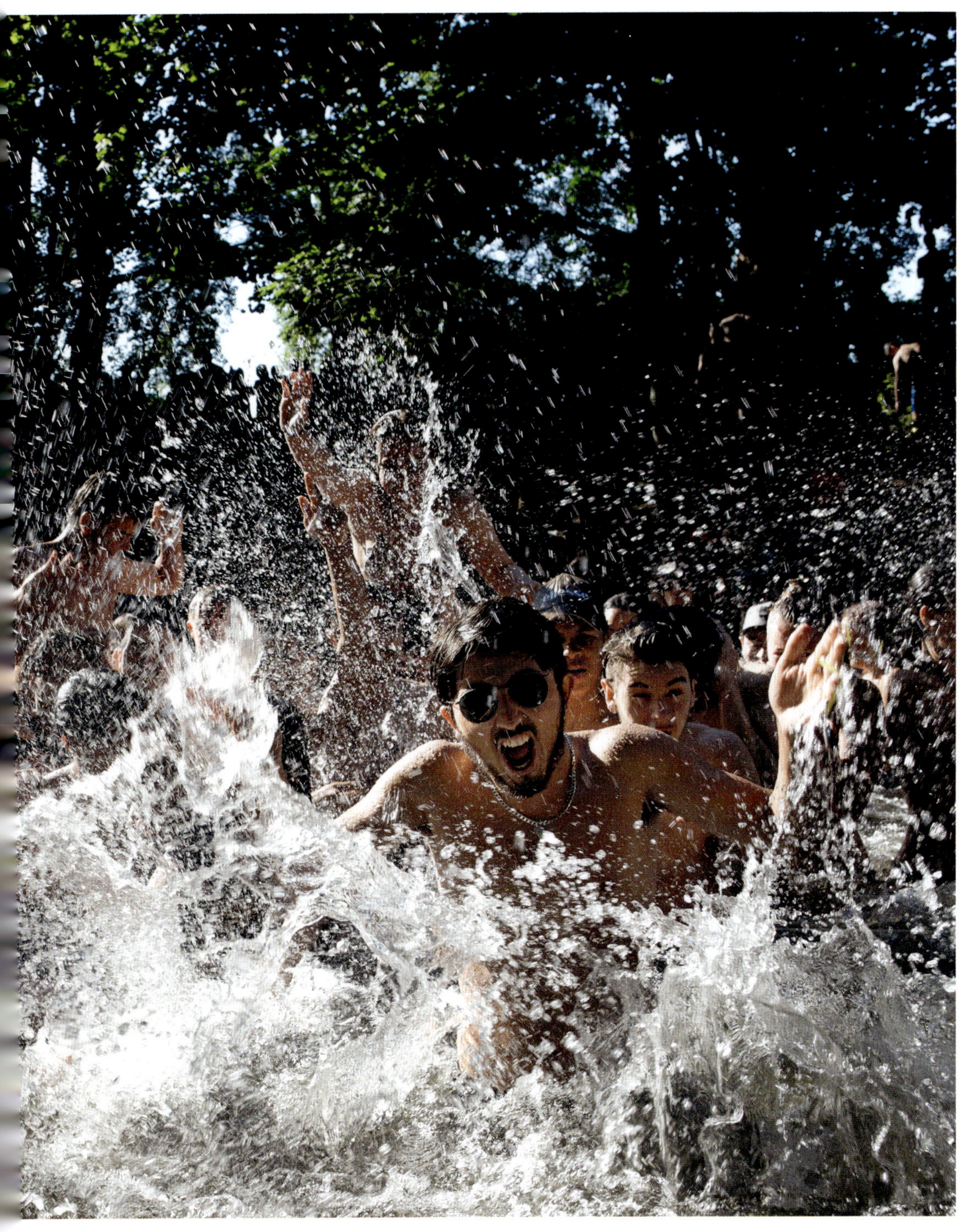

*Splashing to Colombian salsa music, June 2020*

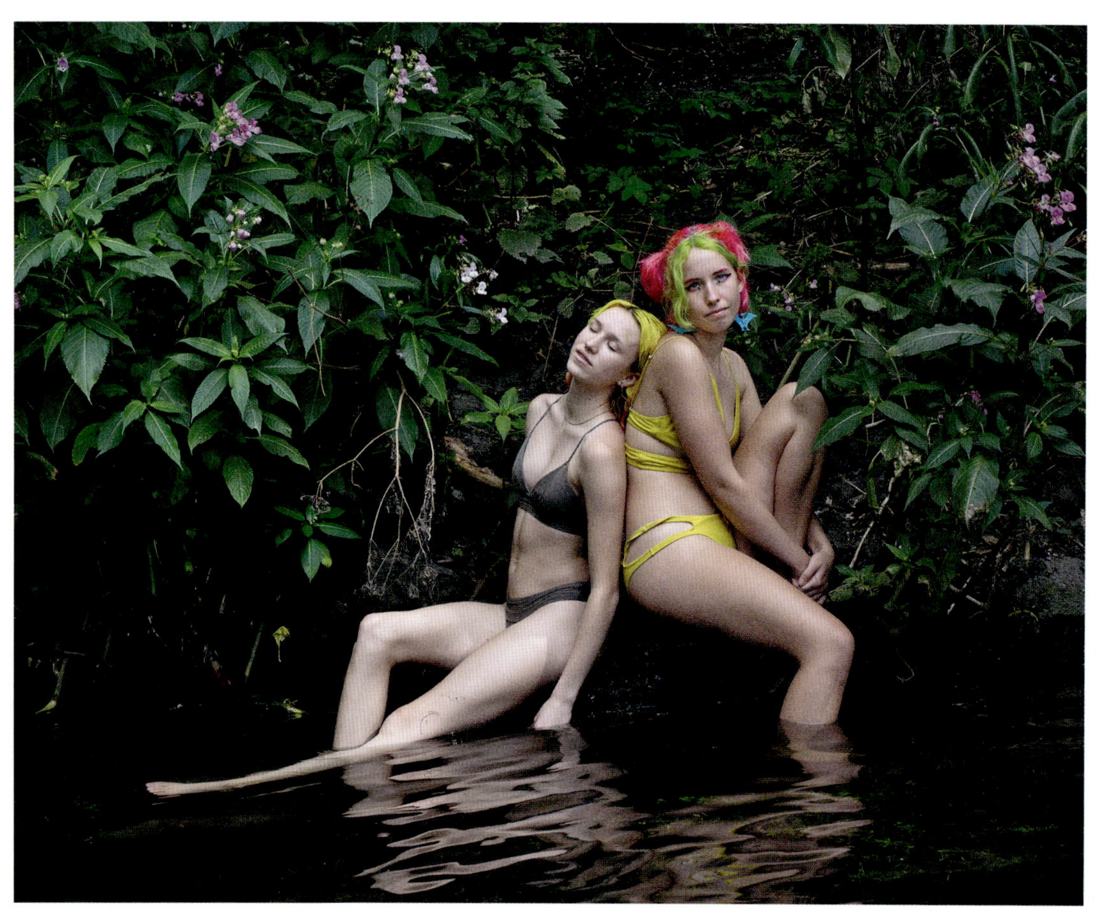

*Daisy and Polly, July 2020*

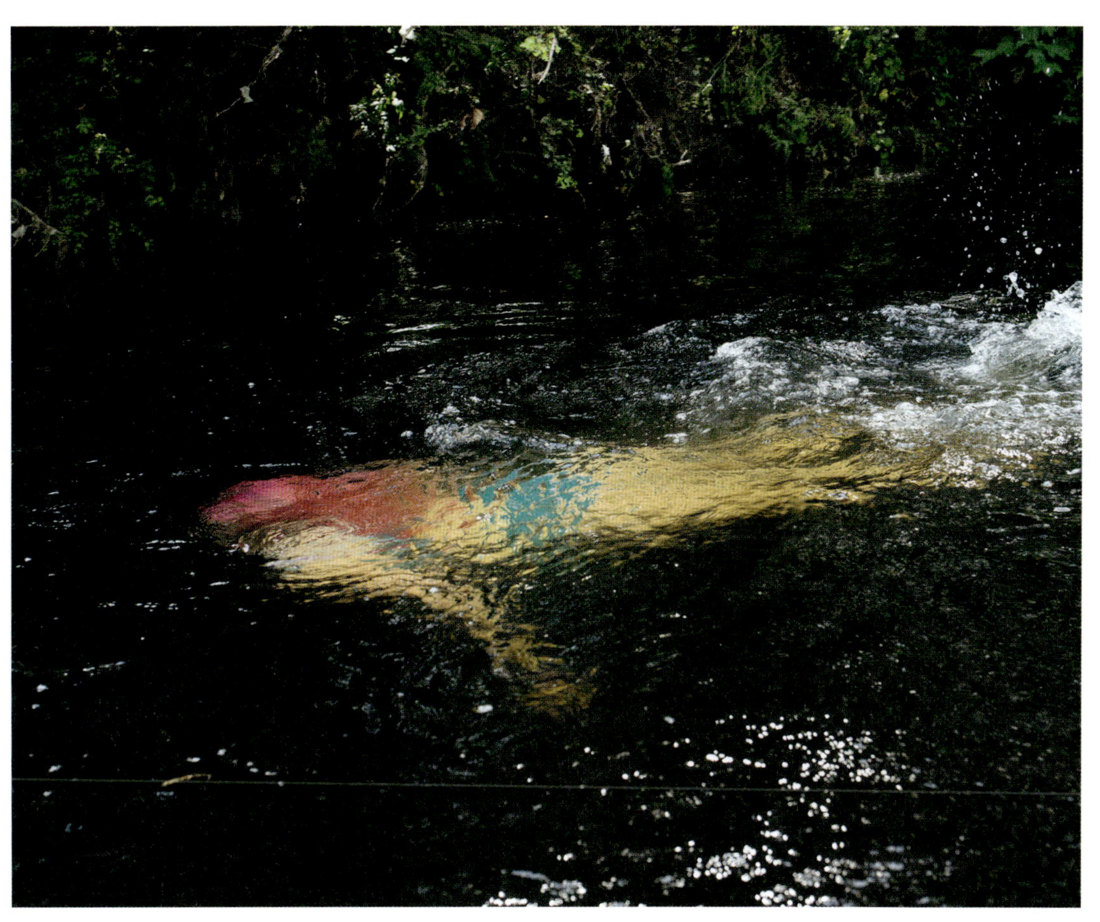

*Lockdown mermaid, May 2020*

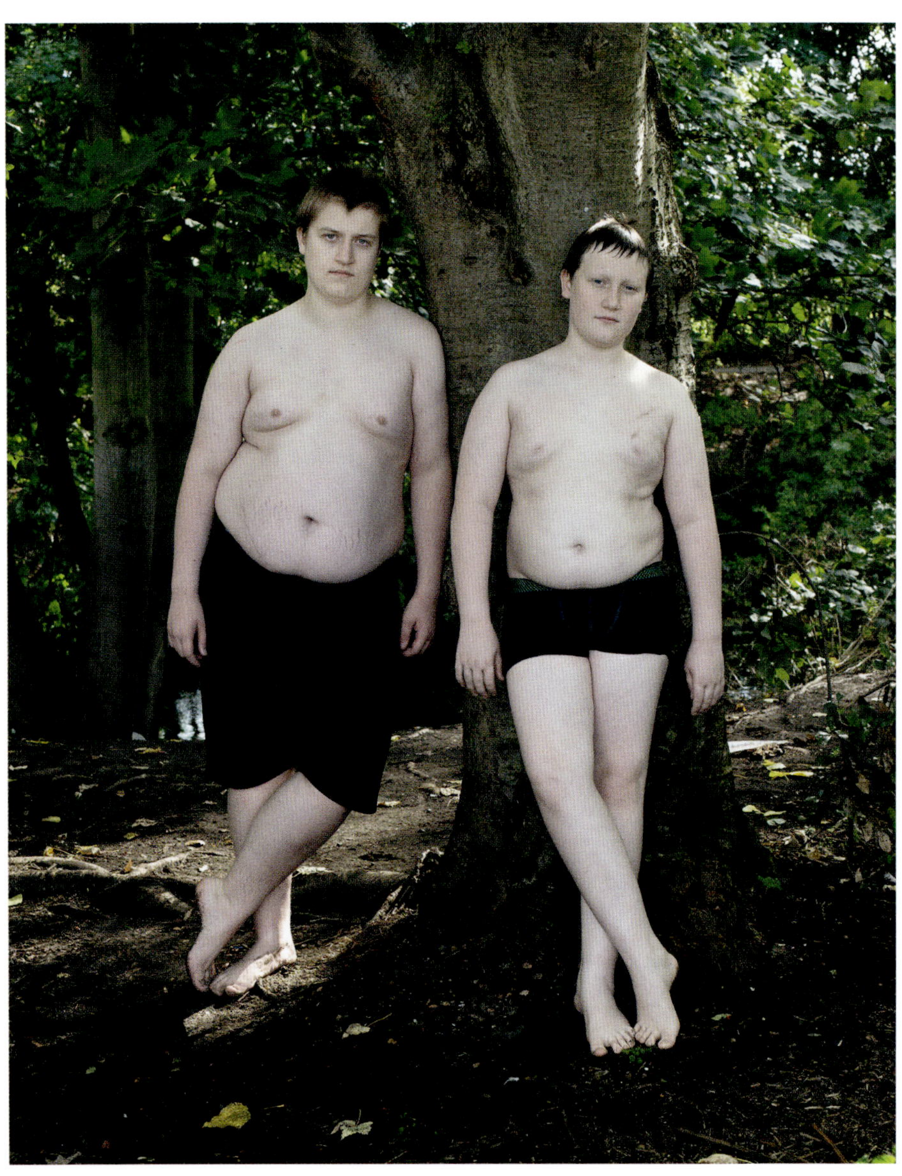

*Aaron and Cameron, August 2020*

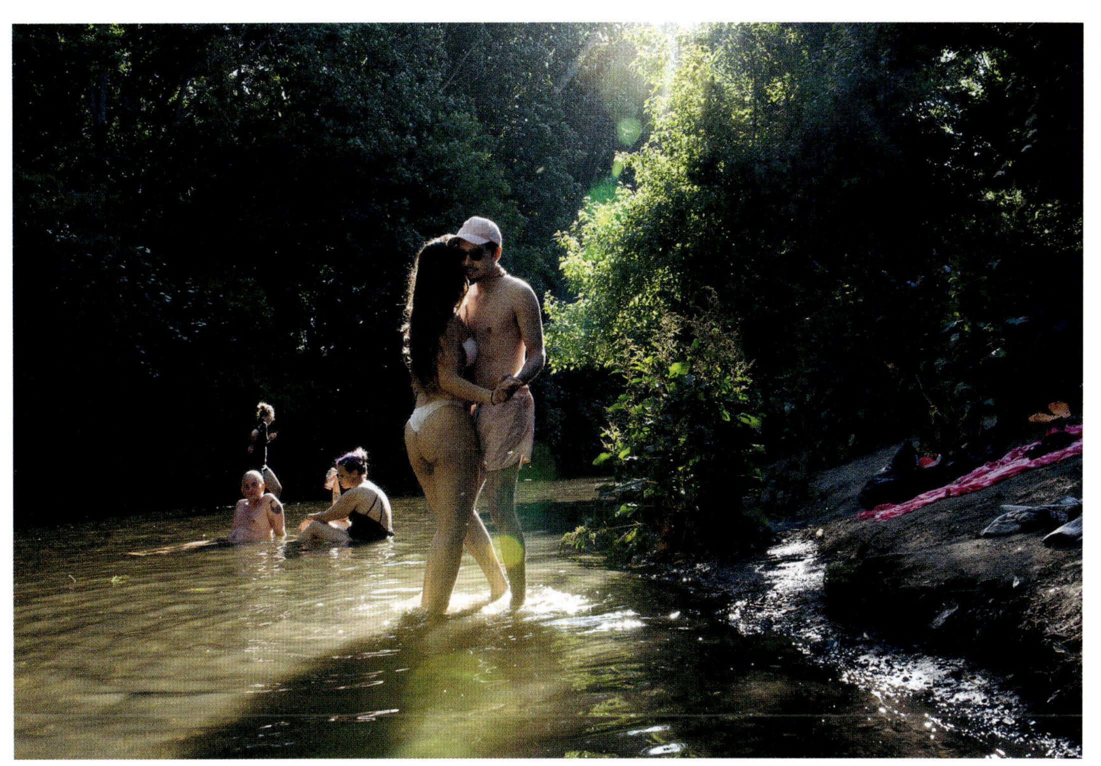

*Marta and Camilo, May 2020*

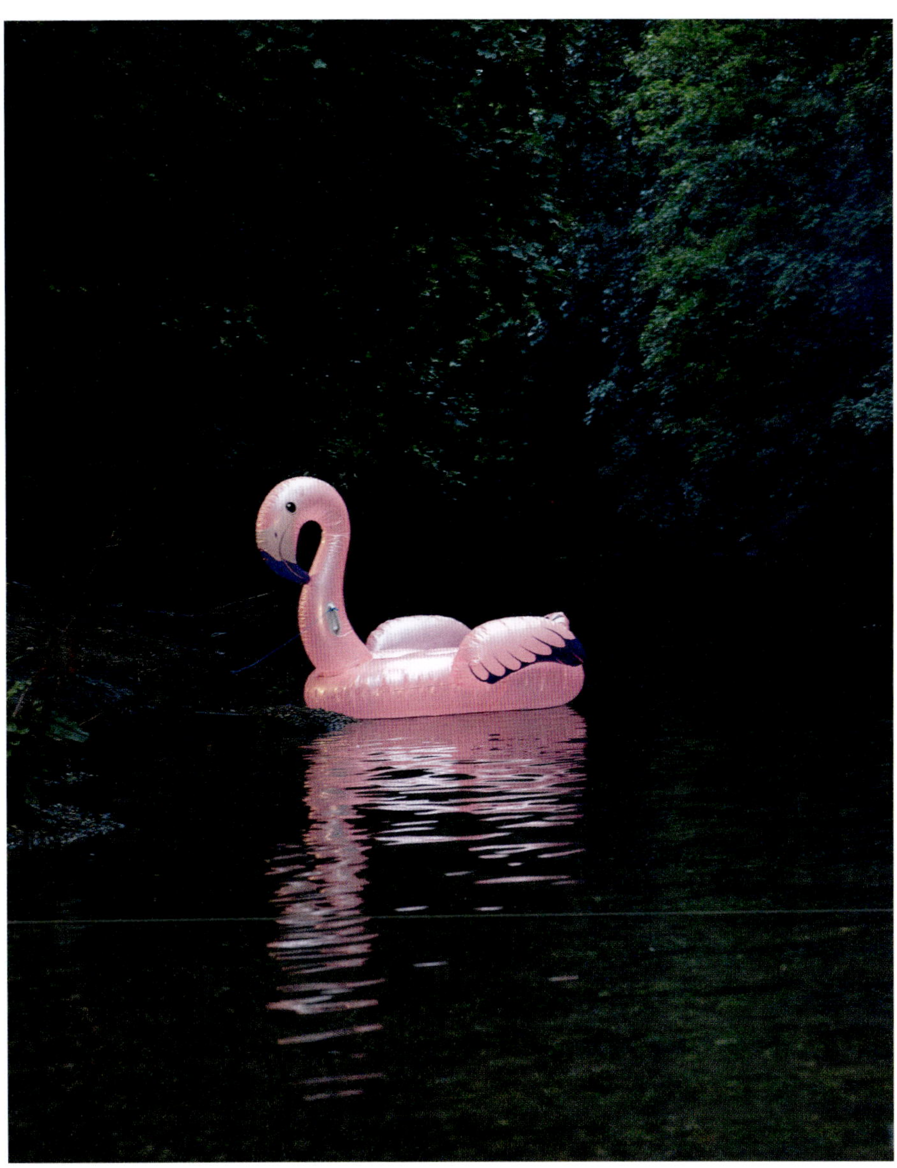

*Flamingo left behind, July 2020*

# Roy Mehta
## *Lockdown*

Roy Mehta's arresting images of the natural world are a visceral response to the strange days of the early pandemic, when an unusually beautiful spring contrasted with media coverage of an impending catastrophe – giving rise to a peculiar tension between stillness and chaos. Propelled by an urge to capture this feeling, Mehta turned to the natural landscape to ease his sense of discomfort with the future. 'I love the slowness of the garden, of growing my own food,' he wrote at the time. 'Like so many of us I have noticed a real change in the quality of the air, a lack of traffic noise, a greater awareness of birdsong and the sensation of time itself being slower.' Inspired by literature, poetry and other readings that poeticise our relationship with the natural world, Mehta's nearly spiritual photographs draw on twilight as a metaphor for transition and mirror his search for inner peace during an unsettling time.

To Mehta, really looking at nature (as many of us perhaps only did for the first time during lockdown) means being witness to everyday unfolding dramas in an endless cycle of decay and renewal. In this simultaneous appreciation of beauty and loss, of seeing ourselves as part of the bigger picture, these photographs not only offer a bittersweet reflection on the experience of the pandemic, but also a political commentary on the collective (mis)use of our natural environment that has led to this point of global devastation.

*'In April the springs are full with water and the bee swarms leave their hives, threshed wheat is eaten and the early barley is gathered in for the store. […] On the sixth day of this month sets the star Spica of the constellation of Virgo which, according to the Arabs, is the third of the fortunate constellations. The grass is dry now but the ten days of rain will come before the month's end.'*

Extract from the 12th-century text *A Moorish Calendar* from the *Book of Agriculture* by Ibn al-'Awwām

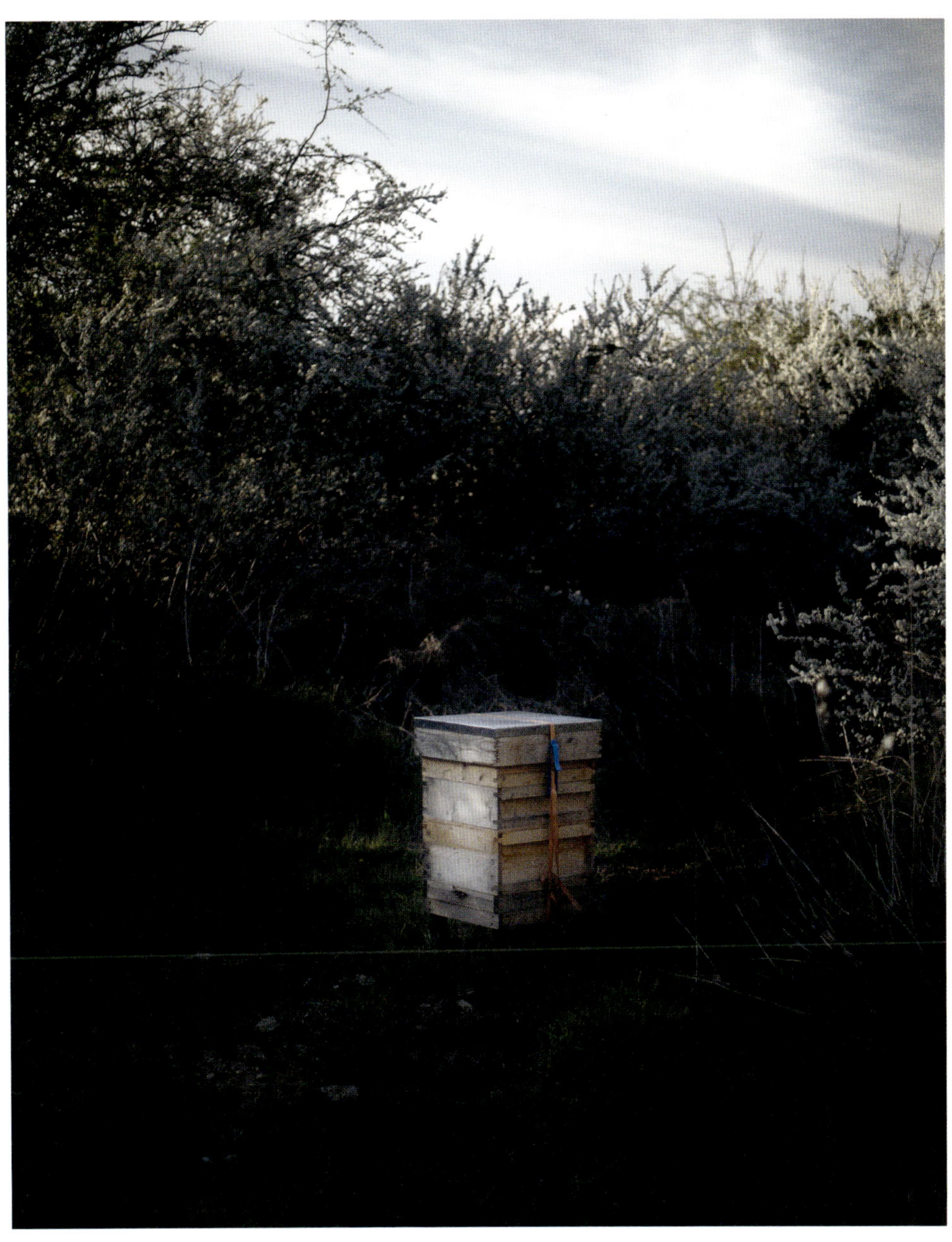

*Beehive, Watford, April 2020*

*'Slow bleak awakening from the morning dream*
*Brings me in contact with the sudden day.*
*I am alive – this I.'*

Extract from the poem *Living* by Harold Monro

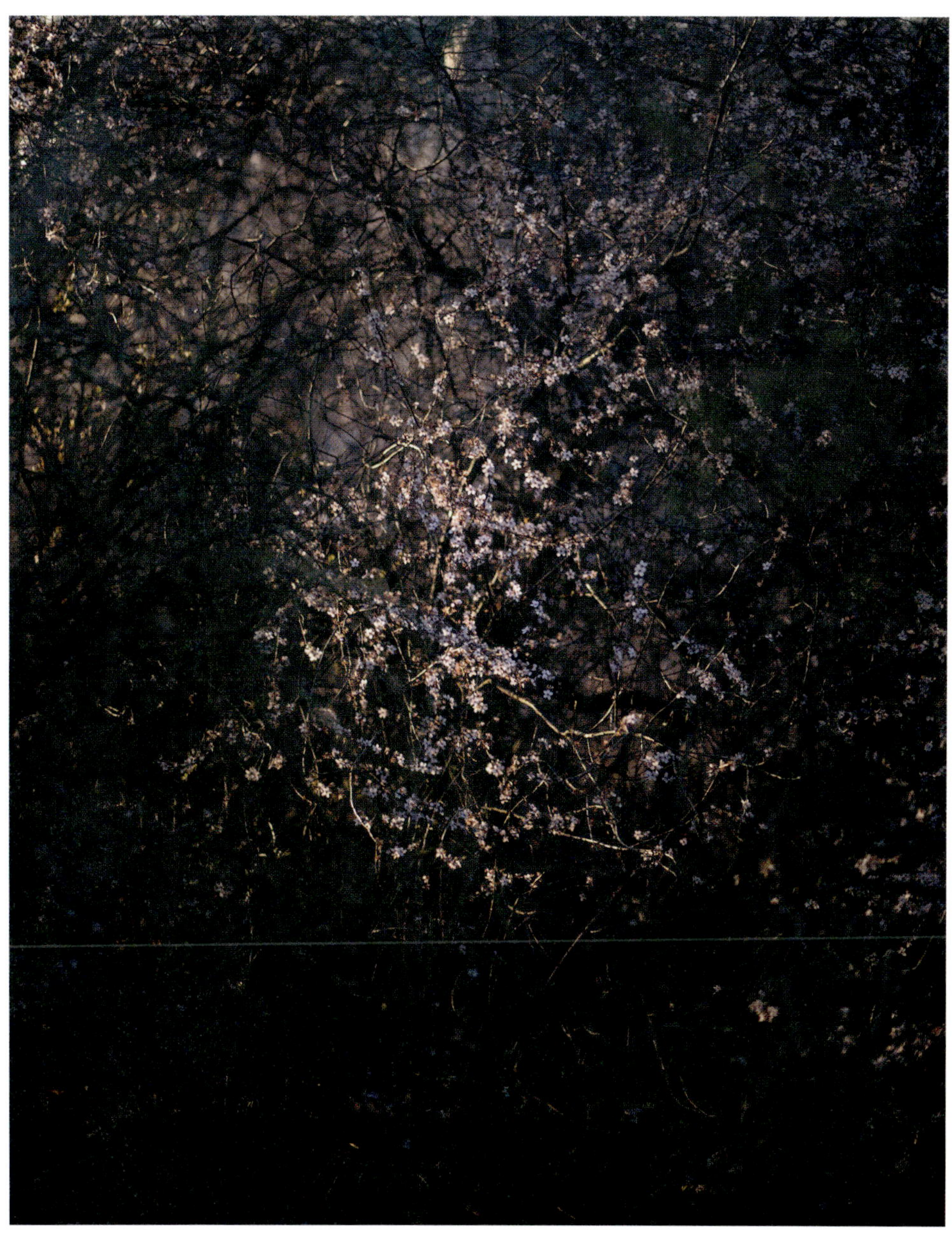

*Living, Watford, April 2020*

*'Our minds are still racing back and forth, longing for a return to "normality",
trying to stitch our future to our past and refusing to acknowledge the
rupture. But the rupture exists. And in the midst of this terrible despair,
it offers us a chance to rethink the doomsday machine we have built for
ourselves. Nothing could be worse than a return to normality.*

*Historically, pandemics have forced humans to break with the past and
imagine their world anew. This one is no different.*

*It is a portal, a gateway between one world and the next.*

*We can choose to walk through it, dragging the carcasses of our prejudice
and hatred, our avarice, our data banks and dead ideas, our dead rivers
and smoky skies behind us.*

*Or we can walk through lightly, with little luggage, ready to imagine
another world. And ready to fight for it.'*

Extract from the article *The Pandemic is a Portal* by Arundhati Roy,
first published in the *Financial Times* on 3 April 2020

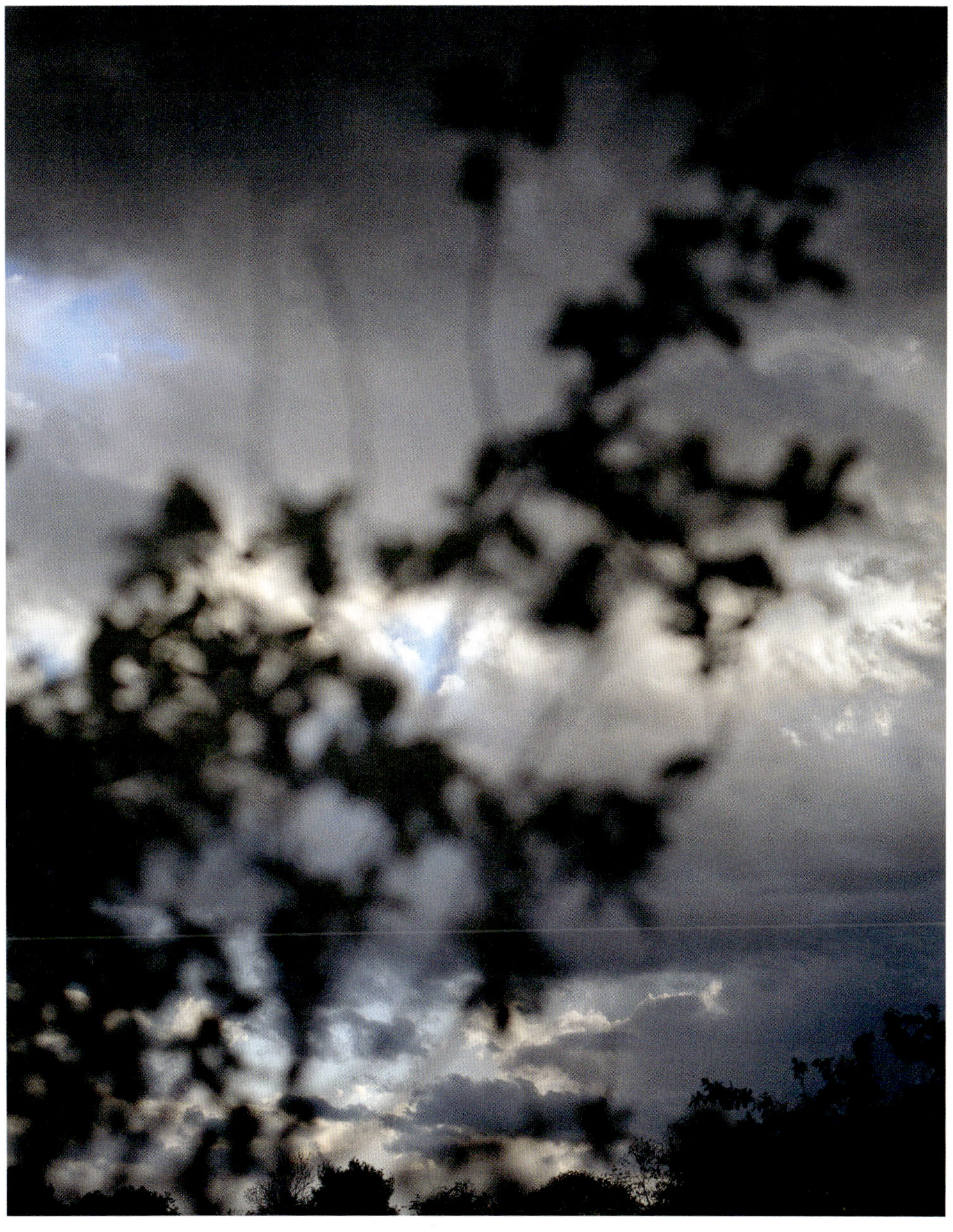

*Pandemic, Watford, May 2020*

*Loveliest of trees, the cherry now*
*Is hung with bloom along the bough,*
*And stands about the woodland ride*
*Wearing white for Eastertide.*

*Now, of my threescore years and ten,*
*Twenty will not come again,*
*And take from seventy springs a score,*
*It only leaves me fifty more.*

*And since to look at things in bloom*
*Fifty springs are little room,*
*About the woodlands I will go*
*To see the cherry hung with snow.*

*Loveliest of Trees, the Cherry Now* by A.E. Housman

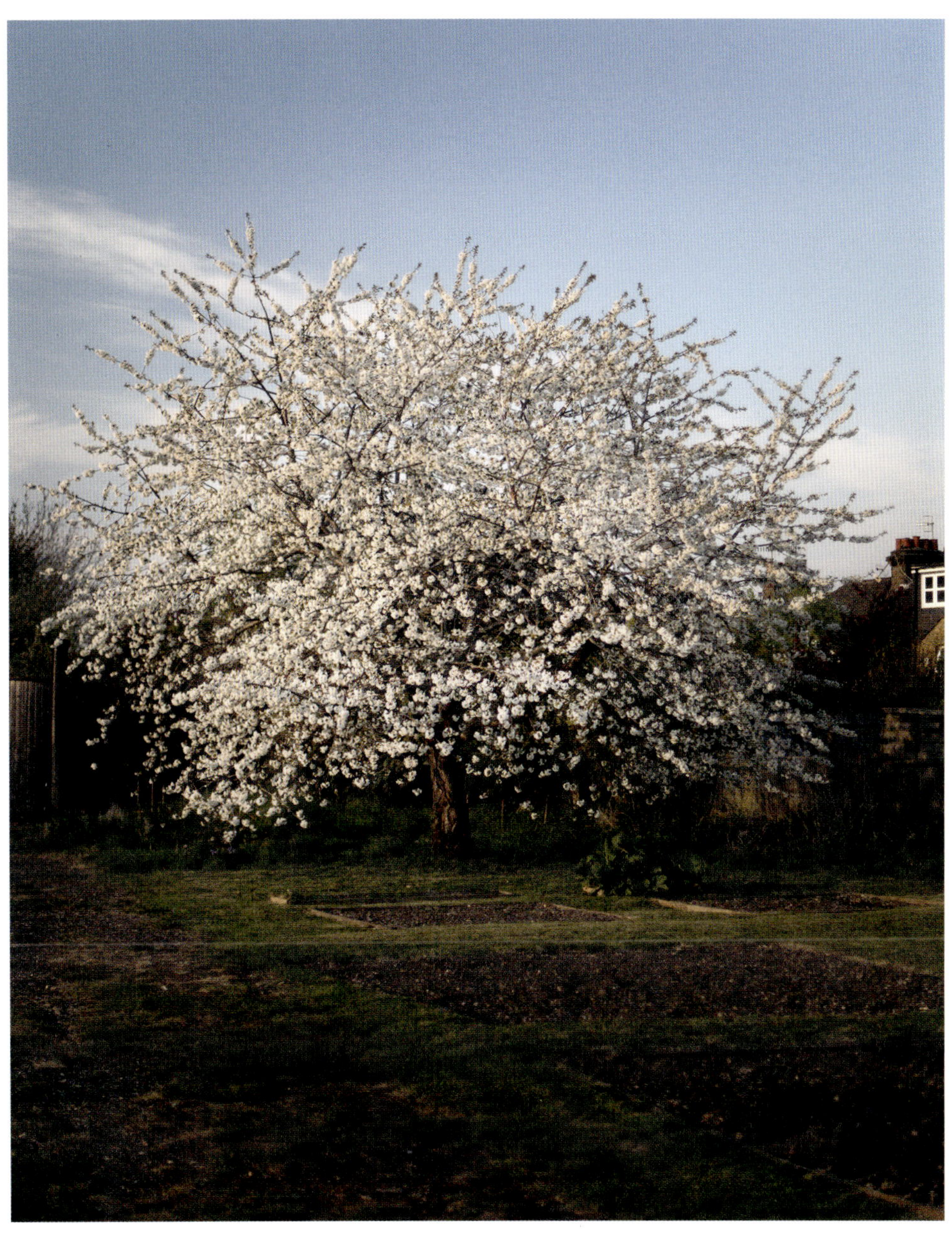

*Cherry Tree, Watford, April 2020*

# Alys Tomlinson
## *Lost Summer*

With exams cancelled and the economy on a downturn, many school-leavers saw their hopes and dreams for the future evaporate or put on hold as a consequence of the pandemic. The summer of 2020 – which was meant to be one of joy and celebration, of looking ahead to a future full of promise and potential, relishing their brief time on the cusp of adulthood – became instead one of missing out on seeing friends and saying last goodbyes. Photographer Alys Tomlinson, whose practice has explored themes of pilgrimage, faith and ritual, was caught by the idea of the cancelled prom as an irretrievable rite of passage for this age group.

Tomlinson's series *Lost Summer* captures 44 individuals between the ages of 15 and 19 in outfits they would have worn to end-of-school celebrations. Shot on a large-format analogue camera, these portraits examine what it meant for her subjects to miss this milestone and graduate at such an uncertain time; the resulting images are unexpectedly still and solemn, depicting the teenagers in moments of quiet contemplation in the midst of a tumultuous period. We feel their loss and vulnerability, but also their spirit. 'It was a very unsettling time for them, but I was surprised at how rational and positive a lot of the teenagers were,' says Tomlinson. 'They seemed to have this real inner strength and resilience that I very much admired. I wanted that to come through in the portraits.' Many of Tomlinson's subjects told her that, despite its difficulties, the lockdown had created space for them to discover new passions and ways of being.

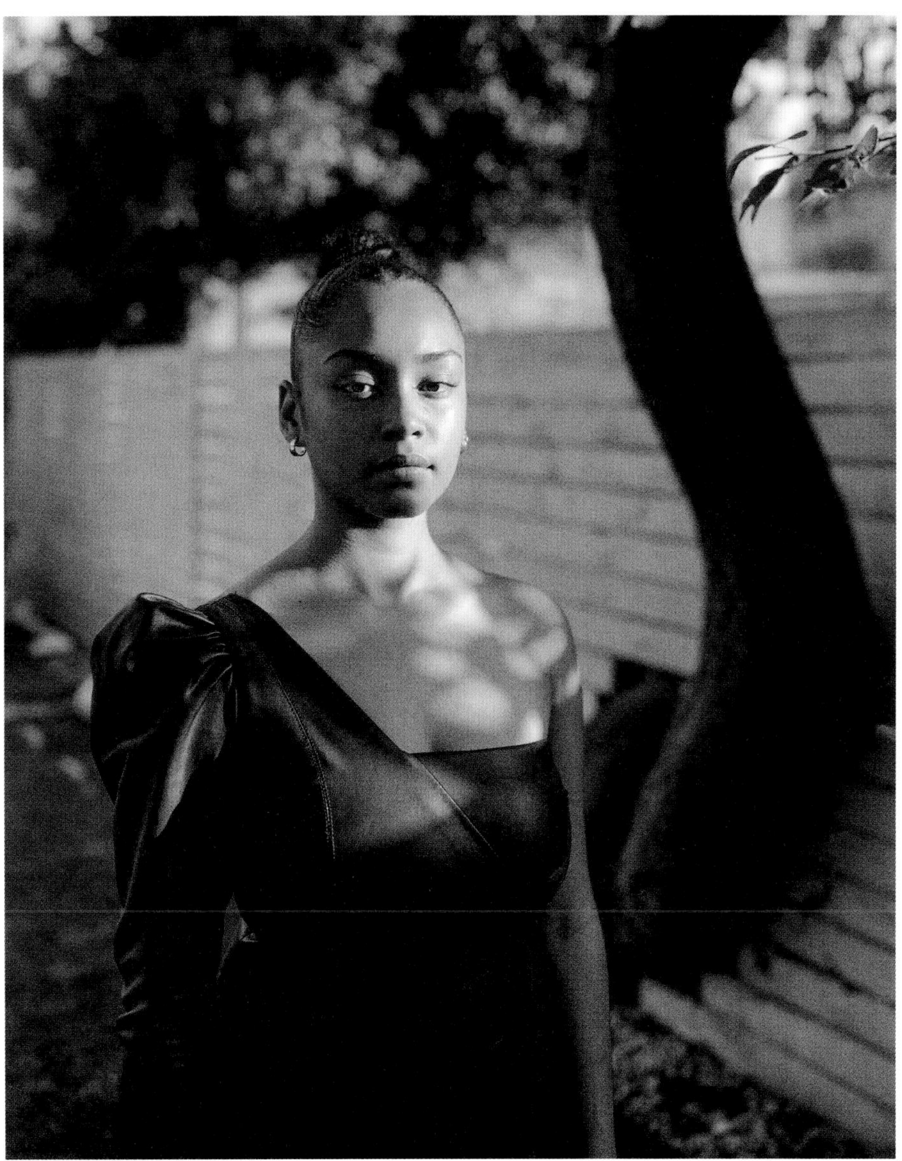

*Precious*

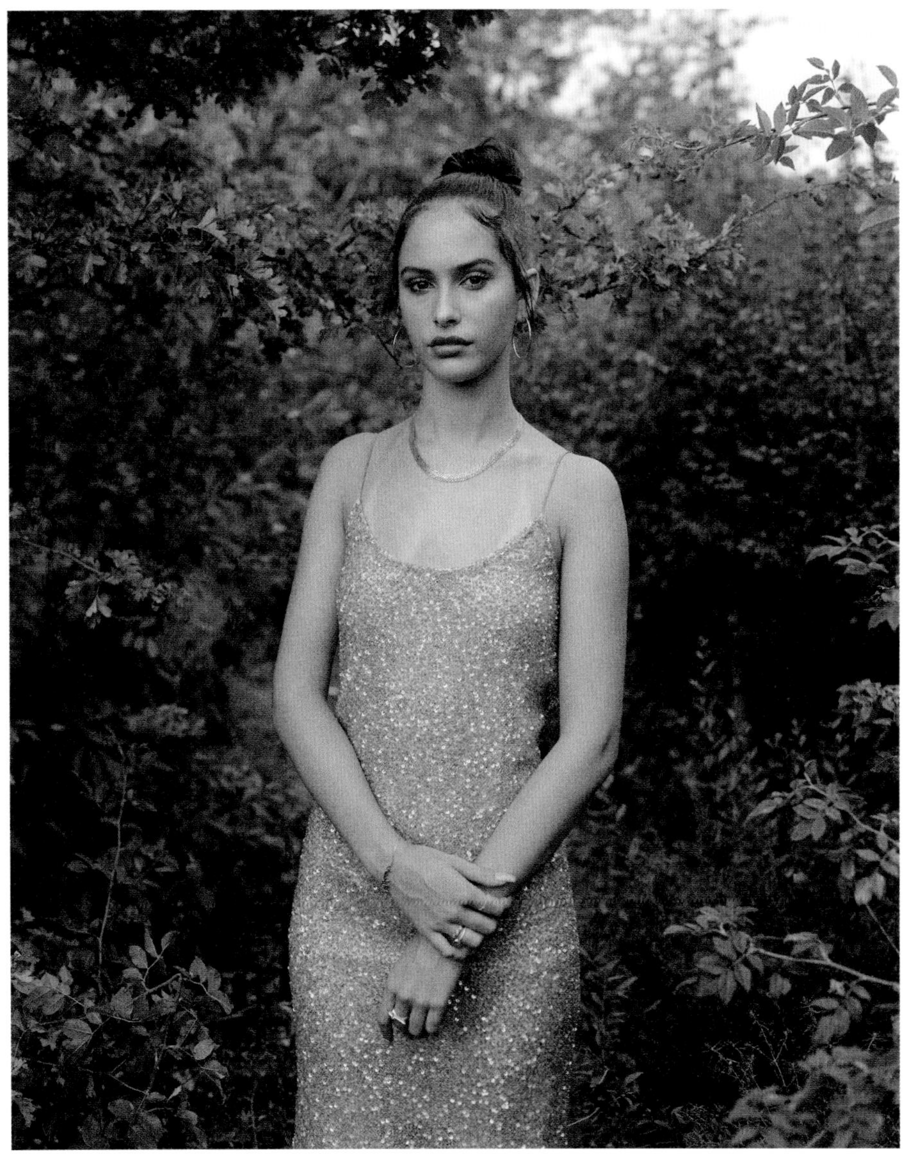

*Ruby*

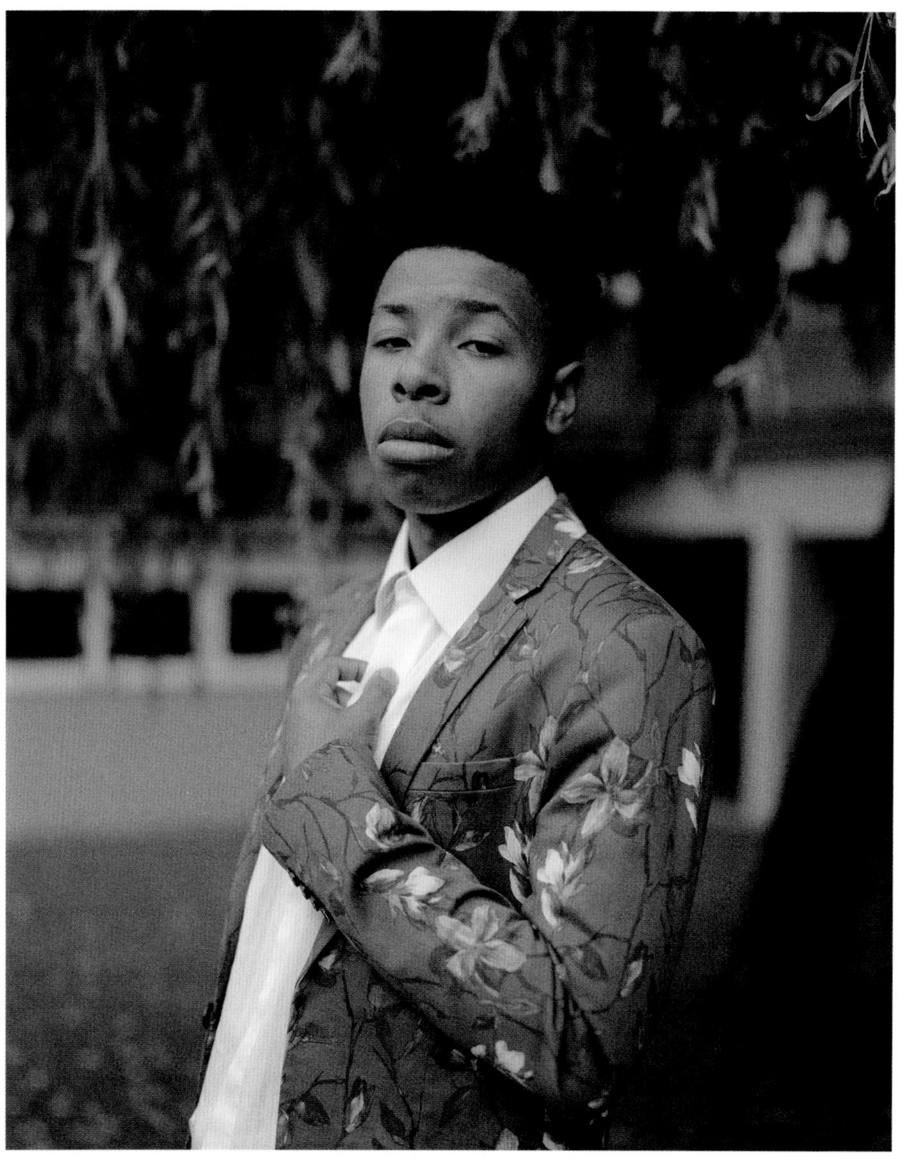

*Fabian*

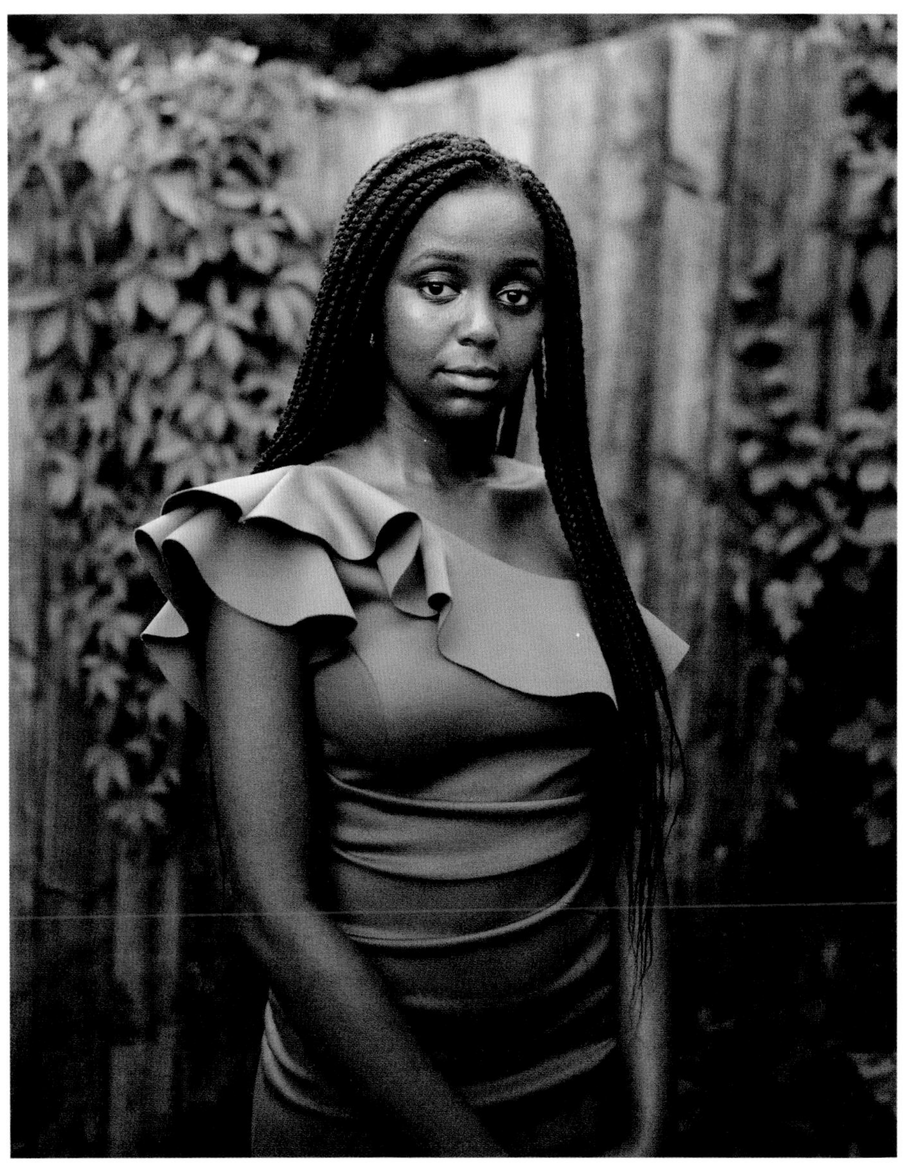

*Ruthann*

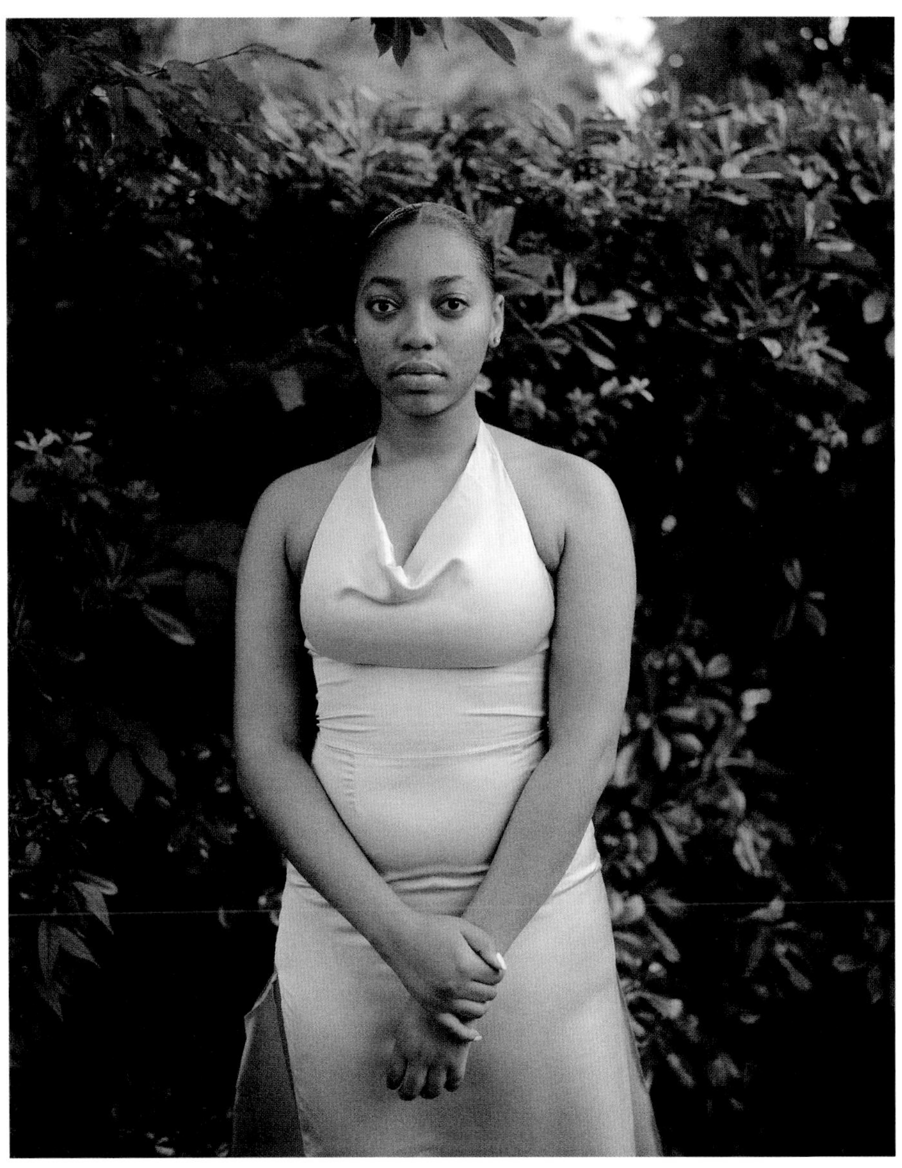

*Jameela*

Samuel

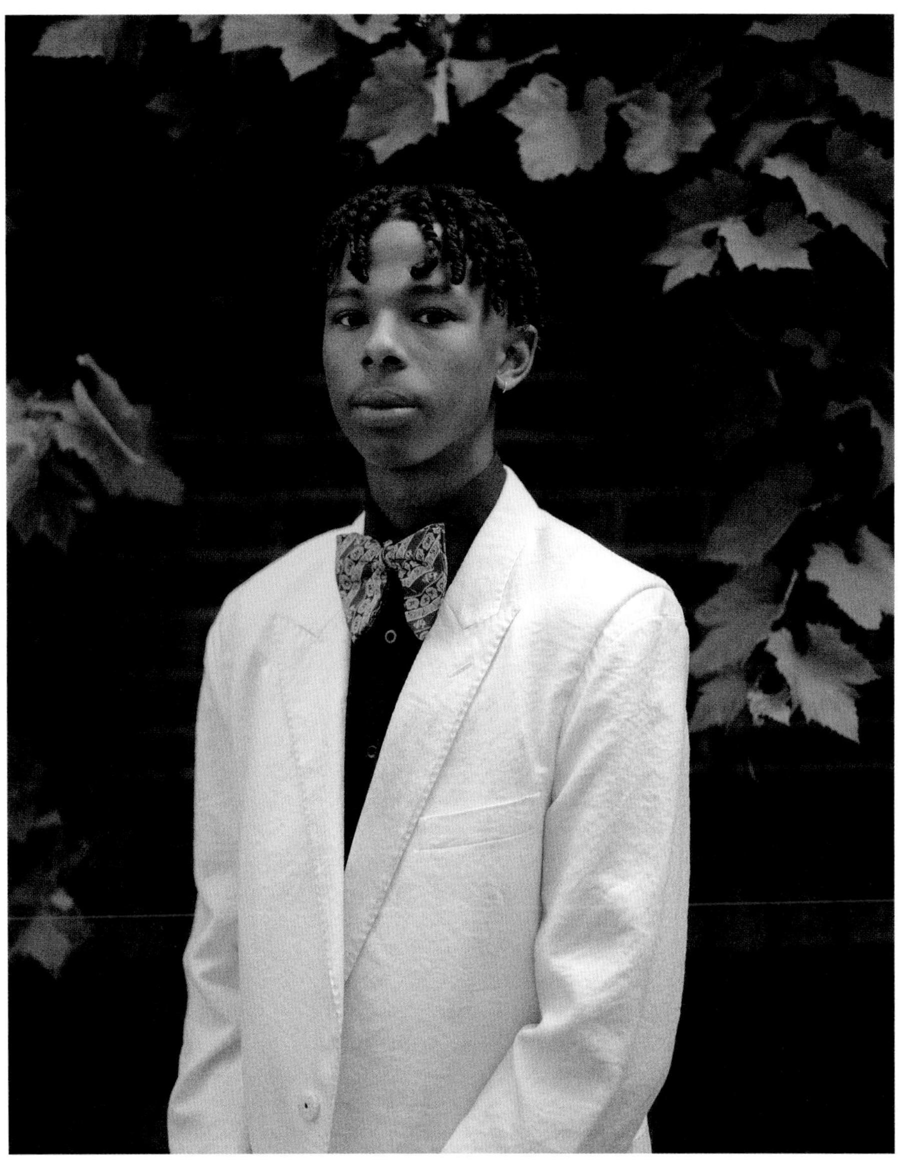

Samuel

# Philipp Ebeling
## *Closer*

The transformative experience of parenthood – that immeasurably
gratifying and at the same time endlessly challenging adventure – changed
Philipp Ebeling's relationship to photography. After the birth of his
children, he no longer travelled as he used to and instead spent a lot of
time at home discovering what it means to be a parent. His new situation prompted him to use the camera lens as a way of creating a sense
of distance between himself and the overly familiar things in the
microcosm of his home. The beginnings of his project *Closer* are rooted
in the period before the lockdown, but when the pandemic hit and
Ebeling's feelings of isolation as a parent collided with the shared
experience of collective confinement, the ongoing series was cast in
a different light.

'The lockdown gave the work a new sense of urgency and different
framing; being stuck at home became a global affliction,' says Ebeling.
'Sometimes in order to see the things closest to you, you are forced to wear
blinkers from everything else. My world shrank and became larger at
the same time.' In *Closer*, Ebeling lets us into his world – we share his loving
gaze towards his children and his wife, experiencing the minute details
of their everyday existence. The result is a far-reaching, elegiac document
of tenderness and wonder that reveals the mundanities of life in all
their beautiful and revolting glory, exposed as if seen through a magni-
fying glass.

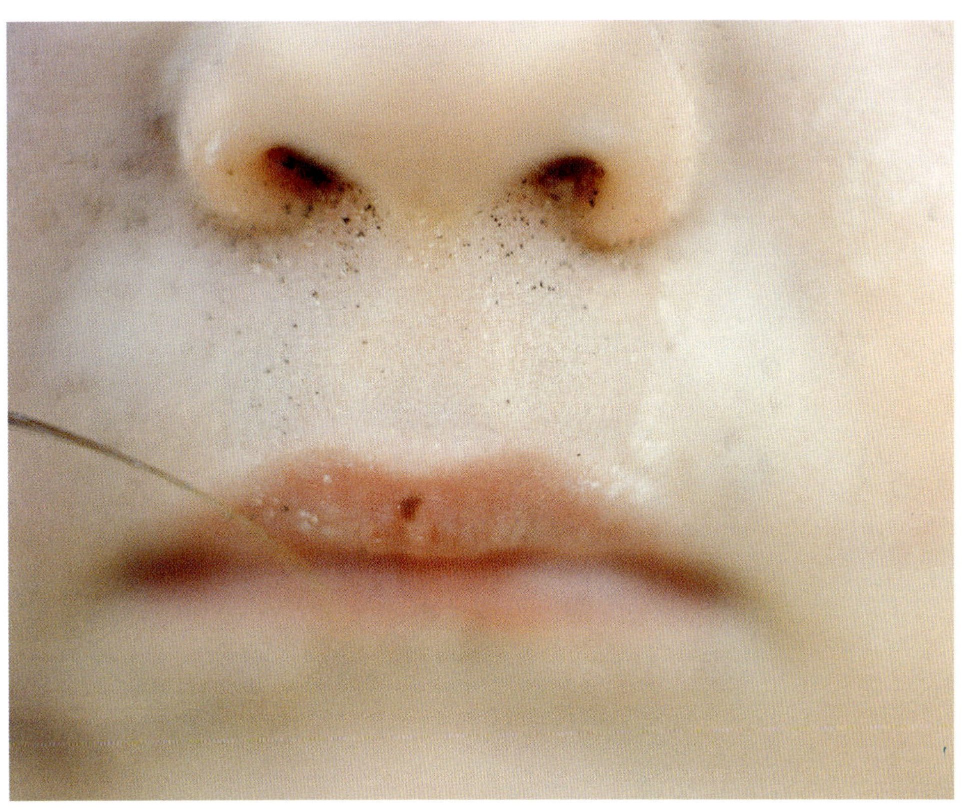

*Birthmark*

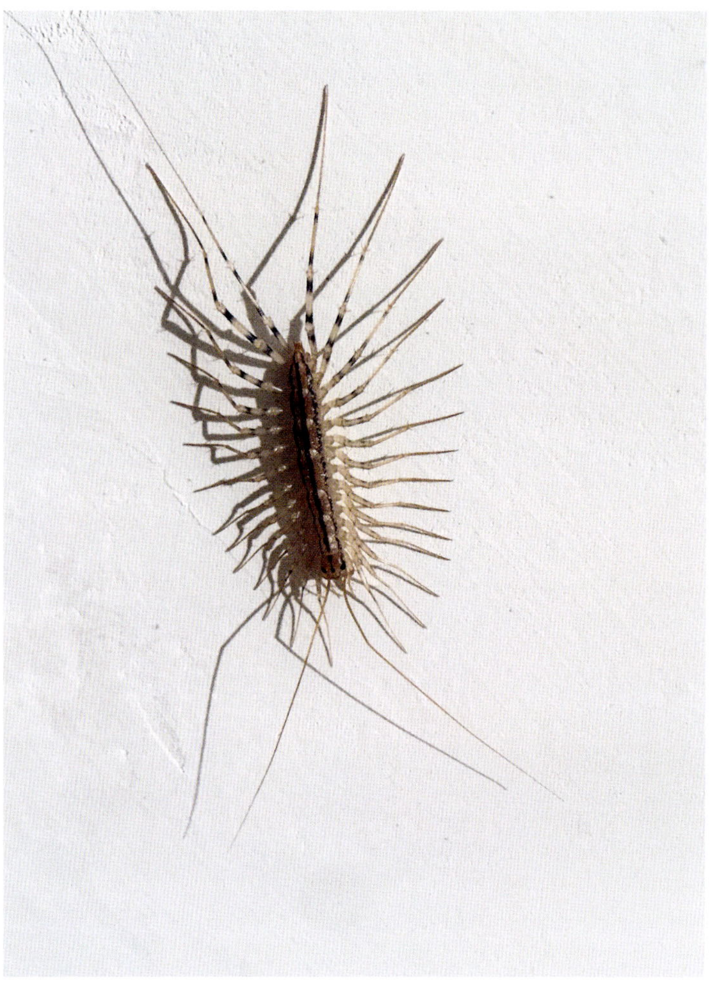

*Centipede*

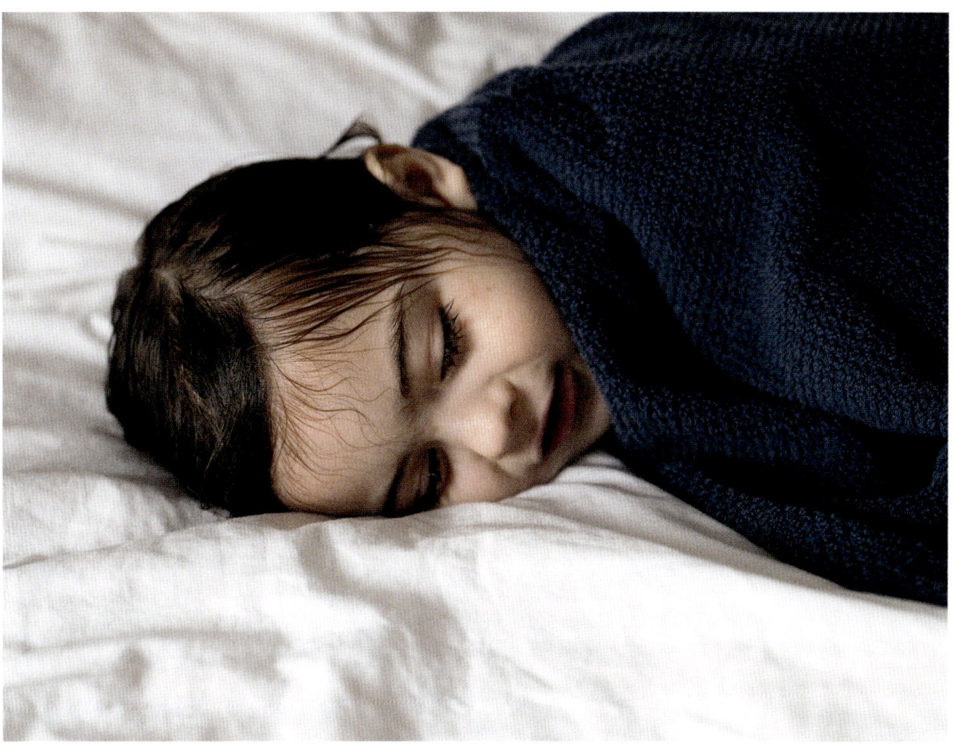

*Thea*

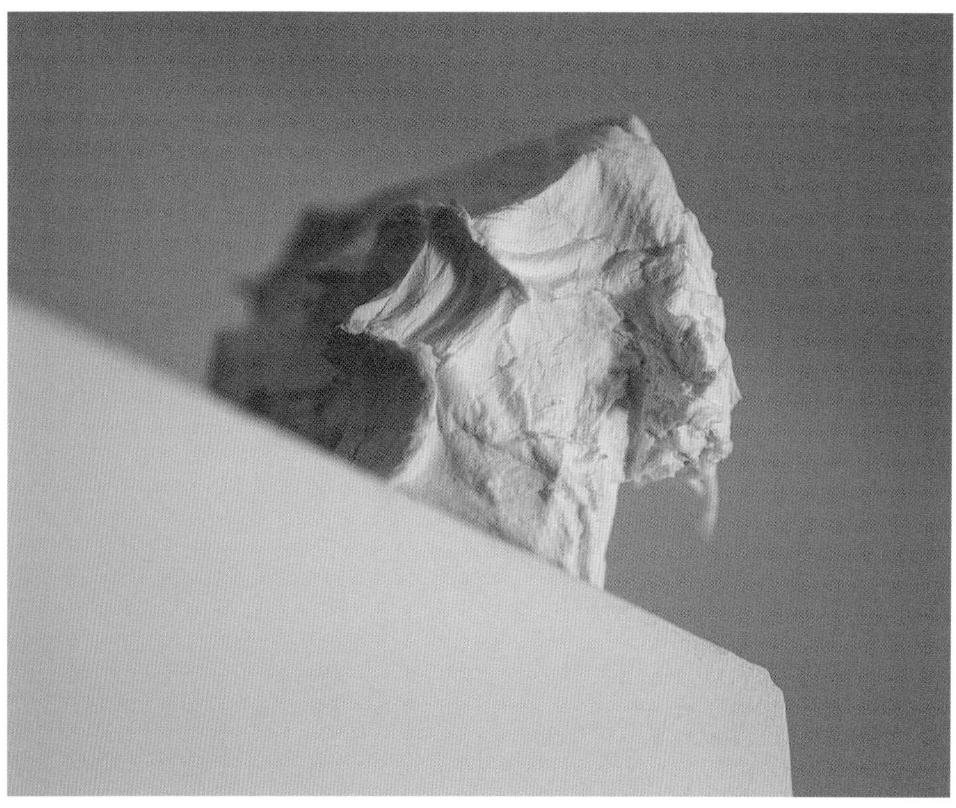

*Loo Roll I*

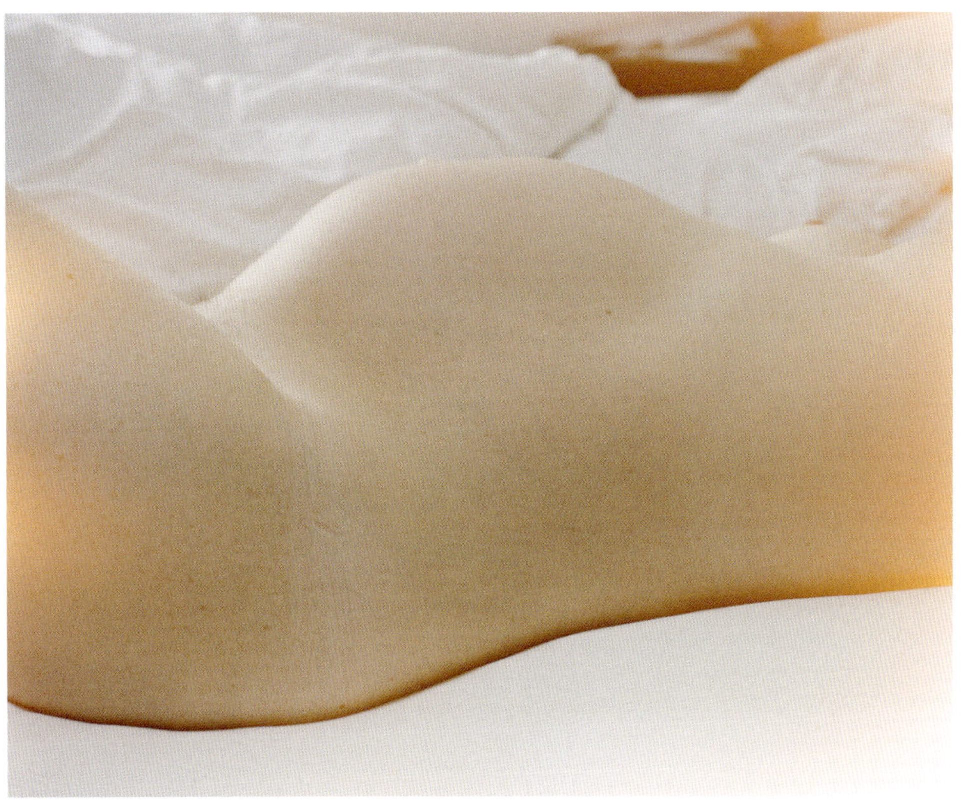

*Liv's Belly*

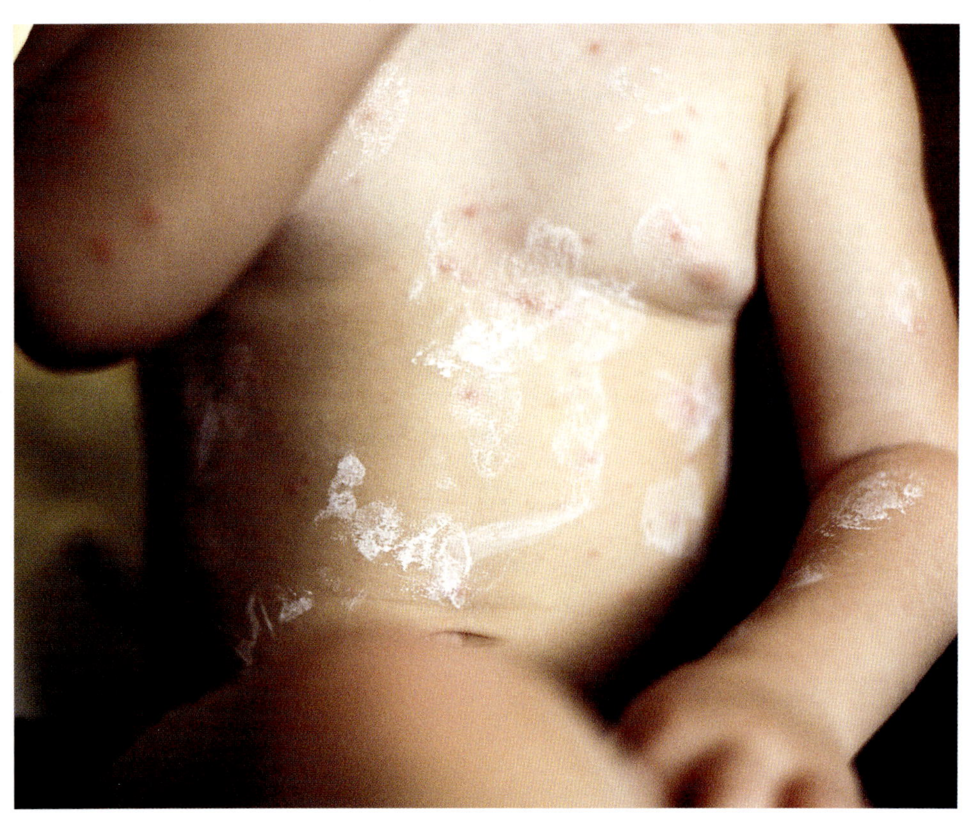

*Chicken Pox*

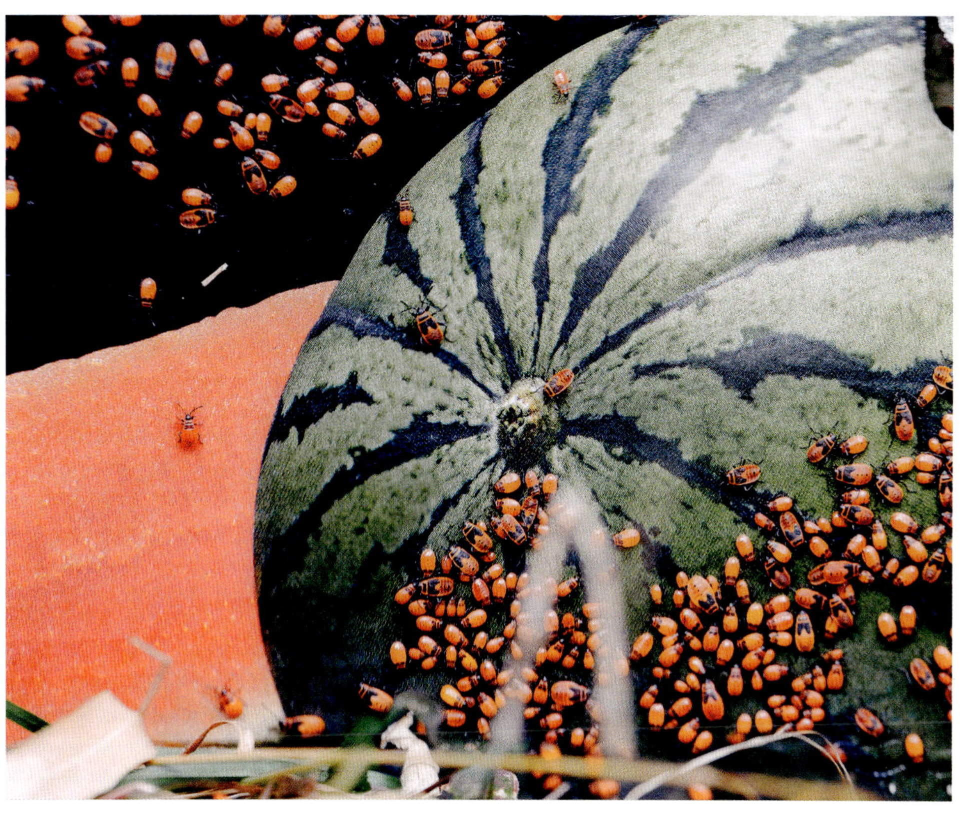

*Shield Bugs*

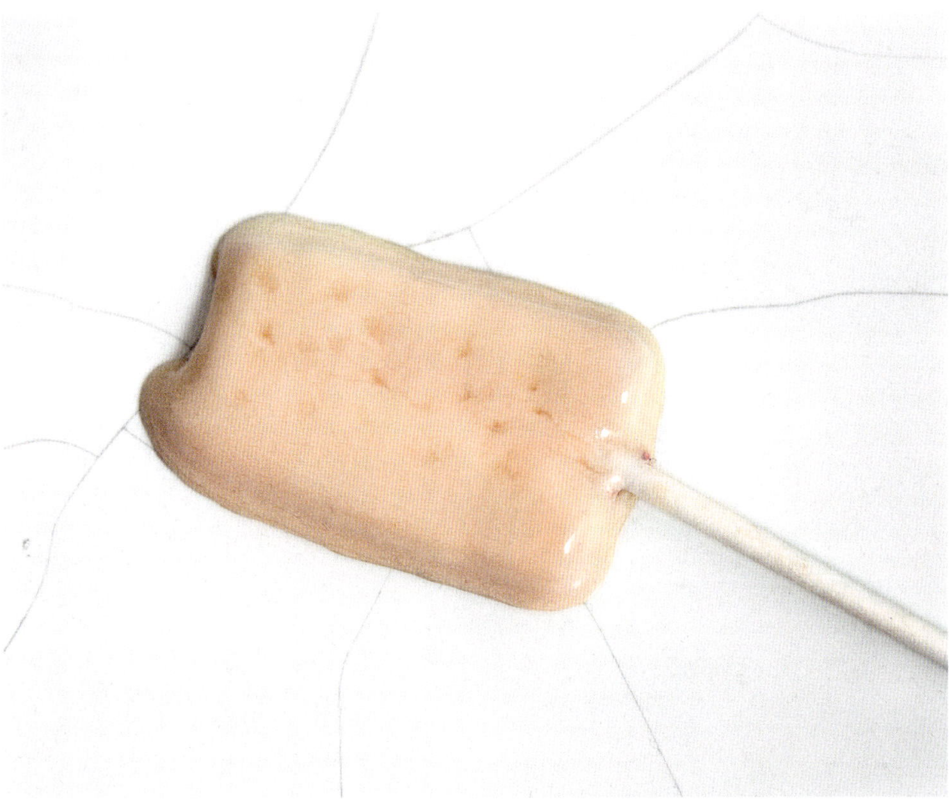

*Lollipop*

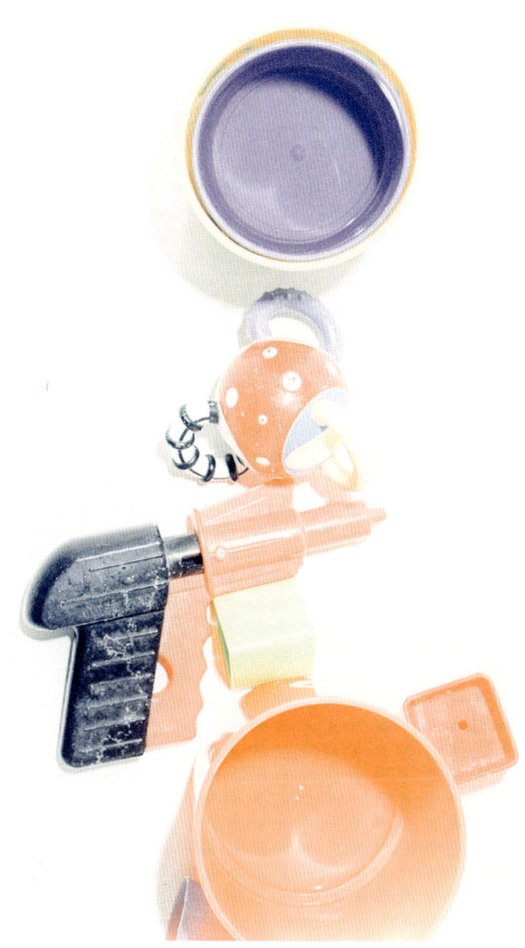

*Bath Toys*

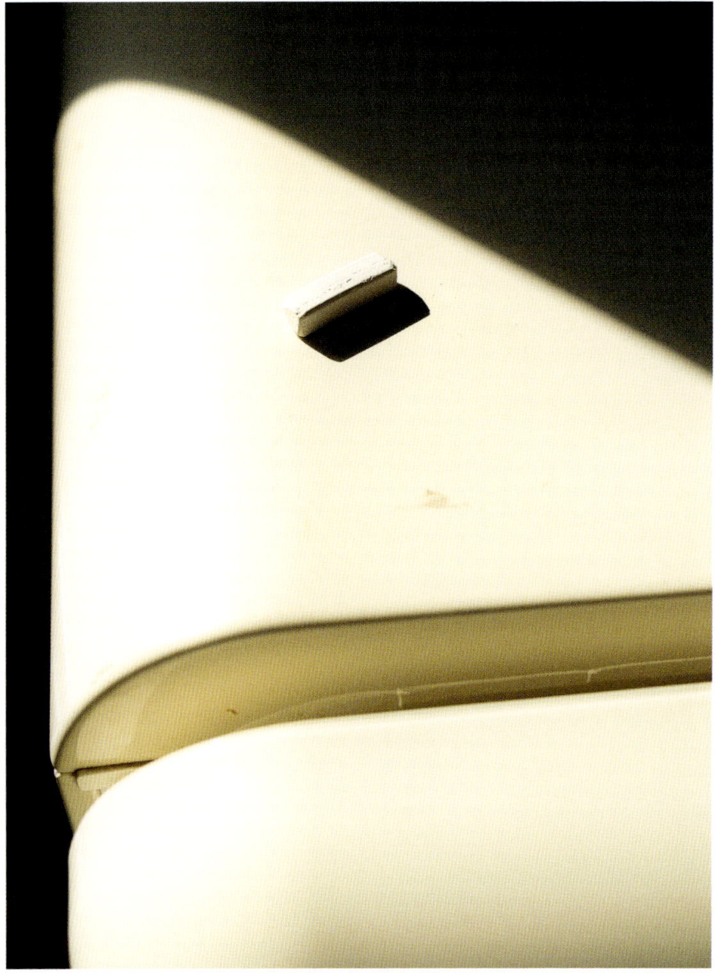

*Misplaced Chalk*

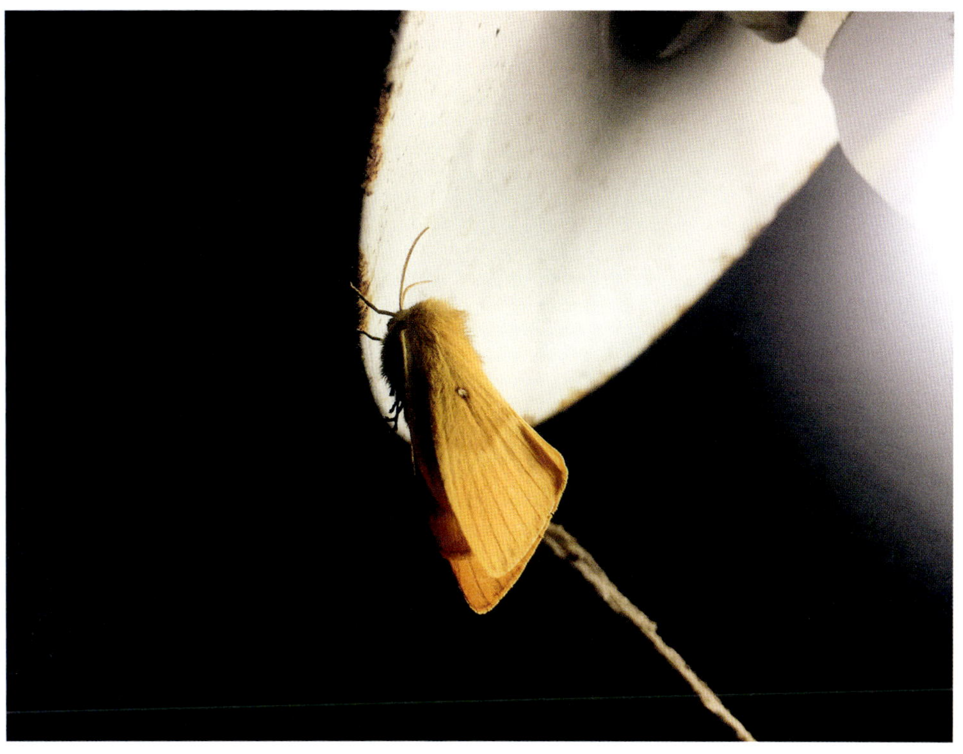

*Orange Moth*

# Celine Marchbank
## *Shot in Isolation*

When Celine Marchbank contracted Covid-19 ahead of the first nation-wide lockdown, she began exploring her home for a subject that felt worth photographing. With spring unfolding, it was the flowers she picked from her garden and allotment, placed in little pots around her house, that caught her attention. For Marchbank, these plants encapsulated the bittersweetness of that strange, uncertain period when the world came to a halt; a time of bulk-buying and communal panic. Cast in a soft evening light reminiscent of 17th-century still-life paintings, Marchbank portrayed her delicate blooms in varying stages of wilting and decay. They are symbolic of her acute awareness of both her own and the world's mortality: 'We were being bombarded with the language of death constantly. Every day we were talking about how many people had died and how many people were in hospital. I was interested in how the flowers reflected that in some way. I noticed that each day the flowers were slightly more aged, more petals dropped. And in that weird atmosphere, it was the only visual way of noticing time was passing.'

The process of making these photographs was therapeutic for Marchbank; it gave her a routine and brought consolation, beauty and joy in a time of gloom. Flowers are a common thread throughout her work – they serve as a point of connection to her late mother whose love for nature and gardening also runs through Marchbank's veins. 'My work is a lot about emotions and feelings: it reflects the time and mood that I'm going through. I was interested in the idea that things were still ticking away during the lockdown, even though the world very much felt at a standstill. It made me feel hopeful.'

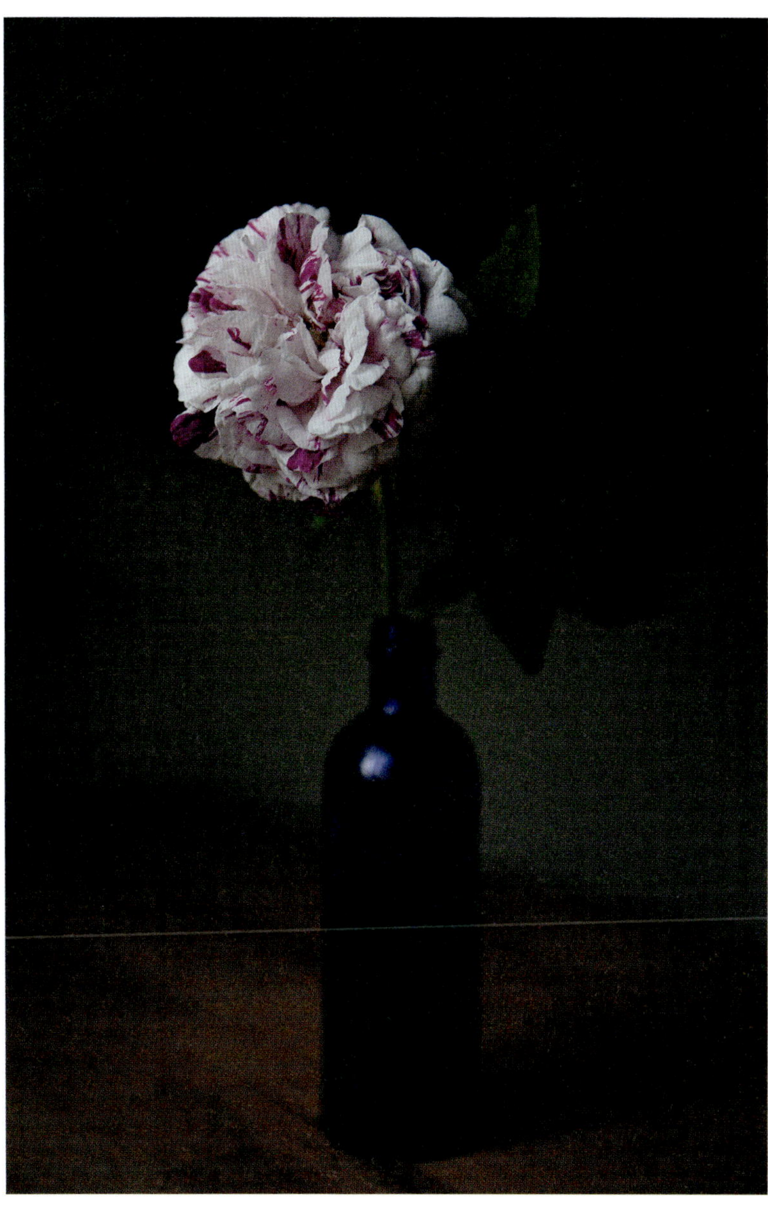

*14 May, 2020*

*13 April, 2020*

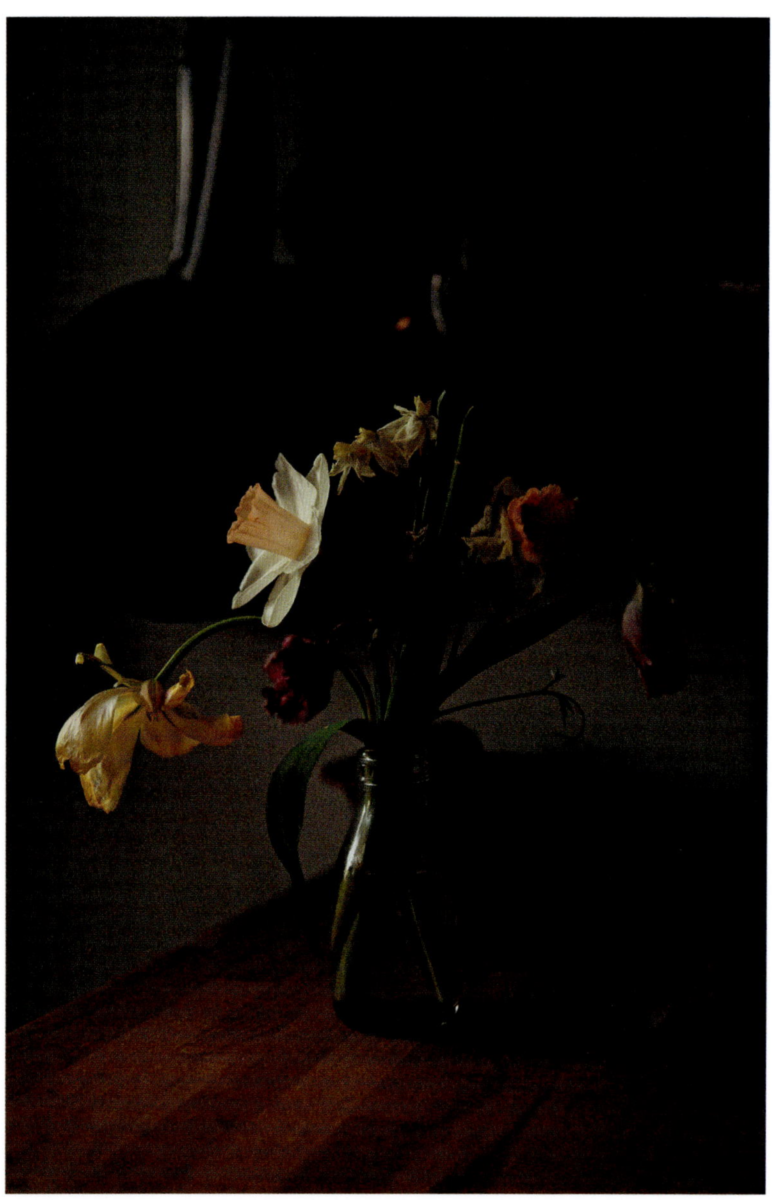

*13 April, 2020*

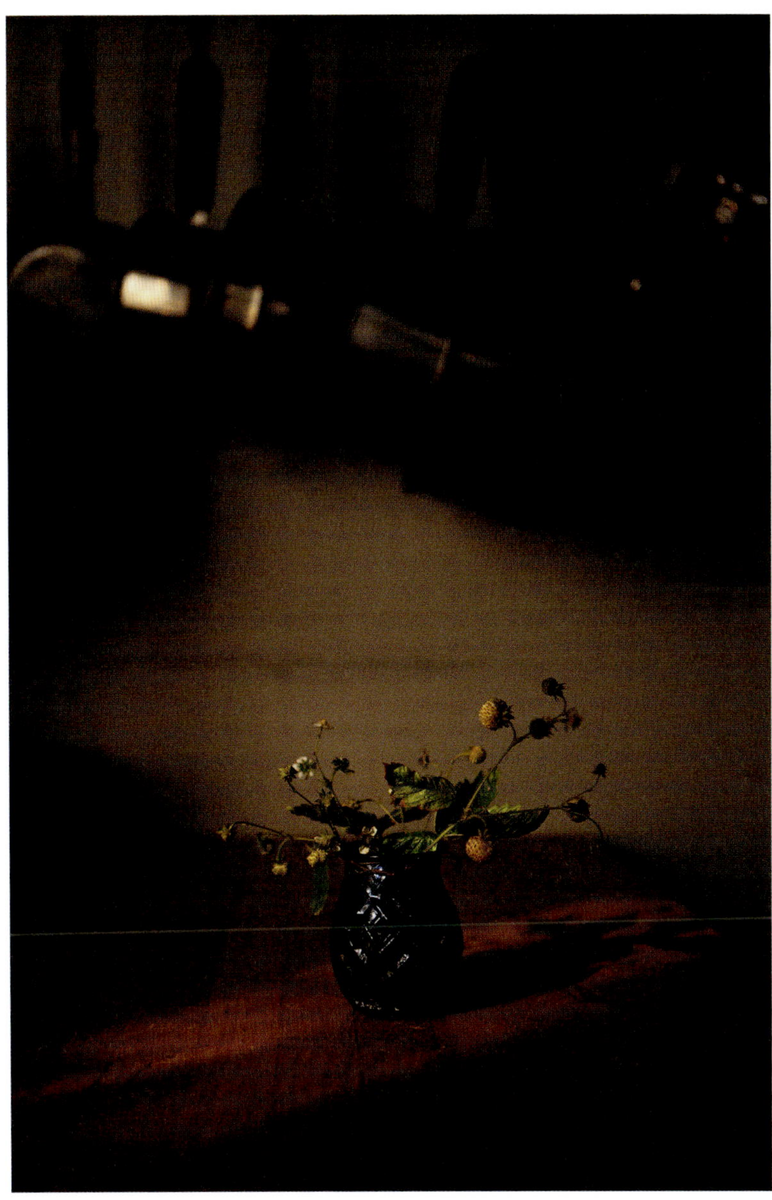

*19 May, 2020*

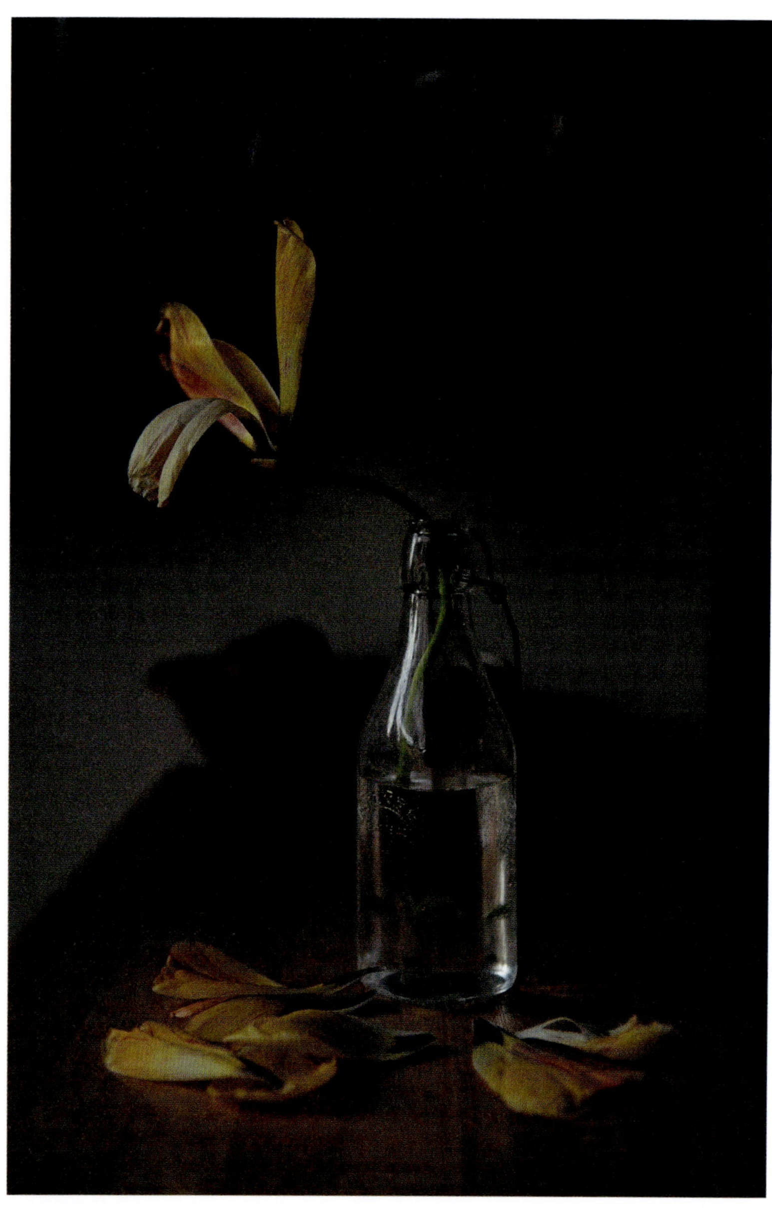

*15 April, 2020*

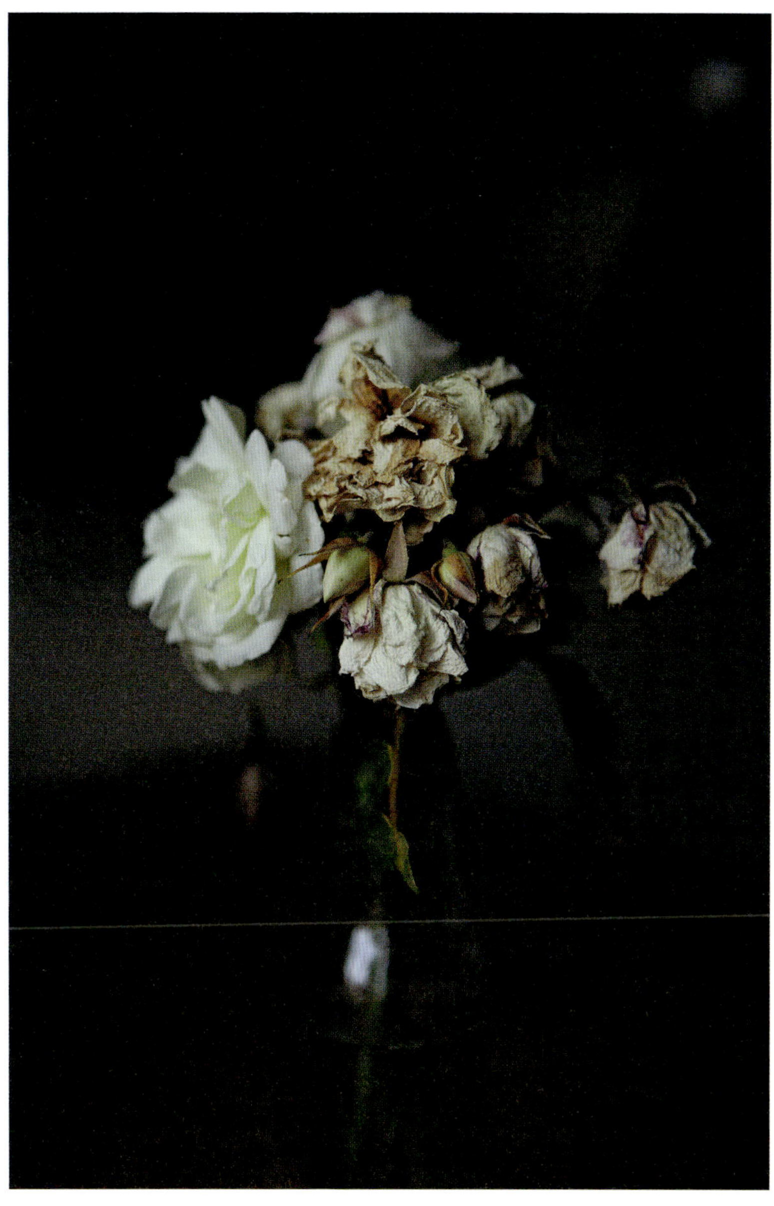

*29 May, 2020*

# Sophie Wedgwood
## *City Parks*

Lonely hearts, oddballs, teenage romances, young families, old friends: in Sophie Wedgwood's eyes, London's parks are a captivating stage set for an eclectic cast of characters. Both curated and natural, she thinks of parks as ambiguous spaces of recreational freedom and performative constraint in which city dwellers can be alone together. 'In the first lockdown,' she says, 'I started walking around parks and saw all these really intimate and personal moments, while big events and huge shifts were happening across the world. There was a lot of escapism. But it also showed in a way how lonely London can be.'

Loneliness and longing for connection form an undercurrent to the work – reflecting not only the shared experience of the pandemic, but Wedgwood's own personal state of being at the time: lockdown meant she was away from her husband for more than a year. Captured in this arresting portrait series, curated in collaboration with casting director Lisa Dymph Megens, Wedgwood's fleeting encounters with strangers in the park reveal great empathy and emotional depth. The influence of neorealist cinema on Wedgwood's aesthetic is palpable: somewhere between fiction and documentary, these timeless portraits depict the interplay between Wedgwood's own creative imagination and the personalities posing in front of the lens. Her subjects' voices whisper to us through small, handwritten notes that record their hopes for the future.

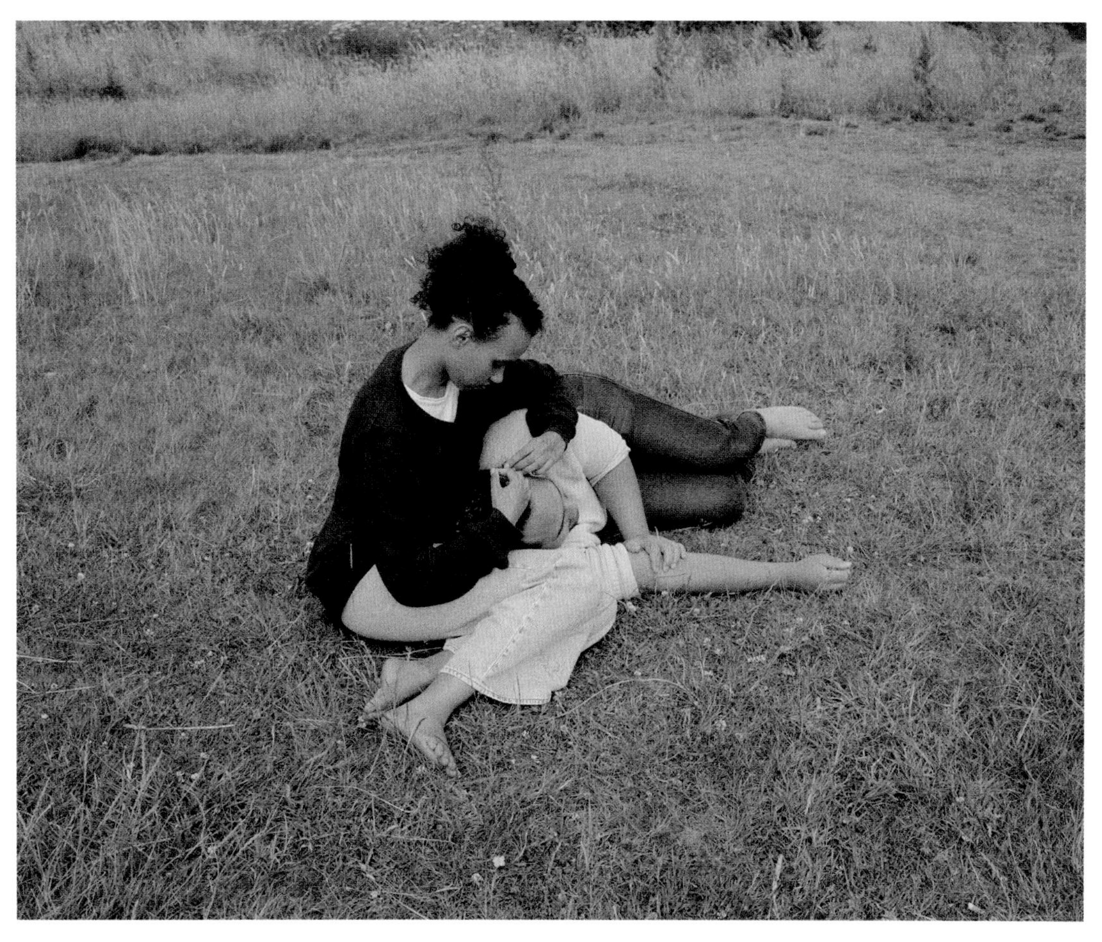

I want to be happy.
this time has shown
me all the things that
bring down my mood.

I hope that instead of merging back
into thoughtless, unstable and unsustain-
able 'normal' ~~and instead we~~
society can pause, ~~reset~~ contemplate,
and use this time to reset, and to
become a more conscious and
harmonious world.

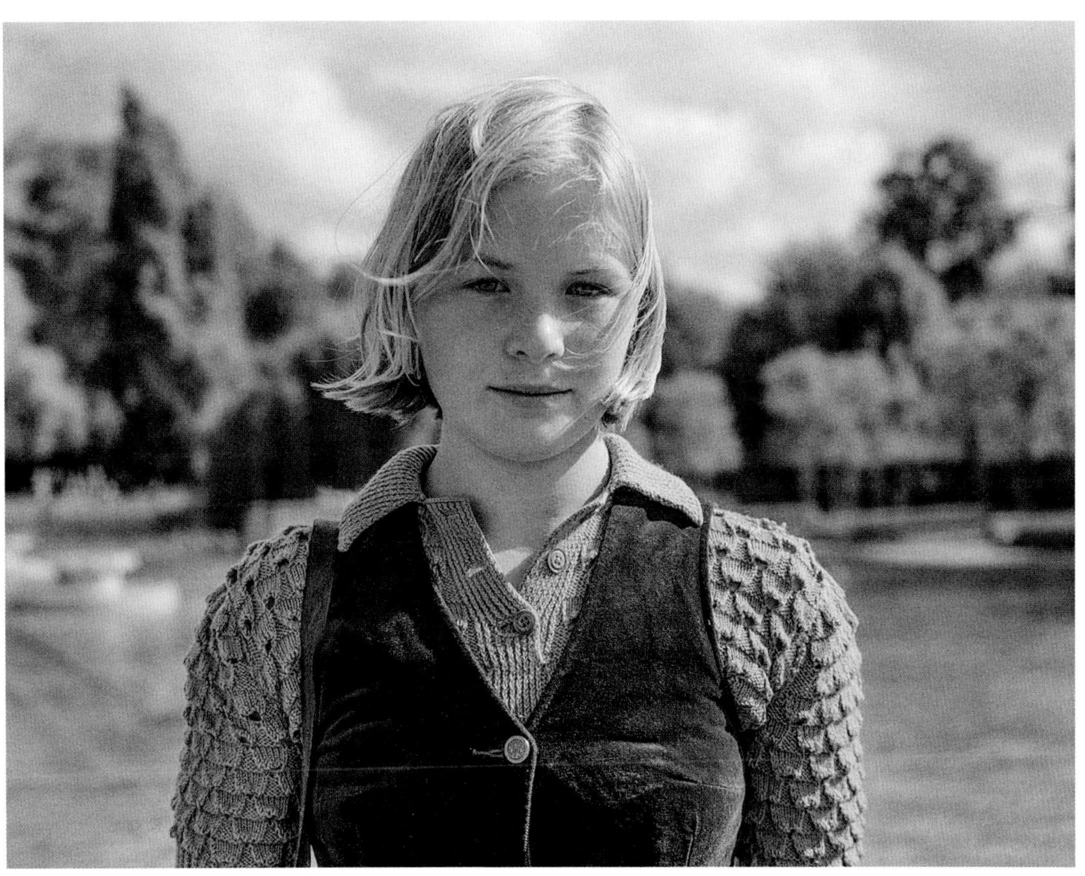

I hope to travel as much as possible around the world and help to raise more awareness about the injustices I face as a black woman in a Capitalist society. We should learn to work together to help those who can't be helped regardless of age, gender, race and religion

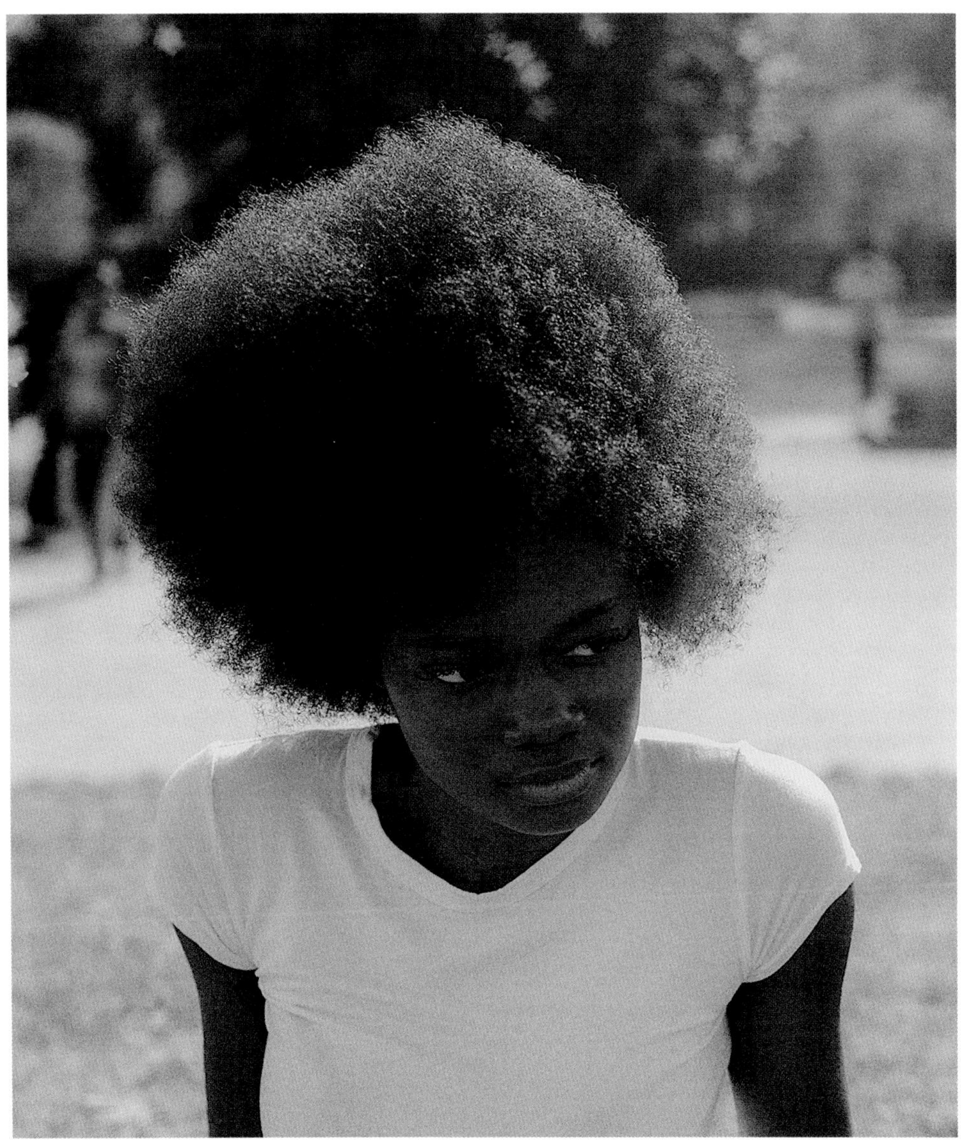

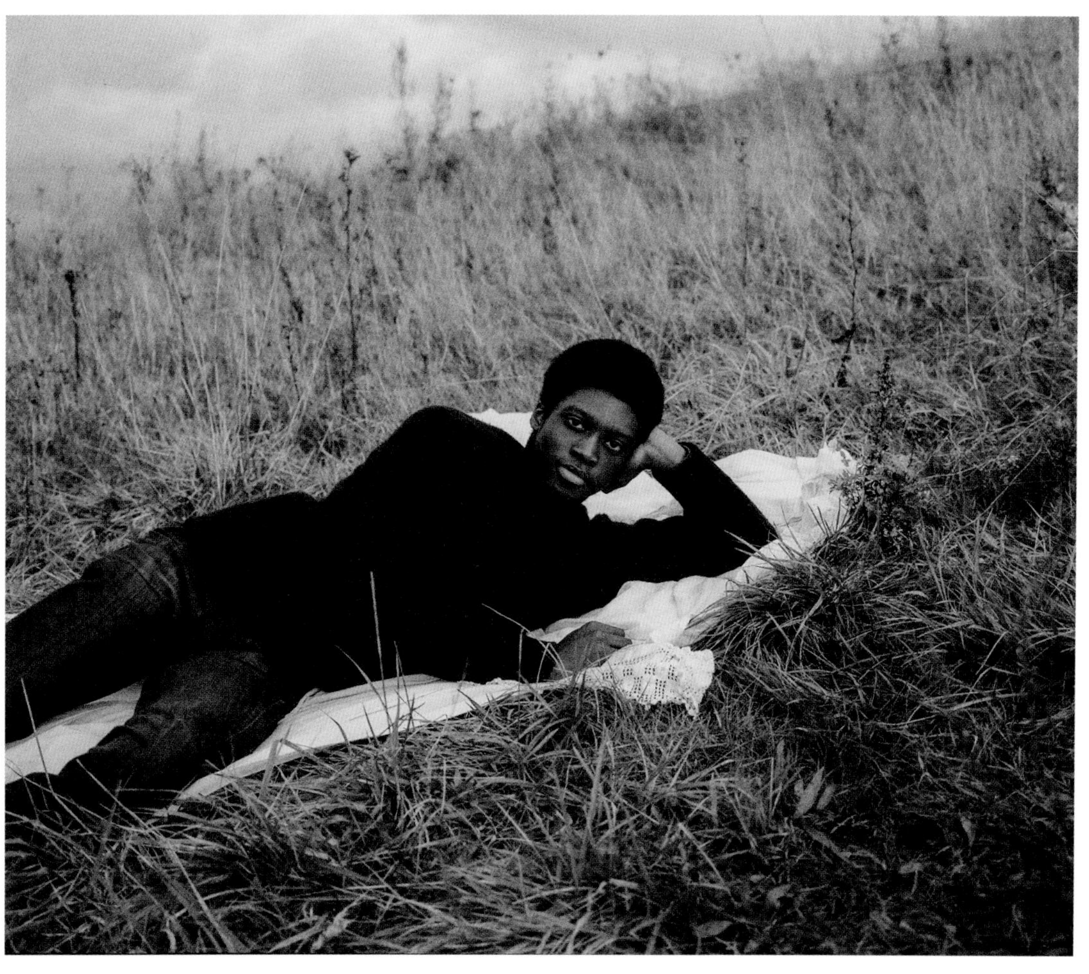

I hope to do something that will inspire people and ~~hopefully~~ hopefully make the world a tiny bit better

Anthony

Tender hopes and wild dreams. Let the creativity rise and people's voices be heard.

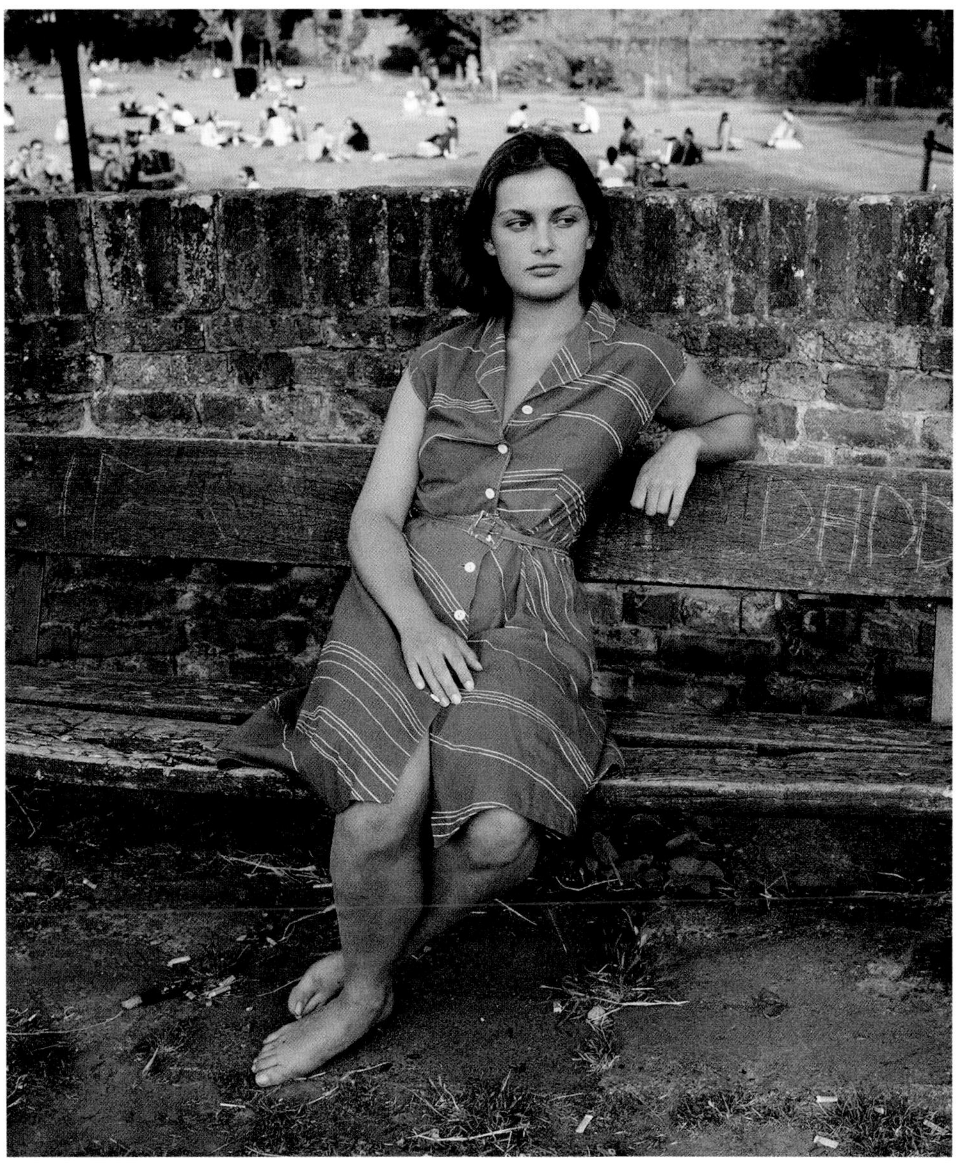

# Greg White
## *Interregnum*

The evaporation of commercial projects during lockdown led Greg White to approach photography in a way reminiscent of when he first picked up a camera as a teenager: loose and free, unburdened by the constraints of assignments or static equipment, and motivated by observations made on his daily walks around the neighbourhood. He found that the light on these early morning explorations lifted his mood and counter-balanced the gloominess of the pandemic year, with the camera acting almost as a therapeutic tool in his search for moments of peace and calm in a world thrown into disarray. 'You take a step back, and notice things you'd never noticed before,' says White. 'It was the smallest things that gave me energy and helped me through the rest of the day of home schooling, et cetera. It wasn't just the physicality of walking, it was the mental visualisation of what I was seeing that improved or helped me.'

White's changing feelings during that year – the sadness, confusion and joy – all found their way into the frame, imparted in often graphic or geometric compositions that hint at his subconscious efforts to create order from chaos. As the project evolved, many of the images accrued metaphorical meaning: cracks in the pavement, a murder of crows taking flight, dropped petals and leaves – each became subtly representative of the dark realities of the pandemic. Shot with spontaneity and intuition, this is a personal account of a collectively experienced liminal state – an interregnum – during which our lives were temporarily placed on pause, and we learnt to look just a little harder at the things around us.

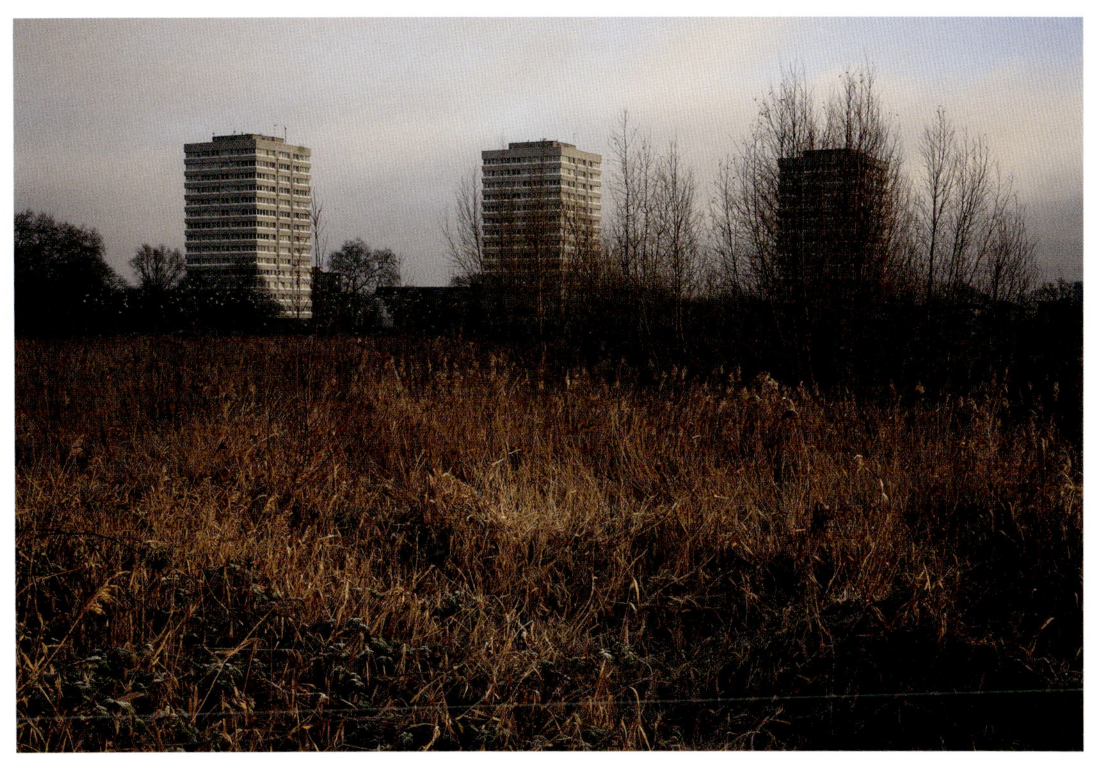

Greg White

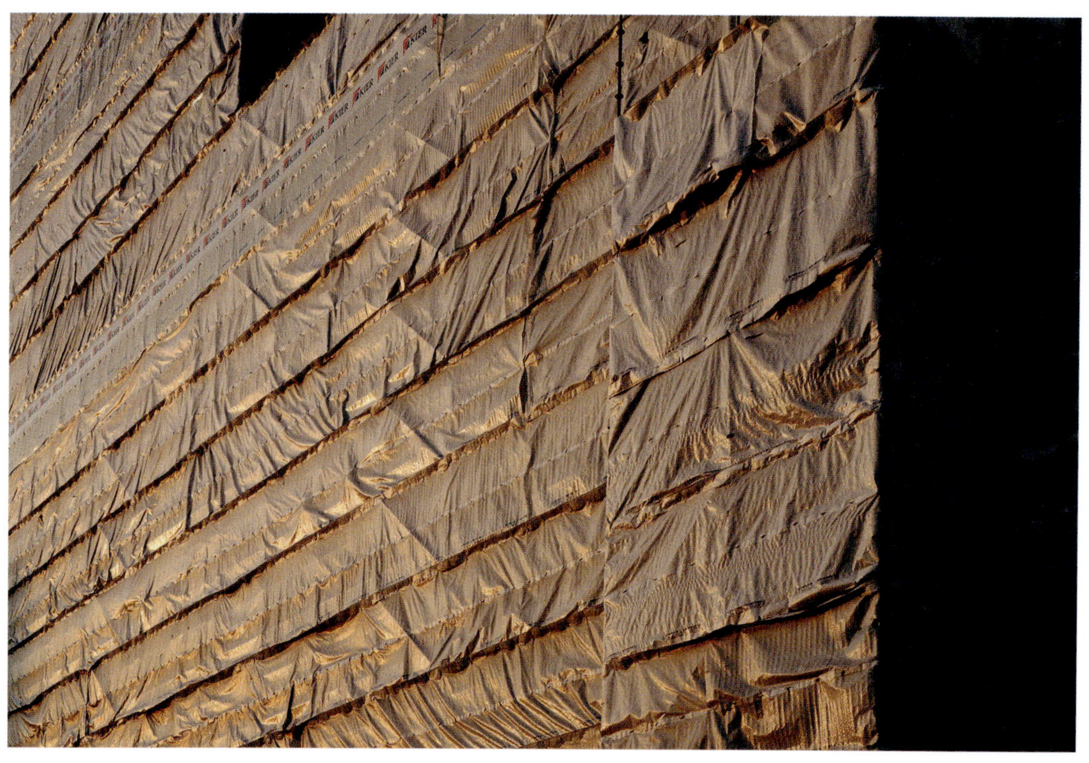

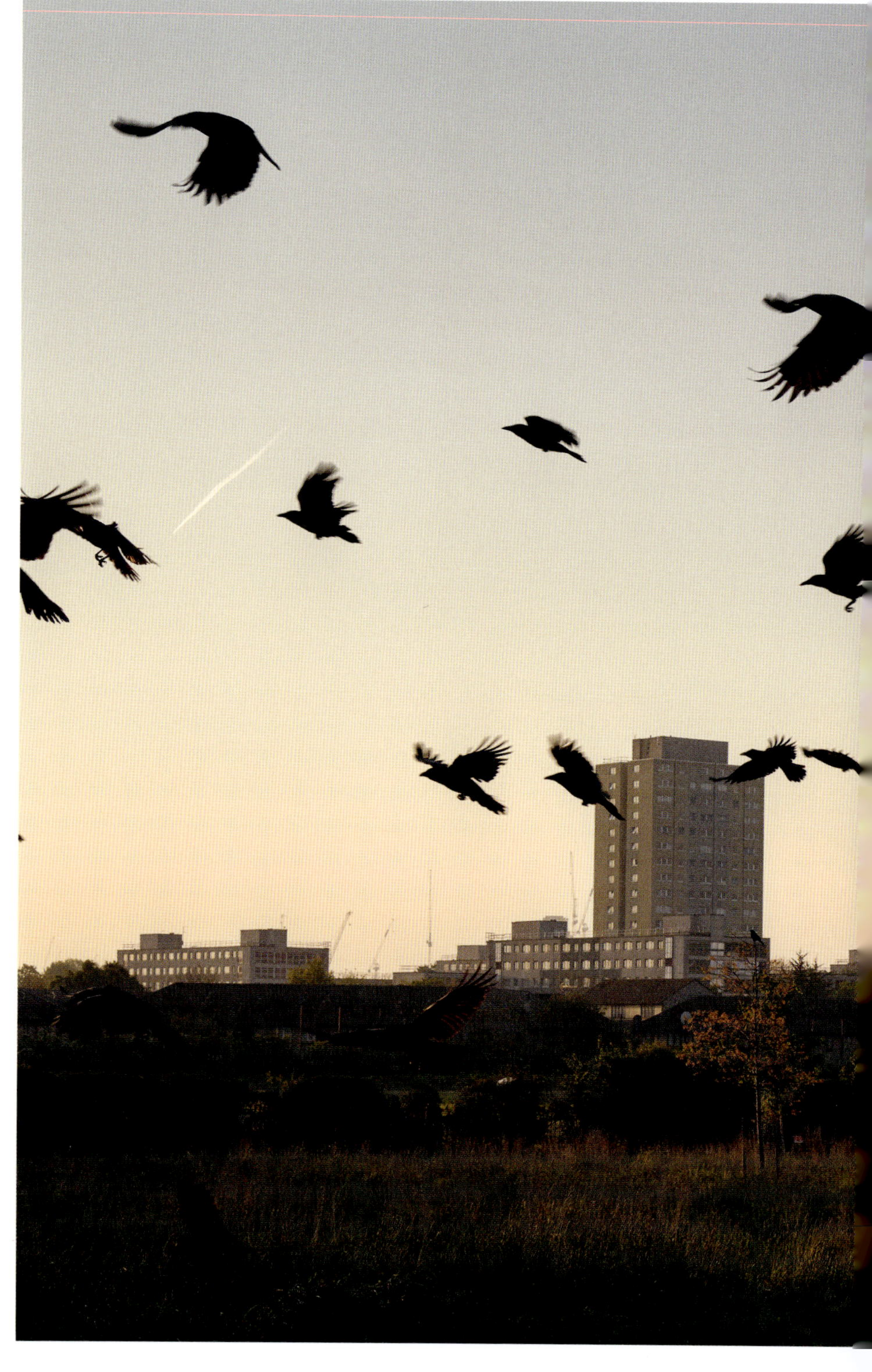

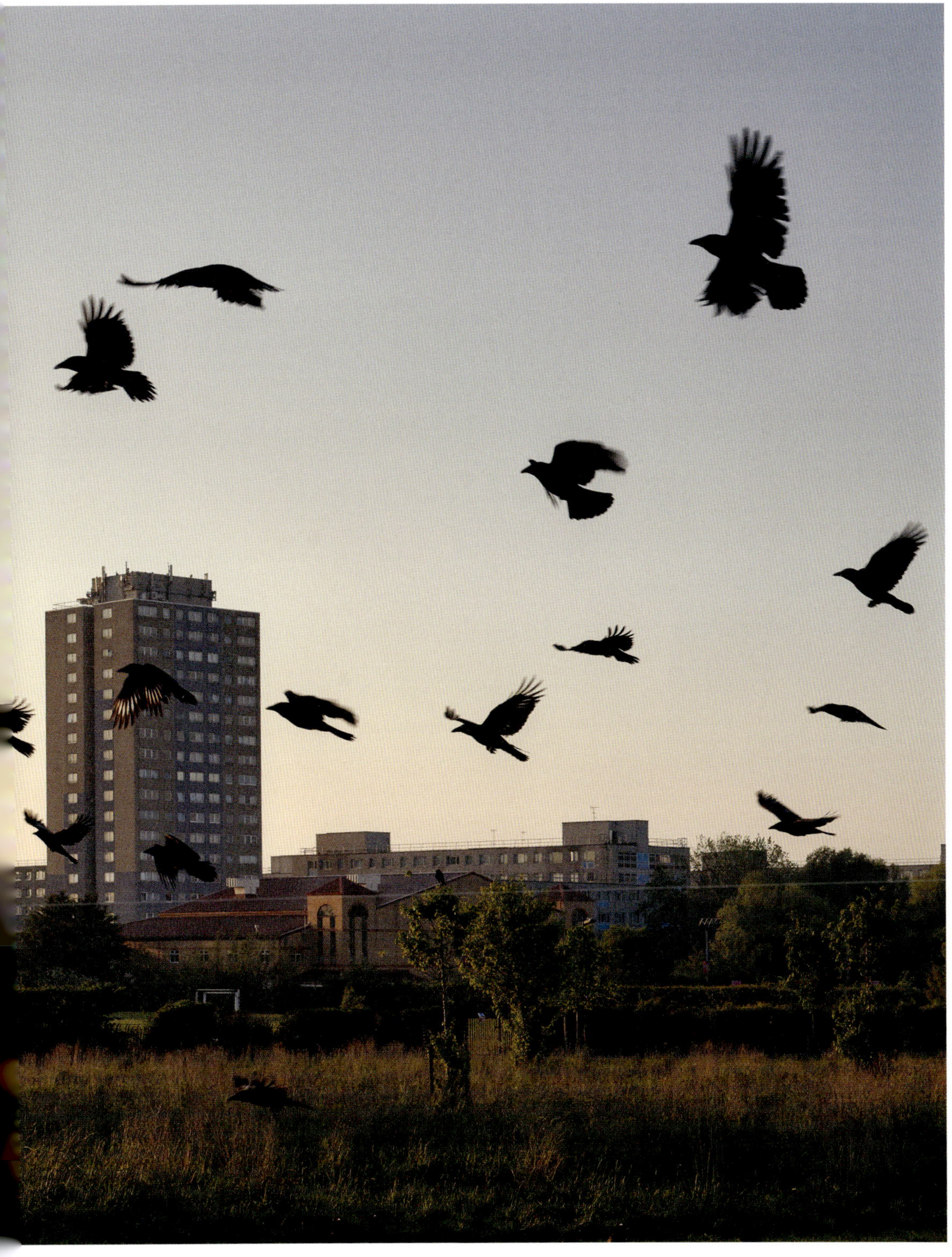

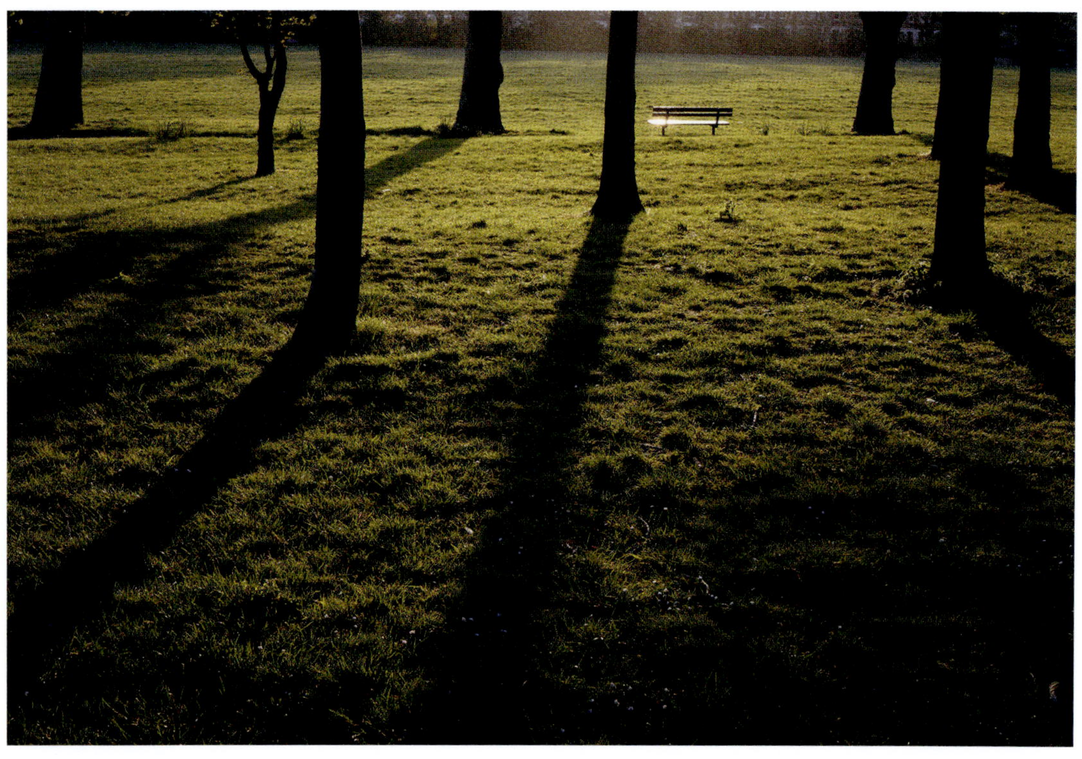

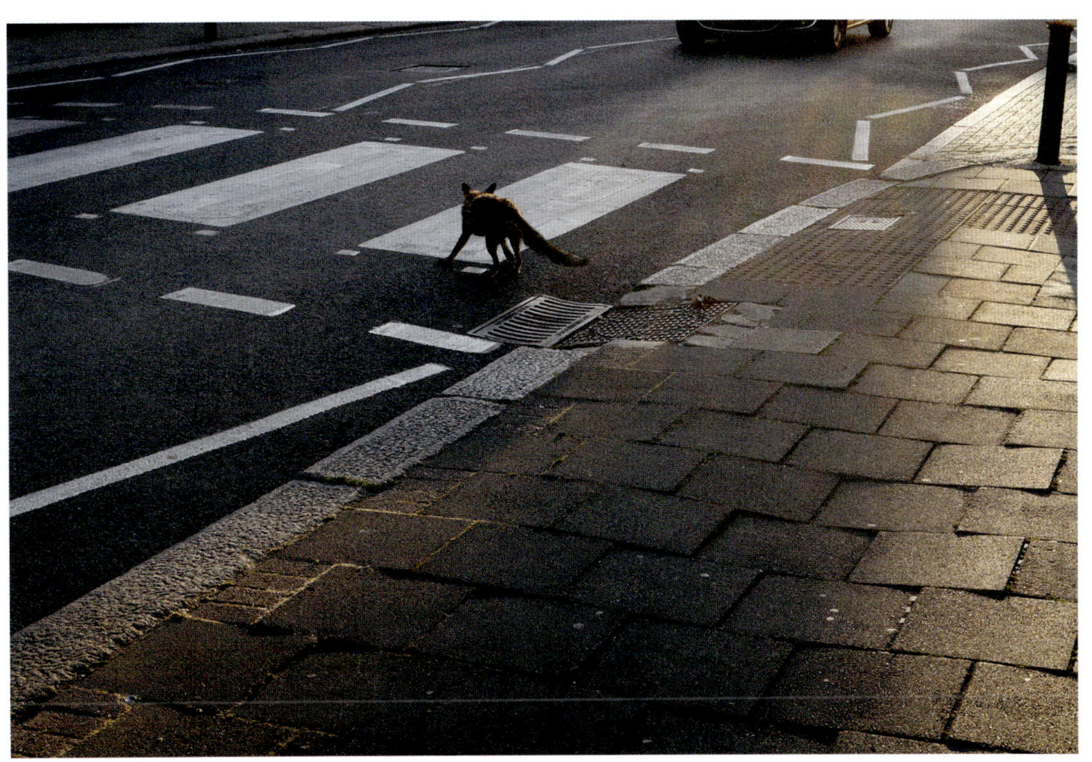

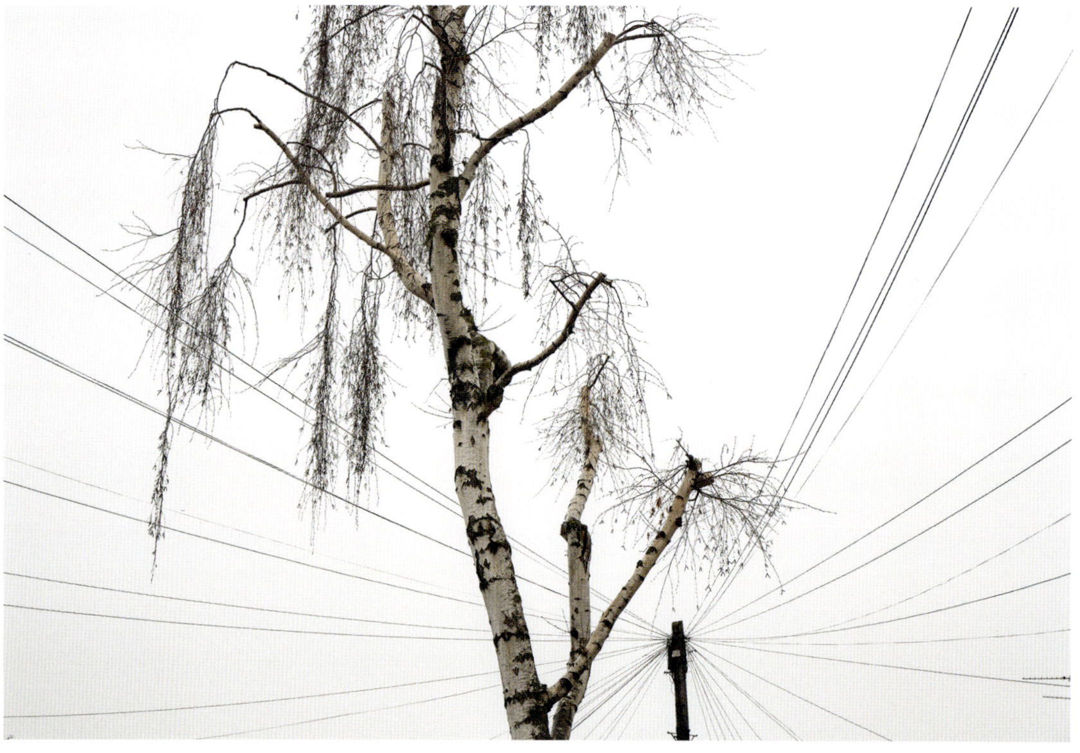

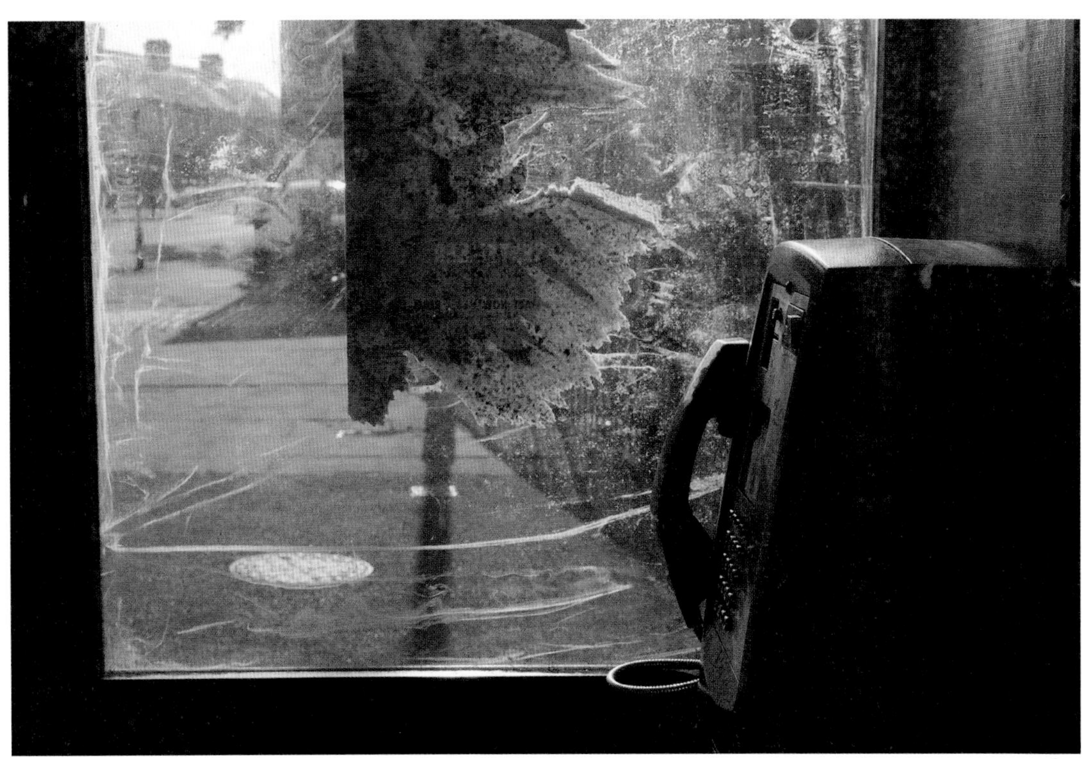

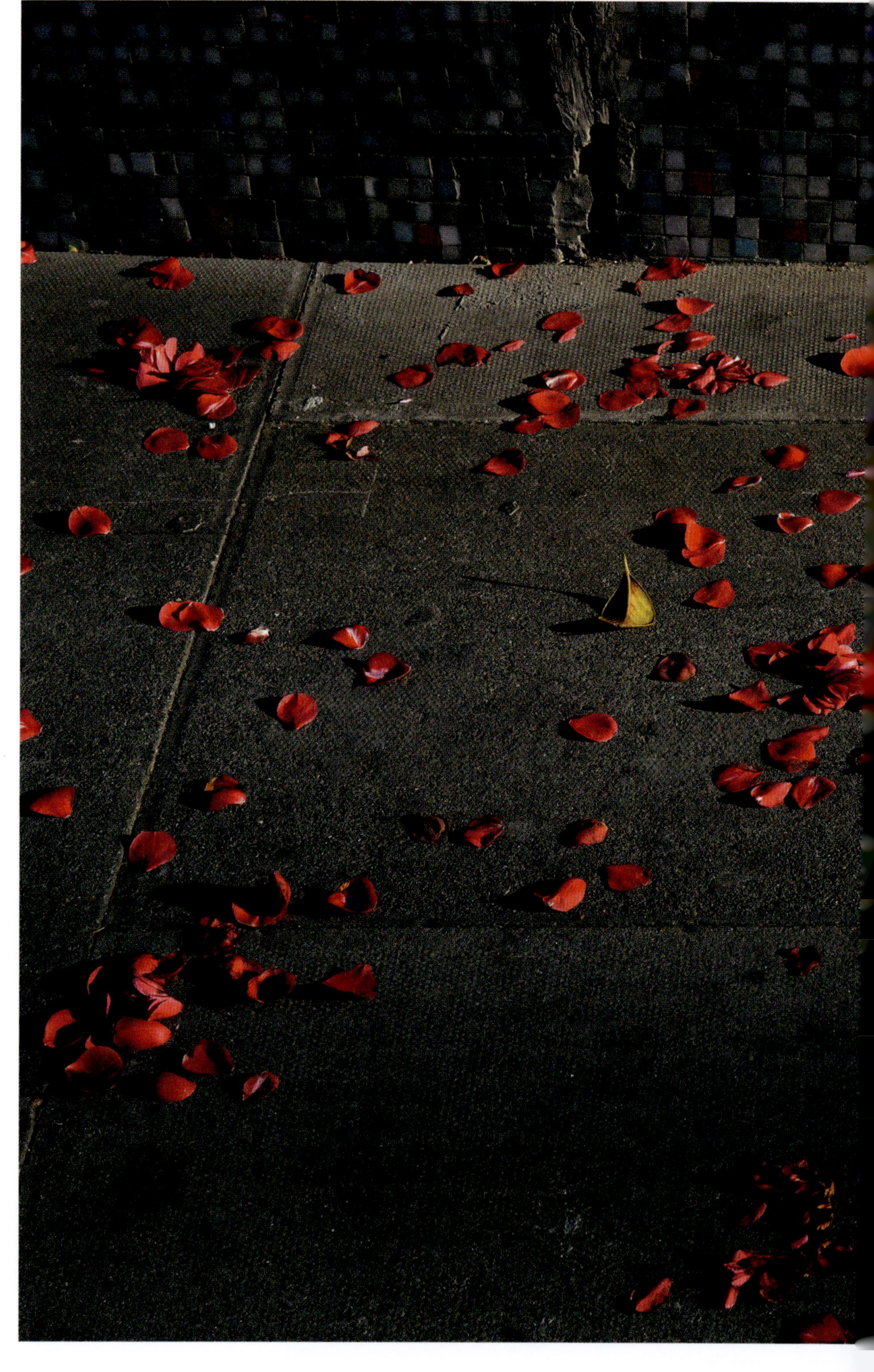

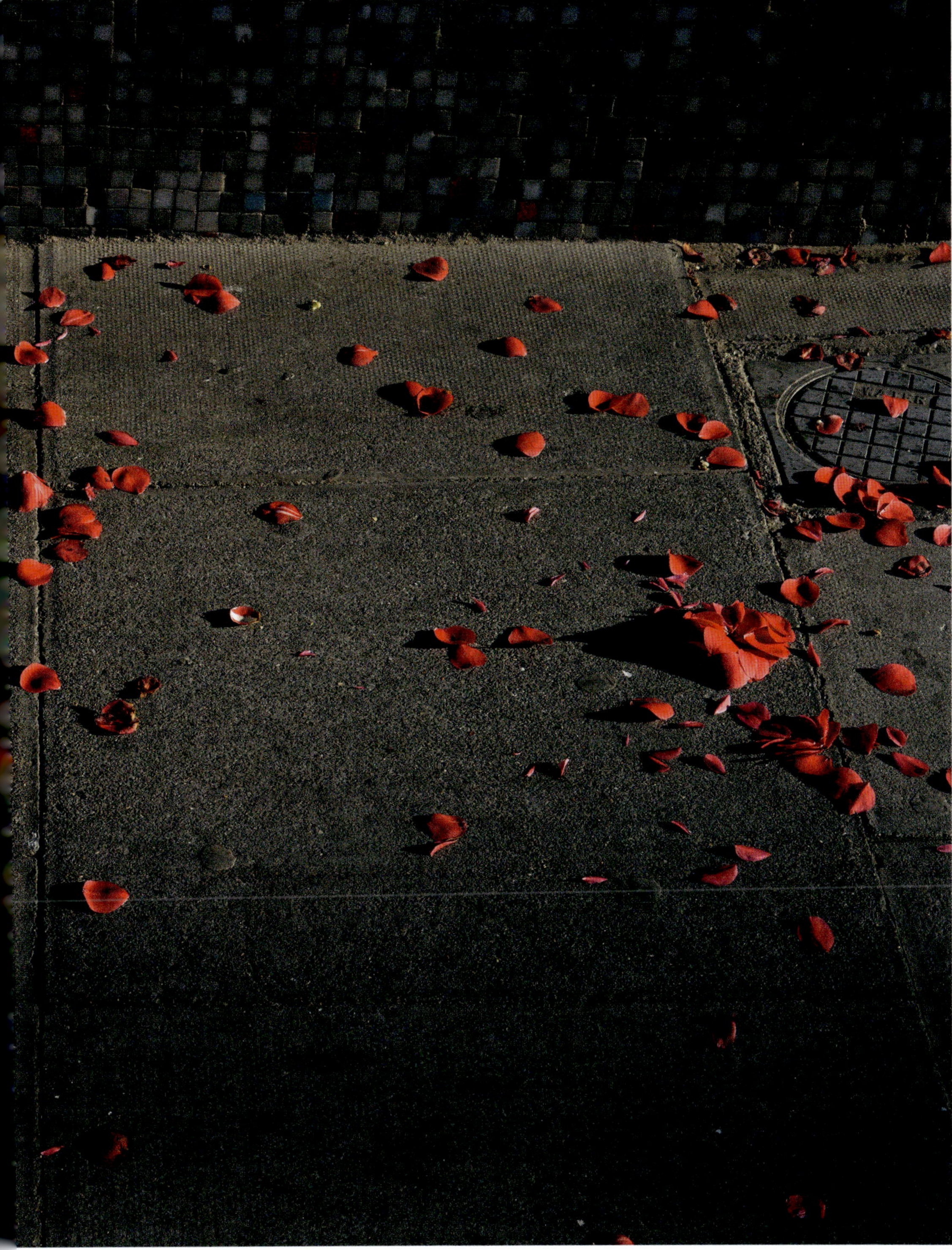

*London in Lockdown*
First Edition

Published in 2021 by Hoxton Mini Press, London
Copyright © Hoxton Mini Press 2021. All rights reserved.

Text and interviews by Jilke Golbach
Front cover photograph by Lydia Goldblatt
Back cover photograph by Chris Dorley-Brown
Design and colour repro by Daniele Roa
Sequence by Jilke Golbach and Hoxton Mini Press
Copy-editing by Florence Filose
Project management and production by Anna De Pascale

Photography credits: *City Parks* © Sophie Wedgwood (casting: Lisa Dymph Megens); *Closer* © Philipp Ebeling; *Custodians for Covid* © Joanna Vestey; *Days on Repeat* © Olivia Harris; *Deserted London* © Chris Dorley-Brown; *Empty City* © Hannah Starkey (originally published in *Wallpaper** magazine, October 2020 issue, *Empty City* photography portfolio in Issue 22 of *Wallpaper** China Edition); *Evering Road* © Christian Sinibaldi; *Field* © Jemima Yong; *Food Banks* © Andy Sewell; *Fugue* © Lydia Goldblatt; *Growing Up in Quarantine* © Morgana Secco; *Inside the Red Zone* © Giles Duley / Imperial College NHS Trust; *Interregnum* © Greg White; *Lockdown* © Roy Mehta (courtesy of the artist and Laura Noble Gallery; the photograph on p.187 was produced as part of Historic England's project *Picturing Lockdown,* 29 April–5 May 2020); *Lost Capital* © Simon Norfolk / Michael Hoppen Gallery; *Lost Summer* © Alys Tomlinson; *Moon City* © Mimi Mollica; *Our Bullet Lives Blossom as They Race Towards the Wall* © Spencer Murphy; *River Lea* © Sophia Evans; *Shot in Isolation* © Celine Marchbank; *Small Changes* © Olivia Arthur / Magnum Photos; *Tale of the Tape* © Peter Dench / Getty Images; *The Ties That Bind* © Grey Hutton (Grey Hutton's work was supported by the National Geographic Society's Emergency Fund for Journalists); *While You Were Sleeping* © Will Hartley (subject: Chiara Soletti).

A CIP catalogue record for this book is available from the British Library.

ISBN 978-1-910566-96-1



This book is 100% carbon compensated according to ClimateCalc (climatecalc.eu).
Offset purchased from: Stand For Trees.

Printed and bound by: Livonia, Latvia.

For every book you buy from our website, we plant a tree:
www.hoxtonminipress.com